The Professional Counselor

A Process Guide to Helping

Second Edition

L. SHERILYN CORMIER
West Virginia University

HAROLD HACKNEY
Fairfield University

ALLYN AND BACON
Boston   London   Toronto   Sydney   Tokyo   Singapore

To Jay and Janine

Series Editor: Ray Short
Production Editorial Assistant: Christine Shaw
Production Administrator: Marjorie Payne
Editorial–Production Service: Chestnut Hill Enterprises, Inc.
Cover Administrator: Linda Dickinson
Composition Buyer: Linda Cox
Manufacturing Buyer: Megan Cochran

Copyright © 1993 by Allyn & Bacon
A Division of Simon & Schuster, Inc.
160 Gould Street
Needham Heights, MA 02194
Copyright 1987 by Prentice-Hall, Inc.

Library of Congress Cataloging–in–Publication Data

Cormier, L. Sherilyn (Louise Sherilyn),
    The professional counselor : a process guide to helping / L.
Sherilyn Cormier, Harold Hackney.— 2nd ed.
        p.   cm.
    Includes bibliography references and index.
    ISBN 0–205–14156–0
    1. Mental health counseling. 2. Counseling I. Hackney, Harold,
    II. Title.
RC466.C67   1993   92–15098
616.89—dc20   CIP

Printed in the United States of America

10 9 8 7 6 5 4 3 2   98 97 96 95 94 93

Contents

5 Developing Counseling Goals   103

6 Defining Strategies and Selecting Interventions   123

___ Preface ___

The process of learning how to counsel others involves many different experiences. At an early stage, the learner will become involved in the examination of self and personal agendas as a way of defining one's personal philosophy. Other experiences are directed toward understanding the many varieties of personal problems that people experience, how problems develop, and how people can change. This causes the future counselor to identify and define a personal theory. Next, one must study the process of counseling, what successful counselors do to help clients, how clients interact and respond to the process, and how the process is applied to different types of clients. Finally, one cannot become a good counselor except by practicing, first in the practicum or internship under the tutelage of a skilled supervisor, then in post-training environment of a school, agency, or private setting, again (it is hoped), under the supervision of a skilled therapist. *The Professional Counselor* is written for the counseling student who is already in the process of identifying a personal philosophy and theory of helping, and who now seeks to develop the skills and insights of the counseling process.

Scope of the Book

We begin with an overview of counseling—the context in which counseling occurs. The overview includes the counselor's personal philosophy, counseling theory, necessary basic conditions under which change is most likely to occur, and the characteristics of effective helpers. In Chapter 2, we provide the reader with a structure for the remainder of the book and for the process of counseling. That structure is a five-stage process that includes establishing a helping relationship, assessing the problem, helping the client identify goals for change, identifying interventions that will help the client to achieve the desired outcomes, and terminating the relationship. We offer this structure as a "roadmap" for the counselor.

Chapters 3 through 6 develop and expand the first four stages of the counseling process. In each chapter, we have included

xi

descriptions of issues and case examples to illustrate the concept. Chapters 7 through 10 give in-depth examinations of four classes of counseling interventions, affective interventions, cognitive interventions, behavioral interventions, and systemic interventions. Again, we have included case illustrations of each intervention and discussions of how clients respond to each type of intervention. Finally, in Chapter 11, we address the important, but often underplayed process of the termination of counseling. We believe this stage to be as important as the initial establishment of a counseling relationship. Chapter 12 examines a number of issues that affect the practice of counseling. Many of these issues are not well understood even today. They include racial and ethnic factors that affect the outcome of counseling, gender issues, the effect of physical disabilities upon counseling process and outcome, resistance to change, and the ever-present prospect of counselor burnout and renewal.

Each chapter includes case illustrations drawn from actual practice, exercises to help the learner rehearse the skills that are described, discussion questions that are intended to help the learner develop and appreciate the deeper meanings of the process of helping, and recommended readings that provide greater in-depth exploration of topics.

Finally, as students explore the many issues surrounding both the practice of counseling interventions and the outcomes, they may find that ethical questions arise as they discuss these with colleagues or classmates. We have included the Ethical Standards of the American Counseling Association as an example of professional guidelines for reference. A second appendix provides additional integrative practice exercises as students rehearse and develop their counseling skills.

Intended Audience

This book is designed to be used as a primary learning source for students in such courses as counseling theories, techniques of helping, pre-practicum, practicum, internship, and/or case management. In addition, the book may be used as a reference source for helpers already practicing as helping professionals.

The authors wish to express their appreciation to Gary Vatcher, Ph.D. and Charles Thompson of the University of Tennessee for their helpful review.

Harold Hackney

L. Sherilyn Cormier

1

The Context
for Counseling

We approach this chapter, and this book, from the perspective of
the beginning counselor. Perhaps we should restate that as the
various perspectives of novice counselors because some of you will
view counseling as an intriguing, almost glamorous profession;
others will sense that counseling is a demanding, often frustrating,
emotion-laden experience; a few may not have any expectations
until they have seen their first client. While it is virtually impossible
to describe precisely what the counseling experience will be like
for you, there are some general parameters of the counseling process that certainly will be part of your experience. How you choose
to fit counseling into your personal life view, how you relate,
interpersonally, to other people, and how you value process and
outcome, these are the touchstones of beginning counselors. In
addition, there are specific skills and learning experiences that make
initial contacts with clients less awkward, more comfortable, and
most of all, more productive.

What is Counseling

Surprisingly, counseling is not an easy concept to define. For one
thing, it is a much overused term. We have financial counselors and
employment counselors, camp counselors, retirement counselors,
legal counselors and nutrition counselors. If there are as many
types of counselor as there are adjectives, then it becomes apparent
that we must somehow differentiate the practice of interper-
sonal/intrapersonal counseling from this myriad of other activities.

Thus, we identify the process and the person in the title of this book, *The Professional Counselor*.

Professional counseling involves an interpersonal relationship between someone actively seeking help and someone willing to give help who is capable of or trained to help in a setting that permits help to be given and received. This definition does not totally satisfy the need to differentiate counseling from other processes. For example, it does not address the issue of whether or not counseling is the same as or different from advising or consulting. So we must add that the process of counseling is directed toward people who experience difficulties as they live through the normal stages of life-span development. Thus counseling is a process that "insist(s) upon the necessity of viewing clients as basically healthy individuals whose problems are essentially developmental in nature" (Brooks & Gerstein, 1990, p. 477). It helps us "stay on track" as we grow up, accept new life challenges, mature in wisdom, and prepare for our lives to end.

Why Counseling?

It may be necessary to remind aspiring counselors that the problems of life can be solved in many ways, counseling being only one of those ways. The vast majority of the human race have never experienced professional counseling. Does that mean that they are functioning at some sublevel of life? Of course not. Many people adapt to life's challenges, using personal resources, friends and family, or religious faith. But even with these resources, challenges can sometimes accumulate to the point that an unencumbered, skilled helper can facilitate the process of growth and adaptation to these challenges.

Viewed in this way, counseling can assume the function of change, prevention, or life enhancement. As change, we are concerned with situations that, for whatever reason, have become disruptive to the extent that we are unable to continue through the normal passage of life development without excess stress, dissatisfaction, or unhappiness. As prevention, counseling is able to take into account those predictable life events that produce stress, cause us to draw upon our psychological resources, and ultimately, demand adaptation to changing life forces. Thus, preventive counseling helps us to anticipate and accommodate life. Finally, there is a third form of counseling, enhancement counseling, that goes beyond life's challenges and predictabilities. As a counseling goal, enhancement attempts to open our experience to new and deeper levels of understanding, appreciation, and wisdom of life's many potentialities.

When we consider "why counseling," we realize that the answer is related both to the internal resources of the potential client, the life stage that person may be entering, functioning within, or exiting, and the goals or objectives that person might have in seeking professional direction.

The Parameters of Counseling

As we consider remedial, preventive, and enhancement counseling, it may become apparent that there are many ways to describe what happens. We can talk about counseling as change or growth. Or we can talk about counseling as process or product. If we go very deeply into an examination of these alternatives, it becomes apparent that we are beginning to talk about philosophical issues as well as psychological or interpersonal concerns. And, how we view these issues and concerns will determine what we do in the interview. If I happen to hold an optimistic view of human beings and how they adapt to life's ups and downs, my view of what should happen in counseling will be quite different from that of the person who holds a pessimistic, or even a cautious, view of human beings and how they adapt. If I solve my problems by careful examination and analysis of issues, decisions to be made, appropriateness of outcomes, and so on, then I might naturally assume that others should approach life problems in a similar fashion. Or, if I see life as a multifaceted *gestalt*, then I might feel less urgency to identify, prescribe, and, thus, control the outcomes of counseling.

Occurring simultaneously with the above, counseling addresses the personal concerns of the client. These concerns may have strong basis in reality, or they may be self-generated by the client's discomfort. Whatever the case, the counselor must have a healthy appreciation of the very broad range of behavior, attitudes, self-concept, and feelings that can occur as people develop. In other words, *normal* behavior, *normal* functioning, or *normal* feelings can include occasional flirtations with abnormal, a kind of testing the limits of one's self. It is best observed in the lives of adolescents, but it is found in people of all ages and stages of development. On the other hand, *normal* does not mean the same as *functional*. Functional behavior is that which facilitates growth, problem-solving, and coping. People can behave in ways that are within the range of normal but still not be behaving functionally. When we listen to the personal concerns of clients, we must seek to understand both life as they see it and the reasons they see life as they do. Only then, can we begin to participate as helpers in the counseling relationship. Only then, can clients begin to move toward more functional behavior.

Finally, there is no way to understand human existence if we separate it from the setting or environment in which existence occurs. Children cannot be fully understood separate from their families of origin; adults cannot be understood separate from their families and careers; and individuals cannot be dissected into intellectual selves, occupational selves, affective selves, or whatever. Each of us is an ecological existence within a cultural context, living with others in an ecological system. Our intrapersonal dimensions are interdependent, and, in turn, we are all psychologically interdependent with others who share our life space. A keen understanding and appreciation of this interdependence will facilitate our understanding of ourselves as counselors, and of our clients as people seeking to recover, to grow, or to enhance their lives.

Counseling and Theory

Another way to understand counseling is to refer to a theory that describes it. Currently there are over one hundred such theoretical approaches or orientations to counseling, most of which were developed from the experiences and life views of practitioners. The most commonly used theories of counseling are summarized in Table 1-1. Counseling theories can serve a number of functions. They serve as a set of guidelines to explain how human beings learn, change, and develop; they also propose a model for normal human functioning (and ways in which human dysfunction may be manifested); and they suggest what should transpire in the counseling process and what the outcomes of counseling should be. In short, a counseling theory offers a "map" of the counseling process and the route its participants should take to achieve certain goals. Since there is much room for alternative viewpoints on such matters as normal human functioning, how people change, and what is a desirable outcome, different theories have emerged to reflect these various viewpoints. On a more practical level, counselors use theories to organize information and observations, to explain or conceptualize client problems, and to order and implement particular interventions with clients.

One might conclude that some theories are more valid than others, but that does not seem to be the case. Using a meta-analysis approach for analyzing the effects of over four hundred psychotherapy outcome studies, Smith and Glass (1977) concluded that the "results of research demonstrate the beneficial effects of counsel-

TABLE 1-1 Synopsis of Theoretical Approaches to Counseling and Psychotherapy

Theoretical System	General Category	Founder or Major Contributor	Personality Theory Base	Key Philosophic, Conceptual, Process, and Relationship Identifiers
Psycho-analytic Therapy	Psycho-dynamic Approach	Sigmund Freud	Psycho-analysis	Deterministic, topographic, dynamic, genetic, analytic, developmental, historical, insightful, unconscious, motivational
Adlerian Therapy	Social-Psychological Approach	Alfred Adler	Individual Psychology	Holistic, phenomenological, socially oriented, teleological, field theoretical, functionalistic
Person-Centered Counseling	Humanistic, Experiential Existential Approaches	Carl Rogers	Person-Centered Theory	Humanistic, experiential, existential, organismic, self-theoretical, phenomenological, person-centered, here-and-now oriented
Gestalt Therapy	Humanistic, Experiential Existential Approaches	Frederick Perls	Gestalt Therapy	Existential, experiential, humanistic, organismic, awareness-evocative, here-and-now oriented, client-centered, confrontive
Transactional Analysis (TA)	Cognitive, Behavioral, Action-Oriented Approaches	Eric Berne	Trans-actional Analysis	Cognitive, analytic, redecisional, contractual, interpretational, confrontational, action-oriented, awareness evocative, social-interactive
Behavioral Counseling, Therapy, and Modification	Cognitive, Behavioral, Action-Oriented Approaches	B.F. Skinner J. Wolpe D. Meichenbaum	Behavior Theory and Conditioning Theory	Behavioristic, pragmatic, scientific, learning-theoretical, cognitive, action-oriented, experimental, goal-oriented, contractual
Rational Emotive Therapy (RET)	Cognitive Behavioral, Action-Oriented Approaches	Albert Ellis	Rational-Emotive Theory	Rational, cognitive, scientific, action-oriented, relativistic, didactic, here-and-now oriented, decisional, contractual, humanistic
Reality Therapy	Cognitive, Behavioral, Action-Oriented Approaches	William Glasser	Reality Theory	Reality-based, rational, anti-deterministic, cognitive, action-oriented, scientific, directive, didactic, contractual, supportive, nonpunitive, positivistic, here-and-now oriented
Trait and Factor Counseling	Trait, Factor, and Decisional Approach	E.G. Williamson D. Paterson J. Darley D. Biggs	Trait-Factor Theory	Scientific, empirical, decisional, informational, educational, vocational, evaluative, data-based, past-present-future-oriented, action-oriented, technological, person-environment interactive, problem-solving, objective, systematic, didactic, interpretative

TABLE **1-1**   *(Continued)*

Theoretical System	General Category	Founder or Major Contributor	Personality Theory Base	Key Philosophic, Conceptual, Process, and Relationship Identifiers
Eclectic Counseling and Psychotherapy	Integrative Approach	F.C. Thorne S. Garfield J. Palmer A. Ivey R. Carkhuff A. Lazarus	Eclecticism	Integrative, systematic, scientific, comprehensive, organismic-environmental, cognitive, past-present-future-oriented, behavioral, educational, developmental, humanistic, analytic, decisional
Systemic Therapy	Ecological Approach	J. Haley S. Minuchin M. Bowen M. Selvini-Palazzoli	Ecological Theory	Total system, boundaries, equilibrium, systemic "rules," cohesive, joining, family structure, dysfunctional system, paradoxical intervention, reframing, prescription, therapeutic directive

Source: Adapted from Burl Gilliland, Richard James, Gayle Roberts, and James Bowman, *Theories and Strategies in Counseling and Psychotherapy*, pp. 2–3. © 1989. Reprinted by permission of Prentice-Hall, Englewood Cliffs, N.J.

ing and psychotherapy. Despite volumes devoted to the theoretical differences among different schools of psychotherapy, the results of research demonstrated negligible differences in the effects produced by different therapy types . . . " (p. 760).

In recent years, the counseling profession has witnessed an increasing convergence among theorists and a growing realization that no single theory can explain or fit all client problems. The result is an emerging view that theory is meant to serve the user, and when no single theory totally fits the counselor's needs, then a blending of compatible theories is an acceptable practice. The result is referred to as an eclectic or integrative approach.

The following list represents certain elements about counseling that are common to the major theoretical approaches described in Table 1-1:

1. Counseling involves responding to the feelings, thoughts, and actions of the client. Thinking of this in another way, the counselor deals with both attitudes and behaviors of the client. Existing theoretical approaches differ with respect to emphasis and order of responsiveness to feelings and behavior. Some approaches (person-centered, existential) favor an emphasis on feelings; others (rational-emotive, reality therapy, behavioral) emphasize the importance of behaviors and actions; an eclectic approach would acknowledge the importance of being able to identify and respond appropriately to feeling states, behaviors, and relationship patterns.

2. Counseling involves a basic acceptance of the client's perceptions and feelings, irrespective of outside evaluative standards. In other words, you must first accept who the client is before you can begin to consider who the client could be. Clients need your understanding of their current situations and concerns before they can anticipate growth and change in a new direction.

3. Confidentiality and privacy constitute essential ingredients in the counseling setting. Physical facilities that preserve this quality are important.

4. Counseling is voluntary. Ordinarily, it is not effective when it is something that the client is required to do. Regardless of how the client is referred, the counselor never uses coercion as a means of obtaining or continuing with a client.

5. London (1964, p. 45) notes that the counselor operates with a conservative bias against communicating to the client detailed information about his or her own life. Although there are times when counselor self-disclosure is appropriate, counselors generally do not complicate the interview by focusing attention on their personal life.

6. One skill underlying all systems of counseling is that of communication. Counselors and clients alike continually transmit and receive verbal and nonverbal messages during the interview process. Therefore, awareness of and sensitivity to the kinds of messages being communicated is an important prerequisite for counselor effectiveness.

Counseling Conditions and Their Effects

Clients often invest significant amounts of time, energy, and money to see a counselor. Counselors also make investments of time and energy. For counseling to be effective, both parties must know that they are moving in some purposeful direction and not just spinning their wheels. This feeling of accomplishing something is more likely to occur if certain things happen to clients during the process. Clients feel encouraged by such things as feeling support and understanding from another person, beginning to see a different and more hopeful perspective, or experiencing a more desirable level of relating to others. Similarly, counselors feel rewarded because their efforts at helping have been productive and therapeutic.

Clients can, do, and should gain from counseling, but such gains need to be realistic in proportion to their ability, skills, problems, life experiences, and time spent in counseling. Although different theoretical orientations emphasize somewhat different counseling outcomes, most practitioners agree on some rather basic outcomes. As Cavanaugh (1982) explains, "All theorists agree explicitly or implicitly that counseling must be a new experience that provides opportunities for people to perceive themselves and life differently, to experience and express their feelings differently, and to behave in ways that are new for them" (p. 11).

When counseling has been successful, clients often experience the following types of outcomes:

1. *They begin to own their problems and issues.* "Owning" is an important word in counseling. It means that clients begin to accept responsibility for themselves, their problems and solutions, and for their lives. Many clients come into counseling blaming their problems on other people, situations, or circumstances. **Example:** A client whose pre-counseling style was to blame her parents for her problems might change her response through counseling to say, "My parents did give me a pretty tough start in life, but now that I no longer live with them, there must be things that I do to perpetuate their effect on me." Being able to say "there must be things that I do" is the process of owning problems and behaviors. Owning one's problems is the beginning step toward resolving them.

2. *Clients develop a more useful understanding of problems and issues.* Once clients begin to accept some responsibility for problems, they frequently develop some understanding or insight into the problem. There are four aspects of problem awareness that understanding brings into clients' awareness: feelings and somatic reactions (affect), thoughts (cognition), problem-related behaviors, and interpersonal or systemic effects. Understanding these different dimensions of a problem helps clients to perceive their reality more clearly and to gain or experience more control over their reactions to an issue. **Example:** Jim, a college student, complains of being depressed since his girlfriend ended their relationship. He describes his situation as feeling down, hurt, lonely, and unlovable. He shows no clinical signs of depression, e.g., sleeplessness, weight loss, or isolation. Rather, he has taken on a "mopey" demeanor, looking for all the world like someone who needs to be taken care of. Through counseling, Jim begins to realize that his reaction is similar to how he would respond as a child when his mother would get on his case. Then, he reports, she would start to feel sorry for her effect on him and would try to repair the obviously damaged relationship. In other words, Jim began to realize that his style of dealing with stressful relationships was to manipulate the other person into repairing the damage. In so doing, Jim never had to assume any responsibility either for the initial issue or for the solution to the relationship problem. Thus, his reaction involved feelings, how he explained the problem to himself (as someone else's doing), his mopey appearance, and how he would manipulate relationships. Through counseling, Jim also began to understand the relationship between his problem resolution style and his resulting behaviors that reflected passivity and inertia. Finally, Jim came to understand that his interactional patterns with his mother were intruding and controlling his relationships with women.

3. *Clients acquire new responses to old issues.* Many counseling theorists now agree that, for most clients, insight or understanding of problems is not sufficient. In addition to developing greater understanding of issues, clients also need to acquire more effective ways of responding, verbally or otherwise, to the situation. Otherwise, they tend to repeat their ineffective interactional style and fail to make any connection between what they think and what they do, or between what they do and the result of their interaction. **Example:** Mary and John see a counselor because of "poor communication" in their marriage. Gradually, they realize that part of the problem is that John is at work all day in a very intense environment and wants to come home to relax, to sit down with the TV or paper, and to be left alone. Mary, on the other hand, has been at home alone all day with a young child. She has lacked adult contact and is feeling a strong need to establish her "adult self" by the time John arrives home. She pursues John for conversation until he puts her down. She retreats in tears. While an understanding of this scenario may be useful to both Mary and John, it is unlikely that they will be able to alter the interaction through understanding alone. They must also develop new behavioral patterns or interactions to avoid repeating the scenario.

4. *Clients learn how to develop effective relationships.* For a great number of people who end up in a counselor's office, adults and children alike, effective and satisfying interpersonal interactions are nonexistent or rare. Since change is often created and supported by a network of social support, it is essential for clients to begin to develop more adequate relationships with other persons. Often the counseling relationship is the initial vehicle by which this occurs. **Example:** Renee comes to see a counselor because she wants to lose a significant amount of weight. In talking to her, the counselor discovers that her obesity has also shielded her from having significant relationships with other people, particularly males. It is unlikely that Renee will have much success in losing weight unless she also learns to feel more comfortable in initiating and developing a greater social support network.

To summarize, counseling usually results in more than one single, all-inclusive outcome for clients. Effective change is multi-faceted and comprehensive and includes greater responsibility, new insights, different behavioral responses, and more effective relationships.

Case Illustration of Possible Counseling Outcomes: The Case of Margaret

Margaret is a thirty-year-old woman who has been married for ten years and has two school-aged daughters. She is employed as a mail clerk in a large business office. She describes her job as satisfying and her relationship with her children as adequate. Her presenting (initial) complaint is about her marital relationship, although she states that her husband has refused to come to counseling with her. She reports that she feels dependent upon her husband or upon acquaintances because she never learned to drive a car and has never really developed any interests or friendships on her own. At the same time, she feels increasingly angry and upset about the way he "orders her around" and tries to keep her "under his thumb." Recently her emotions have become so frayed that she cries easily at home and at work and has developed a pre-ulcerous condition.

Given an effective counseling experience, Margaret might realistically expect to see some of the following kinds of changes:

1. Development of more positive perceptions of herself
2. Greater awareness and understanding of her conflict between being dependent on and independent of her husband
3. Improved family and marital relationships
4. Less digestive upset
5. Greater awareness of and ability to think, feel, and act as an individual, using her own internal resources

Characteristics of Effective Helpers

In order to help clients achieve desired outcomes, counseling must offer clients a new or fresh experience, one somewhat different from the normal range of experience in their lives. Counseling is a reciprocal interaction in which both the counselor and client create and shape the process. Being the trained helper, the counselor has the greater responsibility for ensuring that the counseling process is beneficial and therapeutic for the client. To a large extent, the degree of helpfulness found in the relationship is related to the person of the counselor. Much research evidence amassed over the years indicates that a helper's personal qualities can enhance or detract from the helping process and are as essential (or even more essential) as specific skills or knowledge (Bergin & Lambert, 1978; Jevne, 1981).

In this section, we discuss eight qualities associated with effective counselors. Some are based on results of research (Corrigan, Dell, Lewis, & Schmidt, 1980; Loesch, Crane, & Tucker, 1978; Rowe, Murphy, & DeCsipkes, 1975). Others are based on our clinical and supervisory observations of both good and poor counselors. These eight qualities include:

Self-awareness and understanding
Good psychological health
Sensitivity
Open-mindedness
Objectivity
Competence
Trustworthiness
Interpersonal attractiveness

Self-Awareness and Understanding

On the road to becoming an effective counselor, a good starting place for most counselors is a healthy degree of introspection and self-exploration. Specific areas we suggest you attempt to explore and understand about yourself include:

Awareness of your needs (for example, need to give or to nurture, need to be critical, need to be loved, need to be respected, need to be liked, need to please others, need to have approval, need to be right, need for control).

Awareness of your motivation for helping (for example, what do you get or take from helping others? How does helping make you feel good?)

Awareness of your feelings (for example, happiness, satisfaction, hurt, anger, sadness, disappointment, confusion, fear).

Awareness of your personal strengths, limitations, and coping skills (for example, things about yourself you do well or like, things about yourself you need to work on, how you handle difficulties and stress).

Self-awareness and understanding are important in counseling for a variety of reasons. First, they help you see things more objectively and avoid "blind spots," that is, difficulties that may arise because you do not understand some aspects of yourself, particularly in interpersonal interactions. One such difficulty is *projection*. Counselors who do not understand their needs and feelings may be more likely to *project* their feelings onto the client and not own them for themselves (for example, "I had a very angry client today," instead of "I felt angry today with my client"). Projection is one example of a process we discuss later in this chapter called *countertransference*, or the emotional reactions of the counselor to the client.

Self-awareness and understanding also contribute to greater security and safety for both counselor and client. Lack of self-awareness and understanding may cause some counselors to personalize or overreact to client messages and respond with *defensiveness*. For example, a client questions whether counseling "will do her any good." The counselor's needs to be respected and approved are jeopardized or threatened, but the counselor is not aware of this. Instead of responding to the *client's* feelings of uncertainty, the counselor is likely to respond to personal feelings of insecurity and portray defensiveness in his or her voice, words, or other nonverbal behavior.

Good Psychological Health

While no one expects counselors to be perfect, it stands to reason that counselors will be more helpful to clients when they are psychologically intact and not distracted by their own overwhelming problems. White and Franzoni (1990) report that studies of the psychological health of psychiatrists, psychologists, and psychotherapists in general reveal higher rates of depression, anxiety, and relationship problems than the general population. Even master's-degree-level counselors-in-training "show evidence of higher levels of psychological disturbance than does the general populace" (White & Franzoni, 1990, p. 262).

Unfortunately, some persons either do not recognize when their own psychological health is in jeopardy, or else realize it but continue to counsel anyway, often using counseling as a defense mechanism to reduce the anxiety they feel about their own issues. At selected times in their lives, counselors may need to refer clients with similar life problems to other counselors and/or seek out the services of a competent counselor for themselves.

Sensitivity

Counselors who possess sensitivity are more aware of themselves, their clients, and even of subtle dynamics in the counseling relationship (Cavanaugh, 1982, p. 89). Sensitivity means that the counselor is aware of clients' resources, coping styles, and vulnerabilities. As a result, the counselor can challenge the clients sufficiently without pushing them beyond reasonable limits. The counselor who has greater sensitivity typically is better able to decode client verbal and nonverbal messages and also better able to select and adapt interventions and strategies for each unique client. Sensitivity, in this respect, creates flexibility on the part of the counselor.

Open-Mindedness

Open-mindedness suggests freedom from fixed or preconceived ideas that, if allowed expression, could affect clients. Open-mindedness does not mean that counselors are amoral or have no personal values or beliefs. Open-minded counselors are aware of their belief systems, are able to separate them from those of their clients, and are not driven to push clients to adopt their beliefs or values.

Open-mindedness serves a number of significant functions in counseling: First, it allows counselors to accommodate client feelings, attitudes, and behaviors that may be different from their own. Second, it allows counselors to interact effectively with a wide range of clients, even those regarded by society at large as unacceptable or offensive. Finally, open-mindedness is a prerequisite for honest communication. Anderson, Lepper, and Ross (1980) found that people who are not open-minded continue to believe incorrect things about a client, even in light of new and different information.

Objectivity

Objectivity refers to the ability to be involved with the client and, at the same time, stand back and see accurately what is happening with the client and in the relationship. It has also been described as a part of *empathy*—the ability to see the client's problem *as if* it were your own without losing the "as if" quality (Rogers, 1957, p. 99). It is extremely important to maintain objectivity for the client's sake. Most clients are bombarded with views and advice from many well-meaning people, such as friends and family who are also part of the problem and thus are not objective. Counselor objectivity gives the client an additional set of eyes and ears that are needed in order to develop a greater understanding or a new perception (or reframe) of the issue.

Objectivity also helps the counselor avoid getting caught up in certain client behaviors or dysfunctional communication patterns. For example, clients may try to get the counselor to "rescue" them by playing on the counselor's sympathy with excessive tears and helpless behaviors. Counselors who remain objective are usually able to recognize this behavior pattern for what it is and respond therapeutically. Counselors who lose objectivity may not recognize this and give clients the response they want, thereby reinforcing their dependency and dysfunctional ways of asking for help.

Objectivity also is a safeguard against developing dysfunctional emotional feelings about a client or overidentifying with a client. Counselors must learn to recognize when countertransference develops in the relationship. As we mentioned earlier, countertransference involves either a counterproductive emotional reaction to a client (often based on projection) or the entanglement of the counselor's needs in the therapeutic relationship. Some of the more common ways in which countertransference may manifest itself include need to please one's clients, overidentification with client problems, development of sexual or romantic feelings toward clients, need to give constant advice, and a desire to form friendships with clients (Corey, Corey, & Callanan, 1988). Astute counselors gradually learn to identify certain kinds of clients who consistently elicit strong positive or negative feelings on their part and also certain kinds of communication patterns that hook the counselor into giving a less objective and nonhelpful response.

Competence

According to Egan (1990), competence refers to whether the counselor has the necessary information, knowledge, and skills to be of help. Cavanaugh (1982) observes that competency of the helper is what distinguishes counselors from friends. He asserts: "Effective counselors have a combination of academic knowledge, personal qualities, and helping skills. It would be rare to find a friend with this combination. If a counselor does not possess strengths in all three areas, the counseling relationship is no different, and therefore no more helpful, than any other relationship" (p. 75).

Effective counselors not only appear competent to clients at the beginning of counseling, they also demonstrate competence by their behaviors throughout the counseling process.

1. They call the client by name.
2. They talk on the client's level, using language the client can understand.
3. They appear relaxed and demonstrate attentive behaviors.
4. They listen carefully to the client.
5. They speak fluently and confidently and with vocal and facial animation.
6. They provide direction to the session.
7. They ask questions or make comments that relate directly to the topic or to the client's expressed concerns (Strong & Schmidt, 1970).

Competence is necessary to transmit and build confidence and hope in clients. Clients need to develop positive expectations about the potential usefulness to them of the counseling process. Competent counselors are able to work with a greater variety of clients and a wider range of problems. They are also more likely to be of benefit to their clients and to make inroads more quickly and efficiently.

Competence (sometimes referred to as expertness) is often associated with a model of counseling known as the *social influence model* (Strong, 1968; Strong & Schmidt, 1970; Strong & Claiborn, 1982).

The two basic assumptions of this model are:

1. The helper must establish a power or a base of influence with the client through a relationship comprising three characteristics or relationship enhancers: competence (expertness), trustworthiness (credibility), and attractiveness (liking).
2. The helper must actively use this base of influence to effect opinion and behavior changes in the client.

An increasing amount of evidence on this model suggests that clients' respect for the counselor increases in direct proportion to their perception of the counselor's expertness or competence (Goldstein, 1980).

Trustworthiness

Trustworthiness means that the counselor is reliable, responsible, and avoids any responses or behaviors that could threaten or injure the client. Trustworthiness can be hard to establish, yet it can be destroyed by a single action and in a split second. Counselors who trustworthy are honest, reliable, dependable; they safeguard client communications, respond with energy and dynamism to the client, and "never make a person regret having made a revelation" (Cavanaugh, 1982, p. 79). The essence of trustworthiness can be summarized in one sentence: Do not promise more than you can do, and be sure you do exactly as you have promised. Trustworthiness is essential, not only in establishing a base of influence with clients, but also in encouraging clients to self-disclose and reveal often very private parts of themselves. The counselor cannot *act* trustworthy. The counselor must *be* trustworthy.

Interpersonal Attractiveness

Clients perceive counselors as interpersonally attractive when they see them as *similar* to or *compatible* with themselves. Clients often make this assessment rather intuitively, although probably based on selected dimensions of the counselor's demeanor and attitude, particularly likeability and friendliness. In other words, it is helpful to be down to earth, friendly, and warm rather than formal, stuffy, aloof, or reserved. Counselors who are perceived as attractive become an important source of influence for clients and may also inspire greater confidence and trust in their clients.

Perhaps the most important point we should make about the qualities of effective helpers involves awareness and growth. Few beginning helpers will feel prepared, either technically or personally, to begin working with clients. In part, this is a matter of developing self-confidence in the new skills that have been learned. But, it is also associated with their personal growth as human beings. Experienced counselors find that they learn much about themselves and about the process of living through their work with clients. We have certainly found that to be the case. Each new client reintroduces us to ourselves. Very often, that encounter reveals aspects of our own life adjustment which merit attention and exploration. When this happens, we become increasingly aware of both our strengths and our limitations. It is around those personal strengths that effective counselors build their approach to helping. And it is around those personal limitations that we attempt to structure growth experiences, with the expectation that we will either reduce the limitations or we will attempt to circumscribe their effect upon our clients and our counseling practices.

The Developmental Nature of Learning to Counsel

Over the years, counselor educators have participated in a recurring debate regarding the experience of learning to counsel. The two poles of this debate are that: (a) potential counselors already possess the "skills" of counseling but must learn how to differentiate these skills and use them selectively with clients; or (b) that the skills of counseling have been rather specifically defined and can be taught to potential counselors with a reasonably high degree of success, whether or not they possessed the skills initially. Obviously, most counselor preparation programs fall somewhere between these two poles. But regardless of the source of those skills, whether they are inherent in the candidate's personhood, or whether they are imbedded in the curriculum of the preparation program, the process of bringing them into dominance is worthy of our attention.

We have all known someone who was untrained, but yet a natural counselor. In getting to know such people, we often find that they assumed the helper role as children. They may even have been identified by their families as the peacemaker, the facilitator, the one to whom other family members could turn. Such a role emerges both from temperament and from expectations. Such helpers evolve into the role as their sensitivities, skills, and confidence grow over time. Similarly, students entering counselor preparation programs find that the process is a developmental experience. That is to say, early in the training, the focus tends to be on professional issues external to the person, and like this chapter, the context for helping. Gradually, the focus of preparation turns to the personal qualities of helpers and the process becomes more personal. From this, attention turns to the skills of counseling— what effective counselors are doing and thinking as they work with clients. Finally, preparation begins to integrate these skills with the practical experience of counseling clients in professionally supervised settings.

Summary

In this chapter, our aim has been to describe the various parameters of the counseling process, to relate the process to counseling theory, to illustrate the purposes of effective counseling, and to highlight the major personal characteristics of effective counselors. The counseling relationship has certain features that set it apart from other professional or social relationships or even friendships. One of the most significant features of the counseling relationship is that the counselor is a trained professional capable of providing help in a competent and trustworthy manner.

In Chapter 2, we take a more focused look at the "landscape" of the counseling process. Following chapters examine segments of this landscape in greater detail. The larger intent of this book is to provide the skills dimension of the learning process, and to offer some structure for the implicit and explicit interactional nature of these skills. Each chapter will conclude with suggested exercises to assist your integration of the content and a list of suggested readings that would allow you to explore certain topics in greater depth.

Exercises

I. Purposes And Goals Of Counseling

Two client case descriptions are presented in this activity. Based on the case description for each client, identify possible counseling outcomes that also appear feasible and realistic. You may wish to share your responses with an instructor or another student.

1. You are a middle-aged (early forties) man. You have been fairly happily married for the last fifteen years and have two children. You also have been pretty satisfied with your job as a business executive. During the last year, however, you have begun to question just about everything in your life. Your work seems boring and unchallenging, and your marriage and relationship with your wife have become very routine. About the only thing you still feel very interested in are your two kids. Lately, you have also been feeling very attracted to one of the young female secretaries in your company. You are starting to wonder if something is wrong.

2. You are an older woman (in your seventies). You are hard of hearing and consequently talk loudly to the counselor and often ask her to repeat herself. You have had several bad falls in the last year, one of which resulted in your breaking your hip. You are living by yourself in a two-room apartment, and receive only a social security check. You have no car and have few friends or relatives. You often complain of loneliness and boredom.

II. Qualities Of Effective Counselors

Listed below are the eight qualities of effective counselors we described in this chapter. With a partner or in a small group, discuss what you believe is your present status with respect to each variable. For example, how open-minded are you? What makes it easy (or difficult) for you to be open-minded and relatively tolerant of different values and ideas? Then identify several areas which you may need to work on during your development as a counselor.

1. Self-awareness and understanding

2. Good psychological health

3. Sensitivity

4. Open-mindedness

5. Objectivity

6. Competence

7. Trustworthiness

8. Interpersonal attractiveness

Discussion Questions

1. Counseling has been described by some as a "purchase of friendship." How do you believe counseling differs from a good friendship?

2. Whom do you know that possesses the qualities to be an effective counselor? What are some of these qualities?

3. Considering your age, background, and life experiences, what do you think you have to offer to clients that is different from what they would receive from their friends or family members?

4. What are the most important reasons you want to be a counselor? How might a typical client react to your reasons for choosing counseling as a career?

5. How likely are you to see a counselor yourself? In what ways do you think counseling could help you in your own development as a counselor? For which reasons might you resist getting involved in this experience?

Recommended Readings

Belkin, G.S. (1984), *Introduction to Counseling* (Dubuque, IA: Wm. C. Brown), Chapter 6, Facilitating Growth and Change.

Cavanaugh, M.E. (1982), *The Counseling Experience* (Pacific Grove, CA: Brooks/Cole), Chapter 4, The Person of the Counselor.

Frey, D.H. & Raming, H.E. (1979), "A Taxonomy of Counseling Goals and Methods," *Personnel and Guidance Journal 58,* 26–33.

Gladding, S.T. (1988), *Counseling: A Comprehensive Profession* (Columbus, OH: Merrill Publishing Co.), Chapter 2, The Effective Counselor: Personal, Theoretical, and Educational Factors.

2

Stages and Skills of Counseling

For many years counseling was viewed as a process that did not lend itself to concrete behavioral analysis. For this reason, some people began to think of counseling as having almost mystical qualities. In the 1970s, through the work of people like Robert Carkhuff, Allen Ivey, and Stanley Strong, this mystic character began to disintegrate and be replaced by more specific definitions. Gradually, counseling has taken on a much more defined character.

In this chapter we shall examine the helping process from the counselor's vantage point and from the client's experience. We shall consider how two strangers meet and begin to establish understandings that gradually evolve into a meaningful and productive relationship. These instrumental stages and the counseling skills indigenous to them are presented as a conceptual base for the chapters to follow.

The Stages of Counseling

Counseling is often described as a "process" (Hansen, Stevic, & Warner, 1986). The implicit meaning of this process is a progressive movement toward an ultimate conclusion, that conclusion being the resolution of whatever precipitated the need for help. This progressive movement is often described as a series of "stages" through which the counselor and client move. These stages include: (1) rapport or relationship building; (2) assessment or definition of the problem; (3) goal setting; (4) initiating interventions; and (5) termination and follow-up. The stages overlap in such a way that assessment begins while the relationship is still developing, or early goal setting begins even while assessment is continuing (see Figure 2–1). Just as these five stages collectively describe the process of helping, each stage can be described in terms of progressive movement.

Establishing the Relationship

The term *relationship* has many inferential meanings, including the ties between two people in love, kinship within the family, the bond between close friends, and the understanding that can develop between humans and animals. In the counseling setting, *relationship* takes on a more specific meaning. When the counselor establishes rapport with a client, the relationship includes such factors as respect, trust, and a sense of relative psychological comfort. In other words, rapport refers to the psychological climate that emerges from the interpersonal contact between you and your client. Consequently, good rapport sets the stage for positive psychological growth, while poor or bad rapport leads to undesirable or even counterproductive outcomes.

  Obviously, this psychological climate will be affected by a number of factors, including your personal and professional qualities and the client's interpersonal history and anxiety state. In other words, even the best-trained, best-adjusted counselor still faces a variety of challenges when meeting a new client. Many of these

FIGURE 2-1 Stages of Counseling

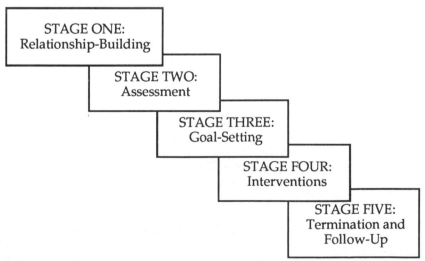

preexisting conditions can be anticipated. For example, few of us like the prospect of asking others for assistance. Thus, when we are forced to admit to ourselves that we need help, we approach it with two sets of feelings: (1) "I know I need help"; and (2) "I wish I weren't here." This conflict is quite common in the early stages of counseling and particularly evident in the rapport-building stage.

Other preexisting client conditions relate to the client's previous experience with sharing personal information, interaction with authority figures, with older persons, with the opposite sex, and so on. In Chapter 1 we referred to some of these factors within the context of interpersonal attraction, trustworthiness, competence, and sensitivity. The sensitive client will read your nonverbal and verbal messages and make inferences about these qualities. The resulting first impressions influence rapport building and may need to be reexamined later when you and your client have reached a more comfortable level with each other.

These reactions sometimes assume overriding control of the situation and begin to influence the process of counseling. When this happens, we refer to the psychological dynamic as transference or countertransference. *Transference* occurs when the client associates certain fictional qualities with the counselor. For example, if the counselor's demeanor reminds the client of his nurturing mother, demanding boss, or arrogant colleague, the client may come to think of the counselor as being like this person, or in extreme circumstances, being this person. Transference can be either positive (favorable comparison) or negative (unfavorable comparison). *Countertransference,* which we mentioned in Chapter 1, describes the same psychological condition, except that it is the counselor who is associating fictional qualities with the client. While this might seem less likely, in fact it is not uncommon.

While we have suggested that relationship building is a critical stage in the counseling process, we do not mean to imply that once the counselor has established a relationship with the client, he or she must live with the product. On the contrary, the relationship is a living, evolving process. Impressions made in the early stages of counseling often change and mature as the two persons work together. The critical determinant in this maturing process is the counselor's ability to recognize psychological dynamics, interpersonal assumptions, and the subterranean emotions that are part of the relationship.

The skillful counselor develops a self-congruent style for meeting clients, a style that reflects both the counselor's personal qualities and counseling experience. Even though there is no "generic" style for establishing rapport, some guidelines and skills are associated with this stage of counseling.

The process begins with adequate social skills. Introduce yourself. Hear the client's name and remember it. Invite the client to sit down, and see to it that he or she is reasonably comfortable. Address the client by name. If the client appears highly anxious, engage him or her in some initial social conversation and watch to see if the anxiety begins to dissipate. Notice nonverbal behavior and use that information to try to understand the client's emotional state. Invite the client to describe his or her reason for coming to talk to you. Allow the client time to respond. This behavior is often described as *attending* or *active listening*. It communicates to the client that you are interested in the person, what she or he has to say, and that you will try to understand both the spoken and the unspoken meanings of the communication.

The relationship is not established in a single contact. Several sessions may be required before the client becomes comfortable with you and begins to admit you into his or her inner world. During these several sessions, consistency is an important quality. Your behaviors, your attitudes and opinions, your promptness and attention to detail will all be observed by the client. If you vary from session to session in these details, the client will find you less predictable and will find it more difficult to become comfortable with you.

While it is not the same as friendship, rapport in counseling shares some qualities with good friendships, and this often proves confusing. As clients begin to know a little about you and your patterns, they will allow a relationship bond to develop. On the other hand, you must also relate to your client for rapport to develop. If you assume a role or a posture that doesn't reflect what you feel about yourself or the client, then you will find the relationship to be insincere or shallow. That may sometimes feel quite uncomfortable to do, but the alternative—to pretend to be someone you are not—is a self-defeating and ultimately nonhelpful approach to establishing a therapeutic relationship with clients.

Assessing the Problem

Even as you and your client are in the process of establishing a relationship, a second process is beginning. That process involves the collection and classification of information related to the client's reason for seeking counseling. We have labeled this the *assessment stage*, though it might also be thought of as the problem-definition process. In this context, we can think of assessment in two ways. First, assessment depends on the counselor's theoretical and philosophical view of human problems. Second, assessment depends on the conditions present in the client's situation and the counselor's understanding of those conditions.

Client problems may be conceptualized as *needs* (something is missing in my life and its absence is disturbing the natural flow of life forces); stressors (something unpleasant has entered my life and its presence is producing distress and distraction); *misinterpretations* (the way I am thinking about my life limits my alternatives); maladaptive interpersonal *patterns* (I am a better person with some people than I am with others); or more likely, a combination of needs, stressors, misinterpretations, and patterns. Counseling theories tend to classify these client conditions as either *affective, behavioral,* or *cognitive* in origin (Corsini & Wedding, 1989). In other words, the client's problems emerge from emotional sources, undesirable behavioral contingencies, or cognitive misrepresentations of reality.

For many years psychologists debated among themselves which was the most accurate representation of human problems. That debate has subsided but remains an issue even today. Perhaps the most viable resolution of that debate is to suggest that the alternative that makes the most sense to you is the approach that would be most appropriate for you to follow. If you think in terms of behaviors and their consequences, then you will find it most natural and logical to use a linear approach to problem assessment. If emotional undercurrents, themes, and the affective domain are natural, then you will be most comfortable assessing problems within that context. And if you think that the way people analyze their life events is the source of their problems, then you will seek cognitive explanations to their life situations. Yet a fourth alternative has been introduced by recent systemic family theorists. Their assessment of client problems is defined by the client's familial environment and the interaction patterns within that environment.

In actual practice it is important to attempt to assess problems in more than one way to avoid the constraints of personal bias or theoretical blind spots and to think of the problem in the client's context as well as a theoretical context. While the "source" of a problem may be conceptualized as emotion based (affective), behavior based (behavioral), thought based (cognitive), or relationship based (systems), the impact or consequences of the problem may be felt as feelings, worries, undesirable consequences, and missing or unsatisfactory interpersonal relationships (see Chapter 4).

The assessment stage is, first, a data-collecting time. You will want to open all of your communication channels to receive information that the client is communicating. At first you may sense no patterns, no meaning to the information. As you continue to work with the client, however, patterns will emerge, and you will begin to understand how the client perceives and tries to affect reality. You will also begin to see your client in the larger context of his or her environment, social setting, or world of relationships. And as the subtleties become increasingly obvious, either by their repetition or by their inconsistencies, you will begin to recognize how you can help your client.

Many views exist as to how assessment should be conducted. Our view is that you should have some blueprint to follow. Otherwise, the amount of detail will begin to overwhelm the process, and you will either overlook important information to solicit or will become distracted from your purpose, which is to determine just what the problem is before you begin to provide solutions. In Chapter 4, we offer an approach to problem assessment which is widely used in clinical settings.

The process of clinical assessment involves several specific skills, including observation, inquiry, making associations among facts, recording information, and forming hypotheses or clinical "hunches." *Observation* includes taking notice of the client's general state of anxiety or comfort, gestures or movements that suggest either emotional or physical dysfunctions, the manner in which the client frames or alludes to his or her problems (for example, some tend to diminish while others inflate aspects of a problem), verbal and nonverbal patterns, and so on. What may appear an insignificant detail at the moment can prove to be part of a significant pattern over time. Thus, observation, mental attentiveness to the persona of the client, is a significant component of the assessment process.

Inquiry is equally important. Beginning counselors have a tendency not to ask for complete details, while experienced counselors pursue certain topics in great detail. Issues related to health, medication, feelings of despair and depression, self-destructive thoughts, and even interpersonal conflicts are examples of such topics. Inquiry is the skill of asking for the finer points, the details behind the event, the information that provides the meaning to an event. Open-ended questions explore processes; closed questions provide specifics. Both are important inquiry tools.

Collected information must somehow be organized and recorded. Some counselors take notes as they acquire information. Others record sessions on audio or videotape. Some do neither, but allow time immediately following the session to write down observations and impressions. The recording of information is a disciplined process. If not done systematically and promptly, it is lost and therefore useless. It is a common counselor lament that information previously given is unavailable because it was not recorded promptly.

When the counselor utilizes observation and inquiry to collect information related to the client's presenting problem, the result is a huge quantity of material. The more observant the counselor, the greater the amount of data. Somehow this information must be synthesized so as to make it usable. This synthesis is conducted within a context. The context may be a counseling theory, or it may simply be the counselor's view of life. Whatever the case, the process involves associating facts and events, constructing possible explanations for events, and making educated (or intuitive) guesses. This assimilation process condenses a large quantity of information into a more usable form. These hypotheses, hunches, and educated guesses become the foundation stones for the next stage, identifying and setting counseling goals. Finally, you might ask the client what he or she thinks the problem is. This simple question often elicits the most important information, the most accurate insights of the entire process. It is surprising that counselors often fail to ask this straightforward question

Goal-Setting

Setting goals is very important to the success of counseling. Some clients and even some counselors resist setting goals. The act of setting a goal involves making a commitment to a set of conditions, a course of action, or an outcome. Sometimes the highly stressed client or the disoriented client may find goal-setting difficult to do. Even in this situation, the goal ultimately becomes one of setting goals.

Why are goals so important? The best answer is a simple one. We set goals in order to know how well counseling is working and when counseling should be concluded. Isn't it enough to let the client decide these questions? Yes and no. The client is an important source of information and reaction to counseling. However, we mentioned earlier that counseling can generate dependent relationships. When that happens, the immediate desire to hold on to a rewarding relationship may overshadow the more appropriate objectives of counseling. Furthermore, as will be evident later, the kinds of things that are done in counseling, the interventions, are often determined by the counseling goal.

The process of setting goals is mutually defined by the counselor and client. The counselor has the advantages of greater objectivity, training in normal and abnormal behavior, and experience in the process. The client has the advantages of intensive experience with the problem and its history, potential insights, and awareness of personal investment in change. Thus, the client needs to be involved in the thinking as well as the decisions about what should happen.

The skills involved in goal-setting may be divided into three classes. First are the counselor's inferential skills. A counselor must be able to listen to a client's vague descriptions of existing and desired conditions and read between the lines of those messages. Rarely are clients able to describe crisply and concisely what they would like to accomplish through counseling. On the contrary, most clients describe their reasons for seeking help in generalities. The typical client is more likely to conceptualize concerns as "I don't want to feel this way any longer," rather than "I want to start feeling that way." So, given this condition, the counselor must be able to think of alternative behaviors and attitudes even as he or she listens to clients describe their concerns.

The second skill involves differentiation between ultimate goals, intermediate goals, and immediate goals. Most of us think in terms of ultimate goals: for example, when I grow up; when I graduate from college; when I get that promotion; when my boat comes in. But if we are to accomplish ultimate goals, we must be able to think in terms of intermediate goals (in the next six months I plan to . . .) and immediate goals (I will do the following things tomorrow). Intermediate and immediate goals provide the strategies necessary to accomplish ultimate goals and are the real vehicle for change in counseling.

The third skill of the goal-setting process involves teaching clients how to think realistically in intermediate and immediate terms. In other words, the counselor may need to teach clients how to set goals that are attainable. In Chapter 5 we discuss ways in which you can use these three sets of skills to help clients set realistic goals for counseling.

Finally, it should be emphasized that counseling goals are never chiseled in granite. Goals can be altered when new information or new insights into the problem call for change. Sometimes a goal is identified inappropriately and must be dropped. It is important to remember that the major function of goals is to provide direction to the counselor and the client.

Initiating Interventions

There are different points of view concerning what a good counselor should do with clients. These viewpoints are, by and large. related to different counseling theories. As you are aware from Chapter 1, a variety of counseling theories exist, each of which can be used by counselors to organize information, define problems, and select intervention strategies. For example, a person-centered orientation would suggest that the counselor involves rather than intervenes by placing emphasis upon the relationship. The existential counselor would view intervention as encouraging clients to recognize and assume personal responsibility for their choices. The behavioral counselor seeks to initiate activities that help clients alter and manage personal contingencies, both in the counseling session and in the clients' real world. The cognitive counselor intervenes by introducing conditions that invite cognitive dissonance or disrupt static cognitive states. The systemic counselor intervenes by challenging interpersonal "rules" or interrupting systemic sequences. In short, all counselors, regardless of theoretical orientation, have a therapeutic plan that they follow, a plan that is related to the assessment of the presenting problem, to their view of human nature and change processes, and to the resulting goals that have been agreed upon.

The real issue in talking about interventions is change and how it occurs. The whole object of counseling is to *initiate and facilitate desirable change.* Thus, when you and your client are able to identify desirable goals or outcomes, the next logical question is, "How shall we accomplish these goals?" In Chapters 7–10 we shall discuss specific types of interventions used in counseling. For the moment, let us consider briefly the process a counselor goes through in identifying counseling interventions based on the assessment process.

Having defined the "problem," the first thing you should do is ask clients what solutions or remedies they have already tried. Most of the time, clients will be able to describe one or more things they have done which were to no avail or only minimally successful in alleviating the problem. This information not only saves you from suggesting alternatives that will be rejected; it also gives you a sense of the client's past efforts to remedy difficulties and the client's resourcefulness as a problem solver. Occasionally clients will report that something they attempted did work but for one reason or another, they discontinued the remedy. Client-induced interventions that were temporarily effective can sometimes be modified and made more effective.

Assuming all client-induced interventions were ineffective, the next step is to relate problems to interventions, depending on the character of the problem. That is to say, problems that appear to be a result of how the client is viewing a life situation may be defined as cognitively determined problems. This would suggest that interventions that are directed toward cognitive change should be considered. If the problem appears to be related to the client's social environment, (family, work, friends), then interventions that are designed to alter interdependent social systems should be considered. If the problem appears to be couched in terms like "hurt," "sadness," or "anger," then it may be affectively based, in which case interventions that facilitate affective disclosure and exploration should be used. Or if the problem's character appears related to the client's actions or efforts to affect others, the problem may be behaviorally based. Then the most effective interventions may be designed to help the client achieve more successful behaviors. The intervention strategies described in Chapters 7, 8, 9, and 10 are grouped around these dimensions of client problems. Chapter 7 examines affective strategies; Chapter 8 presents cognitive strategies; Chapter 9 addresses strategies for behavioral change, and Chapter 10 explores strategies and interventions designed to bring about system change.

Choosing the right intervention is often a process of adaptation. Not all interventions work with all clients, or as well as one might predict. Sometimes the "perfect" intervention turns out to be perfectly awful. It is important that you approach selection of interventions tentatively, prepared to change strategies when the intervention of choice is not working. This process is similar to the treatment of medical problems. When one treatment does not produce the desired response, the practitioner should have an alternative treatment in reserve or reevaluate how the problem is defined.

The skills related to initiating interventions are: (1) competency in using a specific intervention; (2) knowledge of appropriate uses of a specific intervention; (3) knowledge of typical responses to that type of intervention; and (4) observational skills related to the client's response to the intervention. Developing the skills necessary to use different interventions requires that the counselor be able to practice in safe surroundings under expert supervision. Typically, this kind of practice occurs in a counseling practice or supervised clinical field practice. Counselors who try interventions on clients without the benefit of supervised practice are fooling themselves about their potential harmful effect on clients or about their ability to recover from destructive situations.

The counselor also needs to know how clients normally react to a specific intervention. Usually this is expressed in terms of a range of typical reactions. The object is to recognize the abnormal reaction, the unpredictable response, the result of which might intensify the problem rather than alleviate it. For example, the "empty chair" (discussed in Chapter 7) is a gestalt technique often used to help clients recognize and expand their awareness of alternative feelings or reactions. It is a powerful technique, one that sometimes provides access to hidden and possibly frightening feelings. Occasionally this technique will unlock an overwhelming amount of emotion for the client. In such a case, the counselor must be able to recognize that the client's reaction is more than the typical response to this treatment. Related to this awareness of potential effects are the counselor's observational skills. It matters little that the counselor knows the warning signs if he or she does not see them flashing. These three characteristics—skill with a specific intervention, knowledge of its effects, and ability to "read" client reactions—constitute the skills inherent in effective counseling interventions.

Termination and Follow-up

It is difficult to get beginning counselors to think of termination. They are so much more concerned with how to begin counseling, that ending the process seems a distant problem. However, all counseling has as its ultimate criterion the successful termination of the client. With this in mind, let us consider the significance and subtleties of the termination process.

Counseling, and especially good counseling, becomes a very significant event for most clients. The relationship to the counselor may well be the most important relationship in the client's life at that moment. Thus, it is imperative that the counselor acknowledge how important he or she is to most clients and how much his or her actions affect them. Some counselors will find this situation flattering. Others may find it uncomfortable. Some will find it incomprehensible that they could become so important to a stranger in so short a time. However, the fact that the relationship is important does not negate the fact that the relationship must eventually end.

How does a counselor terminate a counseling relationship without destroying the gains that have been accomplished? It must be done with sensitivity, with intention and forethought, and by degree. As the client begins to accomplish the goals that had been set, it becomes apparent that a void is being created. The temptation is to set new goals, create new activity, and continue the counseling process. However, even this may not succeed in filling the void. Eventually, the client begins to realize that the original purpose for seeking counseling no longer supports the process. At this point a creative crisis occurs for the client.

Long before the client reaches this awareness, the counselor should be recognizing the signs, anticipating the creative crisis, and laying the groundwork for a successful termination. As a general rule, the counselor should devote as many sessions to the active terminating process as were devoted to the rapport-building process. This is what is meant by termination by degree. When it is apparent that the counseling relationship may not last more than four to six more sessions, it is time for the counselor to acknowledge that the relationship will eventually end. This can be done simply by saying, "I think we are soon going to be finished with our work."

It is not uncommon for this early acknowledgment to provoke a denial or even a temporary crisis. Up to this point, the client may not have been thinking about facing his or her problems alone. If the client denies, allow it. The denial is part of the recovery process and will dissipate. On the other hand, if the counselor resists the denial by assuring the client that he or she is much stronger, it may only intensify the crisis. It is important to remember that the client must get used to this new thought. In succeeding sessions, the opportunity may arise to introduce the thought again. Gradually, the client will come around, will begin to let self-resourcefulness fill the void, and ultimately will "decide" that counseling can end soon.

Occasionally, clients need a bit of security to take with them, even though they feel ready to terminate. This can be accomplished by making a follow-up appointment six weeks, three months, or even six months in advance. It may be a good idea to ask clients to decide whether they feel the need to keep the appointment as the date approaches. If they do not, they can call and cancel and let the counselor know that they are doing well. On the other hand, it is also important to communicate to clients that if new counseling needs arise, they should feel free to call before the appointment date. In Chapter 11 we discuss in greater depth the skills and concepts associated with termination and follow-up.

Using the Stages to Plan for Counseling

Counseling begins with relationship-building and then moves to assessment, and from assessment to goal-setting, and so on. The fact that one begins assessment before completing the rapport-building stage does not negate this progression. Perhaps the best use of stages is to provide a blueprint for the beginning counselor. For example, as you begin working with a client, you may expect to devote the early sessions to developing a helping relationship. This is not wasted time. When the client begins accepting and trusting you, this may be a signal to move on to the assessment stage and from that to goal-setting, and so on. With experience this blueprint becomes second nature, until it is no longer necessary to think in terms of stages. However, even experienced counselors find occasionally that cases are not progressing well. It is not uncommon for a case to stall or for a sense of lack of movement to take over. When that happens, it is a good idea to return to the blueprint, analyze the progress of the case in terms of stages, and redirect the counseling process where appropriate.

The Client's Experience in Counseling

Very early in the development of his client-centered approach to counseling, Carl Rogers described how the client experiences positive change in psychotherapy. This description became formalized as the Process Scale (Rogers & Rablen, 1958) and was used for many years to study client change. The scale describes seven kinds of client reaction as change occurs. Typically, the client begins counseling by talking about externals rather than self. This gradually changes to include references about feelings, albeit past feelings or those that are external to the client. In the third stage, the client elaborates on feelings, but these are historical rather than current. At the fourth level the client begins to talk about present feelings and acknowledges ownership of these feelings. The fifth stage is one in which the client allows himself or herself to experience current feelings in the present moment of the session. In the final two stages the client begins (1) to experience previously denied feelings and (2) to be accepting and comfortable with those feelings.

The client's experience can be similarly described within the context of the five stages of counseling. As we noted earlier, most clients approach counseling with mixed feelings. While they want to improve their life situation, they are reluctant to become involved in the counseling process. This is the first obstacle for many clients to overcome. In the following sections, we discuss some typical responses clients may have during these five stages of counseling.

Rapport and the Client's Experience

Inexperienced clients enter counseling without knowing exactly what to expect or what will be expected of them. Because of this information deficit, they may feel uncertain, vulnerable, or even embarrassed. A helpful word of direction from the counselor—whether it be a suggestion of where to sit, how long the session will be, or a description of what takes place when people are counseled—will be welcomed. This is not to suggest that all clients will react tentatively to the newness of the situation. Some task-oriented clients begin as though it were already the third session and give little indication that they are anxious or uncertain. This does not mean that rapport has been established, however. The issues of trust, respect, and safety have been suspended temporarily as the client rushes into the process. Those issues will arise later as the client begins to look to the counselor for reactions.

By the end of the first session, many clients have begun to relax and take in the environment of the counseling setting. They may notice and comment upon such things as furniture, pictures, and room arrangement. The client is taking mental pictures and forming first impressions. Between the first and second session, these mental pictures have a significant role. They are the bridge between sessions. If the mental pictures are inaccurate, as is often the case, the client will enter the second counseling session with erroneous perceptions that will lead, once again, to heightened anxiety.

Usually the second session begins on a somewhat better footing than did the first. At the least, the client understands some of the conditions surrounding the counseling process, for example, time limits, responsibility, and so on. But the client must also check out the impressions recalled from the first session and, of course, discover what direction the second session will take. As a result, the second session might be another nervous experience. If the counselor is still attending to relationship issues, the client will become reassured once again, and the focus of the session will gradually shift to substantive issues. This same development will be repeated for several sessions. But as the client and counselor become better acquainted and more comfortable with one another, the progression from relationship to substantive issues takes less and less time.

Assessment and the Client's Experience

Most clients expect assessment to take place, but their expectations are often quite different from what actually happens. It is not uncommon for a client to ask somewhere in the first sessions, "What do you think is wrong with me?" This expectation probably is fostered by the medical model. One goes to the family physician with a fever, swollen glands, and aching joints, and expects to leave with a prescription for medication and some advice on how to treat the symptoms. A more analogous situation would be one in which the patient undergoes lab tests to determine the source as well as the appropriate treatment. In fact, neither analogy adequately describes the assessment process in counseling. For that reason, it is a good idea to explain the process early in counseling, thereby informing the client as well as soliciting the client's assistance.

Clients also have a strong interest in determining what or who "caused" their problems. Very often this question is pursued with such vigor that one would expect the answer to be the solution. In fact, the cause of most client concerns is rarely the solution to the problem. Knowing why a set of conditions exists will not make those conditions go away. Nevertheless, many clients have a strong inclination to think in terms of causes rather than solutions. Perhaps this relates to a need to establish blame for a problem. The client may be saying to himself or herself, "I may have to live with this problem, but at least I don't have to accept the blame for it." Other clients may believe that one can reverse causal relationships, making them go backwards, and ultimately retrack a series of life events.

Whatever the reason, clients tend to approach assessment with mixed feelings. While the solution to the problem may be found in the process, so might the cause and the responsibility for the problem. Worse still, what if the problem is unsolvable? This process of assessment leads the counselor and client to the next stage, setting goals to deal with the client's situation.

Goal-Setting and the Client's Experience

As counseling progresses, and as the client and counselor grow in their understanding of the dynamics and interrelationships that are part of the client's problems, appropriate alternatives are often a natural byproduct. Very often the desirable alternative appears unreachable without the counselor's help. Thus, the client will look to the counselor for assistance in identifying interventions or strategies that will lead to the desirable outcome. Although this involves a certain amount of trust in the counselor's ability to assist, it may also be accompanied by some suspicion. The client probably does not intend to be suspicious of the counselor. Rather, the suspicion grows from the fear that the problem cannot be solved, the situation cannot or will not change, or the prospect of change is too threatening to contemplate. This latter resistance is described in Chapter 10 as homeostasis, a tendency to maintain the status quo. Thus, some clients will resist setting goals. It is as though their rule of thumb is "Nothing ventured, nothing lost." Only as they experience some success in counseling will these reservations begin to dissipate, but that takes both time and wise direction by the counselor.

Will the client accept your assistance and direction? One criterion clients use in determining this is the extent to which the counselor appears to understand the client or the "problem." The client may express this condition as, "She understands my problem in the same way I understand it," or "He really understands what makes me tick." Thus, goal-setting is intimately connected to the process of assessment. And, of course, goal-setting is intimately connected to action.

Interventions and the Client's Experience

Many clients enter counseling vacillating between hope and doubt. Having already failed at solving their problems, they find it difficult to imagine that someone else could find the magic key. On the other hand, the need to find relief demands that they continue their search. In this context, the counselor begins to suggest, to assign, to challenge, to encourage, and to monitor. Many clients have an early rush of hopefulness as positive rapport is established and assessment begins. Soon, however, they begin to look for change and may become discouraged if none is apparent. There are many ways to help clients through this period. Some counselors begin by cautioning their clients that a lull sometimes occurs before change. Other counselors handle this phenomenon by carefully planning goals and objectives so as to assure some level of early success. Another approach would view this as a natural crisis in the counseling process, one in which the client is beginning to address the issues of personal responsibility for change.

Change is a vulnerable process. We do not let go of old ways until we have new ways to put in their place. When the new is forced upon us, we often resist or retreat until we can make the necessary personal adaptations. It is not uncommon for clients to react enthusiastically to interventions, to make major strides, and then to regress. Typically, the regression is less than the original gain and is temporary. Nevertheless, as clients observe first their progress and then their regression, they can begin to doubt the process, or more accurately, their prospects for change through counseling.

As they recover from these temporary setbacks, clients regain their confidence and new patterns become more stable. By this time, some clients can begin to anticipate a new kind of crisis, the crisis of termination. They are feeling better about themselves, about their ability to handle problems, and about the counseling process. A cognitive dissonance emerges, taking the form of

> *Through counseling I am stronger, more satisfied, more in control. Thus, I soon may need to end that which has proven so helpful. But I'm not sure I would be as strong, as satisfied,*

*as in control without counseling. On the other hand, I will
never know if counseling is propping me up or if I have
really changed unless I leave counseling.*

The resolution of this conflict is critical to the success of the counseling process. Only when the client decides to take the risk of
ending counseling can it ever be established that counseling
helped. It is critical at two levels. First, counseling gains must be
supported and maintained in the client's real environment. And
second, the client must be able to view himself or herself as a
changed person.

Termination and the Client's Experience

Termination is a natural outcome of counseling, whether that counseling be successful, unsuccessful, or only partially successful. Said
another way, counseling is an impermanent act. When termination
occurs as a result of successful counseling, the process is one of
both accomplishment and regret. Feeling self-confident, integrated,
and forward-moving, the client experiences a sense of optimism
about the future. At the same time, the client is saying good-bye to
a significant relationship, unique in that it allowed the client to be
the center of attention, concern, and effort. One does not give up
such relationships easily. Thus, there is also a sense of loss blended
into the termination. These two emotional undercurrents will alternately surface as the client and counselor discuss the ramifications
of terminating. Some clients may even be confused by these seemingly contradictory feelings. Under these circumstances, they
probably are misinterpreting the loss reaction as weakness or non-
readiness to terminate.

When termination occurs as a result of unsuccessful counseling, the critical factor is who initiated the termination. If the
counselor initiates it, either because he or she lacked the competencies to work with the case or because the relationship between
counselor and client was counterproductive, then ethical and personal issues must be acknowledged. The ethical issues relate to professional responsibility for the client's well-being. Usually this is
handled by making an appropriate and successful referral. Personal
issues are those which deal with client interpretations of why referral is necessary. As was noted earlier, clients are quite vulnerable
when they seek counseling. If the experience turns out unsuccessfully, some are likely to turn on themselves as having failed again.
Others will conclude that counseling will not work, just as they had

feared. The counselor must acknowledge and help the client work through these reactions as part of the termination process.

On the other hand, if the client initiates termination, a different set of dynamics arises. In this situation, both the client and counselor are vulnerable. The counselor's responsibilities are no less real, however, and include referral considerations, and if possible, personal considerations.

Perhaps the most difficult of termination situations is that in which counseling has been partially successful but cannot be continued. This might occur as a result of the counselor or client changing residence, as a result of client decisions to discontinue or postpone counseling, or as a result of the counselor's conviction that the client should begin working with another counselor or therapist. In this case, the client experiences loss even more intensely than when counseling was successful. That loss may be expressed as frustration, anger, or fear. The frustration is probably justifiable. The anger is a means of adapting to the new circumstances. But the fear is a potentially debilitating condition and must be addressed for successful termination to occur.

Whatever the reason for termination, you are professionally obliged to extend a helping relationship to the client until you are replaced by another helping professional. This may take the form of providing an opportunity to make future appointments, calling the client at a future date to check in, or contacting the professional to whom the client is being referred. Follow-up may also take the form of an evaluation of services, either in the form of a mailed questionnaire or telephone interview.

Dependence and Growth

Throughout the counseling process, psychological dynamics are present and are affecting the development of the relationship, the progress toward goals, and ultimately, the outcome. We have already discussed such issues as trust, respect, and psychological comfort in this context. One further dynamic should be addressed: dependence.

As you and your and client begin to understand one another and the counseling relationship unfolds, a state of client dependency develops. Typically, this dependency begins at a low level, while the client is deciding whether to become involved. As confidence in you grows, so does the dependency upon both you and the process. Through the relationship-building and assessment stages, this dynamic is particularly noticeable. Even in the goal-setting stage, many clients will lean as much as possible on the counselor to make the decisions, to point the direction counseling "should" take. However, an important transition occurs during this stage as clients begin to realize that the decisions they are making, the goals they are setting, are very important personally. It is at this time that dependency begins to shift from the counselor toward self-responsibility. This transition becomes increasingly obvious in the intervention stage as the client assumes more and more responsibility for changes in behavior, attitudes, and emotions. The final accomplishment in this evolution from dependence to independence is reflected in the client's decision to terminate. Even as the client wrestles with the conflicting desires to keep the relationship and let it go, there is an underlying awareness that success means termination, cutting the bonds, and becoming self-responsible.

Summary

In this chapter we described a set of guidelines for counseling. Beginning with building the relationship, the counselor moves on to assessment, goal setting, planning and initiating interventions, and then termination. These stages are never accomplished without the full participation of the client. Within each stage, there is much to be considered. Often two stages will overlap. Occasionally, the counselor and client will need to take stock and move back to an earlier stage. Throughout these stages, evaluation is an important activity, whether it be considering how well the relationship seems to be developing, whether the problem has been correctly identified, whether the goals that have been identified are appropriate (or achievable), how well the interventions seem to be working, and of course, what needs are part of the process of ending the relationship.

Finally, we considered the client's part in this experience called counseling. How does the typical client react to this passage from initiation to termination? What are "normal" expectations? These many facets of the counseling experience are important but often are intangible. Thus, while you attend to the progress of counseling, it is also imperative that you attend to the client's experience, listening for the intangible, the unique, the nonconforming aspects of each client's passage.

Exercises

1. Select a partner and role-play a counseling relationship. Determine in advance which of the five stages you will illustrate in

the role-play (relationship building; assessment; goal-setting; intervention; termination). Have other class members observe and then identify the stage. Continue this exercise until you have illustrated all five stages.

2. Using the same partner, develop a role-play in which the assessment stage is enacted. After the enactment, plan three different goal-setting approaches, one for a cognitive interpretation of the problem, one for an affective interpretation, and one for a behavioral interpretation.

3. Select a partner and determine which of you will be the counselor, which will be the client. Then enact the following role-play.

   You and your client have been working for five months and have reached a plateau. Most of the client's presenting problems at the outset of counseling have been resolved. In your judgment, based on the client's report, the client is functioning well and could really terminate counseling at this point. The client both agrees and disagrees with this assessment. He or she has no new problems to address, but really hates to see counseling end. You have no desire to terminate prematurely, but your concern is that the client accept that he or she is functioning well and is not in need of further counseling at this time.

   Following the role-play, discuss among yourselves the dynamics that seemed to arise during the session. What were your feelings? The client's feelings? Were you able to stay on task? Could you see the client's ambivalence? Could you help the client with that ambivalence? Where do you think the relationship was heading?

Discussion Questions

1. How is assessment different from goal-setting? What counseling activities are part of assessment but not part of goal-setting? What activities are common to both?

2. Discuss the ramifications of the relationship-building stage. How does it affect the assessment stage? The goal-setting stage? The intervention stage? Termination?

3. If counseling interventions do not seem to be working, what might be the problem? How would you know?

4. What do you think is the most important stage in the counseling relationship? Why do you choose this stage? How does your choice reflect your theoretical biases? Would you consider yourself more behavioral? More cognitive? More affective?

5. How does one "know" when counseling should terminate? Is there more than one way of knowing?

Recommended Readings

Egan, G. (1990), *The Skilled Helper* (Pacific Grove, CA: Brooks/Cole), Chapter 2, Overview of the Helping Model.

Hackney, H. and Cormier, L.S. (1988), *Counseling Strategies and Interventions* (Englewood Cliffs, NJ: Prentice-Hall), Chapter 9, Conceptualizing Problems and Setting Goals.

Hansen, J.C., Stevic, R.R., and Warner, R.W., Jr. (1986), *Counseling Theory and Practice* (Newton, MA: Allyn & Bacon), Chapter 14, Continuing the Relationship.

Nugent, F.A. (1990), *An Introduction to the Profession of Counseling* (Columbus, OH: Merrill), Chapter 4, Individual Counseling.

3

Rapport and Relationship

People who are helpers are able to offer a rather unique kind of relationship to their clients. It incorporates many elements of a social relationship, a friendship relationship, and an intimate relationship, and yet it is none of these. It is a relationship created and maintained by both parties, yet it develops and continues primarily to serve the needs of only one of the participants. It is built upon many of the dimensions found in the best and most intimate friendships—trust, safety, openness, and sharing—yet to protect the welfare of the recipient, distinct boundaries exist.

As you are learning to be an effective helper, you may feel pressure to learn the strategies and techniques needed to facilitate client growth. However, the relationship you establish with your client is the beginning point, the foundation for all that will follow in the counseling process. Deffenbacher (1985, p. 262) observes that "Clients . . . need to feel cared for, attended to, understood, and genuinely worked with if successful therapy is to continue." To meet such needs, the counselor must seek to build rapport, bring interpersonal anxiety in the relationship to a functional level, provide the genuineness and self-confidence that engenders client trust, and create a counseling atmosphere that communicates respect for the client, a warmth and accepting disposition, and a willingness to commit to a serious effort to help. This may sound like a major task. But it is important to note that counseling skills are only part of the construction of this relationship. Perhaps the larger portion of the structure draws upon your personal qualities, which includes your self-comfort, your liking of other people, your sense of what constitutes "personal failure" in life, your willingness to get involved in other people's lives without being able to control the outcome. A third dimension of relationship is the client's personal qualities and how they interact with your own. It is possible for you to bring major personal strengths and yet the interaction between you and your client produces a chemistry that is not therapeutically facilitative. Thus, relationship is a composite of therapeutic skills, counselor personal qualities, and client personal qualities. In the remainder of this chapter, we shall address the therapeutic skills and qualities that you can learn and/or develop in preparation for your role as a helper.

Characteristics of an Effective Therapeutic Relationship

It has been proposed that there are six counseling conditions that are both necessary and sufficient to produce constructive client personality change (Rogers, 1957). Although the notion that any "conditions" may be sufficient in and of themselves is arguable, it is beyond argument that certain conditions do facilitate a beneficial relationship and others do not. It follows that clients are more likely to achieve their goals when a good relationship exists.

Conditions that have been identified as important in the establishment of an effective counselor-client relationship include *accurate empathy, counselor genuineness, and an unconditional caring or positive regard for the client*. These variables are derived from person-centered therapy (Rogers, 1957; Holdstock & Rogers, 1977; Meador & Rogers, 1984). Proponents of diverse theoretical orientations join on this one issue, that effective counselors are open, value the client, and are able to understand how and what the client is experiencing.

A constructive counselor-client relationship serves not only to increase the opportunity for clients to achieve their goals, but also serves as a potential model of a good interpersonal relationship, one that clients can use to improve the quality of their other relationships outside the counseling setting.

Empathy

Accurate empathy implies just this: that you "understand what the other person (the client) is experiencing, thinking, and feeling, and how the other perceives his or her behavior" (Holdstock & Rogers, 1977, p. 139). There is some question as to whether empathy is a "learned" counseling response, a personal quality, or some combination of the two (Hackney, 1978). Quite possibly, all human beings are born with a capacity to relate to others and their tribulations. If that is so, it is also possible that our early life experiences either bring out that capacity or leave it dormant. Whether or not this is the explanation, it is a fact that not all would-be counselors are able to listen with the empathic ear, to project themselves into their client's experience in such a way as to experience, vicariously, the client's world. Curiously, actors tend to be highly empathic. They are able to project themselves into the role and bring it to life. Perhaps it is the creative imagination, paired with a sensitivity to feelings and nuances that allow this to happen for the actor. Certainly, it is a product of experience as well. For these reasons, we believe that counseling students can develop strong and effective empathic skills through their preparation and experience.

The next step is taking action on that empathic experience. How do you know when the client feels that you have understood? Clients often give you the answer through their responses. It isn't unusual for a client to react with some surprise or relief. Expressions like "Yes, that's exactly how I'm feeling" or "Yes, that's it" indicate recognition of the level of your understanding. When clients say something like that after one of your responses, you are assured that they sense your strong identification with them and their feelings or their problem.

Strong empathic relationships are such that one person may begin a thought and the other complete it with accuracy, sensitivity, and emotion.

Learning to understand is not an easy process if it does not come naturally. It involves the capacity to switch from your set of experiences to that of the other person, as though you actually viewed the world through that person's eyes. It involves accurately sensing that person's feelings, as opposed to feelings you had or might have had in the same or a similar situation. It involves skillful listening, so you can hear not only the obvious but also the subtle shadings of which perhaps even the client is not yet aware.

Counselor empathy contributes to the establishment of rapport, the conveying of support and acceptance, and the demonstration of respect and civility. It helps the counselor and client clarify issues and contributes immensely to the collection of relevant client information (Cormier, Cormier & Weisser, 1984; Egan, 1990).

Genuineness

Genuineness refers to the counselor's state of mind. It means that the counselor can respond to the client "as a full human person and not just in terms of the role of therapist" (Holdstock & Rogers, 1977,

p. 140). Egan (1990) describes genuine people as being "at home with themselves and therefore (being comfortable as) themselves in all their interactions." It includes being congruent, spontaneous, non-defensive, open to the experience, consistent, and comfortable with those behaviors that help clients (pp. 69–71). In short, it is being who you really are, without pretenses, fictions, roles, or veiled images. It suggests a large amount of comfort with self; thus, it is a quality that we acquire through life experience.

It is often referred to as *congruence,* which means that your words, actions, and feelings are consistent—that what you say corresponds to how you feel, look, and act. Helpers who attempt to mask significant feelings or who send simultaneous and conflicting messages are behaving incongruently. For example, if I say that I am comfortable helping a client explore his or her sexual orientation issues, but show signs of my discomfort with the topic, then I am in a state of incongruence. Such incongruence can contribute to client confusion and to unnecessary distance in the relationship.

The word *spontaneous* was also used in reference to genuineness. This is the ability to express oneself easily and with tactful honesty without having to screen your response through some social filter. It does not mean that you will verbalize every passing thought to your client; nor does it give you license to blurt out whatever is on your mind. Spontaneity communicates your "realness" to the client and provides the client with a basis for establishing a meaningful relationship with you.

Helpers who are genuine are often perceived by clients as more human. Clients are often more likely to discuss private views of themselves when the counselor possesses a degree of non-threatening self-comfort. Counselor genuineness also reduces unnecessary emotional distance between the counselor and the client. This is why it is referred to as a "facilitative condition."

Positive Regard

Positive regard, also referred to as *respect,* means the ability to prize the client as a person with inherent warmth and dignity, regardless of such external factors as the client's behavior, demeanor, appearance, and so on (Rogers, 1957). Positive regard is often misconstrued as agreement or disagreement with the client. It is an attitude of valuing the client, rather than a measure of level of agreement. To show positive regard is to express appreciation of the client as a unique and worthwhile person. Positive regard serves a number of important functions in developing and establishing a therapeutic relationship. Among these are:

1. To communicate a willingness to work with the client
2. To communicate interest in the client as a person
3. To communicate acceptance of the client
4. To communicate caring to the client (Cormier, Cormier, & Weisser, 1984; Egan, 1990)

Skills Associated with the Relationship Conditions

As we mentioned earlier, three facilitative conditions (empathy, genuineness, and positive regard) have their roots in the Rogerian or client-centered approach to helping. Although the Rogerian approach is typically viewed as "devoid of techniques that involve *doing* something to or for the client" (Gilliland, James, & Bowman, 1989), in more current writings, Rogers (1977) asserts that these three core conditions represent a set of skills as well as an attitude on the part of the helper. In this section, we describe the major skills associated with these three relationship conditions.

Skills Associated with Empathy

As we noted earlier, empathy is a *communication state* reflecting the listener's success in perceiving the client's world *as if* you were the client. However, many writers have noted that empathy has no impact on the counseling process if the client does not recognize that you are empathic. Therefore, there are two types of skills associated with empathy: (a) skills associated with accurate perception of another person's world view; and (b) skills associated with the communication of one's empathic perceptiveness to another person. The primary skills associated with the communication of empathy include:

Nonverbal and verbal attending behaviors
Paraphrasing content of client communications
Reflecting client feelings and implicit client messages
Pacing or synchrony of client experience

Nonverbal Attentiveness

Clients often determine whether a helper is attentive by observing the helper's nonverbal behavior. In fact, even if a helper *states* "Go ahead and talk—I'm listening to you," the client may not believe this verbal message if the counselor is looking away, leaning back in the chair, or generally appearing disinterested. Whereas verbal communication is intermittent, nonverbal communication is constant. When verbal and nonverbal messages are in contradiction, the client will usually believe the nonverbal message (Cazda, Asbury, Balzer, Childers, & Walters, 1984). This is due, in part, because so much of the communication that occurs between people is expressed nonverbally rather than verbally.

Effective nonverbal attentiveness includes the use of appropriate eye contact, head nods, facial animation, body posture, and distance.

Good eye contact—eye contact that reinforces clients and makes their communication easier, lies somewhere between the fixed gaze and "shifty eyes," or frequent breaks of eye contact. Look at clients when they are talking. Occasionally, permit your eyes to drift to an object away, *but not far away*, from the client. Then return your eyes to the client. Let yourself be natural. Do not be afraid to invite the client into the world of your vision.

The affirmative head nod also indicates to clients that you are listening and being attentive. When overdone, however, it can become distracting. You do want clients to be aware of your attentiveness. The use of occasional head nods, paired with good eye contact, will reassure (reinforce) clients of your involvement and commitment.

Animation in facial expression gives clients the feeling that you are alert and responding to ongoing communication. It may be that your facial expressions serve as a mirror for clients' feelings as well as an acceptance of them. Certainly, an absence of facial expressions (the proverbial "deadpan") will suggest a lack of interest, awareness, or mental presence to clients. The most noticeable expression is the smile. The appropriate use of smiles can have a powerful effect upon clients particularly when paired with occasional head nods (Hackney, 1974). But continuous smiling becomes a negative stimulus. Frequent frowns can communicate disapproval. Occasional frowns, on the other hand, may communicate your failure to follow or understand a particular point, and are therefore useful.

The key to body communication is the amount of tension that you are feeling. A relaxed body posture indicates comfort, both with the counseling setting and with the topic being discussed. Body tension communicates action. It may reflect a "working" moment for you, involvement with the client, movement toward a goal, or preparation for something new. Or it may reflect your discomfort with yourself, with the topic, or with the client. Continuous body tension probably will communicate the last-named discomfort; selective body tension will indicate the first. In order to manipulate or use body tension as a message, it is important to begin from a relaxation base.

Another important aspect of nonverbal attentiveness relates to the physical distance between the counselor and the client. A distance of three to four feet seems to generate ease, comfort, and verbal expression on the part of the client. Too little distance (two feet) or extreme distance (seven to nine feet) between counselor and client may produce anxiety and inhibit client communication.

It is important to keep in mind that attentive behaviors, while generally useful, need to reflect both the situation and the individual client. High levels of attention may be too intense for some clients, especially during an initial contact. Nonverbal attentiveness particularly should be adapted to the situation because the impact of such behaviors varies across cultures.

Nonverbal Attentiveness and Cultural Differences

In recent years, awareness of the effect of cultural differences on the process of counseling has grown significantly; even so, it still is considered a relatively new field of study. We do know that many of the traditional assumptions about the counseling process do not fit neatly into cross-cultural counseling practices. This is particularly apparent when talking about nonverbal behavior and its effect upon the process. Ivey (1988, pp. 11–12) has summarized some of the cultural differences found in expressions of nonverbal behavior:

> One of the critical issues in interviewing is the fact that the same skills may have different effects with different individual and cultural backgrounds. Eye contacts differ, for example. In our culture, middle-class patterns call for rather direct eye contact, but in some cultural groups, direct eye contact is considered rude and intrusive. Some groups find the rapid-fire questioning techniques of many North Americans offensive. Many Spanish-speaking groups have more varying vocal tone and sometimes a more rapid speech rate than do English-speaking people. It is also important to remember that the word culture can be defined in many ways. Religion, ethnic background (for example Irish-American and Black-American), sex, and lifestyle differences as well as the degree of a client's developmental or physical handicap also represent cultural differences. There is also a youth culture, a culture of those facing imminent death through AIDS or cancer, and a culture of the aging. In effect, any group that differs from the mainstream of society can be considered a subculture. All of us at

times are thus part of many cultures that require a unique awareness of the group experience.

The real issue in cross-cultural counseling relationships is the counselor's *awareness* of the effect cultural differences can have and attempt to utilize that awareness to assess the current relationship communication variables. These cultural differences include not only ethnic differences but also economics and social class, religious affiliation, and gender (Sue, 1981, p. 73). With so many variables to consider, e.g. Asian/middle class/middle-aged female; Black/economically deprived/young male; Hispanic/middle class/male, it becomes apparent that being aware of the *potential impact* of cultural characteristics is the real objective for the beginning counselor. Only through extensive experience with multicultural populations can one even hope to become proficient as a multicultural counselor.

Lacking proficiency, what is the beginning counselor to do when working with culturally different clients? Recent research suggests that synchrony of body movements between helpers and their clients contributes to rapport and also conveys empathy (Maurer & Tindall, 1983). Synchrony can be achieved by bringing your own nonverbal behavior into some similarity of pattern with that of your client. We will discuss this in greater detail later in this section.

Verbal Attentiveness

Nonverbal attentiveness is supported by verbal attentiveness—that is, what is said to clients that demonstrates an interest in them. There are different ways of expressing verbal attentiveness.

One way to show verbal attentiveness is to allow clients to complete sentences. Cutting off a client's communication by interrupting may seem punitive and may discourage full expression, unless of course the client is rambling or telling stories, in which case an interruption can be useful. According to Gordon (1969), interruptions are not always verbal expressions; they include any behavior that distracts the client or interferes with the client's ability to continue with the interview at a particular pace.

Another way to demonstrate attentiveness is through the occasional use of short "verbal encouragers" such as "Mm-hmm," "I see," "Go on," and so forth. When used selectively, these short phrases can have a powerful effect in gaining trust and encouraging expression. Overuse of these responses, however, can induce a "parroting" effect in the session and can be irritating or frustrating to clients.

Another aspect of verbal attentiveness is called *tracking* or verbal following (Minuchin, 1974, p. 127). A helper engages in tracking by following the content and actions expressed in the client's communication. Minuchin likens the therapist's use of tracking to "a needle tracking grooves in a record" (1974, p. 127). The interviewer is nonintrusive and leads by following, accepting, and encouraging the client's communication rather than initiating or changing topics.

Tracking can be used in a variety of ways. It is not restricted to just one type of response. It may be a statement or a question, and it may take the form of any number of different verbal responses, such as a clarification, paraphrase, reflecting of feeling, and open-ended question. The critical element in tracking is to maintain the focus on the topics expressed by the client.

Another aspect of verbal attentiveness is the use of the voice. The voice can be a very powerful tool in communicating with clients. It is important to learn to use your voice effectively and to adapt the pitch, volume, rate of speech, and voice emphasis to the client and to the situation, as clients will differ in their reaction to the same stimulus. As Ivey (1988) observes, "(s)ome people will find one voice interesting, whereas others find that same voice boring, and still others may consider it warm and caring" (p. 28).

An important concept to consider in the use of the voice is that of *verbal underlining*—the manipulation of volume and emphasis (Ivey, 1988). Verbal underlining is a way of using the voice to match the *intensity* of your nonverbal behaviors with those of the client. For example, if the client is speaking loudly about a situation that angered her, you can also speak louder and emphasize key words in your response with your voice.

Paraphrasing and Reflecting Client Messages

Another skill that helpers use in conveying empathy is to show the clients by the use of selected verbal responses that they understand or are attempting to understand the clients' feelings and experiences.

In responding to any client message, helpers must choose which part of the message is the most important and deserving of response. Client messages may contain an objective or cognitive component and a subjective or affective component. The *cognitive* component includes thoughts and ideas about situations, events, people, or things; it answers the question "What happened?" The *affective* component refers to the emotions or feelings of the client; it answers the question "How does the client feel about what happened?" Notice the cognitive and affective portions of the following client message:

> *I really care for and respect my husband. He gives me just about all I need in the way of food, clothes, and so on. If only he could give me more affection. Sometimes even when I'm with him, I feel lonely.*

The cognitive part of this message—"What happened?"—refers to this client's experiences of being taken care of by her husband. The affective component—"How is she feeling about what happened?"—refers to her emotional experience of loneliness.

Not all client messages contain easily recognized cognitive and affective components. Some messages may have only cognitive content, as when a client says "I think my professors here are just average." Other messages may contain only the affective portion; for example, a client may state "I feel lousy today." In both of these examples, the other component was omitted from the message and must be discovered through indirect inquiry or inference.

Paraphrasing Client Communication   Another way to convey empathy is through the use of verbal responses that "mirror" or rephrase to clients the essential part of their communication. The response used to rephrase cognitive client messages is the *paraphrase*. The response used to rephrase affective client messages is the *reflection of feeling*.

A *paraphrase* is saying the client's primary words and thoughts another way (Cormier & Cormier, 1991; Ivey, Ivey, & Simek-Downing, 1987). Paraphrasing involves selective attention to the *cognitive* or objective part of a message—with the client's key words and ideas translated into other words in a shortened and clarified form. An effective paraphrase thus does more than simply parrot back what the client has said. "The goal should be to rephrase what has been said in such a way that it will lead to further discussion or to increased understanding of the topic" (Jessop, 1979, p. 63).

Consider the following interchange:

> *Client:*   I know I shouldn't be so hard on myself. But I can't seem to stop second-guessing everything I do.

> *Helper:*   You know you shouldn't be so hard on yourself but
> you can't stop second-guessing whatever you do.

In this example, the counselor merely parroted the client's words. The likely outcome of such a response is that the client may merely say "Yes" or "I agree" and not elaborate, or that the client may feel belittled or ridiculed by the counselor.

A more effective paraphrase would involve a concise rephrasal, such as "You're aware that being critical of yourself isn't helpful, even though you haven't yet found a way to give it up." When a paraphrase is accurate or on target, the helper is likely to be rewarded with a "Yes" or "That's it!" Then the client will either explore the topic in greater depth or will feel finished with it, content to finally be heard (Ivey, 1988).

There are four steps in formulating an effective paraphrase: recall identification of content, rephrasal of key words and constructs, and perception check. First, listen to and recall the entire client message by restating it covertly in your own mind. This process helps to ensure that you have heard the message in its entirety and that you do not omit any significant parts. Second, identify the content part of the message; that is, decide what event, situation, idea, or person the client is talking about. Third, rephrase the key words and constructs the client has used to describe this concern in fresh or different words. Be as concise as possible in your rephrasal. Long paraphrases border on summarizations—a skill we describe in Chapter 11. Finally, include a perception check that allows the client to agree or disagree with the accuracy of your paraphrase. The perception check not only gives clients the opportunity to correct any errors of perception you might make, but also aids you in your discrimination process about what to focus on next. A perception check often takes the form of a brief question. However, helpers also check their perceptions of client messages by phrasing their statements in a tentative manner and by identifying client nonverbal reactions to their paraphrase.

Some helpers are hesitant to paraphrase for fear they might be wrong. Yet, as Gilmore (1973) observes, "(w)ithin limits, it is better to risk giving an inaccurate paraphrase and stopping for clarification than to sit there with an all-knowing look, nodding your head as if you understand" just to avoid being wrong (p. 242). Moreover, clients are not likely to lose respect for you if you paraphrase inaccurately, as long as you convey your efforts to understand and give the client an opportunity to clarify and correct your perceptions. Finally, your willingness to be fallible may actually help, not hinder, the development of rapport (Moursund, 1985, p. 20).

Reflecting Client Feelings

Whereas paraphrasing involves a rephrasal of the nonaffective or cognitive parts of a client's message, the *reflection-of-feeling* response rephrases the affective or emotional tone of the message. According to Jessop (1979), "reflection of feeling consists of verbalizing the client's *present feeling states* as they are observed in the interview" (p. 54).

Learning to reflect client feelings involves three steps. The first step is to identify the client's feelings or the affective or emotional tone of the client's communication. The second step involves reflecting these feelings back to the client in fresh or new words, and the third step involves a perception check.

In order to identify the client's feelings accurately, you need to become more aware of and sensitive to certain *verbal* and *nonverbal* cues that are elements of the client's communication. Some of these cues are referred to as *leakage,* since they communicate messages the client did not deliberately intend to have communicated (Ekman & Friesen, 1969). Other cues, primarily verbal, are more deliberately intended and are more easily recognized and identified.

In the case of affective leakage, it is important to account for the inferences you may draw. For example, when you say "The client seems happy," that is an inference. If you say, instead, "The client is smiling and that may mean that he is happy," then you have accounted for your inference.

The total impact of a client's message includes both verbal and nonverbal elements. The verbal element refers to certain nouns, adjectives, adverbs, and verbs that express the client's feelings about something or someone; for example:

I am really worried *about school.*

The verbal element associated with the client's feelings in this example is the word "worried." These kinds of words can be called *affect* words. They express some feeling that the client possesses. If an adverb such as *really* or *very* precedes the affect word, this indicates an even stronger intensity of emotion.

Nonverbal cues can be seen from such elements of the client's communication as head and facial movement, position of body, quick movements and gestures, and voice quality. Although no single nonverbal cue can be interpreted accurately alone, each does have meaning as part of a larger pattern, or gestalt. Thus, relationships exist between nonverbal and verbal aspects of speech. In addition to the relationship between nonverbal and verbal parts of the message, nonverbal cues may also communicate specific information about the relationship of the people involved in the communicative process, in this case the counselor and the client. Nonverbal cues differentially convey information about the *nature* and *intensity* of emotions, sometimes more accurately than verbal cues. (Ekman & Friesen, 1967). Remember, too, that the meaning of nonverbal cues varies across cultures. Nonverbal cues to feelings are especially important when the affect is implied and not directly stated.

After the counselor has identified the client's feelings from the kinds of verbal and nonverbal leakage, the next step involves verbally reflecting or mirroring the feelings back to the client, using different words that convey the same or similar emotional tone. The choice of words used to reflect the feelings is critical to this skill because the words can reflect either the same or different level of intensity of feelings experienced by the client. For example, if a client states that she is feeling *irritated* at someone, affect words that are similar in content and intensity would be "annoyed," or "ticked off." Words such as "angry" or "outraged" add to the intensity expressed by the client's word. Because of this varying intensity of affect words, the reflection-of-feeling response can occur at two different levels. That is, the counselor may, at the most obvious level, reflect only the surface feeling of the client. At a deeper level, the counselor may reflect an implied feeling with greater intensity than that originally expressed by the client.

The more obvious level occurs when the counselor reflects an affect message that is *overtly* present in the client's message by using a *different* affect word that captures the same feeling and intensity expressed by the client, as in the following example:

> *Client:* I feel really mad that you interrupted me.
>
> *Counselor:* You're angry with me.

The second kind of reflection occurs at a deeper level. This one mirrors an affect message that is only *covertly* expressed or implied in the client's message. Consider, for instance, the implied affect message in "I think we have a really good relationship." The feeling inherent in the words refers to a positive affect message of *like, enjoy, pleased,* and so forth. Thus, a reflection that picks up on the implied feeling in this communication might be:

> *"You're feeling satisfied with the way the relationship is developing."*
>
> *"You're pleased with the relationship."*

The reflection that occurs at a deeper level not only mirrors the *covert* feeling but also reflects greater intensity of feeling. Furthermore, the most effective reflection is one that emphasizes what it is the client *anticipates;* in other words, one that acknowledges the *implied admission* of the client's message. Consider this sort of reflection in the following example. (Note that the counselor reflects back the covertly implied feeling with a greater intensity of affect, and acknowledges the implied admission; that is, what the client would *like* to do or feel.)

> *Client:* I feel like I have to be so responsible all the time. . . .
>
> *Counselor:* Sometimes you'd feel relieved just to forget all that responsibility—to say 'to hell with it'—and really let go.

This kind of reflection not only mirrors the implied affect but also the behavioral *implications* of the feelings.

The third step in reflecting client feelings involves a perception check. You can check out the accuracy of the reflection by asking the client a brief question or by recognizing client nonverbal reaction to the reflection. As with the paraphrase response, clients will usually express confirmation and/or relief once their feelings have been accurately identified and understood. Occasionally, however, clients may respond by denying their feelings. In this case, you must decide whether the reflection was inaccurate or simply ill-timed. As Ivey (1988) concludes, "(t)hough noting feelings in the interview is essential, acting on your observations may not always be in the best interest of the client. Timing is particularly important with this skill" (p. 112).

Skills for Conveying Genuineness

Genuineness can also be conveyed to clients with appropriate sets of corresponding skills. The primary skills associated with genuineness include:

> Supporting nonverbal behaviors
> Congruence
> Openness and self-disclosure
> Immediacy

Nonverbal Behaviors Associated with Genuineness

There are three nonverbal behaviors that seem to communicate genuineness to clients:

Direct eye contact
Smiling, interested facial expression
Leaning toward clients while seated

These nonverbal behaviors should be used discreetly and gracefully by counselors. For example, there is a fine line between maintaining eye contact with clients and gazing at them intently. Some clients may interpret a helper's gaze as staring in a rude fashion. Similarly, continual smiling or always leaning toward clients may be viewed as phony and artificial rather than genuine and sincere. Recall too from our discussion of empathy that it is important to utilize nonverbal behaviors that parallel or are in synchrony with the client, particularly in the initial stage of helping.

Congruence

Congruence means simply that your words, actions, and feelings all match or are consistent. For example, when counselors become aware that they are bored by a client's rambling, they acknowledge this—at least to themselves—and do not try to pretend or feign interest when it does not really exist.

Clients may respond to counselor incongruence with confusion or irritation and may view the incongruence as an indicator of counselor deception (Graves & Robinson, 1976). Incongruence by the helper may reduce the extent to which the client feels psychologically close to the helper and may interfere with the client's ability to perceive the helper as genuine and sincere. In contrast, congruence of helpers is related to both client and counselor perceptions of counselor facilitativeness (Hill, Siegelman, Gronsky, Sturniolo, & Fretz, 1981).

Congruence implies that counselors need to be good observers of their own internal reactions and resulting behaviors; otherwise, they may send incongruent or mixed messages to clients. For example, a helper may state, "Sure, I want to hear what you have to say about this" while simultaneously fidgeting, looking away, or tapping her feet impatiently. Clients are very sensitive to even very tiny signals the counselor sends, noticing every shift or blink made.

Awareness of your words, feelings, and responses will help you convey your own meanings more clearly and will lead to cleaner interventions on your part. Moursund notes that: "As you notice contradictions between the words you are saying and the way your body is responding, you can clarify your emotional reactions to the client and to the process that is unfolding between the two of you" (1985, p. 17). You can become more congruent by sharpening your observation of your own experience and by noticing signals that may indicate incongruence or discrepancies. Physical or bodily sensations and underlying feelings or emotional responses often prove to be more accurate guides to incongruities and discrepancies than do words.

Openness and Self-Disclosure

Expression of your thoughts, ideas, and feelings necessarily follows your awareness of them. This process can be reflected either through *openness* or *self-disclosure*. Either one may serve to let your client know that you are a real person and not just a role. Ivey (1988) notes that self-disclosure, when used with timeliness, "can encourage client talk, create additional trust between counselor and client, and establish a more equal relationship in the interview" (p. 253).

Certainly timeliness is a critical variable. The *nature* and *degree* of self-disclosure is similarly critical. Self-disclosure does not imply that you should talk about your own problems, since that would shift the primary focus of the interview from the client to you. It may also serve to reduce the client's confidence in your ability. Thus, self-disclosure is a mixed bag. In their study of the effect of self-disclosure, Donley, Horan and DeShong (1990) concluded that "our data do not support the supposition that counselor self-disclosures have a favorable impact on either counseling process or outcome (and that) counselors ought to be quite circumspect about its use" (p. 412). On the other hand, counselor openness is related to genuineness. For example, clients may sometimes ask questions about the counselor. "Are you married?" "Why did you become a counselor?" "Are you in school?" It is usually best just to give a direct, brief answer and then return the interview focus to the client. However, if this is a frequent occurrence with the same client, there are other ways of responding. Such client behavior may indicate that the client is anxious or insecure in the relationship and needs some common ground on which to establish relationship with you. If the request for personal information seems to be excessive, then there are some better ways to respond to the client's queries. For example, it may be more helpful if you speak to the obvious by saying something like:

1. "You seem anxious about talking about yourself now."
   Reflecting upon the client's feelings of anxiety.
2. "You've been asking a lot of questions about me."
   Reflecting upon the process.
3. "I think you might feel as if you've been on the 'hot seat' and asking me questions is a good way for you to get off it."
   Making a statement about what you see happening.

Limited amounts of self-disclosure can be very useful for giving clients necessary "breathing space." The verbal skills associated with empathic understanding that we described earlier all maintain a primary focus on the client. In contrast, self-disclosure shifts the focus to the helper. Limited use of it can actually relieve pressure on the client. Just "as blinking one's eyes helps one to see more clearly, so this brief shift gives the client a chance to come back to his own reactions with a better focus . . . [and] the contrast of the therapist's response with that of the client allows the client to hear his own comments more clearly" (Moursund, 1985, p. 22).

Self-disclosure can be achieved by the use of sharing responses—responses that reveal something about the helper to the client. The most effective sharing or self-disclosing responses are those that are similar in content and mood to the client's messages. Ivey and Gluckstern (1976, p. 86) refer to this similarity as *parallelism*, meaning that the helper's self-disclosure is closely linked to the client's statements. For example:

> *Client*: I just wish my father was more understanding and less critical of me. He always seems to want me to do better than I can or to be someone I'm not.

> *Helper*: (Parallel sharing response): I've also felt the sense of hurt and anger that results when you feel one of your parents doesn't accept you. Sometimes I find myself thinking, "Wouldn't it be nice to have parents who are perfect" although then I realize I don't really know any who are.

> *Helper*: (Nonparallel response): Sometimes I feel bothered, too, about the reactions of other people to me. It's not pleasant when you don't know if people approve of you.

Immediacy

Immediacy can be thought of as a special case of self-disclosure, involving a particular kind of sharing with clients. It is a verbal response that describes something *as it occurs in the helping session.* Although immediacy involves self-disclosure, it is limited to self-disclosure or sharing of *current* feelings or of feedback about what is occurring at the *present* time in the relationship or in the session.

The expression of immediacy is important for conveying both genuineness and positive regard. As Cormier and Cormier (1991) note: "(w)hen persons avoid being immediate with each other over the course of a developing relationship, distance sets in and coldness can quickly evaporate any warmth formerly established" (p. 31). Immediacy is useful for bringing covert, implicit feelings into the open and for providing discussion of or feedback about aspects of the helping relationship. Gottman and Leiblum (1974) point out that this kind of sharing aids not only in the development of the relationship, but can also be a highly effective kind of therapeutic intervention:

> *Rather than hide his own reactions from the client, the therapist's reactions should be used as relevant data. If the therapist tells the client about reactions to him, the client is better able to understand others' reactions to his communications and may better monitor his behavior. Acceptance of all of a client's behavior without comment is neither realistic in terms of generalization to the extra-therapy world nor respectful of the client (Gottman & Leiblum, 1974, p. 126).*

Instances in the helping relationship in which the tool of immediacy is particularly useful include:

1. *Hesitancy or carefulness in speech or behavior:* "Mary, I'm aware that you [or I] seem to be choosing words very carefully right now, as if you [or I] might say something wrong."

2. *Hostility, anger, resentment, irritation:* "Joe, I'm feeling pretty irritated now because you're indicating you want me to keep this time slot open for you but you may not be able to make it next week. Since this has happened the last two weeks, I'm concerned about what might be happening in our relationship."

3. *Attraction:* "At first, it seemed great that we liked each other so much. Now I'm wondering if we're so comfortable that we may be holding back a little and not sharing what's really on our minds."

4. *Feeling of being stuck, lack of focus or direction:* "Right now I feel like our session is sort of a broken record. We're just like a needle tracking in the same groove without really making any music or going anywhere."

5. *Tension:* "I'm aware there's some discomfort and tension we're both feeling now—about who we are as people and where this is going and what's going to happen" (Cormier & Cormier 1991, p. 32).

Immediacy expressions of genuineness are often characterized by sharing and feedback statements—statements that convey to the client your sense of what is going on and your feelings about it:

"I am glad you shared that with me."
"If that happened to me, I think I'd feel pretty angry."
"I don't feel that we're getting anywhere right now."

Sharing and feedback communicate to the client that you have heard or seen something going on, and that you have certain thoughts or feelings about it that you want to communicate. Sometimes you will want to say not only what you feel about a specific instance or experience, but also how you feel about the client. This will be more effective if your feelings are expressed as immediate ones; that is, expressed in the *present* rather than in the past or future. This is the meaning of keeping the process of relationship in the "here and now," using what is going on from moment to moment in each session to build the relationship. It is represented by the type of statement that communicates, "Right now I'm feeling . . ." or "Right now we are. . . ."

There is some evidence that helpers tend to avoid immediacy issues even when raised directly by clients (Turock, 1980). This may be especially true for beginning helpers, who are unaccustomed to talking about relationship issues as they are occurring. Unfortunately, helpers who avoid using this skill are likely to contribute to the development of a somewhat stagnant therapeutic relationship. True contact in the therapeutic relationship is possible only when helpers also allow themselves to be a person, owning their thoughts and feelings and sharing them when significant with their clients.

Skills for Conveying Positive Regard

Although positive regard involves an expression of caring and nurturance for the client, this condition also can be conveyed to clients with the appropriate use of selected skills, including the use of supporting nonverbal behaviors and enhancing responses. Both of these skills may be used to communicate *warmth* to clients. Warmth is a key ingredient of positive regard. According to Goldstein (1980), without the expression of warmth, specific procedures "may be technically correct but therapeutically impotent" (p. 39). Although warmth itself is a hypothetical construct, the expression of warmth and regard can be detected from the presence of selected skills.

Nonverbal Behaviors Associated with Positive Regard

David Johnson has described some very specific nonverbal behaviors associated with the expression of positive regard and warmth (1981, p. 136):

Tone of voice: soft, soothing
Facial expression: smiling, interested
Posture: relaxed, leaning toward the other person
Eye contact: looking directly into the other person's eyes
Touching: touching the other softly and discreetly
Gestures: open, welcoming
Physical proximity: close

One supporting nonverbal behavior that can convey positive regard is the use of touch. Many clients respond favorably to the use of a well intentioned touch from the helper. (Touch that is not well-intentioned arises out of sexual attraction or from a desire to be overly protective of a client.) A handshake or a pat on the shoulder can convey the helper's concern and caring for the client. An occasional client may resist being touched or may attach a different connotation or meaning to the touch than the helper intended to send. Thus, touch "can interrupt a client's process as well as advance it" (Moursund, 1985, p. 73).

When and why helpers touch a client is actually more critical than whether or not they do (Moursund, 1985, p. 73). To help you assess the probable impact of your touch on the client, consider asking yourself the following three questions:

1. How does the other person perceive this? Is it seen as genuine or as a superficial technique?
2. Is the other person uncomfortable? (If the other person draws back from being touched, adjust your behavior accordingly.)

3. Am I interested in the person or in touching the person? Whom am I doing it for—me, the other person, or to impress those who observe? (Gazda, Asbury, Balzer, Childers, & Walters, 1984, p. 111).

Enhancing Responses

There is one thing that all clients need from the helper, particularly in the initial stage of helping, *acceptance.* Helpers convey acceptance by responding to client messages with nonjudgmental or noncritical verbal and nonverbal responses. Thus, when a client states, "I know I'm pregnant again. It will make my fifth abortion. But I don't know who the father is, and I can't stand to use contraception," the helper does not respond by raising her or his eyebrows in surprise, becoming flushed, or expressing judgment about the client's behavior or moral character. On the other hand, the helper does not need to agree with or condone the client's behavior. Acceptance involves the use of responses that are essentially supportive of the *person,* though not necessarily supportive of the behavior.

A verbal skill involved in the communication of positive regard and acceptance is the use of *enhancing statements* (Ivey, Ivey, & Simek-Downing, 1987). Enhancing statements are those that comment on some positive aspect or attitude about the client and provide encouragement to the client in some fashion. Enhancing statements usually focus on process rather than outcome; for example, "I can see you've really worked hard on this issue," rather than "You did a great job on resolving this issue." Other examples of enhancing statements include:

"I think you're expressing your ideas well."

"You're allowing yourself to get close to your feelings now."

"You have a very complete understanding of this issue."

"I can see you really put a lot of time and energy into completing this homework assignment this week."

"You're willing to take a risk now, even if it means finding out something uncomfortable or painful."

"You're starting to take a step forward."

Enhancing statements can have a strong effect on the client and on the relationship. They are most effective when used *selec-*

tively and *sincerely*. You know the feeling you have about someone who *always* is saying nice things—these statements lose their effect when used constantly.

Functions of a Therapeutic Relationship

The core conditions and associated skills we describe in this chapter are derived from the person-centered approach to helping. Most other helping approaches or theoretical orientations also stress the importance of a sound therapeutic relationship in effective helping, even though other approaches differ in the degree of importance and reasons for importance of the relationship. For example, Adlerian and transactional analysis approaches emphasize the necessity of establishing a democratic and egalitarian relationship with the client. Behavioral approaches identify the importance of a good relationship as a potential reinforcing stimulus to the client.

One of the key ingredients of reality therapy, that of *involvement*, is based on the notion of the helpers' ability to relate effectively with their clients. According to Brammer and Shostrom (1982), the relationship is important not only because "it constitutes the principal medium for eliciting and handling significant feelings and ideas," but also because it often is the determining factor for "whether counseling will continue at all" (p. 143).

We believe there are at least four primary functions that an effective relationship serves for clients. First, the therapeutic relationship creates an atmosphere of trust and safely. This kind of atmosphere is necessary to reduce client cautiousness, suspiciousness, and hesitancy about taking risks. In turn, this atmosphere facilitates the client's disclosure of very personal and sensitive material without experiencing aversive or punitive consequences. Without such disclosure, counseling is likely to have little impact on clients because the pertinent issues are not being explored.

Second, the relationship provides a medium or vehicle for intense affect. It permits and protects the client who needs to express strong feelings. Often, expression of strong feelings is the initial step in diminishing their intensity and handing back some control to the client.

Third, an effective therapeutic relationship provides a model of a healthy interpersonal relationship. Such a model can assist clients in identifying and enhancing the quality of their interpersonal interactions with significant others. For example, through the helping relationship, clients can learn that it is OK to say how you feel, ask for what you need, and share thoughts and feelings with others. Clients learn more direct forms of communication that do not involve game playing.

Finally, the relationship serves an important motivational function for clients. Active involvement with the helper implies confidence and gives hope to the discouraged clients who need some additional impetus to continue the change process, which they may experience as difficult and painful. An effective therapeutic relationship can provide the groundwork for the various change-oriented intervention strategies "to yield their intended effects" (Goldstein, 1980, p. 20).

Effects of a Therapeutic Relationship on Clients

Clients' reactions to the helper's level of involvement can range over a number of dimensions. Some clients initially will feel pleased and satisfied about the quality of this interpersonal relationship. They may feel relieved that someone finally seems to understand, and that they have an opportunity to get burdensome or painful material out in the open and "off their chest." They also may feel hopeful that someone finally seems to care enough to get involved.

Not all initial client reactions will be this positive. Some clients, unaccustomed to the informality or intensity of the exchange, may feel threatened, intimidated, or scared by the therapeutic relationship. They are uncomfortable with so much focus on themselves, with the helper's expression of caring and concern, and with what they perceive as an insufficient amount of role distance.

Still a few other clients may question the counselor's motives and view the counselor and the relationship with a degree of skepticism. They may have trouble believing that the helper's intentions are good or that the helper's sincerity is "for real." They may wonder how committed the helper really is to them and to working on their behalf. These clients are often looking for assurance that counseling will be structured to meet their needs and that the counselor will not in any way exploit their vulnerability (Johnson, 1981). Often, such clients express their concerns with indirect or mixed messages designed to collect data about the helper's trustworthiness. If counselors fail to respond to the underlying issue of trust and skepticism, the relationship may deteriorate or even terminate, with the counselor still unaware that the real issue was lack of trust (Fong & Cox, 1983).

Counselors need to be careful about assuming that the conditions and quality of the therapeutic relationship always produce favorable client reactions. Current interpretations of empathy, for example, view it as a multistage process consisting of multiple elements (Barrett-Lennard, 1981; Gladstein, 1983). As such, empathy may be more useful for some clients and less useful at other times or with other persons. As Gladstein (1983) observes, in the counseling process empathy "will be helpful in certain stages, with certain clients, and for certain goals." However, at other times, it "can interfere with positive outcomes" (p. 178).

When clients respond to the therapeutic involvement with apprehension or skepticism, it does not mean that the helper stops reacting therapeutically or that the helper denies involvement with the client or withdraws from the other person. It does mean that the counselor makes a concerted effort to pay close attention to the client's feelings and attempts to relate to the client in a way that paces or matches the client's feelings and frame of reference. Initially, this might mean moving a little more slowly, not pushing as much, or not conveying implicit or explicit demands for client progress and change. Your understanding of the skills and concepts of the therapeutic relationship may be enhanced by reading the following case. (Case examples are provided throughout the book to illustrate the major stages and strategies of the helping process. The case examples should help you in the application of the material you read.)

Case Illustration of the Relationship Stage: The Case of Lenore

Lenore is a forty-five-year-old woman referred to you by her physician because of failure to find any organic basis for Lenore's frequent headaches, which the physician attributed to "stress—particularly in her family life."

In the initial interview, Lenore admits that her constant headaches have been a source of frustration for her. At the same time, she expresses skepticism about how counseling can help her. She hesitantly reveals that she experiences a great deal of stress in her family because of her husband's verbally abusive behavior toward her and toward her two daughters. Yet she feels powerless to do anything to change the situation, partially because her husband has refused to come for counseling. She also feels hopeless about whether counseling will be helpful. Throughout most of the initial interview, she is somewhat passive and reticent, as though she is holding back a barrage of unexpressed ideas, concerns, and emotions.

Your response to her behavior during this initial interview is not to push her or persuade her to see how helpful counseling will be, but simply to try to pace or match her experience and understand her frame of reference. This means that you acknowledge and reflect her skeptical feelings directly. "Lenore, I'm aware that you're feeling discouraged about how talking together like this can really help you in your situation." It also means that you attempt to pace or match her nonverbal behavior—in terms of body language, voice tone, and so on.

At the same time, without pressuring her to be more self-revealing, you are somewhat disclosive yourself and use the tool of immediacy to convey to her how difficult it can be to discuss painful feelings with a stranger: "Lenore, sometimes I too am in a situation where I really want to let go, but I find myself holding back. Sometimes it's very difficult to know where or how to start."

Lenore returns for a second session and, although she still expresses some skepticism, her body language is much more relaxed this time and she speaks more freely and with greater animation and energy. You continue to pace her body language and voice tone, making sure your nonverbal behavior also reflects increased energy.

Lenore returns a third time. This time, she begins to reveal some of the pain in her family, particularly in her relationship with her husband. You continue to attempt to communicate understanding of her feelings by pacing her language (which is primarily visual) and by reflecting her feelings: "Lenore, it is clear to me that you're feeling disappointed not only with your husband, but also with yourself." At this point, Lenore begins to sob as though a flood of pent-up emotions has finally been released.

During this time, you respect her need to cry by offering permission and protection: "Go ahead and cry—don't rush this—take some time to let these feelings and the tears come out." You attempt to respond with both warmth and spontaneity to the expression of her feelings and to let her know that you are not uncomfortable with the intensity of her feelings, even though she might be: "Sometimes these feelings can be pretty overwhelming, especially if you've been holding back for a while. It may be helpful to try to express them in any way that you can."

At the end of the third session, Lenore has revealed many feelings and has disclosed a lot of specific material regarding her family situation. She indicates that the opportunity to talk to someone who appears to understand has been very helpful. Although she still feels somewhat discouraged about her ability to effect change in her marital situation, she wants to continue with counseling. She is also starting to be aware of some issues she wants to work on that are somewhat independent of the marital relationship, such as discovering more about herself as an individual and being less dependent upon her role as a wife and mother in determining her own identity. The two of you agree to work together for the next ten weeks and then at that point to stop and assess what is happening and where Lenore wants to go from there. Additionally, you provide an opportunity for her two daughters to see a helper.

Children and the Counseling Relationship

Thus far, we have discussed rapport and relationship from an adult context. Much of what we have observed may also apply to the adolescent, although the issue of trust is inherently more complex with adolescents who are actively seeking to differentiate self from parents. However, the matter of relationship is more variable for younger children. With them, the issue is more likely to be whether or not to trust a stranger. Thompson and Rudolph (1988) observe that "Making friends with the children you counsel may be the key to the entire counseling process" (p. 23). This may be done through play media, pets (fish, turtle, cat, and so on), or the use of video vignettes of the type seen on "Sesame Street" or "Mr. Rogers' Neighborhood." In using such enhancements, the counselor is creating a shared experience with the child that may serve as a common ground on which to build relationship.

There are other developmental issues to take into account. The younger child has not learned many of the subtleties of adult communication. But at a less subtle level, younger children also lack the vocabulary of the adult world. It is important that you modify your adult behavior to match that of the child. This means matching the child's vocabulary level. A second type of matching relates to the physical domain. To young children, adults look like giants. Their appearance serves as a reminder of the child's vulnerability and powerlessness. Thus, you may want to reduce this physical contrast by sitting more on the child's level. Finally, we must remember that the child's attention span is briefer than that of adults. This has two implications. First, younger children will not be topic-bound for more than two or three minutes at any one time (they may return to a topic several times during a session). Secondly, the counseling session will not be as long as an adult session. You may want to think in terms of 20-minute counseling sessions for the younger child. Beyond these immediate concerns, the establishment of rapport and relationship with younger children also involves understanding, acceptance and a "liking" of children, and genuineness. Genuineness is especially critical. If young children sense that you are being disingenuous or not taking them seriously, their basis for trusting you will be destroyed and rapport will not occur.

Summary

In this chapter, we discussed a number of conditions and ingredients important for conducting the initial stage of building a therapeutic relationship with clients. The three most powerful relationship conditions are *empathy*, or accurate understanding; *genuineness*, or being yourself; and *positive regard*, or acceptance. While these three relationship conditions are conveyed by the helper's attitudes, they are also expressed by selected helping skills, which include the presence of supportive nonverbal behaviors that match or pace those of the client and selected verbal skills such as paraphrasing, reflecting, self-disclosure, immediacy, sharing, and enhancing responses.

The most obvious danger in this initial phase of helping is the "hurry up and fix something or make something change" attitude. This attitude can be experienced both by clients and counselors. It is precipitated by clients who want relief from pain and by helpers, particularly beginning ones, who may need to prove something to clients and to themselves. Because of eagerness to be helpful and get results, "it is all too easy to overlook the importance of creating a situation in which the client can begin to discover his own strength, his own rhythm of change and growth, his own self. And yet it is that internal process, not some set of quick tricks from the therapist, which will allow him to change in the most lasting and meaningful ways" (Moursund, 1985, p. 51). Moursund passes along the best advice she knows for handling this initial stage of helping most effectively—slow down and take time!

Exercises

I. Attentiveness and Empathy

Find another person you can work with in the following two interactions. Each interaction will last about five minutes. After both have been completed, assess the impact of each interaction. Ask the person for his or her reactions to each situation. In which one did he or she feel most comfortable? In which did he or she feel like stopping or leaving?

1. You are to listen carefully to what your partner is saying, but are to send your partner nonverbal signals that indicate bore-

dom: look away, doodle, slump in your chair or sprawl on the floor, twist and fidget, clean your fingernails, fiddle with your clothing, or such. If your partner accuses you of being uninterested, insist that you are interested—you may even review what has been said—but continue to send nonverbal signs of boredom. Do not discuss or share these instructions at this time.

2. This time, you are to listen carefully to what your partner is saying and to send nonverbal signals that indicate your interest and attentiveness—eye contact, head nodding, facial animation, and so on. Make some attempt to ensure some synchrony between your partner's nonverbal behavior and your own.

II. Identifying Nonverbal and Verbal Affect Cues

To give you practice in identifying nonverbal and verbal affect cues, complete the following exercises:

1. Pick a partner. One of you will be the speaker; the other will be the respondent. After you complete the exercise, reverse roles and repeat the exercise.

   The speaker should select a feeling from the following list:

   contented, happy
   puzzled, confused
   angry
   discouraged

   Do not tell the respondent which feeling you have selected. Portray the feeling through nonverbal expressions only. The respondent must accurately identify the behaviors you use to communicate the feeling and should infer the feeling you are portraying. After he or she has done so, choose another feeling and repeat the process.

2. The speaker should select a feeling from the following list:

   surprise
   elation or thrill
   anxiety or tension
   sadness or depression
   seriousness or intensity
   irritation or anger

   Do not inform the respondent which feeling you have selected. Verbally express the feeling in one or two sentences. Be certain to include the word itself. The respondent should accurately identity the feeling in two ways:

   a. Restate the feeling using the same affect word as the speaker.

   b. Restate the feeling using a different affect word but one that reflects the same feeling, for example:

      Speaker: I feel good about being here.

     Respondent: a. You feel *good?*
                 b. You're *glad* to be here.

3. Choose another feeling and complete the same process.

III. Paraphrasing and Reflecting

    Respond in writing to each of the following three client messages. (Feedback follows the chapter exercises.)

1. Identify the cognitive and affective part of each message.

2. Write a paraphrase that reflects the cognitive part of the message.

3. Write a reflection of feeling that rephrases the affective part of the message.

   1. Client: "I'm tired of sitting home alone, but I feel so uptight in going out by myself."
      Cognitive part of message:
      Affective part of message:
      Paraphrase of content:
      Reflection of feelings:

   2. Client: "I don't know why we got married in the first place. We're basically quite incompatible."
      Cognitive part of message:
      Affective part of message:
      Paraphrase of content:
      Reflection of feelings:

   3. Client: "The pressure from my job is a lot to contend with, but I expected it" (said with strained voice, furrowed brow, twisting of hands):
      Cognitive part of message:
      Affective part of message:
      Paraphrase of content:
      Reflection of feelings:

IV. Identification of Representational Systems

    Following is a practice worksheet listing ten words or phrases. Indicate in the space provided which representational system is reflected in the words, using the following key: V = Visual; A = Auditory; K = Kinesthetic; O = Olfactory; G = Gustatory. (Feedback follows the chapter exercises.)

1. _____ A novel perspective

2. _____ A bitter pill to swallow

3. _____ A harmonious situation

4. _____ A softening trend

5. _____ A better horizon

6. _____ Change your tune

7. _____ A cemented agreement

8. _____ Envision a better tomorrow

9. _____ Rings a bell

10. _____ Things are looking up

V. Pacing of Client's Experience

Using triads with one person as speaker, a second as respondent, and the third as observer, complete the following tasks. Then rotate roles until each person has had an opportunity to react in all three ways.

A. The speaker should begin by sharing with the respondent his or her primary concern about becoming a helper.

B. The respondent should listen to the speaker and identify the speaker's predicates, then verbalize to the speaker what he or she heard, *matching* predicates when responding.

C. The observer should note the extent to which the others accomplished their tasks and whether the respondent matched or mismatched the speaker's predicates.

Following a brief (five-minute) interaction, respond verbally to the following questions:

Speaker: Do you think the respondent heard what you had to say? Did you think he or she understood you? Why or why not? Discuss this with the respondent.

Respondent: *Did* you let the speaker know you understood or attempted to understand? How did you do

this? What blocks within yourself made it difficult to pace or match the speaker's words?

Observer: Discuss what you saw taking place between the
speaker and respondent.

VI. *Self-Disclosure and Immediacy*

Listed below are four client situations. For the first two,
develop and write an example of a *self-disclosure response* you
might make to this client. For the second two, develop and write
an example of an *immediacy response* you could use with this
client. Share your responses with other students, colleagues, or
your instructor or supervisor.

1. The client hints that he wants to tell you something but is reluctant to do so because it is something he feels very ashamed of.

2. The client believes he or she is the only person who has ever
   felt guilty about an issue.

3. You experience a great deal of tension and caution between
   yourself and the client. You both seem to be treating each other
   with "kid gloves." You are aware of physical sensations of tension in your body, which are also apparent in the client.

4. You and the client like each other a great deal and have a lot in
   common. Lately, you have been spending more time swapping
   life stories than focusing on or dealing with the client's presented concern of career indecision.

VII. *Positive Regard and Enhancing Responses*

1. Take a few minutes to think of a person with whom you are
   currently in a relationship and toward whom you experience
   positive regard. What kinds of positive feelings do you have for
   this person? Jot them down.

2. What does this person do that you like and value? Jot these
   things down.

3. Based on your positive feelings for the person and on the things
   he or she does that you like, develop some enhancing statements you could use to convey your feelings to this other person. Make a list of them.

4. How would you feel making these statements to the person?
   What might be the effect on the other person? If your expression of these kinds of statements is infrequent, what might be
   holding you back?

Feedback for Exercises

III. Paraphrasing and Reflecting

Client Message 1

1. The cognitive part of the message is "being tired of sitting home alone." This is the event or situation.

2. The affective part of the message is "feeling uptight in going out alone."

3. Examples of paraphrase responses:
    a. Sitting home by yourself is getting to be an old thing now.
    b. It's not much fun to be waiting around at home by yourself.

4. Examples of reflection responses follow. Note the first two are at the surface level; the second two reflect the implied as well as the obvious message.
    a. You're feeling uneasy about venturing out alone.
    b. You're feeling apprehensive about going out on your own.
    c. You're feeling unsure about going out by yourself. You really wish you had someone to accompany you.
    d. You're feeling anxious about going out by yourself. You'd like someone to be there with you.

Client Message 2

1. The cognitive part of the message is "why we got married in the first place; we're incompatible."

2. The affective part of the message is "don't know why." Don't know reflects uncertainty, confusion.

3. Examples of paraphrase responses:
    a. You find it interesting that you decided to get married, considering that you're two very different people.
    b. Despite all of your differences, you ended up marrying each other anyway.

4. In the following examples of reflection responses, the first two are at the surface level; the second two reflect implied omission or what the client would like to have happen.
    a. You're feeling unsure about why the two of you ever got married anyway.

   b. Given the basic differences that exist between the two of you, it's puzzling that you two ended up together.

   c. You're feeling confused about the reasons for marrying each other. It sounds like you'd feel more comfortable if you two weren't so different and shared more of the same interests.

   d. You're uncertain about how the two of you ever got hooked up together to begin with. Seems like you might be looking for a smoother, less rocky relationship.

Client Message 3

1. The cognitive part of the message is "There's a lot of pressure from my job."

2. The affective part of the message is implied from the client's nonverbal behavior—strained voice, furrowed brow, twisting of hands—all of which suggest tension.

3. Examples of paraphrase responses:
   a. You're finding out just how much there is in your job you have to cope with.
   b. Sounds like you've got an awful lot to manage in your particular job.

4. In the examples of reflection responses, the first two are at the surface level and the second two are at a deeper level.
   a. You expected some pressure in your job. Now it seems like you're feeling the strain of having even added burdens.
   b. You seem to be feeling somewhat tense about everything that is confronting you from your job.
   c. From your nonverbal behavior, you seem to be feeling somewhat tense about your job demands. It appears as though you'd like those demands to ease off a bit.
   d. Even though you expected some pressure in your job, you're feeling concerned that it's more than you expected. You'd like to feel less pressure than you do.

IV. *Identification of Representational Systems*

Check your responses with the identifications here:

1—V	6—A
2—G	7—K
3—A	8—V
4—K	9—A
5—V	10—V

Discussion Questions

1. How do you approach a new relationship? What conditions do you require to be met before you open yourself to a closer relationship?

2. What are the "unwritten rules" in your family about interactions with nonfamily members? How do you think these unwritten rules will affect the way you relate to clients?

3. If you were a client, what kind of relationship would you expect and value? Now try to answer this same question from a cultural perspective different than your own.

4. What do you think is the critical ingredient for establishing rapport with clients?

5. Do you believe that the therapeutic relationship is: (1) a *necessary* condition for effective helping? (2) a *sufficient* condition for effective helping? Explain your responses.

6. What do you see as the greatest obstacles to establishing an effective therapeutic relationship with a client? How might you handle these roadblocks?

7. Is it *always* useful to be genuine with clients? Can you think of any instances in which an expression of genuineness might be inappropriate?

8. How would you handle your feelings and behavior if your realized that you disliked a particular client?

Recommended Readings

Barrett-Lennard, G.T. (1981), "The Empathy Cycle: Refinement of a Nuclear Concept," *Journal of Counseling Psychology 28*, 91–100.

Cummings, Anne L. (1989), "Relationship of Client Problem Type to Novice Counselor Response Modes," *Journal of Counseling Psychology 36*, 331–335.

Donley, R.J., Horan, J.J. and DeShong, R.L. (1990) "The Effect of Several Self-Disclosure Permutations on Counseling Process and Outcome," *Journal of Counseling and Development 67*, 408–412.

Doster, J.A., & Nesbitt, J.G. (1979), "Psychotherapy and Self-Disclosure," in G.J. Chelune (Ed.), *Self-disclosure: Origins, patterns, and implications of openness in interpersonal relationships* (San Francisco: Jossey-Bass).

Frederick, S.L. (1988), "Learning to Empathize with Resistance," *Journal of Counseling and Development, 67*, p. 128.

Gladstein, G. (1983), "Understanding Empathy: Integrating Counseling, Developmental, and Social Psychology Perspectives," *Journal of Counseling Psychology 30*, 467–482.

Hansen, J.C., Stevic, R.R. & Warner, R.W., Jr. (1986), *Counseling: Theory and process. 4th Ed.* (Boston: Allyn & Bacon), Chapter 14, Continuing the Relationship.

Ivey, A.E. (1988), *Intentional interviewing and counseling, 2nd Ed.* (Pacific Grove, CA: Brooks/Cole), Chapter 2, Attending Behavior: Basic to Communication; Chapter 5, Encouraging, Paraphrasing and Summarizing: Hearing the Client Accurately; and Chapter 6, Noting and Reflecting Feelings: A Foundation of Client Experience.

Maurer, R.E. & Tindall, J.H. (1983), "Effect of Postural Congruence on Client's Perception of Counselor Empathy," *Journal of Counseling Psychology 30*, 158–163.

Moursund, J. (1985), *The Process of Counseling and Therapy* (Englewood Cliffs, NJ: Prentice-Hall), Chapter 4, The Early Phase.

4

Assessing Client Problems

In most instances, clients see a counselor (or are "encouraged" to see one) because of concerns or problems that are interfering with their daily functioning or are making them feel bad. Clients hope that, as a result of counseling, they will feel better and/or their life situation will improve. This expectation has both positive and negative implications for counselors. On the positive side, it behooves the counselor to start moving the sessions in some focused direction and to do something in addition to sitting and listening. On the negative side, it can create a trap for both counselor and client, who may feel that counseling is not successful unless the counselor is *always* doing something—usually *for* or *to* rather than *with* the client.

In spite of this potential trap, it is important to remember that the reason most clients seek a helper's services is for relief of symptoms or resolution of problems. Counselors who forget this are likely to have clients who feel that their reasons for seeking help are being ignored or overlooked. It is important to take client complaints seriously. One way to do this is to utilize some portion of the counseling process for assessing client concerns. Assessment of client concerns not only gives clients the feeling that the counselor views their problems with a healthy degree of respect, but also provides valuable information to the counselor about conceptualization of client problems and corresponding treatment or intervention approaches.

Purposes of Assessment

Assessment has two primary purposes. First, it is a systematic way to obtain information about the client's identified problems and concerns. Second, it is useful for identifying the significant variables that contribute to the problems. For example, two clients may come in and present the same initial concern: "I'm depressed." Depression, however, is a construct that has different meanings. Although both clients may feel depressed, assessment of this problem for each is likely to reveal somewhat different descriptions of the problem and different contributing conditions.

It is also important to note that assessment can be *reactive;* that is, the process of obtaining specific information about problems may also effect some kind of change in the problem. For example, a male client who reports that he is self-conscious around women may find that some of his self-consciousness dissipates as he begins to explore his behavior with the counselor and to monitor it more closely outside the counseling sessions. Thus, assessment can also contribute to desired client changes or outcomes.

Components of Assessment

Assessment refers to anything counselors do to gather information and draw conclusions about client concerns. Although most of the major components of assessment occur early in the counseling process, to some degree assessment goes on continuously during counseling, in that counselors are always seeking missing parts of the puzzle and attempting to place them where they fit.

Intake or History Interviews

The first identifiable component of assessment is usually referred to as the intake or history interview. During this session, counselors are interested primarily in obtaining information about the range or scope of the client's problems and about aspects of the client's background and present situation that may relate to these problems.

An assumption behind the intake interview is that the client is coming to counseling for more than one interview and intends to address problems or concerns that involve other people, other settings, and the future, as well as the present. Most counselors try to limit intake interviews to an hour. In order to do this, the counselor must assume responsibility and control over the interview. No attempt is made to make it a "therapeutic session" for the client. The second session can begin to meet those needs.

Because the intake session is different from a regular counseling session, it is helpful if the counselor gives the client an explanation about the purpose and nature of the initial session. You might say something like: "Marie, before counseling gets started, it is helpful if I have some preliminary background information about you. So this time, I'd like to spend the hour getting to know you and asking you some questions about your school, work and family background, and so on. Then at the next session, you will be able to start discussing and working on the specific concerns that brought you to counseling. Do you have any questions about this?"

The following is a suggested outline to follow for an intake interview:

  I. *Identifying data.*
      A. Client's name, address, and telephone number at which client can be reached. This information is important in the event you need to contact the client between sessions. The client's address also gives some hint about the conditions under which the client lives (large apartment complex, student dormitory, private home, etc.).
      B. Age, sex, marital status, occupation (or school class and year). Again, this is information that can be important. It lets you know if the client is still legally a minor, and provides a basis for understanding information that will come out in later sessions.
 II. *Presenting problems, both primary and secondary.*
      It is best that these be presented in exactly the way the client reported them. If the problem has behavioral components, they should be recorded as well. Questions that help reveal this type of information include:
      A. How much does the problem interfere with the client's everyday functioning?
      B. How does the problem manifest itself? What are the thoughts, feelings, etc., that are associated with it? What observable behavior is associated with it?
      C. How often does the problem arise? How long has the problem existed?
      D. Can the client identify a pattern of events that surround the problem? When does it occur? With whom? What happens before and after its occurrence?

  E. What caused the client to decide to enter counseling at this time?

 III. *Client's current life setting.*

  How does the client spend a typical day or week? What social and religious activities, recreational activities, etc., are present? What is the nature of the client's vocational and/or educational situation?

 IV. *Family history.*

  A. Father's and mother's ages, occupations, descriptions of their personalities, relationships of each to the other and each to the client and other siblings.

  B. Names, ages, and order of brothers and sisters; relationship between client and siblings.

  C. Is there any history of mental disturbance in the family?

  D. Descriptions of family stability, including number of jobs held, number of family moves, etc. This information provides insights in later sessions when issues related to client stability and/or relationships emerge.

 V. *Personal history.*

  A. Medical history: any unusual or relevant illness or injury from prenatal period to present.

  B. Educational history: academic progress through grade school, high school, and post-high school. This includes extracurricular interests and relationships with peers.

  C. Military service record.

  D. Vocational history: Where has the client worked, at what types of jobs, for what duration, and what were the relationships with fellow workers?

  E. Sexual and marital history: Where did the client receive sexual information? What was the client's dating history? Any engagements and/or marriages? Other serious emotional involvements prior to the present? Reasons that previous relationships terminated? What was the courtship like with present spouse? What were the reasons (spouse's characteristics, personal thoughts) that led to marriage? What has been the relationship with spouse since marriage? Are there any children?

  F. What experience has the client had with counseling, and what were the client's reactions.

  G. Alcohol and drug use: Does the client currently use, or has the client in the past used alcohol or drugs, and to what extent?

  H. What are the client's personal goals in life?

 VI. *Description of the client during the interview.*

Here you might want to indicate the client's physical appearance, including dress, posture, gestures, facial expressions, voice quality, tensions; how the client seemed to relate to you in the session; client's readiness of response, motivation, warmth, distance, passivity, etc. Did there appear to be any perceptual or sensory functions that intruded upon the interaction? (Document with your observations.) What was the general level of information, vocabulary, judgment, abstraction abilities displayed by the client? What was the stream of thought, regularity, and rate of talking? Were the client's remarks logical? Connected to one another?

VII. *Summary and recommendations.*

In this section you will want to acknowledge any connections that appear to exist between the client's statement of a problem and other information collected in this session. What type of counselor do you think would best fit this client? If you are to be this client's counselor, which of your characteristics might be particularly helpful? Which might be particularly unhelpful? How realistic are the client's goals for counseling? How long do you think counseling might continue?

In writing up the intake interview, there are a few cautions to be observed. First, avoid psychological jargon. It is not as understandable as you might think! Avoid elaborate inferences. Remember, an inference is a guess, sometimes an educated guess. An inference can also be wrong. Try to prevent your own biases from entering the report.

Problem Definition

The second dimension of clinical assessment involves a more extensive definition of the problem. This may begin as part of the intake interview but will continue into the next one to two sessions. Problem definition differs from intake information in that specific details regarding the nature and context of the presenting problem(s) are explored. These details may include not only the one(s) presented initially by the client (referred to as the *presenting problem*), but also may include any others that may have been mentioned during the intake or during subsequent sessions.

Frequently, clients will identify a presenting problem as their reason for seeking help and then, during the subsequent sessions, reveal something else that is the real object of their concern. In these instances, the client has been "testing" the counselor or the counseling process to determine whether or not this is a safe or appropriate environment in which to explore such issues. For this reason—and also because a sound therapeutic relationship is an important prerequisite to the proper identification of goals—it is usually a good idea to have one or more counseling sessions with the client before attempting to define the problem too specifically. The following are areas to explore in reaching a useful understanding of the client's problem:

I. *Components of problem* (ways in which the problem manifests itself primarily and secondarily).
   A. Feelings associated with problem (major feeling or affect categories to assess include confusion, depression, fear, anger, also bodily or somatic reactions).
   B. Cognitions associated with problem (including thoughts, beliefs, perceptions, and internal dialogue or self-talk).
   C. Behaviors associated with problem (specific actions observable not only to the client but also to others, including counselor).
   D. Interpersonal aspects of problem (effects on significant others and on the client's relationships with others, including family, friends, relatives, colleagues, peers; also effects significant others may have on problem).
II. *Pattern of contributing events* (Can the client identify a pattern or sequence of events that seems to lead up to problem and also keeps it going or maintains it?).
   A. When does problem occur?
   B. Where?
   C. With whom?
   D. What is happening at this time?
   E. What happens before its occurrence?
   F. What happens after its occurrence?
   G. What makes problem better? Go away?
   H. What makes problem worse? More intense?
III. *Intensity of problem* (extent to which the concern makes client feel bad and/or interferes with client's everyday functioning).
   A. How long has problem existed?
   B. How often does problem occur?
   C. How long does problem last when it does occur?
   D. What about problem caused client to see a counselor at this time?

      E. In what ways does problem interfere with client's daily functioning?

  IV. *Client coping skills, strengths, resources.*

      A. How has client coped with problem? What has worked? Not worked?

      B. How has client successfully coped with other problems?

      C. What resources, strengths, and support systems does client have to help with change efforts?

In addition to this kind of information collected from problem definition interviews, counselors also can obtain additional assessment information about clients and their problems by using *adjunctive data*, such as psychological tests, self-ratings, and so on. While it is beyond the scope of this book to discuss them, it is important for counselors to remember that the information obtained from intakes and problem-definition interviews is sometimes corroborated with additional assessment tools.

Clinical Assessment with Children

Children pose a unique assessment challenge to the counselor. On the one hand, children are less inhibited than adults in talking about their concerns to a trusted counselor. On the other hand, children, especially young children, lack the cognitive development to describe problems with causal and contextual sophistication. As a consequence, you must phrase questions in such a way as to draw out the kinds of information that will allow you to conceptualize the child's world. Children's problems tend to fall into three areas: (a) environmental factors affecting healthy growth and development; (b) self-concept issues; and (c) relationship issues.

Once you have established a safe and trusting relationship with a child, you can begin the intake/problem definition process. This will differ from the adult intake interview described earlier. Depending upon the child's emotional state, intake information may be drawn from other significant sources as well as the child, e.g. parents, teachers, siblings, peers. Thus, the first contact with the child may find you already involved in problem definition questions that draw out the child's emotional state, environmental factors contributing to the child's feelings, self-views, and significant relationships with others. The highly verbal child will be able to respond to open-ended questions about self, family, friends, and environment. However, the less verbal child may need structured questions, e.g. Who? What? Where? How? When?, in order to respond to the counselor. Some child counselors prefer to avoid these types of questions since they also restrict the child's response, and thus the range of information that is gained.

The most important factors are: (a) that you know in advance what type(s) of information you wish to gain from the session; (b) that questions are asked at the child's vocabulary and conceptualization level; and (c) that information obtained is specific rather than general. Laing (1988) points out that this type of assessment is limited by four factors: (1) the client understands what information is being requested; (2) the client possesses the information that is requested; (3) the client is willing to provide the information; and (4) the counselor accurately interprets the client's response. Osberg (1989) has added to this list an important fifth factor, that the client possess a minimal amount of introspectiveness to be able to respond to the questions. These factors are particularly appropriate to child counseling.

The intake process has also been used with group guidance activities in elementary schools. Morse and Bockoven (1989) describe the use of an intake interview as a precursor to guidance curriculum projects using the DUSO-R.* They suggest questions such as "What goes well between you and your mom (dad, friends)?" "What do you do that helps it go well between you and your mom (dad, friends)?" Such questions address both relationship issues and personal involvement issues and "provide a sense of the children's goals or desired outcomes for participating in the DUSO-R program" (p. 106).

Clinical Assessment with Couples and Families

Most professional literature on marital and family therapy emphasizes a systemic approach to working with couples and families (See Chapter 10). With this approach, Sluzko (1978) has observed that:

> *The qualitative shift in the conceptual framework that characterizes the interpersonal systems approach to the couple requires that one utilize the transactions between individuals, rather than the characteristics of each given individual, as primary data. Even when, for one reason or another, attention is zeroed in on one person, his/her behavior is analyzed in*

---

* The DUSO-R is a guidance curriculum developed by Dinkmeyer and Dinkmeyer (1982) containing teachers' manuals, discussion pictures and objects, audio cassettes of songs and stories, other activity suggestions such as role-playing, career activities, puppetry, and discussion topics.

terms of its power to affect and shape the behavior of other members of the system and in terms of the variables of the ecosystem that may have affected it (p. 366).

Given this "qualitative shift in conceptual framework," the types of questions that would characterize the intake and problem definition interview would reflect an orientation to the relationships and transactions occurring within those relationships. While it would still be important to obtain demographic information and medical information about the couple or family, the counselor would quickly refocus to factors reflecting effects rather than intentions, the effects of "behaviors upon behaviors, (and) the way interpersonal sequences are organized" (Sluzko, 1978, p. 367). Questions that would reflect this orientation would include:

"Whenever Charles does this, how are you likely to respond, June?"

"When June reacts, what is the next thing you are likely to do or say, Charles?"

Note that the counselor does not ask "Why do you respond this way?" The reason or "intention (for a particular response) is considered irrelevant to the understanding of interpersonal processes" (Sluzko, 1978, p. 367).

Using Assessment Information

Counselors develop different approaches to using the information collected from intake and problem-definition sessions. Some counselors look primarily for patterns of behavior. For example, one counselor noted that his client had a pattern of incompletions in life: he received a general discharge from the Army prior to completing his enlistment, dropped out of college twice, and had a long history of broken relationships. This observation provides food for thought. What happens to this person as he becomes involved in a commitment? What has his client come to think of himself as a result of his history? How does he anticipate future commitments? Another counselor uses the assessment information to look for "signals" that suggest how she might enter the counseling relationship. Is there anything to indicate how the client might relate to females? Is there something current in the client's life that common sense would suggest is a potential area for counseling attention? For example, is the client in the midst of a divorce; is the client at a critical developmental stage?

The information counselors collect during assessment is also invaluable in planning relevant counseling strategies and approaches to use with problems. For example, one client who reports depression describes the problem primarily in cognitive terms: "I'm a failure, I'm not good at anything, I can't stand it when people don't approve of me. When something goes wrong, it is all my fault." This client has internalized a set of beliefs and self-perceptions that are erroneous, are not based on data or facts, and are self-defeating. The counselor would probably decide to use an approach or strategy with this client that deals directly with this client's cognitions, beliefs, and internal dialogue. (See Chapter 8 for a discussion of cognitive change strategies.)

In contrast, suppose another client who complains of depression is depressed because of a perceived inability to make friends, to form new relationships, and to maintain existing ones. In this instance, the counselor might target her or his approach toward behavioral strategies (see Chapter 9) that emphasize acquisition of social skills and interpersonal or systemic strategies (see Chapter 10) that deal with relationships between people.

Counselors who fail to conduct assessment interviews are more likely to formulate erroneous conclusions about client problems and irrelevant or nonworkable counseling approaches and strategies. As a result, not only is more time spent on "hit or miss counseling," but ultimately clients may leave with the same set of problems they came with in the first session.

To help you tie together the information revealed from assessment of a client with corresponding counseling strategies, we have organized the strategy chapters (Chapters 7 through 10) around the four components of the problem described in Section I of our outline on page 84. For example, strategies that deal primarily with feelings or have an affective focus are presented in Chapter 7. Cognitive-based strategies are described in Chapter 8, while Chapter 9 presents behavioral strategies. Strategies with an interpersonal or systemic focus are found in Chapter 10.

Skills Associated with Assessment

In assessing client concerns, the counselor relies on all the skills described in Chapter 3 that are used to build rapport and to establish a good therapeutic relationship. Some of the skills that are used most frequently during intake and problem-definition interviews include *verbal and nonverbal attending, paraphrasing content*, and *reflecting feelings*. In addition, the counselor relies heavily on the use of *questions* to facilitate the assessment process.

In this section, we describe and provide examples of three specific kinds of questions useful in assessment:

1. Clarifying questions
2. Open-ended questions
3. Closed questions

Clarifying Questions

Sometimes client responses sound cryptic or confused and the counselor is left wondering just what the client was trying to say. It can be very important to seek clarification in these moments rather than guessing or assuming that the communication was unimportant. The clarifying question asks the client to rephrase the communication, and can be stated in several ways.

"Could you try to describe that feeling in another way? I'm not sure I am following what you mean."

"When you say 'fuzzy,' what's that feeling like?"

"I think I got lost in that. Could you go through the sequence of events again for me?"

Clarifying questions are self-explanatory. The important point is that they can be overused or underused. When overused, they become distractors. Sometimes the counselor is reluctant to seek clarification lest it impede or distract the client from the topic. If you are simply unable to follow the client's train of thought, it is more important to seek clarification than it is to allow the client to proceed. Otherwise, you run the risk of drawing inaccurate conclusions. Other examples of clarifying questions include:

"Could you go over that again for me?"

"Is there another way you could describe that feeling?"

"What did you mean a while ago when you said your parents were pretty indifferent?"

Open-Ended Questions

Open-ended questions require more than a minimal one-word answer by the client. They are introduced with *what, where, when, who,* or *how.* The choice of the opening word in open-ended questions is important because each word tends to elicit different kinds of responses from clients. *What* questions solicit facts and information; *how* questions are used to inquire about emotions or sequences of events; *where* and *when* elicit information about time and place; *who* elicits information about people (Ivey, Ivey, and Simek-Downing, 1987). It is important to vary the words used to start open-ended questions depending on the type of material you want to focus on and solicit from the client.

You may have noticed that we omitted the word *why* as a suitable stem. This is because *why* questions tend to focus on intentions and often have an accusatory ring to them, making a client feel put off, threatened, or defensive.

You will find that it is very difficult to ask questions that clearly place the focus upon your client. Fairly often, counselors ask questions that allow the client to respond with either a "yes" or a "no." The result is that the client assumes no responsibility for the content of the interview. The purpose of open-ended questions is to prevent this from happening. Examples of open-ended questions are:

"What are you thinking when you are silent?"

"How do you plan to find employment?"

"When do you feel anxious?"

"What do you like about it?"

"What is keeping you from doing it?"

"How do you feel about it?"

"How is it helping you?"

"When do you feel that way?"

"Where does that occur for you?"

Specific times when open-ended questions are very useful during counseling sessions include:

1. *Beginning an interview*
"What would you like to talk about?"
"How have things gone for you this week?"
"Where do you want to begin today?"

2. *Encouraging client elaboration*
"What happens when you lose control?"
"Who else is invested in this problem?"
"When do you notice this?"

"How could things be better for you?"

3. *Eliciting specific examples*
"What do you do when this happens?"
"Exactly how do you feel about it?"
"Where are you when you feel down?"

Closed Questions

When your objective is to get the client to talk about anything, the closed question is not a good response. However, when you want the client to give a specific piece of information, it can be the best response available because it narrows the area or focus of discussion. Consider the following examples of closed questions:

"How old were you when your parents died?"
"Are you an only child, or do you have brothers or sisters?"
"Are you taking any medication now?"
"Have you ever received counseling or therapy?"

Closed questions should be used sparingly. Too many closed questions can cause clients to avoid sensitive topics and can discourage client discussion and elaboration because the counselor assumes too much control of the session.

Effects of Assessment on Clients

The assessment stage of counseling is likely to have a number of possible effects on clients. Although each client may react somewhat idiosyncratically to an intake or problem-definition interview, it is also possible to describe some fairly predictable client reactions. Some of these are positive; some are negative. On the positive side, assessing client concerns helps clients to feel:

Understood: "Wow—someone finally understands how terrible these last few months have been for me."

Relieved: "What a relief to get that off my chest."

Hopeful: "Now at least maybe something can be done to help me feel better or get a handle on things."

Motivated: "Now that I have someone to talk to, I have some energy to do something about this."

On the negative side, assessment can result in client reactions and feelings such as:

Anxious: "Am I really that bad off? I guess so. Wow, this is heavy, so much to cope with and deal with at once."

Interrogated: "Boy, do I feel like I'm on the spot. There are so many questions being thrown at me. Some of them are so personal, too."

Vulnerable: "How do I know if I can trust him with this? Can he handle it and not share it with anyone else?"

Evaluated: "I wonder if she thinks I'm really messed up? Crazy? Stupid? Maybe something really is wrong with me."

Given these possible reactions, it is important to assess client concerns carefully and with much sensitivity. The ideal outcome is when the client's positive reactions to assessment outweigh the negative reactions. When this occurs, assessment has become a very useful and productive part of counseling without jeopardizing the rapport and relationship the counselor and client have worked so hard to establish prior to this time. Client reactions to assessment are likely to be more positive when the counselor uses questions that are directly relevant to the client's concerns and also used in proportion to other skills and responses.

Nothing can make a client feel defensive and interrogated more quickly than asking too many questions. Sometimes the same information can be gleaned by nonverbal attending behaviors, verbal following, or statements that paraphrase content or reflect feelings. Counselors seem to have a natural tendency to use questions more frequently than any other response (Spooner and Stone, 1977) and must be especially careful during assessment not to let this skill take over while their other newly learned skills "go by the wayside."

Case Illustration of Assessment: The Case of Mary

Mary appears to be a middle-aged female who works full-time as a teacher. She reports that she is divorced and has not remarried, although she maintains custody of two teenage children. She states that the reason she is seeking counseling at this time is to learn to have better control of her moods. She indicates that she often "flies off the handle" for no reason, with her own children or with her students in the classroom. She also reports that she cries easily and "feels blue" much of the time for no apparent reason.

Intake Interview

The intake-history interview with Mary revealed the following information:

I. *Identifying data:*
Mary is forty years old. She lives with her two children (ages twelve and fifteen) in a trailer outside a small town. She has been divorced for six years. She teaches English to high school sophomores.

II. *Range of problems:*
In addition to the problems first presented (feeling out of control and blue), Mary also feels she is a failure as a wife and a mother, primarily because of her divorce and her mood swings. Her self-description is predominantly negative.

III. *Current life setting:*
Mary's typical day consists of getting up, going to work. coming home, doing something with her children, and then grading papers or watching TV. On the weekends, she stays at home a great deal. She has few neighbors, only one or two close friends, and does not participate in any recreational, religious, or social activities on a regular basis. She reports a great deal of difficulty in carrying out her regular routine on days when she feels "down." Occasionally, she calls in sick and stays home and sleeps when this happens.

IV. *Family history:*
Mary is the youngest of three children. She describes her relationship to her two older brothers and to her mother and father as quite good. Additionally, she observes that her entire family treats one another with a great deal of respect. She also reports that as the youngest child and the only girl, she was protected and pampered a great deal by her parents and her brothers while growing up. Currently, she lives a day's drive away from both her parents and her brothers and sees them only three times a year. To her knowledge, none of her immediate family members have had any significant mental health problems.

V. *Personal history:*
   A. Medical

Mary reports that in the last year she has undergone major surgery twice—once for the removal of a benign lump in her breast and once for the repair of a disc. She also indicates she has been diagnosed as having Addison's disease and is on medication for it, prescribed by a general practitioner, but she frequently forgets to take the medication as prescribed.

Mary reports some sleeping problems, primarily when she is distressed. At these times, she has difficulty falling asleep until 2:00 or 3:00 AM. Her weight fluctuates by five or six pounds during a given month. When she is upset or blue, she often eats little or nothing for a day or two.

B. Educational

Mary has a bachelor's degree in English and consistently made good grades in all of her educational work. She appears to be of above-average intelligence and describes herself as a conscientious student to the point of worrying excessively about her grades and performance. As a teacher, she occasionally takes graduate courses to renew her certification.

C. Military

Mary has never served in the military.

D. Vocational

Mary has been a high school English teacher ever since graduating from college, although she reports that she "dropped out" of her teaching after her first child was born fourteen years ago. She resumed teaching again when she was divorced six years ago. Her children were then six and eight, respectively. She describes her present job as marginally adequate although not very challenging and not very financially rewarding. She indicates she stays with it primarily because of job security and because of the "hours" (summers off). She reports satisfactory relationships with other teachers, although she has no good friends at work.

E. Sexual and marital

Mary's first sexual experiences were with her former husband, although she reports she received a good bit of sex education from her parents and her older brothers. She asserts that this is a difficult subject for her to discuss. She states that while she felt her sexual relationship with her husband was adequate, he became sexually involved with another woman prior to their divorce. She indicates that before her marriage, she had had only two other "love" relationships with men, both of which were terminated mutually because of differences in values. She describes her marital relationship as good until the time she discovered through a friend about her husband's affair. She has very little contact with her ex-husband, although her two children see him every other weekend. She reports that the children have a good relationship with their father and that he has been helpful to her by taking the children for periods of time when she is feeling depressed and overwhelmed by her life situation. She repeatedly indicates that she blames herself for the failure of the marriage.

F. Counseling

Mary states that she saw a counselor for depression during her divorce. She saw the counselor for about twelve sessions. She terminated because she thought she had things under control. Now she is concerned about her ability to manage her feelings and wants your help to learn how to deal better with her moods, especially feeling upset, irritable, and blue.

G. Goals

Mary states that she does not have any specific short- or long-term goals other than to keep custody of her children and to be the best mother she can be.

VI. *Counselor's observations of Mary:*

During the intake interview, you observe that Mary generally seems to have little energy and is rather passive, as evidenced by her slouched body position, soft voice tone, and lack of animation in facial expressions and body movements. Mary appears to be in control of her feelings, although she cried much of the time while describing her marital and sexual history to you.

Integration of Material from Intake

Following an initial interview, it is important to tie together the information obtained from the client in some meaningful fashion. In Mary's case, we know that she is a middle-aged female who, although she has been divorced for six years, has not ever really resolved the divorce issue in her mind. Furthermore, her concern with mood fluctuations and feeling so blue appears to be substantiated not only by her nonverbal demeanor but also by her verbal reports of symptoms and behaviors typically associated with depressed mood:

> She perceives herself as a failure, particularly in her role as a wife and mother. She blames herself for the divorce.
>
> She describes herself negatively.
>
> She engages in very few enjoyable activities.
>
> She experiences a reduced level of energy and rate of activity when distressed. She has very few close relationships with others.
>
> She experiences some sleeping difficulties and loss of appetite when distressed. She does not appear to have any concrete goals and plans for the future for herself apart from her role as a mother.

This picture is complicated by her health. She has undergone two operations in the last year and also suffers from a fairly complex endocrinological problem which, because of her lack of compliance in taking prescribed medication, probably makes her mood fluctuations and depression more intense and more frequent. As part of and continuing beyond the intake interview, it is important to continue developing an understanding of the presenting problem. This involves assessment of the components of the problem, intensity, and possible controlling variables associated with Mary's feelings of dysphoria. Some of the information she gave during the intake session will serve as clues on which to build during the problem-definition process.

Problem Definition Analysis

I. Components of the problem:

Feelings: Mary describes her predominant feelings as irritable, upset, and "down" or "blue." Primary somatic reactions during times of stress include loss of appetite and insomnia.

Cognitions: When you ask Mary to describe specific things she thinks about or focuses on during the times she feels depressed, she responds with statements such as "I just think about what a failure I am" or "I wish I were a better wife (or mother)" or "I should have been able to keep my marriage together, and because I didn't, I'm a failure." Her cognitions represent two areas or trouble spots often associated with feelings of depression—shouldism and perfectionism. She does not report any thoughts or ideas about suicide.

Behaviors: Mary has some trouble specifying things she does or does not do while depressed. She finally states she often withdraws and retreats to her room, or becomes irritable, usually to her students or children. She also cries easily at these times.

Interpersonal relationships: Mary notes that once she feels down, no one around her can really pull her out of it. But she also observes she does not really have close friends to talk to about her feelings or problems. She believes her depressed feelings interfere with her relationship with her children because they tend to avoid her when she gets upset. However, she also acknowledges that she can use her feelings to get her children to do things "her way."

II. *Pattern of contributing events:*

When Mary describes what seems to lead up to these feelings, she notes the following:

1. Seems to be worst a week before her menstrual period
2. Failure to take her medication
3. Being reminded or reminding herself about her divorce
4. Hassles with her children and/or ex-husband

In noting what seems to keep the feelings going or make them worse or more intense, she describes:

1. One or two days before her period
2. Continued lapse of medication
3. Feeling sorry for herself
4. Being alone, particularly on weekends when the kids are with their father.

In describing what seems to stop the feelings or makes them better or worse, she observes:

1. Having her period over with
2. Taking her medication
3. Doing something with her children
4. Having to go to work
5. Having telephone or other contact with her brothers or parents

III. *Intensity of the problem:*

With depression, it is important to assess whether it is a long-term, chronic condition or a short-term response to a situation or event. Mary reports that she has felt more depressed for the last six years since the divorce. However, she acknowledges that as a child and even during her marriage she was frequently able to use tears to get her way. Thus, her crying at least had value for her in the past, and even currently she can use it to manipulate her children. She states that, on the average, she gets quite depressed for one week out of every month. She rates the intensity of her feelings at about 8 on a 1 (low) to 10 (high) scale. When she feels down, she usually does so for several days. This is the time when she is most apt to call in sick or to become irritable with her students or her children.

VI. *Client coping skills, strengths, resources:*
Mary is not readily aware of anything she does to deal effectively with her depressed feelings. She seems to believe that the onset and termination of these feelings are somewhat out of her control. She does describe herself as a good student and a good teacher. Her strengths are her reliability and dependability. She does indicate that she has a lot of perseverance and tenacity when she decides she wants something to work out.

Integration of Problem-Definition Information with Treatment Planning

The information obtained from this problem-definition session and initial session are of direct value in selecting and planning relevant counseling strategies to help Mary. In her case, the depression seems partially maintained by two potential physiological problems—Addison's disease and PMS, or premenstrual syndrome. Therefore, part of your planning would involve having her health assessed and monitored by a competent physician. Additionally, it is evident that the cognitive and interpersonal spheres are major components and contributing causes of these feelings. It would thus be important to select counseling strategies that focus on the cognitive and interpersonal modalities. Strategies such as cognitive restructuring, reframing, rational-emotive therapy, transactional analysis, social skills training, and family counseling are all useful possibilities. (These strategies are described in Chapters 8 and 10.)

Summary

Assessment is invaluable for seeking pertinent information about clients and their presenting problems. In addition to the value of information garnered, assessment can also be reactive; that is, it can initiate the process of change for clients. Assessment is usually started by intake sessions that gather information about the client's background and history. Assessment is very important in the early stages of counseling to help counselors formulate hypotheses, but it also is an ongoing process during counseling, as presenting problems and accompanying conceptualizations of issues often change. Specific assessment interviews obtain information about components of the problem, pattern of contributing events, intensity of the problem, and client coping skills. Skills used to obtain such information frequently include paraphrasing content, reflecting feelings, summarizing, and a variety of questions.

Exercises

I. Intake and History Interviews

A. Identify a current or existing problem in your life. It might be a family or relationship conflict, a love or sex issue, a financial problem, or a work or school-related concern. Select someone with whom you feel comfortable discussing this problem. Your task is to discuss how your background and history have affected the development and maintenance of this concern. You may want to refer to the intake and history outline on pages 81–83 in your discussion.

B. Using triads, identify one person as the client, one as the counselor, and one as the observer. The assigned tasks are as follows:

Client—Describe a present or ongoing concern or issue in your life.

Counselor—Conduct an intake or history-taking session with this client following the outline given on pages 81–83.

Observer—the interaction, using the outline on pages 81–83 as a guide. Be prepared to give feedback to the counselor following the role-play and/or to intervene and cue the counselor during the role-play if she or he has difficulty and gets stuck. Rotate the initial roles two more times so that each person has an opportunity to be in each role one time.

II. Problem-Definition

A. Using the same problem you identified for Exercise I A., identify:

   (1) The various components of the problem
   (2) Contributing conditions
   (3) Intensity of the problem
   (4) Your resources, strengths, and coping skills

You may wish to do this alone or in conjunction with a partner, colleague, instructor, or supervisor. It may be helpful to refer to the outline on page 84 and to jot down some key words as you go through this process.

B. Using triads, identify one person as the client, one as the counselor, and one as the observer. If possible, it may be helpful to use the same triads you used for Exercise B. The assigned tasks are as follows:

Client—Describe a current, ongoing problem. You may wish to use the same one you presented for the intake role-play.

Counselor—Conduct a problem-definition session with this client in which you assist the client to identify the components of the problem, the contributing variables, the intensity of the problem, and the client's resources and coping skills. Initially, it might be helpful for you to follow the outline given on page 84.

Observer—Observe the interaction, using the outline on page 84 as a guide. Give feedback to the counselor following the role-play. You also can guide the counselor during the session if he or she appears to need direction.

After the initial role-play, rotate the roles at least two times so that each person has an opportunity to function once in each of the three roles. Additional practice sessions may be necessary in order for you to integrate the skills associated with problem-definition interviews.

III. Questions

A. In this activity, identify whether each of the questions listed is a clarifying question, open-ended question, or closed question. Use the key below to record your answers in the blanks provided. Feedback follows the exercises.

C = Clarifying
O-E = Open-ended
Cl = Closed

____ 1. "What is it like for you when you get depressed?"
____ 2. "Have you had a physical exam in the last two years?"
____ 3. "Are you saying you don't give up easily?"
____ 4. "How does this job affect your moods?"
____ 5. "Do you mean to say that you have difficulty letting go?"
____ 6. "Do you have many children?"

B. In this activity, you are given five client statements. Practice formulating a question for each client statement. Share your questions in your class or with your instructor or a colleague.

1. *Client (a teenager)*: "I've got to graduate with my class. If I don't, everyone will think I'm a failure."
2. *Client (an elderly man)*: "It's just so hard to make it living on a fixed income like this. If I had it to do over again, it would be a lot different."
3. *Client (a young girl)*: "I hate my dad. He's always picking on me."
4. *Clients (a couple married for four years)*: "It's just not turning out the way we thought. We wanted our marriage to really work. But it's not."
5. *Client (a middle-aged person)*: "There are just so many pressures on me right now—from all sides family, work, friends, you name it."

Feedback for Exercises

III. Questions

1. O-E	4. O-E
2. Cl	5. C
3. C	6. Cl

Discussion Questions

1. Intake interviews and the problem-definition process are time-consuming and may seem to delay the counseling process. Assuming you are the clinical director for a private mental health agency, how would you justify the use of these assessment interviews to the administrative director or to the agency's board?

2. Suppose you are seeing a client who presents a crisis situation (e.g. recent rape, decision over abortion, spouse-child abuse). You probably will not have the luxury of devoting a session or more to conduct a complete intake/problem-definition process. What information about the problem and about the client's background and history would be most important to obtain in a fifteen-minute period of time?

3. Assessment with young children (ages 6–10) calls for a different type of interaction. How would you modify your approach to this age group? What kinds of information would you solicit? What do you know about yourself that would either facilitate

the assessment process or provide obstacles to your success
with this age group?

Recommended Readings

Celotta, B., & Telasi-Golubscow, H. (1982), "A Problem Taxonomy for
Classifying Client's Problems," *Personnel and Guidance Journal 61*,
73–76.

Egan, G. (1990), *The Skilled Helper*, (Pacific Grove, CA: Brooks/Cole).
Chapter 7, Helping Clients Tell Their Stories.

Epstein, N.B., & Bishop, D.S. (1981), "Problem-Centered Systems Therapy
of the Family," *Journal of Marital and Family Therapy 7*, 23–31.

Hackney, H., & Cormier, L.S. (1988), *Counseling Strategies and Interventions*, (Englewood Cliffs, NJ: Prentice-Hall). Chapter 9, Conceptualizing Problems and Setting Goals.

Haynes, S.N., Jensen, B.M., Wise, E., & Sherman, D. (1981), "The Marital
Intake Interview: A Multimethod Criterion Validity Instrument,"
Journal of Consulting and Clinical Psychology, 49, 379–387.

Hutchins, D. (1979), "Systematic Counseling: The T-F-A Model for Counselor Intervention," *Personnel and Guidance Journal 57*, 529–531.

Laing, J. (1988), "Self-Report: Can It Be of Value as an Assessment Technique?" *Journal of Counseling and Development 67*, 60–61.

Long, L., Paradise, L., & Long, T. (1981), *Questioning: Skills for the Helping
Process* (Pacific Grove, CA: Brooks/Cole).

Miller, M.J. (1990), "The Power of the "OCEAN": Another Way to Diagnose Clients," *Counselor Education and Supervision, 29*, 283–290.

Osberg, T.M. (1989), "Self-Report Reconsidered: A Further Look at its
Advantages as an Assessment Technique," *Journal of Counseling
and Development 68*, 111–113.

Swensen, C.H. (1968), *An Approach to Case Conceptualization* (Boston:
Houghton Mifflin).

West, J.D. (1988), "Marriage and Family Therapy Assessment," *Counselor
Education and Supervision 28*, 169–180.

5

Developing Counseling Goals

Often counselors (or sometimes clients) will complain, "The session didn't go anywhere" or "I felt like we were talking in circles." As part of the assessment process, it is important to translate general client concerns into specific, desired goals. Goals represent the results or outcomes the client wants to achieve at the end of counseling. Goals give direction to the therapeutic process and help both counselor and client to move in a focused direction with a specific route in mind. Without goals, it is all too easy to get sidetracked or lost. Goals help both the counselor and client to specify exactly what can and cannot be accomplished through counseling. In this respect, goal-setting is an important extension of the assessment process in counseling. Recall that during assessment, clients focus on specific concerns and issues that are difficult, problematic, or are not going very well for them. In goal-setting, clients identify specific ways in which they want to resolve these issues and specific actions they can take for problem resolution.

Functions of Counseling Goals

Goals serve three important functions in the counseling process. First, goals can have a *motivational* function in counseling. When clients are encouraged to specify desired changes, they are more likely to work toward accomplishing those outcomes. This is particularly true when clients actively participate in the goal-setting process. Clients are much more likely to support and work toward changes that *they* create.

Goals also have an *educational* function in counseling in that they can help clients acquire new responses. Goals provide clients with information and standards by which they can encode and rehearse desired actions and responses. As Dixon and Glover (1984) explain, "Once a goal is formulated and selected by a problem solver, it is likely to be rehearsed in the working memory and stored in long-term memory. A goal encoded in this way, then, becomes a major heuristic for the problem solver as he or she interacts with the environment" (pp. 128-129). This is quite evident in the performance of highly successful performers or athletes who set goals for themselves and then use the goal to rehearse their performance over and over in their heads. Concert pianists, for example, will cognitively rehearse the way they want a particular selection to sound; champion divers will see themselves performing a particular feat in the desired fashion.

Goals also meet an *evaluative* function in counseling. The type of outcomes or change represented by the client's goals helps the counselor to select and evaluate various counseling strategies that are likely to be successful for a particular client pursuing a specific direction or set of outcomes. Goals also contribute to the evaluative function in counseling because a goal or outcome represents the difference between the client's *present* behavior and situation and the *desired* behavior and situation. When outcome goals are established, both the counselor and client can evaluate client progress toward the goals in order to determine when they are being attained and when the goals or the counseling strategies may need revision. As Bandura (1969) notes: "When desired outcomes are designated in observable and measurable terms, it becomes readily apparent when the methods have succeeded, when they have failed, and when they need further development to increase their potency. This self-corrective feature is a safeguard against perpetuation of ineffective approaches. . ." (p. 74).

Parameters of Goal-Setting: Process and Outcome Goals

The counseling process involves two types of goals: process goals and outcome goals. *Process goals* are related to the establishment of therapeutic conditions necessary for client change. These are general goals, such as establishing rapport, providing a nonthreatening setting, and possessing and communicating accurate empathy and unconditional regard. They can be generalized to all client relationships and can be considered universal goals. Process goals are your primary responsibility; you cannot expect your clients to help you establish and communicate something like unconditional regard.

Unlike process goals, *outcome goals* will be different for each client. They are the goals directly related to your clients' changes to be made as a result of counseling. As you are able to help your clients understand their concerns, you will want to help them understand how counseling can be used to respond to these concerns. The two of you will begin to formulate tentative outcome goals together. As counseling continues, the original goals may be modified through better understanding of the problems and through the development of new attitudes and behaviors that will eliminate or reduce problems. Goal-setting should be viewed as a flexible process, always subject to modification and refinement. Most important, outcome goals are *shared* goals, goals that both you and your clients agree to work toward achieving.

Outcome goals that are visible or observable are more useful, since they allow you to know when they have been achieved. Yet not all outcome goals are stated as visible goals. For example, consider the two outcome goals:

1. To help your client develop more fully his or her self-actualizing potential
2. To increase the frequency of positive self-statements at home and at work by 50 percent over the next six weeks

Both of these could be considered to be outcome goals. They might even be so closely related as to be the same in terms of outcomes. Your clients may be much more attracted to such goals as developing their self-actualizing potential. You may want to view the development of self-actualizing potential as a composite of many smaller and more specific goals. To state it a little differently, self-actualizing is a hypothetical state that cannot be observed. It can only be inferred through certain visible and audible behaviors. Using this goal, you have no way of knowing the types of activity that your clients will enter into while proceeding toward the goals. As a result, you and your clients know very little about what they could be doing in the relationship, and you have no way of assessing progress toward the desired results. Consequently the first goal (1) is not as satisfactory, in that it does not provide you or your clients with guidelines for change.

When outcome goals are stated precisely, both you and your clients have a better understanding of what is to be accomplished. This better understanding permits you to work more directly with your client's problems or concerns and reduces tangential efforts. Equally important are the benefits you are able to realize in working with specific behavioral goals. You are able to enlist the client's cooperation more directly, since your client is more likely to understand what is to be done. In addition, you are in a better position to select appropriate techniques and strategies when your clients have specific objectives. Finally, both you and your clients are in a better position to recognize progress, a rewarding experience in its own right.

Three Elements of Good Outcome Goals

Perhaps you have noticed from our previous examples that outcome goals are different from process goals in several respects. A well-stated outcome goal includes the behavior to be changed, the conditions under which the changed behavior will occur, and the level or amount of change. One client may want to modify eating patterns; another may wish to reduce negative self-appraisal; and a third may wish to increase assertive requests or refusals.

The second element of an outcome goal indicates the conditions under which the desired behavior(s) will occur. It is important to weigh carefully the situations or settings in which the client will attempt a new behavior. You wouldn't want to set your client up to fail by identifying settings in which there was little hope for success. The client might agree to modify eating habits at home during the evening, but not to attempt to modify eating habits at the company dinner on Saturday night.

The third element of outcome goals involves the choice of a suitable and realistic level or amount of the new behavior. That is to say, *how much* of the new behavior will the client attempt? Some clients enter diets with the expectation that they will reduce their consumption from 3,000 calories per day to 900 calories per day. A more realistic goal might be to reduce to 1,500 calories. This brings us to another thought about goals. As we modify goals, we come increasingly closer to the ultimate goals of the client. Each time we set a goal, it is a closer approximation of the results. Successive approximations are very important. They allow the client to set more attainable goals, experience success more often, and make what might be dramatic changes in their life style.

Obstacles in Developing Specific Goals

Krumboltz and Thoresen (1969) have noted that rarely does a client begin by requesting assistance in achieving specific behavior changes. Instead of saying "I want to be able to talk to teachers without getting nervous," the client is likely to say "I am shy." In other words, a personal characteristic has been described rather than the ways in which the characteristic is experienced. It then becomes the counselor's job to help the client describe the ways in which the characteristic could be changed.

Taking nonspecific concerns and translating them into specific goal statements is no easy task for the counselor, who must understand the nature of the client's problem and the conditions under which it occurs before the translation can begin.

What can you expect of yourself and your clients in terms of setting specific goals? First, the goals that are set can never be more specific than your understanding and the client's understanding of the problem. This means that at the outset of counseling, goals are likely to be nonspecific and nonbehavioral. *But nonspecific goals are better than no goals at all.*

Krumboltz (1966) describes these nonspecific (general) goals as *intermediate* mental states, but he emphasizes that one cannot assume that such goals will "free up" clients to change their overt behavior. The point is that although intermediate goals may be necessary at the outset of counseling or until you have some specific knowledge of the client, such goals must be viewed as temporary. At the earliest possible time, you must strive to identify more concrete and observable goals.

As you and your client explore the nature of a particular problem, the type of goal(s) appropriate to the problem should become increasingly clear. This clarification will permit both of you to move in the direction of identifying specific behaviors that, if changed, would alter the problem in a positive way. These specific behaviors can then be formulated into goal statements; as you discuss the client's problems in more detail, gradually you can add the circumstances in which to perform the behaviors and how much or how often the target behaviors might be altered.

The **GOAL SETTING MAP** (Figure 5-1) is a useful tool to help clients learn to set goals. The map provides a visual representation of the goal-setting process and requires that the client focus on the steps that lead to change. The first step is to help your client establish a desired outcome (*Main Goal*). Then encourage your client to identify three to five things that would have to change for this desired outcome to occur (*Subgoals*), and finally, the client must identify at least three things he or she must do for each of the subgoals to happen (*Immediate Tasks*). When several subgoals are identified, they usually are arranged in a sequence or hierarchy. Similarly, the immediate tasks related to each subgoal are arranged in a logical sequence and are accomplished in that order. The client completes one subgoal before moving on to another. By gradually

FIGURE 5–1 Goal Setting Map

```
                                              1. _____
                         1. _____    2. _____
                                              3. _____

                                              1. _____
                         2. _____    2. _____
                                              3. _____

                                              1. _____
 1. _____       3. _____    2. _____
    Main Goal                                 3. _____

                                              1. _____
                         4. _____    2. _____
                                              3. _____

                                              1. _____
                         5. _____    2. _____
                            Subgoals          3. _____
                                              Immediate Tasks
```

Step #1:   Choose a Main Goal (long-term or short-term)

Step #2:   Write five steps you must take toward achieving this main goal. These are your Subgoals.

Step #3:   For each Subgoal, write down three more steps which must be taken to achieve it. These are your immediate tasks and you can begin *NOW*.

---

completing the activities represented by subgoals and immediate tasks in a successful manner, the client's motivation and energy to change are reinforced and maintained (Hackney, 1973). Successful completion of subgoals also may reduce potential failure experiences by giving the client greater control over the learning process (Bandura, 1969). Subgoals always represent actions that move clients in the direction of the desired goal (Carkhuff & Anthony, 1979). The most effective counseling subgoals are:

1. Built on existing client resources and assets
2. Based upon client selection and commitment
3. Congruent with the counselor's and client's values
4. Identified with immediate tasks the client can be expected to accomplish

Skills Associated with Goal-Setting

Goal-setting involves all of the prior skills learned so far. The skills and conditions associated with an effective relationship are necessary in order to establish *process* goals with clients. For instance, relationship skills such as empathic responding, matching or pacing of the client's language, and nonverbal behavior are useful for process goals of establishing rapport, conveying trust, and communicating accurate understanding to clients.

Careful listening is important in order to hear subtle outcomes or veiled attempts to change the goal. Listening responses can help you hear client messages about their goals more accurately, reflect clients' positive or negative feelings about goal-setting, and summarize desired client changes.

Questions are also an integral part of goal-setting in order to help clients state desired results. Consider, for instance, the following ones:

"How do you want things to change for you?"

"In what ways do you want counseling to help you?"

"What would you like to be doing (thinking or feeling) differently?"

"When do you want to be able to accomplish this?"

"In what situations?"

"What amount of change is realistic, considering where you are right now?

"What are some things you need to do to be able to make this happen?"

"What will your first step be?"

In addition to these skills, there are two other responses that are very useful during the goal-setting process: *confrontation* and the *ability-potential response.* In this section, we describe these skills and provide examples of their uses.

The Confrontation

One of the most useful counselor responses is the confrontation. The word itself has acquired some excess emotional meanings. The confrontation is sometimes misconstrued to mean lecturing, judging, or acting in some punitive manner. A more accurate notion is to regard the confrontation as a response that enables clients to face what they want or feel they need to avoid. The avoidance might be a resistance to the client's own feelings or to another person, including the counselor and counseling relationship. The avoidance is usually expressed as one part of a discrepancy present in the client's behavior. Thus, the confrontation helps the client to identify a contradiction, a rationalization or excuse, and a misinterpretation.

The discrepancy or contradiction is usually one of the following types:

1. A discrepancy between what clients say and how they behave (for example, the client who says he is a quiet type, but in the interview, he talks freely).
2. A contradiction between how clients say they feel and how their behaviors suggest they are feeling (for example, the client who says she is comfortable but continues to fidget).
3. A discrepancy between two verbal messages of the client (for example, the client who says he wants to change his behavior, but in the next breath places all blame for his behavior on his parents or on others).

Operationally, the confrontation is a compound sentence. The statement establishes a "you said/but look" condition. In other words, the first part of the compound sentence is the "you said" portion. It repeats a message of the client. The second part of the compound sentence presents the contradiction or discrepancy, the "but look" of the client message. For example:

"You say school isn't very satisfying, but your grades are excellent."

"You keep putting that job off, and eventually you're going to be back in the same trap of being mad at yourself."

The first part, or the "you said" portion, need not be stated by the *counselor.* It may be implied instead, if the client's discrepancy is obvious. For example:

> *Client:* I just can't talk to people I don't know.
>
> *Counselor:* (You say, etc. *[implied part]*) But you don't know me that well.

Using the confrontation suggests doing just what the word implies and *no more.* The confrontation in both the "you said/but look" conditions *describes* client messages, *observes* client behavior, and *presents* evidence. However, the confrontation should *not* contain an accusation, evaluation, or problem solution.

The confrontation serves several important purposes:

1. It assists in the client's achievement of congruency; that is, a state in which what the client says and how the client behaves correspond.
2. It establishes the counselor as a role model for direct and open communication; that is, if the counselor is not afraid to confront these contradictions, perhaps the client can be less afraid of them.
3. It is an action-oriented stimulus. Unlike the reflection stimulus that mirrors the client's *feelings*, the confrontation mirrors the client's *behavior*. It is very useful in initiating action plans and behavior change on the client's part.
4. It is useful in exploring conflict associated with change and goal-setting.

The Ability-Potential Response

The ability-potential response is one in which the counselor suggests to the client that he or she has the ability or potential to engage in a specified form of activity. It not only reinforces the client's sense of control and management of his or her life and affairs, but also communicates the counselor's faith in the client's ability to act independently. The ability potential can be used to suggest a course of action that is potentially beneficial to the client. As such, it is extremely useful during goal-setting to help clients establish subgoals or action steps. Of course, subgoals must be selected and "owned" by the client. It is important for the counselor not to become overly invested in which actions the client pursues; otherwise, the ability-potential response is likely to be rejected by the client.

If your client were to say: "I don't know where I'm going to get the money to pay that bill," you could say: "You could work for a semester and earn the money." In other words, you are suggesting that the client has the ability to pay the bill, should he or she work for a semester to earn the money. Consider a second example:

> *Client:* I'd like to be able to tell him what I really feel, but if I do, I believe he'll get upset.

Counselor: We could start by anticipating some potential positive ways to talk to him.

Typically, the ability-potential response begins with "you could" or "you can." Like all the other types of counselor responses that you have been learning, it can be overused. When that happens, it begins to sound unreal, hollow, and meaningless. Although the ability-potential response sounds like advice, it is used effectively as a means of identifying alternatives available to the client. It is misused when, in oversimplification, the counselor attempts to suggest or prescribe a panacea; the effect is to negate or hide the client's feelings of concern.

Effects of Goal-Setting on Clients

The process of setting goals can have important effects on clients. Most are positive or helpful, although an occasional client may resist the goal-setting process. The advantages of establishing concrete goals are:

Clients feel less confused, clearer about themselves and their wants and needs. Goal-setting helps clients sort out the important from the mundane, the relevant from the trivial of their lives. Goal-setting encourages them to make decisions and choices that represent their most significant values and priorities. As a consequence, clients often feel more enlightened and more clear about what they really want for themselves.

Clients feel a sense of accomplishment. Goal-setting is often the first time during counseling that clients begin to take specific action in response to a problem or issue. Sometimes the problem has been a long-standing one. Clients reward themselves during goal-setting by overcoming a sense of inertia, by mobilizing their forces, and by starting to set in place a chain of events and behaviors that will lead to problem resolution. As a result, clients often feel a great sense of accomplishment during and after the goal-setting process.

Clients feel better about themselves and their concerns. The process of establishing specific goals can be reactive; that is, the act of selecting and defining results can contribute to desired changes. This is particularly true when clients are heavily invested in the goal-setting process. As Lloyd (1983) notes, "Clients who are aware of their own specific objectives may do better in therapy than those who are not. The more involved both therapists and clients are in the details of goal attainment procedures, the more likely is the system to be reactive" (p. 60). When goal-setting is reactive, clients are likely to feel better about themselves and encouraged about the directions they are choosing to pursue.

Recent research into client perceptions of various aspects of the counseling relationship support the importance of goal-setting (Halstead, Brooks, Goldberg, and Fish, 1990). In their results they found

> . . . that clients perceived the goal portion of the alliance as being stronger than their counselors did. A possible explanation for this finding, again, may be associated with the nature of the client's personal investment. One would expect the counselor and client to have a common understanding of the explicit goals that help to guide the counseling process. These goals, from the counselor's frame of reference, serve as a beacon by which to set a course to help the client. To the client, however, the goals of counseling, especially in early sessions, may get associated directly with a way to relieve emotional pain. The goals in counseling may represent a real sense of hope for the client. Therefore, it is likely that clients form stronger personal attachments to their goals in that goals can serve to create solutions to what may look like overwhelming situations (p. 216).

Occasionally a client may be hesitant about setting goals or reluctant to work toward change. For instance, upon completing a counseling session with her client, a counselor said, "This was the fourth interview, and I still cannot get him to talk about goals." When this happens, the counselor must deal with the question: "What is the client resisting?"

In working with client resistance to goals, it is helpful to realize that such behavior is purposeful; that is, what the client does or avoids doing achieves some desirable result for the client. Consequently, we may find that the client who resists setting goals may be protecting the behavior that is in need of modification because that behavior is also doing something desirable. An example is the chronic smoker. Although an individual may recognize the negative consequences of smoking, he or she also clings to the habit, believing that it is a helpful way to deal with a tense situation, that it is relaxing, that it increases enjoyment of a good meal, and so on.

It becomes your task to get clients to identify what they gain from their current behavior. In so doing, you may help clients determine whether that gain or outcome can be achieved in more desirable ways. For example, a young student may throw paper airplanes out the school window in order to gain attention from peers. Gaining attention may be a desirable outcome; it is the method that is the problem. Therefore, you and your client may consider more appropriate means for gaining increased attention other than throwing airplanes out the school window.

Sometimes clients resist attempts to establish goals because they feel that the counselor (either overtly or subtly) is pushing them in a certain direction. Unless clients can determine some *personal* goals of counseling, the probability of any change is minimal. You can avoid creating client resistance to goals by encouraging active participation by clients in the goal-setting process.

Some clients resist goal-setting because they are genuinely confused about their desired priorities, needs, and wants. They know what is wrong in their lives, but they cannot articulate what they need to modify. These clients resist goal-setting because it puts them in touch with their confusion, and also because there is an implicit demand for them to sort things out, to "get clear." With such clients, it is often very helpful to acknowledge their confusion directly ("Joe, I can sense how hard it is for you to sort things out now" or "Mary, I can see these feelings of doubt and confusion are overpowering to you now"). If you give them overt permission to "go slow," the implicit pressure to "get clear" does not compound their already building sense of frustration and powerlessness. You might say something like, "Don't feel that you have to come up with something right *now*. Take a few minutes (or next week) to think about it. Give yourself time to mull it over."

Other possible strategies to help the "confused" client set goals include:

1. *Language work:* Ask the client to complete open-ended sentences such as, "I want," "I do not want," "I need," "I do not need," "I choose to."
2. *Imagery and visualization:* Ask the client to visualize himself or herself in an ideal situation and describe it—or to visualize someone else who embodies the qualities and behaviors the client desires. What are they?
3. *Role-play and enactment:* Ask the client to attempt to reenact the problem through a role-play.

Other clients may be very conflicted about competing priorities and needs. They may identify several possible directions or options, but be in conflict about which course of action is the best one to pursue. These clients resist goal-setting because it exposes the conflict, which often feels painful or uncomfortable to clients and seems easier to mask or avoid than to deal with head-on. With such clients, it is often helpful to use the skill of confrontation (described earlier in this chapter) to point out the apparent conflict: "Jean, on the one hand, you're saying that you want to have some stability in your life. At the same time. you're saying you are considering a job offer in which you will be required to move every two years."

Confrontation is particularly useful for *identifying* and *describing* the conflict. For actual *working through* of the conflict, additional counseling strategies, such as Gestalt dialoguing (see Chapter 7), Transactional Analysis redecision work (Chapter 8), and reframing (Chapter 10) are usually necessary. It would be important to use such strategies with these clients at this point in counseling, since very little progress is likely to be made until this initial conflict is resolved.

Client Participation in Goal-Setting

Often, goal-setting is construed to mean that you listen to the client, make a mental assessment of the problem, and prescribe a solution or goal. In fact, such a procedure is doomed to failure. The nature of counseling is such that the *client must be involved* in the establishment of goals. Otherwise, the client's participation is directionless at best and interferes with counseling at worst. An example will illustrate this idea.

A beginning counselor was seeing a client who was overweight, self-conscious about her appearance, reluctant to enter into social relationships with others because of this self-consciousness, and very lonely. Realizing that the problem of being overweight was an important factor, the counselor informed the client that one goal would be for her (the client) to lose one to three pounds per week, under a doctor's supervision. With this, the client became highly defensive and rejected the counselor's goal, saying, "You sound just like my mother."

Goal-setting is highly personal. It requires a great deal of effort and commitment on the client's part. Therefore, the client must select goals that are important enough to make sacrifices to achieve. In the above example, the client's resistance could have been prevented if the counselor had moved more slowly, permitting the client to identify for herself the significance of her being overweight and the importance of potential weight loss. At this point, both the counselor and client could then work together to determine the specific goals and subgoals that, when achieved, might alleviate the client's concerns. As with other aspects of the counseling relationship, goal-setting should be an interactive process for which both counselor and client assume responsibility.

Case Illustration of Goal-Setting: Continuation of the Case of Mary

In this example, we illustrate how the counselor could help Mary (from Chapter 4) identify desired outcome goals for counseling. Recall that Mary described her problem as a depressed state in which she perceives herself as a failure, engages in few meaningful activities or relationships with others, and in general, lacks a purpose in life apart from her role as a parent. Also, recall that part of Mary's depressed moods seem to be precipitated and/or maintained by a physiological condition—premenstrual syndrome (PMS).

After you and Mary probe the facets of her concerns, you can consider the specific changes Mary would like to make. Gradually, these changes can be translated into an outline of desired goals (see Figure 5-1). We refer to this as an outline because of the major headings (I, II, III, IV) which represent the four overall or primary outcome goals for Mary; the subheadings (A, B, C, D) reflect the changes Mary believes must occur for the outcome goals to be achieved. And the sub-heading items (1, 2, 3, 4) indicate tasks Mary can do to bring about those changes. Remember that goal-setting is a flexible process, and that the goals listed in this outline might change as counseling with Mary progresses. Mary's goal outline follows.

I. *Outcome Goal 1:* Mary wishes to become significantly more positive about herself over the next three months.

    A. Mary must learn to recognize when she is involved in negative and self-defeating thoughts or self-talk about herself each day.

        1. Mary will start noting the number of times each day she says or thinks something negative about herself.

        2. Mary will begin to keep a list of general topics she tends to use in putting herself down.

        3. Mary will start noting what time of day she finds herself involved in negative and/or self-defeating behavior to determine if she is more vulnerable at certain parts of the day or night.

B. Mary must develop a list of positive or self-enhancing statements about herself.

1. Mary will begin focusing on her positive qualities with the counselor's help.

2. Mary will write each positive quality statement she identifies on a 3 x 5 index card and keep these cards handy during the parts of the day that she has identified as her most vulnerable times.

3. Mary will faithfully read a positive quality statement and focus on it until she has overcome the negative surge each time she finds herself starting to become negative or self-defeating.

C. Mary will examine the setting(s) in which she is most likely to become self-defeating or negative to determine the effect of setting on her moods.

1. With the counselor's help, Mary will look for a time-of-day pattern to her tendency to become negative or self-defeating.

2. With the counselor's help, Mary will look for other conditions that might be associated with her moods, e.g. being alone, having a lot of tasks to do, and so on.

3. With the counselor's help, Mary will identify settings to avoid and develop a list of alternative activities when she finds herself in a self-defeating setting.

II. *Outcome Goal 2:* Mary wishes to control any negative effects from PMS that might contribute to her mood swings.

A. Mary will seek a dependable physician's advice on the effect of PMS on her mood swings.

1. Mary will make an appointment with her gynecologist for an examination and consultation on the possible effects of her PMS.

2. Mary will try to anticipate when she is due for a bout with the blues.

B. Mary must determine what changes of behavior, use of medication, etc., would counteract any effects of PMS on her mood swings.

1. Mary will use this information to identify how her daily habits must change.

2. Mary will begin a preventive program, as prescribed by the information she has obtained.

3. Mary will keep a daily record of her new activities until they become part of her normal routine.

4. Mary will monitor the intensity of her moods on a 1–10 scale in at least three different time periods on a daily basis over the next two months.

III. *Outcome Goal 3:* Mary wishes to be more aware of those daily activities and relationships and their meaningfulness or value to her.

    A. Mary must determine the relative importance of her work and leisure activities and relationships.

       1. Mary will monitor and log all daily work and leisure-time activities for a week and with the counselor's help, will categorize these activities into "pleasant" or "unpleasant" categories.

       2. Mary will determine which of the "unpleasant" activities are within her control to change or reschedule.

       3. With the counselor's help, Mary will attempt to reframe the meaning of those "unpleasant" activities so that they become at least neutral and perhaps pleasant.

       4. Mary will do the same analysis with her relationships.

    B. Mary must establish a more positive balance between negative and positive work/leisure activities and relationships.

       1. With the counselor's help, Mary will analyze her typical weekly schedule to determine whether it is overbalanced by negative activities and relationships.

       2. With the counselor's help, Mary will identify new sources of positive activities and relationships associated with her work and leisure time.

       3. With the counselor's help, Mary will seek to establish and maintain a positive balance in her weekly work/leisure activities and relationships.

IV. *Outcome Goal 4:* Mary would like to have a sense of meaning for her life and some sort of a "plan" for the next five to fifteen years, and she would like to feel like she is working toward fulfilling that plan.

    A. Mary knows that she must have a better understanding of her values, and what kinds of goals and accomplishments are really important to her.

       1. With the counselor's help, Mary will do some values clarification activities to get a better sense of her life priorities.

2.   Mary will begin to look at her present activities and priorities to see if they match her life priorities.

B.   Mary realizes that part of her problem is inertia and being a slave to her habits, and she must fight to overcome this personal quality if she is to have the kind of life she wants for herself.

1.   With the counselor's help, Mary will start a list of things she has always wanted to do.

2.   Mary will select from this list, one activity, will set a date to do it, and will make the plans necessary to carry it out.

3.   With the counselor's help, Mary will evaluate the success of this activity, its effect on her self-concept and self-satisfaction, and its meaningfulness for her.

C.   Mary would like to feel more independent of her ex-husband.

1.   She will attempt to be more resourceful about taking responsibility for the children during times when she is feeling blue.

2.   She will try to view the children's relationship with their father as a positive factor in her life rather than a potentially threatening factor.

Notice the process by which these outcome goals are established:

1. They begin as overall goals that are directly related to the client's specific or general concerns or descriptions of a set of problems.
2. Specific and observable changes (subgoals) are identified which must occur if Mary is to succeed in accomplishing the overall goal(s).
3. Specific tasks are identified that Mary must accomplish if the observable changes (subgoals) are to be accomplished.

Thus, goal-setting moves from general goals (which are related to the presenting problem) to specific goals to specific tasks. The specific goals are directly related to the general goal; the tasks are the activities that must occur to achieve the specific goals.

Summary

Goal-setting is such a central part of the change process that people often take it for granted. And yet, many people (including many helpers) are not very skilled at setting goals or helping others to identify and set goals. In this chapter we have differentiated two types of goals that are part of the counseling process: *process goals* and *outcome goals*. Process goals affect the therapeutic relationship. Outcome goals determine the specific counselor interventions and desired results or changes that the client hopes to achieve. Goals can help motivate clients to make desired changes and can also prove useful as the counselor attempts to evaluate therapeutic progress. Parameters of effective goal-setting include identification of what broad changes the client would wish to accomplish, specific situations that would have to change if this broad goal is to be achieved, and specific "tasks" the client would have to undertake if the intermediate objectives are to be realized. A goal-setting plan was offered in Figure 5-1 that can be used with clients to provide the structure for goal-setting in the counseling session.

Exercises

I. Identification of Client Goals

Tom is a junior in college. He is bright and personable, but a bit shy. He came to counseling with the problem of relating to girls. Specifically, he is concerned that there may be some flaw in his personality that "turns girls off." His reasons for thinking this grow out of his experience with dating. He reports that girls go out with him once or twice and then do not accept any more dates. He admits to getting discouraged when he calls a girl for a date and she says she already has a commitment. If this happens twice, he never calls the girl again, assuming that she does not want to date him, and wishing to spare himself further embarrassment.

1. Put yourself in Tom's position. Identify a few goals which you think might be appropriate objectives in the counseling process, using the suggested goal outline in Figure 5-1.

   Main Goal   Subgoals   Immediate Tasks

2. Are your goals specific or vague? How would Tom know when he had achieved these goals? How would achieving them affect Tom's dating problem?

3. As Tom's counselor, what *process* goals would you set for yourself. How would these process goals relate to Tom's presenting behavior and problems?

II. Outcome Goals

In the following exercise, examples of client-outcome goals are presented. Determine which of the three elements of an outcome goal behavior, condition, or level may be missing. After each example, list the missing parts, using *B* for behavior, *C* for condition, and *L* for level. Feedback will be provided to you at the end of the exercise.

The following example is provided as an illustration: To increase job placement (behavior) of physically handicapped clients seen in a rehabilitation agency (condition) by 30 percent in a one-year time period (level).

Identify the missing parts in the following four outcome goals:

1. To decrease temper tantrums.
2. To increase exercise to two times a week over a six-week period.
3. To decrease the number of nightly arguments at home with your wife.
4. To decrease tardiness.

Feedback for Exercises

II. Outcome Goals

1. The missing elements are the condition *(C)* and level *(L)* of the goal.

2. This goal specifies the behavior and the level; the condition *(C)* is missing.

3. The level *(L)* of the goal is missing here.

4. This goal specifies the behavior; the condition *(C)* and level *(L)* are not present.

Discussion Questions

1. In this chapter we discussed possible reasons for client resistance to goal-setting. Can you think of any reasons why counselors might also resist developing outcome goals with clients?

2. In what ways do outcome goals help you assess client progress during counseling? What would it be like to assess progress when no goals have been formulated?

3. Identify a recent problematic situation for yourself in which you specified and utilized a goal. How did specifying the desired result help you handle the situation?

4. What are some steps counselors can take to maximize client participation in the goal-setting process?

Recommended Readings

Cormier, W.H. & Cormier, L.S. (1991), *Interviewing Strategies for Helpers: Fundamental Skills and Cognitive-Behavioral Interventions* (Pacific Grove, CA: Brooks/Cole), Chapter 9, Selecting and Defining Outcome Goals.

Dixon, D.N. & Glover, J.A. (1984). *Counseling: A Problem-Solving Approach*. (New York: John Wiley), Chapter 8, Goal selection.

Frey, D.H. & Raming, H.E. (1979), "A Taxonomy of Counseling Goals and Methods," *The Personnel and Guidance Journal, 58*, 26–33.

Hackney, H. (1973), "Goal-Setting: Maximizing the Reinforcing Effects of Progress," *The School Counselor, 20*, 176–181.

Hackney, H. & Cormier, L.S. (1988), *Counseling Strategies and Interventions*, 3rd Ed. (Englewood Cliffs, NJ: Prentice-Hall), Chapter 9, Conceptualizing Problems and Setting Goals.

Halstead, R.W., Brooks, D.K., Goldberg, A., & Fish, L.S. (1990), "Counselor and Client Perceptions of the Working Alliance," *Journal of Mental Health Counseling 12*, 208–221.

6

Defining Strategies and Selecting Interventions

Thus far, we have described a process in which the counselor and client meet, a therapeutic relationship begins to take form (Chapter 3), an assessment of the parameters of the problem occurs (Chapter 4), and, from this, goals to be accomplished in the counseling relationship begin to emerge (Chapter 5). In this chapter we shall examine the processes that the counselor uses to determine what should occur in the counseling session. The *strategies* that are identified reflect your "game plan" or counseling plan. The *interventions* you select are the activities that you introduce to accomplish the game plan.

By the time you are ready to identify counseling strategies and interventions, both the problem(s) and the goals or desired outcomes should be defined. These are important prerequisites to the process of strategy selection because both the nature of the problem and the goal(s) influence the type of strategy that may work with a given client. Counselors need to remember that "... there is no single perfect counseling strategy that fits all situations. Different techniques work differently for different individuals, for different problems, and for different goals" (Hosford & de Visser, 1974, p. 97). Your task, aided by significant input from the client, is to select strategies that are likely to be successful for a particular client. This is an important decision since it shapes the direction counseling will take. This decision will be affected by a number of other variables, including how you conceptualize the problem (your personal theory of counseling), what the client's goals may be, client characteristics that may affect the change process, and, thus, the strategy and interventions selected. In this chapter, we discuss six guidelines to help you choose particular counseling strategies and interventions that reflect characteristics of both you and your client.

Identifying Your Own Counseling Theory

We discussed, in Chapter 1, the range of counseling theories that represent our profession. While numerous, these theories reflect a finite number of philosophical viewpoints, personality development patterns, change processes, and relationship alternatives. They may be crystallized into four broad categories: theories that emphasize feelings and affective states; theories that emphasize thoughts and conceptual processes; theories that emphasize behavior and how it shapes our reality; and theories that emphasize relationships and how they interact to manifest and support feelings, thoughts, and behaviors.

Implicit in this process are the personal qualities that you, the counselor, bring to the interaction including: your values; your world view; and your beliefs about how human problems develop and how they are resolved. These personal characteristics will vary among novice counselors. One person will approach a problem by attempting to define the feelings dimension. Another will first look to see what behaviors must change for the problem to recede or disappear. Yet another will examine how the situation has been thought out, and in so doing, look for misperceptions, inaccurate assessments of the problem, and so on. These various approaches to the problem reflect how we tend to approach our own problems. They reveal our problem-solving styles. It will be important for you to examine your own views and style in order to be consistent in your practice of counseling. Do not be surprised if you find that your impressions of how you approach problems are quite different from your practice of problem-solving.

While most counselors develop a broad range of interventions that reflect their particular theoretical orientation, experienced counselors also utilize interventions that reflect counseling orientations other than their theory. In other words, they find that while their choice of strategies is determined by their theoretical orientation, their choice of interventions may reflect different theoretical orientations.

Experience and Competence of the Counselor and Strategy/Intervention Choices

Beginning counselors worry about making the "right" choice of strategy or interventions. Their concerns are appropriate, although their fears may be exaggerated. With most counseling interventions, the potential negative effect upon a client will probably be quite small. There are exceptions to this, of course. Sometimes a particularly vulnerable client, someone who has a very weak self-concept or who is in crisis, may be more susceptible to a counselor's interventions. But most clients tend not to make themselves so vulnerable to the counselor that they would experience emotional harm from the intervention. More likely, if the counselor had chosen an inappropriate intervention, they would conclude that the counselor was inept. That may be little solace to the novice counselor who doesn't wish to appear inept either. But we are speaking of extreme situations in which the counselor's choice of intervention is quite inappropriate. There are a few counseling interventions that can be quite powerful. An example would be the *empty chair* dialoguing intervention which can, with the client's cooperation, reveal rather powerful emotions. It is generally held that such potent interventions should only be used by experienced counselors who have received appropriate training and who have demonstrated sound therapeutic judgment in the use of such methods. Recent research in the marriage and family therapy field (Figley & Nelson, 1990) indicates that a similar view is held regarding the use of certain family therapy interventions by novice marriage and family therapists. Counselors usually suggest strategies they know something about, have some experience with, and feel competent to use. In order to develop new techniques and practices and still provide competent help to the client, it is best to seek out supervision either from a counselor educator, a field supervisor, or from a colleague or professional peer.

Knowledge of Typical Client Responses to Interventions

Counselors can work with strategies more adeptly if they are aware of which strategies are typically used for particular client problems, and of resulting client reactions to the strategy. Most of the strategies and their accompanying theoretical orientations described in Chapters 7 to 10 are supported by varying amounts of documentation in the professional literature. Such documentation ranges from reports of informal case studies of the use of a selected strategy with a particular problem to more formal empirical inquiries on the effectiveness of selected therapeutic procedures for given clinical problems. Obviously, counselors should keep abreast of readings and developments in the field for this reason.

The counselor's past experiences and competence are also important factors. Counselors who use cognitive change techniques, for example, should be prepared for a rather typical client response when they introduce the idea of irrational ideas: "Who me? I don't think irrationally." Counselors who are aware of typical client responses can anticipate them and develop some ways of responding effectively to them.

Similarly, counselors can use information about strategies obtained from literature and their accumulated experience to recognize more unusual client responses to strategies and interventions. For example, Gestalt dialogue work and Transactional Analysis (TA) redecision/script work are useful ways to help clients develop awareness of conflicts, incongruities, and mixed feelings. If over time, however, these strategies intensify rather than resolve the conflict, this client reaction is a clue to the counselor to move slowly and monitor the effects of the strategy with this client very carefully. Counselors need to be aware of client reactions that occur within counseling sessions, as well as reactions that may occur during the week between sessions.

Character of the Problem and Counseling Strategies

Successful interventions are related directly to the nature or character of the problem. Best results are achieved when selected interventions match the components of the problem (Ost, Jerremalm, & Johannson, 1981). Thus, if the client's presenting problem appears to be predominantly affective or emotional in nature, interventions would be targeted to the affective complaints. Similarly, if a client seems to be using his thought processes to sabotage himself, then the counselor would want to select interventions that addressed the cognitive sources. On the other hand, it is important to realize that most client problems are multi-dimensional. A problem with negative "self-talk" ("I'm constantly telling myself I'm no good") is not just cognitive, but would also reflect an affective dimension ("I feel lousy about myself"), a behavioral dimension ("I choose to stay home and watch a lot of TV"), and a systemic dimension ("When I do go out, I avoid contact with others because they find me strange, *or I behave strangely and others react to me accordingly"*).

The fact of multi-dimensional aspects to a problem does not mean that all aspects must be addressed. Frequently, a behavioral aspect, if altered, will lead to different social consequences which will, in turn, alter other people's reaction to a person in a more desirable way. Or, if I am able to *think* more kindly about myself or my problem, I may find that I *worry* less and *behave* less self-consciously. Thus, if the counselor chooses to intervene at the affective door to the problem, changes in the client's affective state will have concomitant effects upon the cognitive, behavioral, and interpersonal aspects of the client's world. This ecological interconnectedness suggests that positive change can occur, regardless of how the problem is *experienced* by the client. However, it may prove less efficient and less effective if you choose to intervene behaviorally, when the client is experiencing the problem affectively. Figure 6-1 illustrates how a problem can be explored from different perspectives. Even though these several perspectives will yield different information, the larger context of the problem is the same.

How does one plan a strategy for counseling intervention if multiple choices exist and "all roads lead to Rome?" A general guideline is that clients are most receptive when the choice of strategy matches their experiencing of the problem. That is, if the client experiences the problem as an emotional trauma, then an affective intervention strategy might seem more plausible to the client. Inconsistency between client experiencing of the problem and counseling strategy can lead clients to conclude that the counselor has failed to understand. This is not to suggest that the counselor's strategy would be exclusively affective in this case. As counseling proceeds, and as the multiple dimensions of the problem become apparent to the client, counseling can begin to address these other dimensions. However, the base for this case would remain affective. In a different counseling case, the client's experiencing of the problem might be behavioral (for example, excessive drinking), thus suggesting that the counseling plan should be behaviorally based, with cognitive, affective, and systemic excursions from the behavioral component as appropriate.

Sometimes the client's experiencing of a problem fails to produce the best understanding of how that problem should be confronted and the counseling strategy yields only qualified success. When this occurs, you should re-examine your rationale for selecting a particular strategy. For example, if a woman presents a problem of poor self-concept, the counseling strategy may be to address her cognitive self. However, as she begins to feel and become more competent, her new self may lead to a crisis in her marriage, caus-

FIGURE 6-1 The various ways to approach a problem.

1. How does the problem make your client feel? How do her feelings affect her effort to change the problem? How might her feelings maintain the problem? What different feelings might change the problem?

2. What kinds of things does she do when the problem is "in charge?" How do these behaviors support or maintain the problem? What behaviors could she change and thereby reduce the effects of the problem?

Your client has been experiencing repeated failures in her college courses. She is starting to feel hopeless, thinking about dropping out of college, doesn't know what she might do, wonders if she might try to revive an old high school love and perhaps marry.

3. What kinds of things is your client saying to herself? How might her messages be part of her problem? What different self-statements might alter her self-perceptions?

4. What is her relationship with other students? with men? How do her professors fit into the picture? How have her parents functioned in her absence? In what ways do relationships support the problem?

ing her to back off her recent gains. It may be that her husband's expectations are for her to remain less competent, thus maintaining a relationship in which he is superior. In this situation, the problem may have been experienced as a cognitive and/or affective issue, while the underlying issues really represent a systemic problem.

Character of the Goal and Counseling Strategies

The choice of strategies also depends on what the agreed-upon goal represents. While outcome goals are specific and unique to each client, goals can be defined generally as representative of *choice* or *change*. Clients who commit themselves to *choices* usually have the prerequisite skills and opportunities to take a particular course of action, but have not yet committed themselves to do so. These clients first need to resolve a conflict or make a decision. Clients who commit themselves to *changes* usually lack necessary skills, opportunities, or behaviors (Dixon & Glover, 1984). These clients need to develop new behaviors or modify existing ones.

This global distinction about what client outcome goals represent is important because each kind of goal requires different intervention strategies. Choice-related issues often occur in educational-vocational counseling as well as relationship counseling. Strategies that usually work well with these kinds of goals include information giving, decision making and problem solving, conflict resolution, role playing and role reversal, Gestalt dialoguing, and TA redecision work.

Usually, which of these strategies to use depends again upon the component of the problem reflected by the choice issue. Information giving and problem solving might be directed toward the cognitive dimension of choice and conflict; Gestalt and Transactional Analysis work toward the affective dimension of the choice; role playing and role reversal work toward the behavioral dimension of the choice, and these latter two strategies along with conflict-resolution techniques work toward the interpersonal or systemic part of the choice.

Change strategies are selected that help clients make desired changes. Usually, changes can be thought of as acquiring new behaviors, decreasing unwanted behaviors, or increasing desired behaviors. Change strategies are selected that relate directly to the type of change desired and also to the particular components of the problem or to the "character" of the problem. For example, if the client complains of loneliness, and assessment reveals that the client does not know how to initiate conversations and social interactions with other people, strategies would be selected that are targeted toward the behavioral and interpersonal components of the problem and toward the goal of helping this client acquire various interpersonal initiating skills.

In lieu of changing some facet of the client's internal or external behavior, another option for change-related goals is to decide that the situation is not really a problem. In this case, the client's view of the problem is changed, usually through techniques that focus on a reinterpretation of the problem. When the client cannot initiate change independent of other persons or when the client's problems are maintained by other persons, then systems-oriented interventions rather than individual interventions are usually the treatment of choice (see also Chapter 10).

Client Characteristics and Counseling Strategies

Another major factor to consider in choosing strategies involves client characteristics that may affect the outcome of a strategy or intervention. The choice of suitable interventions is a mutual one that involves both counselor and client input. The selection of therapeutic strategies that meet client expectations and preferences typically results in more positive therapy outcomes (Devine & Fernald, 1973). One reason for this success is probably that clients choose strategies that are congruent with their deeply held values and beliefs. When counselors propose an action plan that is too dissonant for the client's beliefs and values, clients are likely either to resist the plan outright or to work with it superficially but not really invest themselves in the proposed plan. Another reason why clients might resist an action plan is because they perceive it as too risky or threatening.

In the last decade there has been an important change in the client's role and status in counseling. The client has become an active consumer, not just a passive recipient of services. As a result, counselors need to ensure that client rights are made explicit and that clients are informed about and consent to the use of various intervention approaches. Accordingly, counselors need to provide clients with accurate information about all available intervention strategies, including:

1. A description of all relevant and potentially useful treatment approaches for this particular client with this particular problem

2. A rationale for each procedure
3. A description of the therapist's role in each procedure
4. A description of the client's role in each procedure
5. Possible discomforts or risks that may occur as a result of the procedure
6. Expected benefits that will occur as a result of the procedure
7. The estimated time and cost of each procedure (Cormier & Cormier, 1985)

In addition to choosing strategies that reflect client expectations and preferences, counselors also need to consider available client resources and characteristics. For example, does the client have sufficient internal ego strength or self-control to carry out a particular procedure? Does the client live and work in a context in which support from others is fully given or withheld? Is the client likely to apply a particular procedure outside the counseling session? Does a procedure require the client to do something (such as engage in imagery), and is the client capable of doing this?

Proposed strategies also need to take into account previous client attempts to solve their problems. Often in dealing with problems, clients arrive at solutions that are both inadequate and irrelevant. When this happens, an all-too-common situation arises: The solution becomes the problem. This can be illustrated by the person whose world contains so many pressures that sleeping becomes very difficult. After going to bed and lying there for an hour, the client decides to "try a new way to go to sleep." The solution may begin with counting sheep, thinking of "nothing," trying to relax muscles, getting another pillow, getting something to eat, changing the sheets, turning on the radio, turning off the radio, *ad infinitum.* With each new attempt, sleep becomes more elusive. The solutions continue to be more of the same solution; that is, a search for something that will make him or her go to sleep. What is worse, the next night becomes a set of expectations extracted from the previous night, and the solutions become more elaborate. Before long, we have more than just a person with a lot of daytime pressures; we have an insomniac.

It is important for the counselor to understand, as well as possible, the client's world. It is also important to understand the frustrated needs the client is experiencing in that world. Finally, it is vitally important to understand what the client has been doing or thinking to solve the problem of the unmet needs. We often find that clients have a very limited repertoire of "solutions," and they apply these limited solutions indiscriminately. The result is a more complicated, less successful world than even before the "solution" was applied.

By identifying clients' previous unsuccessful attempts to resolve problems, counselors can avoid suggesting strategies that build on or duplicate prior efforts, thus avoiding "problem-engendering pseudo-solutions" (Lazarus, 1981, p. 147).

Categories of Counseling Interventions

Effective counseling intervention selection involves a number of different factors, including assessment of the client's problems and desired goals, the client's preferences, personal characteristics, and learning style. In Table 6–1, we describe a comprehensive list of illustrative counseling interventions (techniques) categorized by domain—affective, cognitive, behavioral and interpersonal. We also describe corresponding characteristics of potential clients in order to give you a brief description of behavior typical of clients with a predominant orientation in each of these four categories:

Affective interventions (described in Chapter 7) involve interventions that focus primarily on feelings and emotions. Additionally, affective strategies may also involve body awareness activities that focus on somatic components of a problem, as emotional states often involve the musculature and the expenditure of physical energy (Zajonc, 1980).

Cognitive interventions (described in Chapter 8) involve interventions that deal with thoughts, beliefs, attitudes, self-talk, and internal dialogue.

Behavioral interventions (described in Chapter 9) involve interventions that focus on skills, actions, habits, and behavioral excesses and deficits.

Interpersonal interventions (described in Chapter 10) comprise systemic interventions that deal with interactions and relationships with significant others such as family, work or school colleagues, friends, and peers. Often, systemic approaches focus upon the context or the ecology surrounding the client's problem.

This categorization system is based on previous classification systems, particularly the T-F-A (thought, feeling, action) model described by Hutchins (1979; 1982; 1984) and the E-R-A (emotionality, rationality, activity model) proposed by L'Abate (1981). In addition, these categories are linked to a conceptual framework of client problems, including the client within social systems. As you may recall from the discussion of assessment in Chapter 4, client problems typically are multidimensional rather than unidimensional. In categorizing counseling strategies and interventions along these dimensions, the intent is to illustrate how

TABLE 6–1 Counseling Strategies and Corresponding Manifestations of Clients' Problems

Affective	*Cognitive*	*Behavioral*	*Systemic*
Person-centered therapy: reflective listening; empathy; positive regard; genuineness.	**Rational-emotive therapy:** "A-B-C-D-E" analysis; homework tasks.	**Behavior therapy:** social modeling; assertion and social skills training; systematic desensitization; self-control techniques; behavior modification strategies; contingency contracting.	**Structural therapy:** instructing about subsystems, enmeshment & disengagement, triangles, alliances, coalitions, roles, complementarity; problem definition; clarifying interactional systems.
Gestalt therapy: awareness techniques; empty chair; fantasy; dreamwork.	**Information-giving:** bibliotherapy; mediatapes; props; charts; handouts.		
Body awareness therapies: bioenergetics; biofeedback; radix therapy.	**Problem-solving and decision-making:** brainstorming; identifying alternatives; reframing.	**Reality therapy:** involvement; action plans; contracting.	**Strategic therapy:** reframing; prescribing the problem; altering interaction sequences.
Psychodynamic therapies: free association; transference; dream analysis.	**Personal construct:** Rep test.	**Cognitive-behavioral:** cognitive restructuring.	**Intergenerational systems:** genogram; maintaining neutrality; coaching; defining boundaries; shifting triangulation patterns.
Experiential therapies: focusing techniques.	**Transactional analysis:** egograms; script analysis; rescripting; reparenting; transactions; contracting.		

Corresponding Manifestations of Clients' Problems

Emotional expressiveness and impulsivity; instability of emotions; use of emotions in problem-solving and decision-making; sensitivity to self and others; receptive to feelings of others.	Intellectualizing; logical rational, systematic behavior; reasoned, computer-like approach to problem-solving and decision-making; receptive to logic, ideas, theories, concepts, analysis, and synthesis.	Involvement in activities; strong goal orientation; need to be constantly doing something; receptive to activity, action, "getting something done"; perhaps at expense of others.	Enmeshed or disengaged relationships; rigid relationship boundaries and rules; dysfunctional interaction patterns.

selected strategies may be most suitable for given dimensions of client problems. The intent is not to pigeonhole clients into one of these areas, nor is it to view any of the strategies or associated interventions in a monolithic or restricted fashion. Nor do we want to suggest that affective strategies work only with affective components of problems, or that cognitive strategies work only with cognitive components. In fact, if one views the person as a system (and we do), then interventions into any of these four dimensions will produce effects in all of the dimensions of the problem. Let us revisit Mary, our fictional client from Chapter 4 to illustrate how strategy and intervention selection is implemented.

Case Illustration of Strategy Selection: Continuation of the Case of Mary

Based upon information derived from an intake interview with Mary, the counselor summarized Mary's complaints, using the four-dimensional analysis (see Figure 6-2).

Next, the counselor examines the six factors for establishing a counseling strategy for this case. These include the following:

1. *The counselor's theory:* The counselor prefers an affective approach, with elements of person-centered theory and existentialism. The counselor also subscribes to systemic explanations of human problems.

2. *Counseling experience:* The counselor has practiced for about four years and has taken several training workshops since completing her formal counselor preparation program. She has worked with several depressed clients.

3. *Character of the problem:* Mary's problem may have a medical dimension in addition to an affective, cognitive, behavioral, and system dimension. Her presenting concern is how to have better control over her moods.

4. *Typical responses to the problem:* Based upon her training and experience, the counselor knows that clients who feel inadequate need to examine their support system, identify what ends their moods serve, and develop alternative and more facilitative behavior patterns.

5. *Character of the goal:* Mary identified three main goals (Chapter 5) that she would like to achieve in counseling: (a) to become significantly more positive about herself over the next three months; (b) to control any negative effects the PMS may be contributing to her moods; and (c) to become more aware of the meaningfulness of her daily activities and relationships.

FIGURE 6-2 Four-dimensional Analysis of the Case of Mary

AFFECTIVE	BEHAVIORAL
Mary often feels irritable, upset, or depressed; feels sorry for herself when things go wrong; feels inadequate; feels that her ex-husband "deserted" her.	Mary retreats into her room when she feels blue; takes her feelings out on her children or students; occasional sleep problems; avoids social contact; has no regular recreational activities.

Mary (see Chapter 4) is seeking counseling to learn how to have better control of her moods. She indicates that she often "flies off the handle" for no reason with her children or with her students in the classroom. She suffers from PMS and occasional difficulties sleeping. She feels she is a failure as a wife and mother, primarily because of her divorce and her mood swings. Her self-description is primarily negative.

COGNITIVE	SYSTEMIC
Mary has a lot of negative self-talk, e.g. failure, perfectionism; she has no goals;	Mary doesn't date; she seems to have no support network; has little contact with her family of origin; 'uses' her children to avoid others; ex-husband takes children when she is overwhelmed.

6. *Client's characteristics:* Mary appears to be functioning at a minimal level, personally and socially. She was raised in a family in which she was not expected to be responsible for attending to her needs, she does not seem to be able to create social support, and she quickly feels overwhelmed when life's demands begin to accumulate. In her former marriage, her husband took responsibility for "cheering her up."

Defining a Counseling Strategy

The first step in developing a counseling strategy is to synthesize what is known about the case and define a plan of action that is consistent with those factors. This synthesis would take into account both the four-dimensional analysis and six factors for establishing a counseling strategy. We note that: (a) Mary presented her problem as affective (mood swings, feels inadequate) and the counselor is predisposed toward an affective approach; (b) the presence of a possible medical concern should be addressed by a physician; (c) Mary set as a goal to become more positive about herself, which corresponds to her cognitive negativity; (d) Mary tends to "retreat" from others (behavioral) as well as from her problem (cognitive) to her affective self when stress builds up; and (e) Mary's problem has spilled over to interpersonal relationships (children, students, social life) which relates to the counselor's systemic interests. In addition, she continues to lean on her ex-husband for help when she is in emotional distress.

Applicable Strategies

The counselor has several fairly obvious choices of direction to take. She might choose to work from an affective context because she suspects that Mary is carrying several unresolved issues from her former marriage (failure feelings) and her mood swings, the effect of which produce increased stress, interpersonal issues, and possible exacerbation of her PMS difficulties. This would seem to be a promising approach, particularly since the counselor does have an affective predisposition and Mary's initial complaints were affective in nature.

Mary's problem could support a different strategy. Rather than address her emotional baggage from her former marriage, the counselor might choose to examine how Mary presently places herself into situations that remind her of her former marriage. In other words, she might address the cognitive links that connect

Mary's present to her past and in so doing, seek to establish more facilitative cognitive responses. In addition, with the counselor's aid, Mary might challenge her self-defeating thinking about her past, her potential, and her interpersonal relationships. This approach might allow Mary to reassess her priorities, view her unchangeable life factors in a more positive light, and identify new goals and activities that would support a more desirable lifestyle. Since the counselor has not shown a strong inclination toward cognitive counseling approaches, this strategy could be more difficult to implement.

Yet a third way that the counselor could conceptualize the case is to focus on Mary's behavior patterns, both in terms of how she responds to herself and to her children, students, and adults. The fact that Mary withdraws when she feels depressed probably exacerbates her affective response and becomes self-defeating. It was noted that Mary appears to be functioning at a minimal level, personally and socially. It may be appropriate to help Mary identify and strengthen certain behavior patterns that she could turn to when she begins to feel overwhelmed, depressed or self-negative. The rationale would be that if she could intervene in this downward spiraling pattern, then she would be spared the undesirable consequences.

Finally, there seem to be clear links between Mary's present functioning and her role in her family of origin and her relationship with her ex-husband. The counselor may wish to explore this linkage with Mary, by seeking to clarify how her interaction patterns reflect her family's views of self-responsibility, how she manifests these patterns with her children and her students, and how her social linkage with her family is similar to her social linkage to other adults. She might encourage Mary to examine how this pattern has repeated itself with her reliance on her ex-husband, and help Mary differentiate more successfully from her old marriage system. The counselor could include the children in the counseling process as a means of revealing patterns of interaction, assumptions, family rules, roles, and structure. This might logically lead to a cognitive reassessment of Mary's approach to family and social groups, using a strategic family therapy model. Because the counselor does subscribe to systemic explanations, this is an attractive approach to Mary's problem.

Selecting Interventions

Each of these four strategies embraces a repertoire of counseling interventions which are theoretically consistent with the assumptions of the strategy. For example, the affective approach places emphasis upon the exploration of feelings in a safe and understanding environment, the development of insight into one's feelings, and ultimately, the acceptance of oneself. Such counselor activities as empathic responding, active listening, acceptance, are endemic to this strategy. Similarly, the cognitive, behavioral, and systemic approaches also identify counselor interventions that support the objectives of these respective strategies. Chapters 7 through 10 examine these interventions and illustrate how they complement the strategy in question.

Choosing the Right Strategy

The character of the problem may be addressed through any one of a variety of counseling strategies, including: behavioral; cognitive; affective; systemic; or any combination of these. Your choice of strategy probably will reflect your personal explanation of human problems and how they can best be resolved (your personal theory). On the other hand, multiple or sequential strategies may be needed to work with the entire character of the defined client problem. For example, anxiety may be experienced somatically (behavioral), cognitively (anticipatory), and affectively (depression). When more than one component is involved, usually more than one intervention is also necessary. You may still approach the case from your preferred vantage point for conceptualization, but you may find that your interventions should address all aspects of the problem.

Strategies for Working with Children

Children pose special issues in the counseling relationship, since they have little power or control over their environment. How a child views herself or himself (self-esteem) is bound to have environmental linkages. Similarly, how a child behaves is interconnected to the behaviors of others in the world. The child's potential to change that environment, be it the home, the neighborhood, or the school, without the involvement of significant others is highly problematic. Consequently, any effort to intervene in a child's problems will necessarily involve relationships with siblings, parents, friends, teachers, and other adults. For this reason, a systemic view of the problem, if not a systemic strategy, will prove helpful. The systemic view involves relationship patterns, and their concomitant behavioral and cognitive components. The counselor can work with the child on an individual basis and seek to produce systemic change *through* the child, or the counselor can involve other participants in the child's system and seek to invoke direct change in the interactional patterns of the system.

The school counselor may include in this systemic counseling process other children, the teacher and child, or the parents, teacher(s), and child. If the problem, and thus the goal, is primarily learning-related, then the process may be contained totally within the school setting. But if the problem is familial, then the counselor's goal may be to generate parental awareness and responsibility for the problem, at which time a referral to a family therapist would be appropriate. Counselors working with children in community settings probably will seek to include the family in the counseling process. Given the more diffuse nature of community counseling clientele, child problems that come to the counselor probably require family participation if successful resolution of the presenting problem is to be achieved.

Summary

Counseling strategies constitute the base upon which most therapeutic work and change takes place. The strategic plan of action must take into account a number of divergent factors, including those related to the counselor's theory, experience, and expertise, as well as the client's presenting problem, goals, and systemic contingencies. In the case of children, the other significant players in the child's world assume a particularly significant role. Counselors must work with clients to identify interventions that will address both the character of the problem and the goals that have been identified. Client expectations, preferences, capabilities, and resources are other important criteria to consider in choosing workable strategies. In the following four chapters, we will examine different counseling interventions, how they are implemented, what they are intended to achieve, and how clients typically react to their introduction in the counseling process.

Exercises

I. Choice or Change Issues and Related Counseling Strategies

A. By yourself or with a partner, list four to six issues or problems you are currently experiencing in your own life. Identify whether each is a choice or change issue. Remember: Choice issues are ones in which you have the skills and opportunities to follow a course of action but feel conflicted about which direction to pursue. Change issues are ones in which you need to develop new options and behaviors or modify existing ones (Dixon & Glover, 1984). Finally, note whether the choice or change for each issue is under your control and can be initiated by you. If not, identify the other people in your life who are also a part of this choice or change.

B. With a partner or in a small group, brainstorm possible strategies that might be suitable interventions for one of the issues or problems from your list in Part A. Next, evaluate the probable usefulness of each strategy. In your evaluation, consider the six guidelines for selection of counseling strategies described in this chapter:

1. Is the strategy consistent with your theoretical orientation?
2. Do you have any expertise and experience in working with this strategy?
3. Are you knowledgeable about typical responses to and effects of this strategy?
4. Does the strategy fit the character or nature of the problem?
5. Does the strategy fit the character or nature of your desired goal?
6. Does the strategy meet your expectations and preferences and does it avoid repeating or building on prior unsuccessful solutions?

Note: You do not have to select complex or sophisticated counseling strategies. If you have not yet been exposed to counseling theories and techniques, rely on common sense approaches and interventions, since the emphasis in this activity is on the process of strategy selection rather than on the actual strategies you select.

C. Continue this activity with your partner or group. For the strategy your group selected in Part B as the best or most effective one, generate the following information about the strategy:

1. A rationale—how it seems to work.
2. A description of the counselor's role in the strategy.
3. A description of the client's role in the strategy.
4. Possible discomfort, negative effects, or "spin-offs" from the strategy.
5. Expected benefits of the strategy.
6. Estimated time involved in using the strategy.

D. Role-play providing the information in Part C about the strategy to a hypothetical client. One person will assume the client's role and present the issue. The other person will assume the counselor's role and suggest the recommended strategy and provide the client with enough information about the strategy to help the client make an informed choice about accepting or rejecting your suggestion. Additional members of the group will function as observers and will provide feedback to the counselor after the role-play.

II. Relationship of Problem Components to Strategy Selection

In this exercise, we present three client cases. For each case, determine the primary component(s) of the problem that would need to be addressed during the intervention strategy phase of counseling. There may be more than one significant component. (Feedback for the exercise can be found on p. 142.)

1. The client is a sixteen-year-old sophomore in high school who wants to lose forty pounds. He states that he has been overweight most of his life and has never really attempted to lose weight before. He notes that he eats just about "whatever he wants, when he wants." He states that he has no real knowledge of diets, calories, or behavior modification techniques for weight loss. Additionally, he asserts that it is hard to refuse food in his family. His parents are also overweight, and he has two teenage brothers who are not overweight but who seem to need to "eat like horses" to keep up their energy. As a result, food is always available and plentiful around the house, with several big meals served daily.

   Primary components:
   Affective
   Cognitive
   Behavioral
   Interpersonal

2. The client is an older (sixty-six-year-old) man who reports vague but distressing feelings of nervousness and anxiety. Apparently, these feelings were precipitated by the death of his wife two years ago and by his recent retirement. He states that he is most aware of these feelings at night when he is alone in the house with nothing to do and no one around to talk to. Additionally, he reports some related somatic symptoms—waking up during the night, loss of appetite, and some stomach distress:

   Primary components:
   Affective

Cognitive
Behavioral
Interpersonal

3. The client is a twenty-two-year-old female. She is currently working as a fashion model in her home town and also lives at home with her parents and her younger sister. After much discussion, she reveals her primary reason for seeking help—that of binge eating. She states that what started out as a rather routine way to keep her weight under control in order to model has turned into a pattern she feels little or no control to change. She describes herself as generally unattractive despite her job as a model. She feels that her parents have constantly compared her to her younger sister and she has always come out "on the short end." She has difficulty describing anything positive about herself. She also indicates that she feels increasingly resentful of the control and strict standards imposed on her by her parents, even though she is no longer a minor.

    Primary components:
Affective
Cognitive
Behavioral
Interpersonal

Feedback for Exercises

II. Problem Components and Strategy Selection

1. There are two major components of this problem that would need to be addressed by treatment or intervention strategies:

   Behavioral—excess weight

   Interpersonal—role of his family in contributing to and maintaining his weight problem.

2. The major component of this problem to address is the affective one. The client presents feelings of distress and anxiety, accompanied by somatic manifestations such as sleep difficulties, appetite loss, and stomach distress.

3. There are three major components of this problem to focus on during the intervention phase:

   Affective—negative feelings about herself

   Behavioral—binge eating

Interpersonal—role of parents in her binge eating (strictness and loss of perceived control and responsibility for her own life)

Discussion Questions

1. Identify and discuss the attributes of good and poor counseling strategies. From your perspective, what factors make a strategy "good" or effective?

2. What do you believe are the most important criteria to use in recommending and selecting counseling strategies for clients?

3. What is your position with respect to the following statement: "Different techniques work differently for different clients, with different problems and goals." Describe your position and reasons to support your views.

4. Recall the last time in an interpersonal or social situation that you felt "roped into" doing something without your input or despite your protests. What was this experience like for you? How did it feel? What was the outcome of it? What steps must you as a counselor take to avoid imposing the use of a particular theoretical orientation or counseling strategy on a client?

5. Try to identify a problem situation of your own in which your attempted solution either became a new problem or made the existing problem worse. How did you recognize this? How did you deal with it? How can you determine the effects of client "solutions" on their presenting problems?

Recommended Readings

Dixon, D. & Glover, J. (1984), *Counseling: A Problem-Solving Approach* (New York: John Wiley), Chapter 9, Selecting an Intervention Strategy.

Egan, G. (1990), *The Skilled Helper*, 4th Ed. (Pacific Grove, CA: Brooks/Cole), Chapter 14, Helping Clients Develop Strategies for Action; Chapter 15, Helping Clients Choose Best-fit Strategies; Chapter 16, Helping Clients Formulate Plans; Chapter 17, Helping Clients Put Strategies to Work.

Hutchins, D.E. (1979), "Systematic Counseling: The T-F-A Model for Counselor Interventions," *Personnel and Guidance Journal 57*, 529–531.

Hutchins, D.E. (1982), "Ranking Major Counseling Strategies with the TFA/Matrix System," *Personnel and Guidance Journal 60*, 427–431.

Hutchins, D.E. (1984), "Improving the Counseling Relationship," *Personnel and Guidance Journal 62*, 572-575.

Lazarus, A.A. (1981), *The Practice of Multimodal Therapy* (New York: McGraw-Hill), Chapter 8, The Selection of Techniques.

Madanes, C. (1981), *Strategic Family Therapy* (San Francisco: Jossey-Bass), Chapter 3, Marital Problems: Balancing Power; Chapter 4, Children's Problems: Three Paradoxical Strategies; Chapter 5, Parental Problems: Changing Child-Parent Interactions.

Zajonc, R.B. (1980) "Feeling and Thinking: Preferences Need No Inferences," *American Psychologist 35*, 151–175.

7

Affective Interventions

Feelings are the affective or emotional dimension of the human experience (Corsini, 1989). We feel happy when things are going well, sad when we experience loss, angry or frustrated when our desires are thwarted, and lonely when we are deprived of contact with others. Many times, feelings can be accessed only indirectly, through the client's verbal expression or behavior. The client may "feel" depressed but only through verbal and nonverbal communication, physical cues, or acting out can the counselor make contact with that feeling state. The impact of this fact is that "... we cannot manipulate emotions in the sense that we can manipulate thinking or behaving" (Corsini, 1989, p. 7). Consequently, the counselor works with client feelings by generating client awareness, and subsequent client valuing and integration of those feelings.

The role that feelings play in counseling and psychotherapy is an unsettled issue. Corsini (1989, p. 7) observes that "Some people see emotions as epiphenomena accompanying but not affecting therapeutic change, while others see emotions as a powerful agent leading to change and still others see emotions as evidence of change." Whichever the case may be, most, if not all, of our thoughts and behaviors have a feeling dimension. Perhaps, because this is so, feelings can be the source, or a significant part, of the problems we experience. We noted above how the counselor accesses the client's affective state, but the client may also lack access to feelings. This "bottling up" of feelings may be due to one's early training or to the intensity of the emotion which threatens and overpowers the person. We know that boys (and sometimes girls) are often taught to deny those feelings that are associated with weakness, failure, or powerlessness. Similarly, girls are often taught to deny feelings associated with such male characteristics as dominance, control, power, or even intellect. Or, consider the child who is raised in a perfectionist environment. If that child internalizes the environmental demands, then the need to be perfect without the skills to do so will lead to excessive threat and emotional difficulties throughout childhood and into adulthood. The result is that when these unacknowledged or even undetected feelings begin to build up, some people are ill-equipped to find release, and counseling or psychotherapy becomes an appropriate recourse.

Helping the individual to develop the capacity to find release of emotional difficulties and to cope better with life demands is a central goal of many therapeutic approaches. The affective theories have made major contributions to the counselor's repertoire of affective interventions. Generally speaking, those theories with an affective orientation rely heavily upon the development of affect awareness, exploration, and integration. They do not discount thought processes or behavior patterns. Rather, they emphasize the emotional context in which thought patterns, beliefs, and behaviors occur.

Affective Theories

Most affective or feeling interventions derive from the *phenomenological* theories. Phenomenologists make a distinction between what is (reality) and our perceptions of what is. This inner world of our perceptions becomes our reality. By far the most dominant of these theories is Carl Rogers' person-centered therapy. Probably next in its impact would be the contributions of Gestalt therapy, followed by the existentialist approaches (Binswanger, Boss, Viktor Frankl, and Rollo May). Other theoretical approaches that are sometimes identified as affective theories include Kelly's psychology of personal constructs (Rychlak, 1973; Hansen, Stevic, & Warner, 1986); Gendlin's experiential counseling (Hansen, Stevic, & Warner, 1986); and psychoanalytic theory (Frey, 1972; Shertzer & Stone, 1980).

All of these approaches place the individual in a context of self-struggle. The internal issues which are experienced may relate to self-identity, self-worth, self-responsibility, or self-actualization. Whatever the issue or the goal, the process involves exploration of feelings, values, perceptions, and meaning in life. It is within this phenomenological context that the affective theories attempt to define the human condition.

In one respect, referring to affective interventions is a philo-sophical contradiction. The affective therapist is more likely to emphasize the personhood of the client and the interpersonal rela-tionship between therapist and client, rather than the techniques that would be used. Nevertheless, the affective therapist is doing things in this process, and it is these "things" that are the focus of this chapter. As we explore these interventions, the reader should keep in mind that the strategies become gimmicky and ineffective if the therapeutic relationship between counselor and client has been given a lesser priority.

The Goals of Affective Interventions

The primary goals of affective interventions are: (a) to help the client express feelings or feeling states; (b) to identify or discrimi-nate between feelings or feeling states; (c) to alter or accept feelings or feeling states; or (d) in some cases, to contain feelings.

Some clients come to counseling with an awareness that some-thing is wrong in their lives but are unable to articulate or discuss that condition. Talking about problems or feelings may be a new experience for them. This is often the case for the person who grew up in a family where problems were never discussed openly, or the expression of feelings was discouraged or forbidden through injunctions such as "Don't be angry," "Don't cry," "Don't feel." Child clients may not have reached the developmental stage where skills and affect sensitivity are acquired; consequently, they may lack both the skills of expression and the awareness that expression of feelings can be helpful.

At a somewhat more complicated level, the client may come to counseling flooded with emotional reactions. When this hap-pens, it is experienced as an emotional overload, and the protective response often is to tune out the emotions, to become emotionless. Or the response may be confusion or disorientation. When this happens, the client must be helped to recognize and sort out or to contain the variety of affect responses that are being experienced. This condition is frequently found when a person has experienced a long period of emotional turmoil, such as occurs in a divorce, death of a family member, poor physical health, or other life tragedy, or it may be a more serious psychopathologic blocking of affect.

At the most complex level of affect intervention, the counselor and client are involved in the integration of or alteration of feeling states. This may include value clarification, acceptance of hitherto unacceptable feelings, reconsideration of old feelings, or even redefinition of self-perceptions. This process is common when the client is beginning to differentiate self from family, self from spouse and children, self from job or career, or is otherwise laboring with the question "Who am I?"

In this chapter we describe and illustrate the more common affective interventions that facilitate the expression and examination of feelings. These interventions include feeling inventories, counselor "modeling," scripting and role rehearsal, dialoguing and alter-ego exercises, identifying affect "blocks," differentiation between competing feelings, role reversal, the "empty chair," affect focusing, and dreamwork.

Helping Clients Express Affect

Experiencing a feeling, even knowing that somehow feelings are related to one's problems, does not lead naturally to the expression and examination of the feeling. A part of the counselor's role is to help clients find ways to express feelings, both in ways that capture the meaning and convey that meaning to others. The counselor's role may be a matter of setting the stage, creating the proper conditions for a reticent client to open up.

Many authors have described the conditions that are necessary for such an involvement. These conditions—an accurate understanding of the client's situation and an unconditional valuing of the client—were discussed in Chapter 3. Beyond the conditions that create the atmosphere of helping, the counselor becomes involved in the client's process of feeling exploration through selective attention and reflective listening, also described in Chapter 3.

The exploration of feelings is a *process* more than a set of verbal responses, involving the counselor's conceptualization of what the client is trying to understand and the acknowledgment of that effort. Sometimes the process also serves to focus the client's awareness on what he or she seems to be saying. And usually, the process involves sharing the satisfaction of having accomplished the task. Given that it is a process rather than a series of behavioral events, the counselor must rely, nonetheless, on verbal interaction with the client and close observation of nonverbal communication. This metacommunication interaction incorporates many stylistic responses characteristic of counselor and counseling.

Nonverbal Affect Cues

Listening and watching for affective cues is part of the counselor's task. Nonverbal cues can be seen from such elements of the client's communication as head and facial movement, position of body, quick movements and gestures, and voice qualities. Although no single nonverbal cue can be interpreted accurately in isolation, each does have meaning as part of a larger pattern, or gestalt. Thus, there are relationships between nonverbal and verbal characteristics of client messages. In addition to these relationships, nonverbal cues may also communicate specific information about the relationship between individuals involved in the communicative process, in this case the counselor and client. Some nonverbal cues convey information about the nature and intensity of emotions more accurately than verbal cues. The nature of the emotion is communicated nonverbally primarily by head cues; for example, setting of the jaw, facial grimaces, narrowing of the eyes. The intensity of an emotion is communicated both by head cues and body cues; for example, muscular rigidity (Ekman & Friesen, 1967).

The counselor may or may not choose to acknowledge these nonverbal cues. In some cases, acknowledging them ("You've been looking very tight since you started talking about this matter.") can invite the client to share the intensity of the emotion. At other times, the counselor's observation may be rejected outright or may bring out a defensive response. Thus, timing as well as accuracy of perception is a factor in what the counselor chooses to say.

Verbal Affect Cues

Although there are many different kinds of feelings, most feelings that we identify by words fit into one of four classifications: affection, anger, fear, or sadness. Many of these feelings can be identified by certain affect word usage. In addition, there are subcategories of affect words for each of the major affect categories. In using words to identify affect, it is important to remember that these words may occasionally mask more intense feelings or even different feelings. As Ivey (1988) notes, "a common mistake is to assume that these words represent the root feelings. Most often, they cover deeper feelings" (p. 113).

Verbal Cues for Positive Affect

Feelings of affection reflect good or accepting feelings about oneself and others and indicate positive aspects of interpersonal relationships. Verbal cues in a client's communication are revealed by the presence of words that connote certain feelings. For example, if a client uses the word "wonderful" in describing an event, a location, or a person, that descriptor suggests an accepting, preferred, or desirable mental set toward the referent. This is a positive affect or affection response. Some examples of word cues that connote this positive affect are shown in Table 7-1.

Often nonverbal cues occur simultaneously with these positive affect cues. The most frequent nonverbal cue correlates are facial ones. The corners of the mouth may turn up to produce the hint of a smile; the eyes may widen slightly; "worry" wrinkles may disappear. There may be a noticeable absence of body tension. The arms and hands may move in an open-palm gesture of acceptance, or the communicator may reach out as though to "touch" the object of the affect message lightly. When clients are describing feelings about an object or event, there may be increased animation of the face and hands.

Verbal Cues of Anger

Anger represents an obstruction to be relieved or removed in some way. Anger may be triggered by frustration, threat, fear, jealousy, or thwarted aspirations. Anger often represents negative feelings about oneself and may be translated as aggression. Most people are well acquainted with the words that represent anger (see Table 7-2). These verbal cues can be classified into four general categories, to which you may want to add other words.

There are certain vocal qualities also associated with anger. Many times the voice will become louder, deeper, or more controlled. The pacing of the communication may become more rapid or more deliberate. What is important is that communicators make distinct variations from their normal communication pattern when anger is expressed.

TABLE 7-1 Positive Word Cues

Enjoyment	Competence	Love	Happiness	Hope
beautiful	able	close	cheerful	luck
enjoy	can	friendly	content	optimism
good	fulfill	love	delighted	try
nice	great	like	excited	guess
pretty	wonderful	need	happy	wish
satisfy	smart	care	laugh(ed)	want
terrific	respect	want	thrill	
tremendous	worth	choose	dig	

SOURCE: T.J. Crowley. "The Conditionability of Positive and Negative Self-reference Emotional Affect Statements in a Counseling-like Interview" Doctoral dissertation. the University of Massachusetts. 1970. Reprinted by permission

TABLE 7-2 Word Cues of Anger

Attack	Grimness	Defensiveness	Quarrelsome
argue	dislike	against	angry
attack	hate	protect	fight
compete	nasty	resent	quarrel
criticize	disgust	guard	argue
fight	surly	prepared	take issue
hit	serious		reject
hurt			(don't) agree
offend			

It is not often that one experiences anger without being aware of it. But it can happen that a person "carries" old anger all the time and releases the anger at inappropriate times. It is also possible that some angry people do not realize that their anger is perceived by others. Thus, the counselor may acknowledge your client's apparent anger either to invite exploration of its source or to provide confirmation that your client is being heard. This can be accomplished by a simple observation, "You sound as though you might be angry." Or you might focus on the affect cues with a statement like "You have referred to him as 'disgusting' several times. Could you talk about how he is disgusting?"

Verbal Clues of Fear

Fear represents a person's reaction to some kind of danger to be avoided. Often this reaction is a withdrawal from a painful or stressful situation, from one's self, or from other people and relationships. The person experiencing the emotion may also feel isolated. Fear can also be described as a negative set of feelings about something that results in a need to protect oneself. Verbal cues that suggest fear in a client's communication may be classified into five categories (see Table 7-3).

As was true with the anger response, there are some physical cues associated with fear. The face may express surprise or suspicion, the body may recoil or appear ready to spring into action. The breathing rate may become rapid and shallow. Or as anxiety and tension increase, the number of speech disturbances, such as errors, repetitions, stuttering, and omissions, may increase. The person may speak at a faster than normal rate, or the voice may take on a more guarded quality.

When the client appears fearful, either at the moment or fearful of a particular situation, the counselor may wish to explore the

TABLE 7-3 Word Cues of Fear

Fear	Doubt	Pain	Avoidance	Mistrust
anxious	failure	awful	flee	doubt
bothers	flunk	hurt	cop out	sneak
concerns	confused	dismay	escape	dislike
nervous	unsure	aches	cut out	suspect
scare	stupid	fester	run from	lie
freak out	stuck	suffer	neglect	
recoil	insecure	torn between		
		struggle		

ramifications of that fear. How realistic is the fear? How physically threatening is the feared situation? How accurate are the client's perceptions of the feared situation? Often the most appropriate intervention is to encourage the client to discuss the fear. But because the fear is so controlling, the client may be inclined to avoid any discussion. Consequently, the counselor may wish to move gently and supportively, but at the same time confrontatively. One way of doing this is through the use of self-disclosure. An anecdote from the counselor's own experience in which fear was felt, confronted, and ultimately overcome can communicate that fear is a normal feeling, that it can be faced, and that it can be defeated. The effect of a brief self-disclosure is like an invitation for the client to approach his or her fear, to talk about it, and to challenge it.

Verbal Cues of Sadness

Sadness, loneliness, or depression are fairly common emotional conditions presented by clients. Such conditions can be a response to relationships, environmental conditions, physiological imbalances, or even diet. Sadness, often associated with loss, is one of the milder forms of this emotional state. It may be accompanied by a tendency to withdraw from social contact in some clients or a dependency reaction in others. Only the most preoccupied counselor will fail to notice some of the behavioral correlates of sadness. Looking "down in the mouth," "whipped," or "about to cry" are common characteristics of sadness. The real issue, perhaps, relates to how sad the client is. Or in other words, is the client approaching clinical depression, thus necessitating a different form of treatment? Table 7–4 lists verbal cues.

Physical cues that accompany these emotions include a poor posture or slouching in the chair, eyes averted downward and little

TABLE 7–4 Word Cues of Sadness

Sadness	*Loneliness*	*Depression*
Unhappy	Alone	Depressing
Adrift	Abandoned	Depressed
Sorrowful	Isolated	Disillusioned
Distressed	Missing	Weary
Grieve	Missed	Listless
Heartsick		Discouraged
		Despondent
		Gloomy

eye contact with the counselor, talking in a monotone, staring into space, or a general lack of awareness or attention to personal qualities or to self-care.

When you become aware that your client is experiencing feelings associated with sadness, loss, or depression, it is appropriate to ask some questions that would reveal the extent of the mood in order to determine whether your client needs medical attention for mood control and to identify self-destructive tendencies. The following are some questions that would help determine the extent of your client's mood.

How well do you sleep at night?
  Do you have difficulty going to sleep?
  Do you wake up in the middle of the night and find it
    difficult to go back to sleep?
  Are you sleeping less (more) than is your pattern?

What are your eating patterns?
  Are you disinterested in eating?
  Are you eating obsessively?
  Do you feel guilty about your eating?

What is the state of your physical well-being?
  Do you feel normal?
  If not, what seems unusual about your physical well-being?
  Is this a recent change?

What kinds of social contact do you have?
  Has your social pattern changed recently?
  Do you prefer to be alone or with people?
What are your self-views like?
  What do you think about yourself?
  When do you tend to think about yourself?
  How much time do you spend thinking about yourself?

What kinds of things distract you from thinking about yourself?

Do you ever think about suicide?
  If so, have you thought about how you would commit suicide?
  Do you have a plan?
  Have you ever attempted suicide?
  Has any member of your immediate family ever attempted or committed suicide?

Questions such as these provide cumulative information about the client's inner well-being. If the client appears to be withdrawing from social contact, sleeping poorly, eating poorly or erratically, focusing extensively on self, then the counselor should seek consultation or refer the client to a physician or clinical psychologist. If the client is contemplating suicide or has attempted suicide before, referral may be made to a clinical psychologist, family physician, or psychiatrist.

Helping Clients Sort Out Feelings

Some clients enter counseling aware of their emotions but overwhelmed by either the complexity or quantity of their unresolved feelings. Such a condition is often triggered by a traumatic life event, such as the death of a parent, spouse or child, a divorce, or the loss of a career. These traumatic events stimulate feelings associated with the event, and perhaps more significantly, feelings associated with the person's self-worth. Typically, the person is attempting to resolve unanswerable questions such as: "Why did it happen?" "Why did it happen to me?" "Could I have prevented it from happening?"

The counselor's role in this situation is that of facilitator, guide, and supporter. The counselor's interventions include being a sounding board as the client attempts to unfold a complex series of feelings, helping the client recognize the source of various emotional reactions, and helping the client develop a sense of emotional control. Sometimes the counselor will begin this process with a simple paper-and-pencil exercise. At other times, the counseling scene takes on the qualities of a play rehearsal. Often the scene is one of intensely experienced emotions, tears, fears, relived hurts, and anger. Ultimately, it leads to hope, clearer understandings, and new decisions.

A second condition can occur in which the client enters counseling with an overload of emotions. When this happens, a common survival mechanism is to deny or screen out the intensity of the emotional response.

Whether the crux of the problem is the quantity or complexity of emotional experience, the solution is to help clients develop some structure or system for managing those feelings. This process is not so simple as it might sound. The tendency, particularly for the inexperienced counselor, is to offer a structure, a way of viewing the client's concerns. External structures may make cognitive sense, but they usually miss the point. The point is, of course, that most emotional overloads are illogically structured by clients. Therefore, when the counselor provides a logical structure, it does not speak to the client's illogic. Instead, the counselor must encourage the client to reprocess situations, personal explanations, and conclusions in such a way that an alternative, and more logical structure may emerge. This process allows clients to conceptualize their life situation in new ways that are personally meaningful.

There are a number of interventions, exercises, and discussions that help clients sort out feelings. No one intervention is effective with all clients. Thus, you must explore and experiment with each new client to find those activities that are acceptable and meaningful for that client. The interventions range from very simple paper-and-pencil exercises to rather complicated and dramatic reenactments of emotional experiences.

Early in counseling, the most appropriate strategy is to use activities that generate expression and classification of feelings. These would include counselor recognition and reflection of clients' expression of feeling, verbal statements, and counselor empathy for the client's emotional description. Chapter 3 contains a full discussion of empathy, verbal reflections, and restatements. Other activities include paper-and-pencil exercises such as the emotional percentages chart, emotions checklist, and the intense emotions diagram.

Emotional Percentages Chart

The emotional percentages chart is an example of an exercise that can be quite effective early in counseling. On a sheet of paper, two circles are shown. One is drawn as a pie graph and illustrates a number of different feeling states and how much of the total "pie" each emotion occupies. Below the two circles is a list of emotional states that the client may use to draw a personal graph (see Figure 7-1).

FIGURE 7–1:   Emotional Percentages Chart

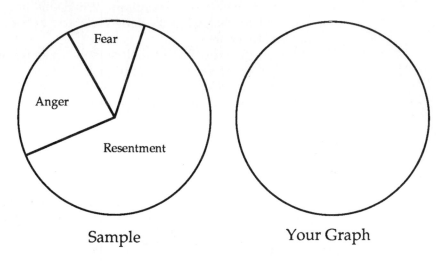

Sample   Your Graph

You might provide the following instructions to the client when introducing the graph:

Most people have a variety of emotions present when they begin to feel "overloaded." Some of these emotions occupy a large amount of their "worry" time. Other emotions are less demanding but are still present. Fill in your graph, indicating what percent of your present life situation is affected by such emotion states as joy, fear, anxiety, guilt, anger, resentment, loneliness, and so on.

FIGURE 7–2:   Emotions Checklist

_____	Discouraged	_____	Confused	_____	Afraid
_____	Optimistic	_____	Uneasy	_____	Mad
_____	Lonely	_____	Relaxed	_____	Insecure
_____	Angry	_____	Doubtful	_____	Uptight
_____	Hurt	_____	Unsure	_____	Furious
_____	Pessimistic	_____	Content	_____	Satisfied
_____	Defensive	_____	Bewildered	_____	Hassled
_____	Skeptical	_____	Outraged	_____	Panicked
_____	Depressed	_____	Hopeless	_____	Cheerful
_____	Unhappy	_____	Disoriented	_____	Irritated
_____	Resentful	_____	Frustrated	_____	Scared
_____	Worried	_____	Excited	_____	Tense
_____	Disillusioned	_____	Annoyed	_____	Offended

Emotions Checklist

The emotions checklist (Figure 7-2) is a good exercise to use prior to beginning or during the first counseling session. It allows the client to identify the various feelings that contributed to seeking help and provides a basis for early discussion and exploration of the client's concerns. The client is instructed to indicate in the checklist those feelings that describe his or her life experience in the past three months, underlining those feelings that are of the greatest concern.

Intense Emotions Indicator

The intense emotions indicator (Figure 7-3) is another paper-and-pencil exercise in which clients are asked to make some discrimination between their feeling states. The exercise can be adapted for use either by children or adults. Clients are given the following instructions about this activity:

> *Sometimes people have several feelings at the same time. Some of those feelings are strong and are very deeply felt, while others are important but are not as intense. Using the illustration, indicate which of your "feeling balloons" are biggest. You can use feelings like Angry, Happy, Lonely, Afraid, Upset, to label your balloons.*

FIGURE 7-3: Intense Emotions Indicator

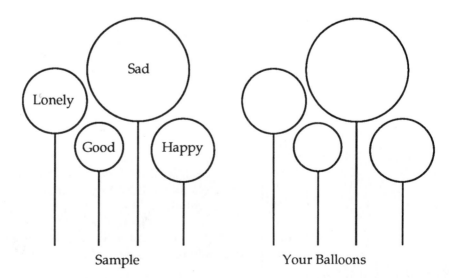

Sample   Your Balloons

Focusing Techniques

Focusing techniques are used to encourage and facilitate introspection in such a way that problems can be clarified and conceptualized by the client. Focusing emphasizes present feelings toward either present or past circumstances. Iberg (1981) describes this process as

> . . . holding one's attention quietly. at a very low level of abstraction, to the felt sense. Felt sense is the bodily sense of the whole problem. In focusing, one doesn't think about the problem or analyze it, but one senses it immediately. One senses all of it, in all its complexity, as the whole thing hits one bodily. (p. 344)

After suggesting that the client find a comfortable position, the counselor invites the client to become quiet and to allow feelings to enter into consciousness. The client is then asked to associate words with this undifferentiated mass of feelings and allow awareness to generate naturally. The instructions for using this intervention that follow have been adapted from Gendlin (1969, p. 506).

Focusing Instructions

> I am going to explain how you can focus on a general or overall feeling you have about some concern or problem. Be silent for a moment and relax . . . (Pause: Have the client close his or her eyes and relax) . . . Now let the tension drain from your body . . . (Longer pause) . . . See what comes to you when you ask yourself, "How am I now?" "How do I feel?" Let any thoughts emerge. Try not to screen your response . . . (Longer pause) . . . Think about what is a major problem or concern for you. Choose whatever seems most meaningful to you . . . (Shorter pause) . . .

Focusing Process

> 1. Try to pay attention (focus) to what all of the problem (concern) feels like. Allow (let) yourself to feel the entire mass of the feeling.
>
>   (Longer pause)
>
> 2. As you pay attention to (or receive) the entire feeling of your problem, you may find that one special concern

comes up. Let yourself pay attention to that one aspect or feeling. Don't explain it or talk to yourself about it. Just feel it.

(Extended pause)

3. Keep following one feeling. Don't let it be just words or pictures. Wait and let words or pictures emerge from the feelings.

(Extended pause)

4. If this one feeling changes, or moves, let it do so. Whatever it does, follow the feeling and pay attention to it. Feel it all. Don't decide what is important about it. Just experience it.

(Extended pause)

5. Now, take your fresh and new feeling about your problem and give it space. Try to find some new words or images or pictures that capture what this feeling tries to say. Find words or images to say what you are feeling now.

(Extended pause)

Following the six steps of focusing, the counselor should ask the client to describe the words or pictures that entered consciousness during the exercise. This description can be continued for the remainder of the session.

Case Illustration of Focusing:
The Case of Maggie

Maggie is a twenty-six-year-old divorced woman who requested counseling to help her deal with an overwhelming sense of anger and despair following her divorce. In the first session, she reported feeling overwhelmed by emotions and the demands of her two-year-old daughter. She vacillated between anger, resentment, guilt, and back to anger (usually directed at her ex-spouse). When this circular process really gained control of her, she would begin to feel "stuck," "caught," or "lost" (her words). She showed strong evidence of being rational, realistic, and in control, except for these emotional bouts. There was no past history of depression or life-threatening acts by either herself or any other family member. She did have her good days as well as her bad days and could say that she believed this terrible time would pass eventually.

Based on this information, the counselor decided that she did not pose a suicidal threat to herself, but did ask her to make an appointment with her family physician for a complete physical examination. The counselor also decided that paper-and-pencil exercises were not needed, since the client seemed quite able to verbalize her feelings and did not seem confused or unable to differentiate between feelings. On the other hand, it did seem desirable to help the client examine these various feelings and to find the meaning or relevance of the pattern in which they seemed to occur (anger . . . resentment . . . guilt . . . anger . . .).

By providing facilitative conditions (understanding, empathy, respect), the counselor gradually produced an atmosphere in which the client began to relax and do some self-confrontation. She was able to talk about her misgivings regarding the causes of the divorce. She began to talk about the heavy burden of single parenthood. Invariably, however, she would reach a dead end (which she referred to as an insurmountable wall) in talking about these feelings.

After three sessions in which this same result occurred, the counselor suggested that they try a focusing exercise. After the counselor explained how it was done and what purpose it might serve, the client and counselor decided to use the next session as a focusing experiment. The client arrived at the next session showing some nervousness, but this soon dissipated. The counselor began the focusing exercise, and the client quickly became a cooperative participant.

At the end of the exercise, the client reported that when she tried to let the anger, resentment, and guilt merge into one larger feeling, the word "responsibility" kept entering her awareness. The counselor wisely suggested that they repeat the exercise, but that the client focus on the "responsible" response this time. At the end of the second round, the client talked with a sense of discovery about the experience:

"I think I have been running away from my responsibilities, my responsibility for the end of the marriage, my responsibility for my daughter, and most of all, my responsibility for myself. In the exercise I reached the point of 'giving these responsibilities away,' but there is no one I would want to give these responsibilities to. They are too valuable to give away."

"What do you mean, they are too valuable?" the counselor asked.

"If I give them away, I must also give away my autonomy. my freedom to be who I am. And that is very valuable to me. I must learn to accept some of these fears about possibly causing the divorce or not liking some aspects of being a mother. If I give these responsibilities away, I'd be right back in the same place I was as a child."

Helping Clients Integrate or Change Feeling States

It was noted in the preceding section that clients sometimes cope with emotions by creating a psychological distance from their feelings. This can happen when the person is bombarded by multiple affect reactions stemming from traumatic life situations. It can also happen when a person is confronted with a strong but unacceptable emotional situation. The result of this psychological distancing is to postpone the immediate demand to respond to the affect. A normal example of this condition is the grieving process. But to postpone an adaptive demand is not a long-term solution. Thus, even the grieving individual must ultimately come to grips with the loss and alter perceptions in whatever way the loss demands.

The process of integrating feeling states, or when appropriate, changing feeling states, can require professional assistance, particularly when the client is insensitive to or unskilled in affective matters. Thus, the process of sorting out and identifying feelings that was discussed in the previous section may lead to a need to integrate those newly identified feelings. A case in point might illustrate this.

Joyce B. was married soon after graduation from college. Within three years, she had a two-year-old daughter and a six-month-old son. She had elected to stay at home during the children's early years and begin her career when both were finally in school. This decision fit her family values and paralleled the situation in her own family of origin.

Since the birth of her second child, Joyce had begun to feel restless and irritable with the children. When this feeling would occur, she would chastise herself and remind herself that this had been a choice based on her beliefs about family needs. Nevertheless, the feelings continued to emerge, and Joyce was finding it increasingly difficult to dismiss these emotional intrusions into her commitment.

Through counseling Joyce became aware that her restlessness was related to some unmet personal needs for achievement and recognition. Fulfilling an important family need was satisfying at one level, but it did not address other levels of her value system. The issue for Joyce was twofold: Should she allow these recurring feelings to be admitted into her perceptions of self and family? And if she did acknowledge these feelings, what would be the implications for the family and for her value system?

Joyce's situation illustrates how emotional undercurrents can intrude into a person's consciousness and disrupt emotional commitments and daily routines. It also illustrates the need to come to some resolution of value conflict and incompatible emotional states.

A number of counseling interventions are derived from client centered, Gestalt, and existential counseling to aid the client with such problems. In this section, we shall examine role reversal, alter ego, empty chair (or two-chair) exercise, and dreamwork.

Role Reversal

The role reversal is a useful exercise when the client is confronting an issue that appears to contradict or conflict with the client's self-image. The purpose of role reversal is to project the client into a paradoxical examination of views, attitudes, or beliefs. This exercise may meet initial resistance, since it asks the client to challenge safe (albeit dysfunctional) roles or attitudes. However, if the client is encouraged to try "playing the devil's advocate," to demonstrate that he or she is, in fact, able to discuss both sides of an issue, the exercise can be quite effective. The case of Bob will illustrate how this technique may be used.

Case Illustration of Role Reversal: The Case of Bob

Bob entered counseling for the purpose of solving "career problems." As counseling progressed, the problem became more clearly defined as an interpersonal conflict between Bob and his boss. Bob found it very easy to explore his feelings toward his boss, even though he liked his job. However, these explorations always seemed to lead up blind alleys if the counselor raised the question of solutions. Bob would become flustered and would jump to the conclusion that the only solution was to change jobs. After this pattern repeated itself for three sessions, the counselor suggested that they try the role reversal exercise. Bob responded somewhat suspiciously, but after some discussion of what the exercise involved, he agreed to participate. The next session began as follows:

> *Bob:* I don't know what this exercise is going to prove. Every time we discuss my problem, I end up at the same conclusion. My boss is insensitive and completely unconcerned about my situation. He'll never change, and I'm not going to change, so the only solution is for me to look for another job.

Counselor: Before we reach that conclusion, let's try the role reversal exercise we discussed last week. It may not change anything, but at least we can say we looked at the problem every way we could imagine. Are you still game?

Bob: Well, I can't imagine what you have in mind, but I'll go along with whatever it is.

Counselor: Good. I'd like you to play devil's advocate with your problem for a few minutes. I'd like you to imagine that you are your boss, and I'll be you. Try to be as accurate in this role as you can. That way, I'll have a much better idea what your boss is like. And I will try to be as accurate as possible in my role as Bob. If I tend to respond inaccurately, stop the role reversal and give me some coaching on how I should respond. Are you ready?

Bob: I suppose so. l know I can imitate him. I know him like the back of my hand. But I don't see how it can do any good.

Counselor: Maybe you're right. Let's give it a try and see what you think. You begin as your boss.

Bob:
(as Boss) Bob, I see you have missed another deadline for the production report. What the hell's going on?

Counselor:
(as Bob) I couldn't get the information I needed, and I didn't want to bother you yesterday.

Bob:
(as Boss) What do you mean "You didn't want to bother me?" If you have to bother me to get the report done, then bother me. But don't miss the deadline.

Counselor:
(as Bob) I wish you wouldn't get so upset with me. I was just trying to take care of you.

Bob:
(as Boss) Look, Bob, you can't have it both ways. If you don't ask for help when you need it and that leads to missing deadlines, then you have to

expect some consequence. And if anger is the consequence, then you've got to understand that it is due to your avoiding me. You've got to stop avoiding me.

(End of role reversal)

Counselor: Well, Bob, what do you think of that scenario?

Bob: I guess it took an unexpected turn. His anger does upset me, but I haven't been thinking about bringing it on myself. Maybe I could learn to handle him better.

As can be seen in this illustration, Bob acknowledges his avoidance in a safe confrontation with his boss. This acknowledgment does not mean that Bob will return to his job with new methods for coping. It may be that counseling will move on to an exploration of how Bob can develop new approaches to working with his boss. For the moment, however, Bob has broken through a resistance that would otherwise impede the resolution of his job difficulties.

Alter Ego

The alter ego exercise is similar to role reversal, but with a novel twist. Webster's (1983) defines *alter ego* as "another side of oneself, another self." The notion is that each of us has another dimension of our personality that is more aware, more honest, more perceptive of personal motives, values, and hidden agendas. It is our alter ego that nags us when we neglect our duties or avoid our responsibilities. Thus, the alter ego knows and is a more honest report of our inner motivations.

In this exercise, the client is asked to become his or her alter ego, and the counselor assumes the client's public self. Because the counselor must produce an accurate portrayal of the client's public self, and because the client must feel safe enough with the counselor to allow the alter ego to emerge, this exercise should not be used early in the counseling relationship. When the alter ego exercise is effective, it allows clients to confront themselves more honestly. This kind of self-confrontation can be far more effective than confrontations provided by the counselor. The result is that the client can introduce issues, refute self-rationalizations, or question self-motives in a therapeutic encounter with the self. The following illustrates the use of the alter ego exercise in a counseling setting.

Case Illustration of Alter Ego:
The Case of Wanda

Wanda was a thirty-five-year-old housekeeper. She was married to a fifty-year-old auto mechanic. She had an eleven-year-old son, Tim, by a previous marriage. Wanda entered counseling because she was concerned about her son's emotional and academic development. The son had been identified as a gifted child by the school he attended. However, his grades had deteriorated in the past six months, and this had become a source of family concern. As Wanda discussed her concerns for her son, she would shift from her personal issues to how she felt her husband did not recognize Tim's needs. When this occurred, she would become angry toward her spouse, and then Tim's issues would become lost.

The counselor had asked her to involve the stepfather and Tim in counseling, but Wanda said her spouse refused and that Tim's school schedule would not permit his participation. While the counselor wondered about Wanda's own reservations about including son and stepfather, she did not question Wanda's report. Because Wanda was a bright and introspective client, the counselor finally suggested that they try the alter ego exercise. Wanda, who liked counseling, readily agreed to the counselor's suggestion.

> *Counselor:* In this exercise, I am going to be you, as I have come to know you. I'll try to represent you honestly and accurately. I want you to be the private you, the person I don't really know yet. In this exercise we are going to talk to each other, the public you (my role) and the private you (your role). We might even have an argument, but that's okay. Do you understand?
>
> *Wanda:* I think so, I'll try.
>
> *Counselor:* Good. I'll go first.
>
> *Counselor: (as Wanda):* I just don't know what to do with Tim (son). He is so bright, but he is wasting his ability.
>
> *Wanda: (as alter ego)* You think you ought to be doing something, but you don't know what to do.
>
> *Counselor: (as Wanda)* Yes, and Bob (husband) ought to be helping me.

Wanda:
(as alter ego) You think Bob should be helping you because you don't want to have to do it alone.

Counselor:
(as Wanda) It's not that I don't want to do it alone. I don't think I can do it alone. And besides, I want Bob and Tim to have a parent-child relationship, and that isn't happening.

Wanda:
(as alter ego) It's not happening because you won't let Bob do the important parenting things.

Counselor:
(as Wanda) What do you mean, "I won't let Bob be a parent?"

Wanda:
(as alter ego) I think you're afraid to let Bob be a real parent because Tim might decide he likes Bob better than he likes you. So you keep Bob away.

Counselor:
(as Wanda) That's not true and you know it. Bob really doesn't love Tim enough to worry about him.

Wanda:
(as alter ego) That's not true, Wanda, and you know it. Bob loves Tim a lot. He worries about Tim. But he worries more about you and your relationship to Tim, and that's why he doesn't get involved.

Counselor:
(as Wanda) I hate it when you say these things.

Wanda:
(as alter ego) I know it hurts, but you better wake up, Wanda, or you're going to lose both of them someday.

The counselor and Wanda ended the exercise at this point. Wanda had said some very self-revealing things and was beginning to show some discomfort with her revelations. Sensing that Wanda was beginning to reach a saturation level, the counselor decided to allow her some time to integrate the ideas and feelings that had been aroused. After stopping the exercise, they took time to discuss the confrontation. During this discussion, Wanda began to relax and look more comfortable with herself. It was a very significant session and proved to be a turning point in Wanda's counseling, when she acknowledged to herself for the first time that her husband was conflicted between his love for Tim and his concern for her relationship with Tim.

The Empty Chair

The empty chair is a dialoguing exercise made popular by Gestalt therapists but used increasingly by counselors from a wide range of orientations. It is used to help clients explore and develop awareness of subtle feelings that are not surfacing but are affecting client functioning. The exercise may be used with interpersonal issues (in which case, the enactment will be between the client and the other relevant person) or with intrapersonal issues (in which case, the enactment will be between the client and the client's "other self").

The counselor begins by explaining that this is a dialogue or imaginary conversation either with oneself or with a specific person who is also involved in the client's problem. The counselor explains that his or her role will be to observe, choreograph the conversation, and at times interrupt to ask questions or share observations. If the client agrees, the next step is to define who the two principals in the conversation will be, that is, who the client will converse with. This might be the "embarrassed self" or the "intimidated self," or it might be the client's parent, spouse, or significant other.

The counselor must be able to recognize the splits in awareness or the potential conflicts in order to define the elements of the dialogue. The next step is to explain to the client how the process works.

> *In this exercise you will be both the "caring you" and the "angry you." And the two "yous" will talk it over and explore both points of view, both sides. Let's start by having the caring you explain why you don't want to talk to your parents about their decision. Then I'd like the angry you to react to the caring you. Is it clear what you will do? Remember, I'll be right here, coaching when you need help.*

Greenberg (1979) refers to this arrangement as the "experiencing chair" and the "other chair." The experiencing chair is similar to what happens in most therapeutic processes. The other chair represents the internal objects—opposing will, conflicting values, or motivations—of which the client is possibly unaware but which have a significant effect on the client's emotions, actions, and choices. The case of Paula illustrates how the counselor helps the client begin this exercise.

Case Illustration of The Empty Chair: The Case of Paula

Paula was a seventeen-year-old high school senior who had recently been invited to go on a skiing weekend with several friends. After much thought and family discussion, her parents had finally agreed to let her go on this "first of its kind" excursion. A few days later, both Paula and her parents became aware that the ski trip was to be unchaperoned. Learning this, her parents reversed themselves and told Paula she could not go. Paula felt both embarrassed and relieved. She also thought she felt insulted that her parents did not trust her enough, but she was not really sure about this latter reaction. In the counseling session following this development, Paula wanted to talk about her conflicting feelings, and the counselor suggested the empty chair exercise. When Paula agreed, the counselor suggested that Paula begin as the insulted self and talk to the relieved self.

Insulted Paula: I am so upset by this whole matter. I don't know why my parents would do this to me. Don't they trust me?

Relieved Paula: Trusting you isn't what they are thinking about. After all, you didn't tell them the trip wouldn't be chaperoned.

Insulted Paula: I didn't know. They didn't tell me that. And whose side are you on, anyhow?

Relieved Paula: I'm not on their side, if that's what you mean. But it would be pretty uncomfortable with this bunch of kids at the ski lodge and no adults around in case someone got hurt.

Counselor: Excuse me just a moment. Why don't you ask the other Paula why she's feeling so good about this decision.

Insulted Paula: Okay, why aren't you mad, too? Didn't you want to go on this ski trip?

Relieved Paula: Yes, I wanted to go, but I didn't want it to be so complicated. I don't really think it would be as much fun if I knew Mom and Dad were worrying, or if I had to worry about things.

Counselor: Okay, now turn the tables. Ask the other Paula what she's so mad about.

Relieved Paula: What are you mad about?

Insulted Paula: I don't know if mad is how I feel. It's just so uncomfortable having to face my friends and admit that my parents won't let me go.

Counselor: Now talk to Paula about her discomfort.

Relieved Paula: Okay. Sure it's uncomfortable. But remember, it would have been pretty uncomfortable at the ski lodge, too. And being mad isn't going to make you feel more comfortable.

Sensing that the transaction had been completed, the counselor ended the exercise at this point and asked Paula what she got out of the dialogue. Paula's response indicated that, while she didn't feel "good" yet about the whole matter. she did think the mad feelings would soon leave.

There are two distinct advantages to be derived from this technique: (a) the client's defenses that characterize the conflicting elements tend to diminish as she enacts the dialogue, thus permitting her to see elements of the relationship that she could not easily let herself see; and (b) the client is unable to maintain the distortion that is part of the relationship as a result of misinterpreting the parents' role in the problem.

Dreamwork

A number of counseling approaches, including psychoanalysis, Gestalt, and Individual (Adlerian) Psychology, make use of dreams in the therapeutic process. In some cases, the dream content is taken as relevant insight into the client's psyche. In other cases, the dream is a metaphor to be used in the session to explore alternative realities. This can be illustrated through the Gestalt treatment of dreams in which the client is asked to explore the different elements of the dream to search for or allow awareness to emerge. The meaning of the elements of the dream is always provided by the client. The following is an example of this type of dream treatment (Dye & Hackney, 1975).

Case Illustration of Dreamwork:
The Case of Linda

A college student (we shall call her Linda) reported that she had had the following dream:

I was picked up by this very expensive limousine. When I got in, I was struck by the plushness of the seats, the fine wood-work on the dashboard, the extreme comfort. It was like all my needs were being taken care of. As we were driving, I turned and noticed the driver for the first time. He was an Oriental and was dressed in this chauffeur's uniform. He was unusually concerned for my welfare and my needs. I really felt taken care of by him too. We drove to this large, impressive house. It sat on a knoll and it had huge pillars in front, like a Southern mansion. We got out of the car and went into the mansion, which turned out to be a restaurant. I was relieved to discover this. Discovering it was a restaurant eased my concerns because I knew how to behave in a restaurant. After we were seated (the Oriental chauffeur and me), the waiter came and offered us menus to study. It was then I realized I was very hungry. We waited and waited for the waiter to return and take our orders, but no one came. As I started to look around for our waiter, I noticed that all the other customers in the restaurant were Orientals, and this surprised me. Finally I spotted our waiter, and I got up from the table and went to him and asked him to come take our order. He said he would be there momentarily. Again we waited for what seemed like a long time. Finally, I got up again and went to the waiter and asked him to please serve us. He apologized for the delay and asked us to move to another table where we would be served immediately. We were led out of the main dining room into another empty room that was all white and had one wall of glass windows. I sat down and then realized that there was only one chair at the table. I looked up to see the waiter and my chauffeur both smiling at me. Then I looked and saw for the first time that the windows had bars on them. I was trapped. For the first time, I realized that I was in a mental institution and I was the patient.

This dream reflects several significant people, objects, and events that the client can be asked to role-play. She could be asked to be the limousine, the chauffeur, the large mansion, the restaurant, the waiter, the Oriental clientele, the white secondary dining room, the table with only one chair, the windowed wall, the bars, the smiling waiter and chauffeur. To try to role-play all of these options would require quite a bit of time. So the counselor might select from this list a smaller number of enactments. In that case, it is best to enact each role-play in the sequence in which it occurred in the dream.

The role-play is a dialogue that the client carries on with herself. As a result, it demands that the client use her imagination, often supplying information or details that were not in the original dream. This may be difficult for some clients to do, and it may be necessary to illustrate what you would have the client do in order that she understand. For example, Linda was first asked to "be" the limousine.

> *Linda:* What do you mean?
>
> *Counselor:* Be the limousine. If you were the limousine and could talk, what would you be saying to Linda.
>
> *Linda:* I still don't think I understand.
>
> *Counselor:* All right. I'll give you some help. Let's pretend that I am the limousine, and this is what I might be saying: "Hi, little one. Get in and let me show you how good I am."
>
> *Linda:* OK. I think I know what you mean.
>
> *Counselor:* Good. Now, you be the limousine. What would you be saying to Linda?
>
> *Linda:* Hello. Linda! Get in and let me show you how good I can be for you. I want to wrap you in comfort and make you feel really good.
>
> *Linda:* Thank you. I would like you to do those things to me. I want to feel safe, secure, and comfortable.

This first segment may be abbreviated (as it was with Linda). Getting into the spirit of the exercise takes time, and the counselor should not push the client to produce more dialogue than she feels is there.

As the client dialogues different parts of the dream, the counselor asks the client to identify any potential relevance of the enactment to her life. For example:

> *Counselor:* Linda, is there any significance in the dialogue between you and the limousine?
>
> *Linda:* No, except that I like to be taken care of, and I think a lot of people would like to have that. That doesn't seem too unusual.

Counselor: OK. Let's go on to the next part of the dream, the driver that you suddenly notice. Can you describe the driver again?

Linda: Yes. He is a large, kindly-looking man. He is Oriental. He doesn't smile or anything. But I can tell that he doesn't mean me any harm.

Counselor: Will you be the chauffeur now, talking to Linda?

Linda: Yes. Hello, Linda. I am glad you joined me. I have been worried about you. I want to help you decide where to go so you will make the right decision. I want to make these decisions for you because you can't make them for yourself.

Counselor: Now be Linda and respond to the chauffeur.

Linda: All right. I will do what you say. I know you can make better decisions than I can. I will do what you think is best.

Counselor: Linda, does the chauffeur remind you of anyone you know?

Linda: Yes, my father.

Counselor: Is he your father?

Linda: Yes, he is.

Counselor: You said he was Oriental.

Linda: Well, I had an Oriental friend who always masked his feelings, and that is the way it was with Dad. He *never* let me know where he was or what he was feeling.

Linda began to find meaning as she progressed through other elements of the dream with increasing investment. She was asked to be the large mansion talking to Linda, and the dialogue led her to identify the mansion as the imposing social system that she had been taught to respect and obey. Linda talked about her mixed emotions regarding the social system. She could feel lost in it, and that brought on anger and resentment that was bigger than she.

Her discovery that the mansion was really a restaurant after she had entered it was also relevant to her. She compared the relief that she had experienced upon discovering the restaurant to the relief she also felt when she realized that the social system was something she was very familiar with and knew how to play. The waiter who appeared so solicitous yet did not serve her was a further extension of her frustration at being unimportant within the system.

As Linda took on the role of the other customers in the restaurant it became apparent to her that they were society sitting in judgment of her. She identified this through the cue that they were faceless; thus she could not read their emotions. She drew the conclusion that they must be reacting to her, and the hiding of their emotions had to mean that judgment was harsh.

It was when Linda began to enact and interpret the final portions of her dream that the gestalt began to emerge. Finding herself alone in the second dining room—the total whiteness (the absence of stimuli), the discovery of the windowed wall that was covered with bars—led her to an intense emotional experience. She cried softly. The counselor asked her to talk about her tears. Where were they coming from? Who was she crying for?

Linda saw the final portions of the dream tying into an old fear. She confided that since she had been in high school, she had feared that she would "go crazy" someday and have to be committed to a mental institution. She said that while she was in high school, her father had had a nervous breakdown and had been in a mental hospital for several months. The mother had kept the details from the children, and they had had to create the details in their imaginations. Linda said she related strongly to her father and feared the same would happen to her. Feeling her weakness and vulnerability, identifying the chauffeur as her father, who wanted to take care of her but on his own terms, feeling the pressure of "society," all of this Linda identified as the constant underlying heaviness that she carried around. She could also see that there were moments of strength, points at which she could exercise control. This came through her sense of the "roles" of society that she understood, and it was apparent to her in her ability to deal with the reluctant waiter.[*]

Dreamwork is not a panacea, whether it be used as a Gestalt therapy intervention, a Transactional Analysis intervention, or a psychoanalytic intervention. It does not always give the client instant relief, but it can offer material that the client can work with and thus generate awareness of underlying tensions. It allows the client to focus.

There are several guidelines to follow while working with dreams:

[*]From H.A. Dye & H. Hackney, *Gestalt Approaches to Counseling* (Boston: Houghton-Mifflin. 1975), pp. 62-67. Reprinted by permission.

1. As a first step, have the client describe the dream from beginning to end without interruption.

2. Describe the procedure for role-playing the dream (dialoguing).

3. If the client appears uncertain about the process, give an example.

4. Be the "director" of the role-play. Ask the client to be each of the several parts of the dream.

5. Proceed with different parts of the dream in the order of their occurrence in the dream.

6. Do not allow yourself to make interpretations of the elements of the dream. Only the client can do that. Ask the client if he or she can find any relationships. If not, proceed to the next part of the dream.

Client Reactions to Affective Interventions

The point was made at the beginning of this chapter that many clients lack the introspective and interpersonal skills to express their feelings accurately and adequately. This does not mean that they do not experience feelings, nor does it mean that they do not need to express their feelings. The inability to express what one is feeling is often experienced as a "pressure cooker" effect in which the bottled up emotions accumulate and add to the person's frustrations. Eventually, the emotions find an outlet, either through psychosomatic illness, substance abuse, physical violence, temper tantrums, or some other socially destructive expression.

Given this kind of condition and its very limited alternatives, most clients experience relief at the expression of feeling states. Some also feel a kind of embarrassment, as though they had broken some unwritten rule about their behavior. The counselor can facilitate this effect by normalizing the feeling. To *normalize* is to point out that this reaction is a normal reaction and will pass in a matter of time. Occasionally, a client will continue, almost without limits, to talk about current and old feelings. It is as though an emotional dam has finally been broken. Whatever the reaction, the most common client response is a sense of relief, catharsis, and renewal that can lead to further change.

Summary

In this chapter we have examined the very complex subject of human emotions and their expressions. You may think of affective interventions as efforts to aid clients in the expression of their innermost fears, hopes, hurts, resentments, and frustrations. Such expression often involves teaching clients how to express their feelings, helping them "give themselves permission" to express emotions. At another level, you may work with clients who are able to describe emotions, but who are unable to sort out or conceptualize what they feel. Finally, at the most complex level, you may become involved in helping clients either to accept or integrate affect states, or to change affect states.

Whatever your involvement might be, it is vitally important to recognize that human emotions are central to human functioning. Consequently, when we work with emotions, we are working near the core of most human beings' reality. Thus, we are creating and walking through what amounts to a highly vulnerable passage for clients. Respect for this condition, and appreciation that clients invite us into their inner world, is both appropriate and essential.

Exercises

1. Choose a partner. One of you will be the speaker; the other will be the listener. The speaker should select one of the four emotions identified in this chapter (positive affect, anger, fear, sadness) and communicate that feeling state to the other person. The listener should record on paper all verbal and nonverbal cues observed, but should not respond to the speaker. After three to five minutes, the exercise should be concluded, and the listener should identify the speaker's feeling state and the cues that support that choice.

2. The following is an exercise in verbal affect identification. Identify the feeling state(s) in each of the four client communications, which have been taken from actual counseling interviews. If more than one feeling state is present in the client response, place an asterisk (*) next to the one that you believe has the greatest bearing on the client's concern. After identifying the feeling states, discuss your choices with other class members.

   A. "Well, uh, I'm happy just being in with people and having them know me."

   B. "And, and, uh, you know, they always say that, you know, some people don't like to be called by a number; well, I don't either."

   C. "In speech, I'm, uh, well, in speech I'm not doing good because I'm afraid to talk in front of a bunch of people . . ."

D. "It seems to me like working in that lab is really harmful; I mean, I enjoy my work, and the people, but that lab, that worries me."

3. Class members should select triads (speaker, respondent, observer/recorder) for the following exercise.
    1. The person designated as the speaker should share a personal concern with the respondent.
    2. The respondent's task is to respond only to affective topics, using one of two responses: the reflection of feeling or the summarization of feeling.
    3. The observer will keep track of the number and kinds of responses used by the listener (for example, first response: reflection; second response: reflection; third response: summarization; and so on.)
    4. After interacting for ten minutes, the three participants should discuss: (a) the observer's record; (b) the listener's experience; (c) how the speaker experienced the listener.
    5. Following this discussion, exchange roles and repeat the exercise.

Discussion Questions

1. Why would phenomenologists take the position that there are multiple realities?

2. Two goals of affective interventions are: (1) to help the client express feeling states; and (2) to help the client identify and discriminate between feeling states. This implies that clients may be able to express feelings but still not be able to identify or sort out those feelings. Do you think this is possible? Isn't it likely that the expression of a feeling carries with it the awareness of what it is? Discuss this with other classmates or colleagues.

3. Which nonverbal cues communicate anger? Do these same cues communicate some other emotion? If yes, what emotion? How would you know which emotion is being communicated?

4. What are the potential therapeutic gains when using role reversal with a client? What kinds of clients might not be able to participate effectively in a role reversal exercise?

5. Referring back to the dreamwork example in this chapter, what was the counselor's role? What was the counselor's most challenging moment during the exercise? What was the client's most challenging moment?

Recommended Readings

Cashdan, S. (1988), *Object Relations Therapy* (New York: W. W. Norton).

Egan, G. (1990), *The Skilled Helper: A Systematic Approach to Effective Helping*, 4th Ed. (Pacific Grove, CA: Brooks/Cole).

Gendlin, E.T. (1984), The Client's Edge: The Edge of Awareness, in J.M. Shlien and R.F. Levant (Eds.), *Client-Centered Therapy and the Person-Centered Approach* (New York: Praeger Publishers).

Gladding, S.T. (1988), The Theory and Practice of Individual Counseling: Affective Approaches, Chapter 4, *Counseling: A Comprehensive Profession*, (Columbus, OH: Merrill).

Johnson, R. (1986), *Inner Work: Using Dreams and Active Imagination for Personal Growth* (New York: Harper & Row).

Knapp, M.L. (1978), *Nonverbal Communication in Human Interaction*, 2nd Ed. (New York: Holt, Rinehart & Winston).

Teyber, E. (1989), *Interpersonal Process in Psychotherapy* (Pacific Grove, CA: Brooks/Cole).

8

Cognitive Interventions

Strategies that are intended to change the way one thinks of self, others, or life situations, are called *cognitive* interventions. In using cognitive interventions, the counselor assumes that people's problematic emotions and observable behavior also are influenced by their beliefs, attitudes, and perceptions, all of which are cognitions or thoughts. Errors in thinking, sometimes called "faulty" thinking, are especially likely to produce distressing emotions and/or problematic behaviors. For example, the person who expects to fail, thinks that she is going to fail, and approaches life events from a "failure" orientation. She could be described as having low self-esteem or lack of confidence, but in fact, she is approaching life with a self-defeating mentality, an "I don't think I can do it" life view. This type of person may benefit from strategies that focus primarily on changing beliefs, attitudes, and perceptions of self and others (Beck, 1976; Lazarus, 1981). In this chapter, we describe a variety of counseling strategies associated with approaches that deal primarily with cognitive change.

One of the major theories to contribute to cognitive counseling approaches is rational-emotive therapy (Cormier and Cormier, 1991; Ellis, 1984; Gladding, 1988; Hansen, Stevic, and Warner, 1986). Some of the counseling interventions described in this chapter are drawn from rational-emotive therapy. Also included are some cognitive interventions that derive from behavioral, communication, and even existential approaches.

The application of cognitive therapeutic techniques is extensive. They have been applied as the primary intervention strategy for such problems as anxiety reduction, stress, anger, habit control, obesity, depression, and sexual dysfunction. Characteristics of clients who seem to have most success with cognitive techniques include:

Average to above-average intelligence.

Moderate to high levels of functional distress.

Able to identify feelings and thoughts.

Not psychotic, in a state of crisis, or severely debilitated by the problem.

Possessing an adequate repertoire of skills or behavioral responses.

Able to process information visually or auditorially.

Goals of Cognitive Intervention

The overall aim of any cognitive intervention is to reduce emotional distress and corresponding maladaptive behavior patterns by altering or correcting errors in thoughts, perceptions, and beliefs. Changes in behavior or affect occur once the client's distorted thinking begins to change and be replaced by alternative, more realistic ways of thinking about self, other persons, or life experiences (Beck, 1976). Thus, a cognitive intervention is intended to alter a client's manner of thinking about a particular event, other persons, self, or life. It also stresses the importance of self-control. Clients are viewed as direct agents of their own changes, rather than as helpless victims of external events and forces over which they have little control, although there are some cognitive interventions that help clients by "nudging" them out of habitualized ways of thinking.

A-B-C-D-E Analysis

The A-B-C-D-E analysis is a cognitive intervention strategy associated with a theoretical approach to counseling known as rational-emotive therapy. This theoretical approach was developed in the 1950s by Albert Ellis, a psychotherapist living in New York City. The major assumption of rational-emotive therapy is that thoughts cause feelings. In other words, it is not events or other people that make us feel bad or upset, but our view or beliefs about these events or persons that create emotional distress. Emotional distress is the result of dysfunctional thoughts that Ellis refers to as "irrational beliefs." Ellis identifies eleven common irrational beliefs:

1. A person must be loved or approved by virtually everyone in the community.

2. A person must be perfectly competent, adequate, and achieving to be considered worthwhile.

3. Some people are bad, wicked, or villainous and therefore should be blamed and punished.

4. It is a terrible catastrophe when things are not as a person wants them to be.

5. Unhappiness is caused by outside circumstances, and a person has no control over it.

6. Dangerous or fearsome things are causes for great concern, and their possibility must be continually dwelt upon.

7. It is easier to avoid certain difficulties and self-responsibilities than to face them.

8. A person should be dependent on others and should have someone stronger on whom to rely.

9. Past experiences and events are the determinants of present behavior; the influence of the past cannot be eradicated.

10. A person should be quite upset over other people's problems and disturbances.

11. There is always a right or perfect solution to every problem, and it must be found or the results will be catastrophic.

According to Ellis, people both create and maintain unnecessary emotional distress by continually "re-indoctrinating" themselves with these irrational beliefs. Self-indoctrination is analogous to playing a tape in one's head over and over again until the one tape is the only one a person hears.

In the A-B-C-D-E analysis, the client learns to recognize *activating* events (A), corresponding *beliefs* about the event (B), and emotional-behavioral *consequences* of these beliefs (C). The client is then taught a variety of ways to *dispute* (D) the emotional beliefs, and to discriminate or attend to new emotional and behavioral *effects* (E) of increased rational thinking. In the actual technique, much of the focus and activity occur with respect to the *D*, or the disputation of existing emotional beliefs.

Getting to the A, or Activating Event

The *activating event* is usually some obnoxious or unfortunate situation or person in the client's life, and often the presence of this situation or person is part of what prompts the client to come for counseling. For example, a client says, "I can't stand my husband. He's a slob" or "My marriage is not turning out the way I hoped at all." In helping clients identify the A, it is important to teach them that this external situation or event does not cause their feelings. For example, "Just because your husband is a slob, or just because your marriage is not turning out as you had hoped, does not mean that you have to feel terribly bummed out or upset."

It is also helpful for clients to discriminate between activating events that can be changed and those that cannot. For those that can be changed, clients can use good problem-solving skills to bring about a change. For those situations that are outside the clients' control, it is important to help clients learn to respond to these situations better and to focus on changing their own reactions. For example, "Since your husband is not here, neither you nor I can be responsible for changing his behavior. However, we can work on changing your feelings and reactions to what he does that is presently so upsetting to you."

Getting at the C

The C represents the emotional *consequences* of the activating event and often is what propels the client into therapy. For instance, "My husband is a real jerk," or "My marriage is failing and I feel really terrible." People cannot tolerate bad or uncomfortable feelings too long, and if such feelings persist, they often motivate them to seek outside assistance. Examples of various emotional consequences that a client may feel include guilt, anger, depression, and anxiety.

In order to identify the C accurately, counselors need to be alert to the presence of affect words the client uses and supporting body language or nonverbal cues indicative of emotions. If an occasional client does not report any Cs and seems to be either very flat in affect or, in the other extreme, very emotionally unstable, these may be signs of pathology that suggest the need for additional assessment techniques such as a mental status exam. The aim of the A-B-C-D-E analysis is not to have the client deny or get rid of all emotions. In identifying the C, the counselor will want to help clients decide if they want to keep or change the emotion.

Getting at the Bs

Identifying the "Bs", or the client's *belief system*, is a major focus of this particular therapeutic technique. The client's beliefs about the activating event may be exhibited in one of two forms—rational beliefs (RBs) or irrational beliefs (IBs). Both RBs and IBs represent a client's evaluations of "reality."

Rational beliefs are those that are truly consistent with reality—in the sense that they can be supported with data, facts, or evidence and would be substantiated by a group of objective observers. RBs result in *moderate* levels of Cs, or emotional consequences, and are useful in helping people attain their goals. IBs are those that are not consistent with reality. In other words, the belief does not match or result from the activating event to the degree that would be substantiated by a group of outside observers. IBs are not based on facts, data, or evidence, lead to disturbed or dysfunctional Cs (emotional consequences), and often interfere with a person's goals.

Most IBs are reflected by one or more of the eleven irrational beliefs listed earlier, although occasionally a client's IBs are more idiosyncratic and do not fit into one of these categories. Usually, Cs, or disturbing emotions, are the result of more than just one IB. The counselor can help the client identify all the existing IBs and then group them into themes such as *needs or have tos, shoulds or musts,* and *awful or catastrophic.* Counselors need to be aware that clients often report IBs as *feelings* and may have trouble responding to counselor queries about their belief system. Some clients may not know what they are thinking or "saying" to themselves either. In these cases, counselors can facilitate the client's identification of IBs by modeling possible IBs or by asking questions similar to the following ones:

> What was going through your mind then?
>
> What are you thinking about?
>
> Suppose you were tape-recording what was on your mind then. Play back the tape. Tell me what is on it.

If, during identification of Bs, the client exhibits an absence of structured thought processes or an excess of loose, fragmented associations, this may be indicative of a thought disturbance that warrants additional assessment, such as a mental status exam.

Disputing (D) the IBs

The real "work" of this therapeutic strategy takes place at the *disputation* stage. Disputation involves issuing a challenge to the client's existing beliefs targeted just toward the IBs and not the RBs. The goal of disputation is twofold:

1. To eliminate the IBs
2. To acquire and internalize a new, more rational philosophy

In order to achieve this twofold goal, disputation occurs in two stages: first, a sentence-by-sentence examination and challenge of any IBs, and second, the development of an alternative and more rational philosophy. The first stage in disputation is, of necessity, highly specific; the second stage is more general.

Disputation can take one of three forms: *cognitive, imaginal,* and *behavioral.* Which form of disputation the counselor selects is usually determined by a consideration of client characteristics that may make one form of disputation more effective than another. However, as Walen, DiGiuseppe, and Wessler (1980) observe, the effects of disputation are likely to be stronger and more enduring when more than one method is utilized with any given client. Regardless of the form(s) used, all disputations involve issuing a challenge to the client's IBs and asking the client to find any evidence to support the IBs.

Cognitive disputation makes use of persuasion, direct questions and logical reasoning to help clients dispute their IBs. This is one time in counseling where "why" questions are permitted. Some examples of questions suggested for cognitive disputation by Walen, DiGiuseppe, and Wessler (1980, pp. 97-99) include:

> Is that true? Why not?
> Can you prove it?
> How do you know?
> Why is that an overgeneralization?
> Why is that a bad term to use?
> How would you talk a friend out of such an idea?
> What would happen if—?
> If that's true, what's the worst that can happen?
> So what if that happens?
> How would that be so terrible?
> Where's the evidence?
> How is a disadvantage awful?
> Ask yourself, can I still find happiness?
> What *good* things can happen if X occurs?
> Can you be happy even if you don't get what you want?
> What might happen?
> How terrible would that be?
> Why would you be done in by that?
> What is the probability of a bad consequence?
> How will your world be destroyed if X happens?
> As long as you believe that, how will you feel?
> "Whatever I want, I must get." Where will that get you?
> Is it worth it?

Counselors who use cognitive disputation need to recognize that this method can lead to client defensiveness. Counselors who rely on this disputation method need to be sensitive to resulting client responses, particularly to their nonverbal cues. Counselors also need to be aware that clients may have difficulty with the disputation process because they are unable to discriminate IBs from RBs. When this occurs, persistence is called for, often supplemented by counselor modeling of the difference between an RB and an IB.

Imaginal disputation relies on client imagery, and particularly on a technique known as *rational-emotive imagery*, or REI. REI is based on the assumption that the emotional consequences of imagery stimuli are similar to those produced by real stimuli. There are two ways this technique can be applied. First, the clients imagine themselves in the problem situation (the A) and then try to experience their usual emotional turmoil (C). Clients are instructed to signal to the counselor (usually with a raised finger) when this occurs. As soon as they signal, the counselor asks them to focus on the internal sentences they are saying to themselves (usually IBs). Next, the counselor instructs them to change their feelings from extreme to moderate. The counselor points out that in doing this they are making the cognitive shift they need to make in real life.

In the second application of rational-emotive imagery, clients are asked to imagine themselves in the problematic situation, and then to imagine themselves feeling or behaving differently in this situation. As soon as they get an image of different feelings and behavior, they are instructed to signal to the counselor. The counselor then asks them to notice what they were saving or thinking to themselves in order to produce different feelings and responses. The counselor points out that these are the kinds of sentences or beliefs they need to use in real-life situations to produce different effects.

According to Maultsby (1984), rational-emotive imagery is "an excellent therapeutic technique for making rational ideas and mental pictures that initially 'feel wrong' begin quickly to start 'feeling right.'" He recommends that for maximum results, clients use REI several times daily for at least a week or two.

Counselors who use REI may do well to forewarn clients not to expect instant success and to remember to be patient with themselves, even to the point of expecting the new feelings and responses generated during the imagery to feel a little strange at first. Some clients may report that distracting thoughts intrude during REI. In these instances, it is usually helpful to encourage clients to let them pass and ignore them, but not to force the distracting thoughts out of their awareness.

Other clients may report difficulty in doing REI work because they cannot generate clear and vivid images during the imagery process. Maultsby (1984) asserts that the production of strong images is not crucial to the success of the technique, as long as clients continue to focus on rational self-talk and on expected new feelings and behaviors as intensely as possible during their daily practice sessions. Also, clients who cannot *picture* rational self-talk and new feelings and behaviors can be instructed to *think about* these aspects of the process instead (McMullin & Giles, 1981).

In *behavioral disputation*, the client issues a challenge to the IBs by behaving in different ways, often in the opposite manner from previous ways of responding. Ultimately, behavioral disputation is almost crucial if the client's adoption of a more rational philosophy is to result in behavior change. Behavioral disputation usually takes the form of bibliotherapy (reading books and self-help manuals) and systematic homework assignments that involve both written and *in vivo* practice. Two specific disputation techniques are discussed in the next section.

Disputation: Desibels Technique

Two additional techniques used for disputation are Desibels (Ellis, 1971) and Countering (McMullin & Giles, 1981). The Desibels technique (which stands for DESensitizing Irrational BELiefs) is used to help clients become aware of disturbances in thinking while simultaneously eliminating consequent distressing feelings. The technique is usually introduced first during the counseling session and then assigned as daily homework. Clients are asked to spend ten minutes each day asking themselves the following five questions and either writing responses on paper or recording their answers on a tape recorder:

1. What irrational belief do I want to desensitize and reduce?
2. What evidence exists for the falseness of this belief?
3. What evidence exists for the truth of this belief?
4. What are the worst things that could actually happen to me if I don't get what I think I must (or if I do get what I think I must not)?
5. What good things could I make happen if I don't get what I think I must (or if I get what I think I must not)?

The Desibels technique may be more effective if daily compliance with it is followed by some form of client self-reinforcement, such as engaging in an enjoyable activity.

Disputation: Countering

Countering involves the selection and application of thoughts that argue against other thoughts. It consists of such activities "as thinking or behaving in an opposite direction, arguing in a very assertive fashion, and convincing oneself of the falsity of a belief" (McMullin & Giles, 1981, p. 6). Clients are asked to identify, both orally and in writing, counters for each of their significant irrational or problematic beliefs, using the following six "rules" (from McMullin & Giles, 1981, pp. 67-68):

1. Counters must be directly *opposite to* the false belief. For example, if the irrational belief is "I'm a failure if my wife leaves me," a directly opposite counter would be, "My wife's behavior is independent of my own success and accomplishments."

2. Counters are *believable* statements of reality. For example, a reasonable or believable statement of reality is, "I don't have to get straight *As* in high school in order to get a reasonably good job," while "I don't have to go to high school to get a reasonably good job" is not.

3. Develop as *many* counters as possible in order to counteract the effects that the irrational beliefs have produced over time.

4. Counters are created and "owned" by the client. The counselor's role in developing counters is limited to coaching. This rule is important because clients are likely to be more invested in counters that they themselves generate. Also, effective counters are often highly idiosyncratic among different people.

5. Counters must be *concise.* Lengthy, long-winded statements are easily forgotten. The most effective counters are ones you can summarize in a few words.

6. Counters must be stated with *assertive and emotional intensity.* As McMullin and Giles (1981) observe, "(m)any clients begin countering in an automatic, mechanical, and unconvincing way. [Instead], we have them repeat a counter nasally, then mechanically (i.e., without feelings), and then with vigor, filling their lungs with air and vehemently stating the new belief. The latter style of countering is what we are trying to produce" (p. 68).

After counters are developed, clients practice them in counseling and at home, often in conjunction with the use of other rational-emotive techniques, such as rational-emotive imagery.

Identifying the Es

If any or all forms of disputation are effective, it will be apparent in new *effects.* New effects typically include diminished emotional distress and changes in behavior. It is important for the client to be made aware of such new effects. Awareness can be highly reinforcing and can motivate the client to continue to use the disputational process in a self-directed fashion even after counseling is terminated.

Counselors may help clients become more aware of new effects from the A-B-C-D-E analysis through the use of self-recording and numerical ratings. For example, on a scale from 1 to 100, with 1 being "not intense distress" and 100 being "very intense distress," clients are asked to record levels of emotional distress during actual situations they experience outside of counseling. Counselors also rely on client self-report and utilize significant others to observe new and different behaviors or responses the client exhibits.

Case Illustration of A-B-C-D-E Analysis: The Case of Yvonne

This case illustrates the use of the A-B-C-D-E analysis that one counselor used with an individual client over a period of time. The client was seen weekly for approximately twenty sessions.

Yvonne is a thirty-year-old woman who presents for counseling because of "mood swings" and "depression." Assessment reveals that Yvonne's depression began about three years ago, following her divorce from her husband. During the last three years, Yvonne reports periodic bouts of depression that seem to stem largely from thoughts of failure and guilt. Specifically, Yvonne blames herself and feels like a failure because of the divorce. She states that she cannot get rid of thoughts that she is a failure and that she is to blame for the breakup of the marriage.

History and intake reveal Yvonne is of above-average intelligence and possesses a master's degree in business. She is currently employed as a marketing analyst for a large chain of fast food restaurants. She dates some men from time to time but has not been involved in a serious or steady relationship since her divorce three years ago. She apparently is in excellent health.

After intake and assessment sessions, the counselor proposes the use of the A-B-C-D-E analysis to Yvonne. The counselor speculates that Yvonne is a good candidate for this technique because her depression seems to be largely the result of errors in cognitive thinking, she processes information dealing with internal dialogue or self-talk easily, she is above-average in intelligence, she is moderately distressed, and she seems willing and able to think logically and to carry out systematic assignments as part of her counseling program.

The counselor first gives Yvonne an overview of the strategy and tells her how it may be helpful, stressing the fact that her continued thoughts of failure and self-blame, not her divorce per se, are largely responsible for creating her moodiness and down feelings. The counselor uses examples and analogies to emphasize how the strategy will help Yvonne acquire more realistic thinking, give up self-defeating ways of thinking, and achieve a state of less emotional distress. As soon as Yvonne indicates that it is plausible to her that thoughts cause feelings, the counselor can begin A-B-C-D-E work with her.

First, the counselor helps Yvonne identify any situations which she feels are responsible for her emotional distress. Yvonne indicates that the primary one is her divorce. She states, "If I were still happily married, I wouldn't feel this way." At this point, the counselor helps Yvonne to explore and determine whether this situation is something she has the control to change or not. When Yvonne indicates she does not, the counselor points out that her thoughts and feelings about the situation can change, even though the external event will not. The counselor also has Yvonne try on the following sentence, "Just because my marriage did not work out does not mean *I have to* feel terribly upset and depressed."

Next, the counselor helps Yvonne identify more specifically the emotional consequences or feelings she is having about the divorce. Yvonne's primary feelings seem to be frustration and depression. These are supported by her nonverbal behaviors: she frequently looks down at the floor, speaks slowly in a low, soft voice, and appears listless or lethargic. The counselor emphasizes that Yvonne can decide whether she wants to keep or change these feelings so that they do not keep producing so much distress for her. The counselor also helps Yvonne explore ways in which these feelings are debilitating to her everyday life situations; for example, to what extent have they been keeping her from getting more involved with other men?

At this point, the counselor and Yvonne are ready to spend some time working with the Bs—her beliefs, thoughts, or internal "self-talk." The counselor reiterates that some beliefs can cause unnecessary levels of emotional distress, particularly those that are self-defeating or cannot be supported by data, facts, or external evidence. The counselor gives some examples of these and contrasts them to more rational or self-enhancing beliefs. Thoughts such as, "I'm a failure," "It's my fault the marriage didn't work out," are presented to Yvonne as examples of self-defeating thoughts. Thoughts such as, "The marriage failed—I didn't," or "The marriage didn't work out—I'm still intact," are presented as examples of self-enhancing thoughts. The counselor encourages Yvonne to identify specific thoughts she has about the marriage breakup by asking Yvonne to close her eyes, imagine or recreate the situation surrounding the divorce, and note what she is thinking about or what is going through her mind at this point. Yvonne indicates again that her primary thoughts are:

"I'm a failure because my marriage didn't work out."

"I was the wife, and I should have kept the marriage together. It's up to the wife to do that. It's my fault we couldn't work things out."

"It's terrible to be thirty years old and divorced."

Yvonne's IBs share common characteristics that are typically associated with depression:

1. Belief in one's inadequacy
2. Horror of not having what you need
3. Awfulness of the way things are

In addition, IBs of depressed clients are usually full of self-blame and self-pity.

Next, the counselor is ready to start helping Yvonne learn how to dispute the emotional beliefs. Because the effects of disputation are usually more long-lasting if a variety of methods are used, the counselor starts with *cognitive* disputation, followed by *imaginal* and *behavioral* disputation.

For cognitive disputation, the counselor uses a series of questions to help Yvonne examine and dispute the IBs on a sentence-by-sentence basis. For example, the counselor takes the first IB on Yvonne's list ("I'm a failure because my marriage didn't work out") and asks Yvonne to challenge this statement using the following kinds of questions:

Can you prove that?
How do you know that?
Where is that written?
Where will this assumption get you?
As long as you believe that, how will you feel?

This same process then occurs with all the other IBs identified by Yvonne and the counselor.

Next, the counselor uses imaginal disputation with Yvonne. First, the counselor instructs Yvonne to relax and close her eyes. Next, the counselor asks her to imagine herself in the problem situation (marriage breakup), but to imagine this time that she is feeling and behaving differently. The counselor instructs Yvonne to focus specifically on what she would like to be feeling and how she wants to be handling this situation. Yvonne is instructed to use a hand signal to indicate when she gets a new feeling and a new image of different behavior. As soon as she does this, the counselor asks Yvonne to focus on what she was thinking or saying to herself in order to produce a different picture or a new feeling. Following this, the counselor encourages Yvonne to identify ways she can use this process and make this shift on a daily basis whenever she starts to feel down or upset about the marriage breakup.

As soon as Yvonne is able to dispute her IBs with the use of cognitive questions and to make a shift to different feelings and responses in imagery, the counselor can introduce systematic homework assignments expressly designed to help Yvonne think and behave in different ways in her real-life environment. One thing the counselor does at this point is to assign *rational self-analysis* (RSA) (Maultsby, 1984) as daily homework, using the form illustrated in Table 8-1. Specifically, Yvonne is asked to engage in RSA at least twice daily during the next two weeks and to apply it with both the divorce as the activating event and to other situations that crop up on a daily basis and result in high levels of emotional distress.

After several weeks of doing RSAs, Yvonne is helped by the counselor to identify new or different effects resulting from the disputational strategies they have been using. The counselor uses imagery and role-play within sessions to help Yvonne increase her awareness of the feelings and behavioral responses she has now acquired to old situations.

Identification of Injunctions and Redecision Work

In a counseling approach called Transactional Analysis (TA), an *injunction* is defined as a parental-like message (verbal and/or behavioral) that tells children what they have to do and be in order to survive and to get recognition. According to TA, children make early decisions based on the kinds of injunctions they hear and accept as true. Although many of these early decisions may have been appropriate in certain situations as children, they are often inappropriate when carried into adulthood. A cognitive TA intervention is meant to help clients become aware of the specific injunctions they accepted as children, to reexamine their effects, and to decide whether they want to continue living according to those injunctions, or to make a new decision. In the application of this

TABLE 8-1 The Standard RSA Format

A. *Activating Event:* What you perceived happened	Da. *Camera Check:* If you perceived anything a video camera would not show, correct that to what a video camera would have shown.
B. *Your Beliefs:* Your sincere thoughts about A, plus your attitudes about each B sentence.	Db. *Rational Debate of B:* Answer "yes: or "no" for each rational question below about each B sentence, or write DNA (does not apply). Then write *rational alternative self-talk* for each irrational B idea, and "That's rational" for each rational B idea.
B_1. B_2. etc.	Db_1. Db_2. etc.
C. *Consequences of B* 1. Emotional feelings 2. Actions	E. *Expected New Behaviors* 1. New emotional feelings 2. New Actions

Five Rational Questions (to be written by client under the Db section)
1. Is my thinking here based on obvious fact?
2. Will my thinking here best help me protect my life and health?
3. Will my thinking here best help me achieve my short- and long-term goals?
4. Will my thinking here best help me avoid my most unwanted conflict with others?
5. Will my thinking here best help me habitually feel the emotions I want to feel?

Source: M.C. Maultsby, *Rational Behavior Therapy*, p. 176. © 1984. Reprinted by permission of Prentice-Hall, Englewood Cliffs, N.J.
Note: For accurate use of this table, complete Section A first, followed by Section B, C, then Da, Db, and finally E. This parallels the RET ABCDE Analysis.

technique, specific attention is given to thoughts or beliefs that occur in conjunction with the early decision that may no longer be true or valid and new or different thoughts that are needed to support a new decision. The strategy uses the following process with clients:

1. When you were growing up—say between the ages of four and eight—what things did Mom say to you that sounded negative or bad to do?
2. Now recall anything that Dad said to you that sounded negative or bad to do.
3. From the following list of injunctions, recall two or three that were used most frequently in your home when you were growing up.

Don't
Don't be
Don't be close
Don't be important
Don't be a child
Don't grow
Don't succeed
Don't be you
Don't be sane
Don't be well
Don't belong
Don't feel

4. Select one of these injunctions. Write or talk about the decision you made about yourself or your life based on that injunction.

5. What thoughts occur to you about this decision? Are they true? Should they affect how you feel and behave?

6. Determine whether this decision is appropriate for you now. If not, rewrite the decision in a way that makes it appropriate for the present. In your new decision, specify what you can realistically do to change your behavior. How will this new decision make you feel?

7. Develop a plan to put the new decision into effect. What could interfere with this? What thoughts could undermine this? What thoughts do you need to support your plan?

Redecision work may be particularly useful with clients whose current behavior is inappropriate in many situations and appears to be based on one or two parental-type messages they still hear or "play" as tapes in their head.

Case Illustration of Injunctions and Redecision Work: The Case of Marie

Marie is a forty-year-old woman who is married, has two teen-aged children, works outside the home as an attorney, and cannot understand why she seems so fatigued, overworked, and generally burned out. Moreover, in the last year she has developed chronic tension headaches and a stomach ulcer. Marie discloses that she has attempted "to do it all and do it all perfectly" and has never really considered asking for help from family or friends, nor has she expressed her growing irritation and resentment over their lack of help and support.

The counselor asked Marie to close her eyes and recall what it was like as a child growing up in her house. Next, the counselor asked Marie to recall anything she remembered Mom telling or showing her not to do when Marie was a child or anything Mom said that sounded negative. Marie disclosed that her Mom always told her to do things as well as possible, preferably without any mistakes, and to do things by herself, without asking for anyone's help. Marie recalled that her mother was a perfectionistic, independent woman who never seemed to have any needs of her own and was always doing things for others.

When the counselor asked Marie to recall what she remembered Dad saying or doing, she stated that Dad always said, "Hold your tongue. Don't get upset or angry with other people, even if they really make you mad." Marie described her father as at least outwardly a very calm, cool, and collected person who never showed much feeling, although he died of heart disease at the age of fifty.

The counselor next helped Marie identify the typical injunctions she heard as a child that she still hears or follows in her present life. Marie identified three:

Don't ask for help or show needs or weaknesses.
Do everything as perfectly as possible.
Don't get angry.

Based on these injunctions, the counselor helped Marie identify any decisions or conclusions she had made about herself and her life. Marie revealed she had decided to "work as hard and as independently as possible," and "keep all negative feelings to myself."

The counselor helped Marie explore how these decisions may have been useful as a child. For example, Marie learned to please her mom and get strokes from her by doing things without error and by not "bugging" her for help. Similarly, she learned to please her dad and obtain recognition from him by being "just like Dad—a chip off the old block—able to handle anything without getting upset." The counselor helped Marie explore whether these two decisions were useful or were interfering in her present life. Marie concluded that her decisions to work independently and contain her feelings not only had resulted in severe stress for her, but also had kept her family and friends at a distance. When she expressed a desire to change these decisions, the counselor helped her decide what new decisions would be helpful and realistic.

Over the next few sessions, Marie decided she would like to continue to work hard but to ask for help and to express negative feelings whenever her stress approached a certain level. The counselor helped Marie develop a plan to supplement the new decisions with specific attention to the thoughts or cognitions that could impede or support the plan. Marie identified the following ideas or cognitions she might think about as interfering to the plan:

> I don't have a right to ask for help.
> I should be able to do it all by myself.
> I shouldn't burden anyone else with my feelings or needs.

Together, Marie and the counselor developed some alternative thoughts to support the plan:

> I am a person who is worthy of asking for and getting help from others.
> It is unrealistic for me to do everything alone.
> I want my family and friends more involved with my life.

During the next few sessions, the counselor continued to work with and encourage Marie while she tried to implement her plan based on the new decisions she had made for herself during the counseling sessions. Gradually, Marie realized she, rather than other people, presented the main obstacles to making the plan a success. She continued to work on ways in which she could support and carry out her new decisions.

Postponement Strategies

Postponement strategies may be more useful thought suppression strategies for clients whose "disturbed thinking" patterns are not tied to particular places or times but occur in more random, less predictable times and places. In all forms of postponement strategies, clients are instructed to do whatever they can to suppress their thoughts for a relatively brief period of time, but to allow themselves to engage in ruminative or unproductive thinking later for a fixed period of time (McLean, 1976).

As an example, a client might be instructed to avoid worrying or thinking such thoughts for the first fifty-five minutes of each hour, then to allow himself to obsess or worry during the last five minutes of each hour. According to McLean (1976), the length of time the counselor suggests for the postponement period depends on the client's estimate of how well he can suppress the thoughts and on how often the thoughts or images appear or crop up. If the thoughts seem to occur frequently and in a great many situations, instructions to the client may be modified in the following way: If you worry during the first twenty-five minutes of every half-hour, do whatever you can to postpone the worry until the last five minutes of each half-hour; for example, do housework, take a walk, or talk on the phone to someone (Biglan & Campbell, 1981, p. 126).

In subsequent sessions, it is important to follow up on the client's efforts to use the strategy and to inquire specifically about what the client did successfully and unsuccessfully to suppress the thoughts during the postponement period.

Case Illustration of Postponement Strategy: The Case of Mr. Neiman

Mr. Neiman is a sixty-eight-year-old widower who lives alone. His wife of thirty-five years died three years ago. In the last three years, he has been quite sad and depressed and cries easily. Assessment interviews reveal that neither the frequency nor intensity of his depressed moods have substantially decreased over the past three years. Assessment also reveals that Mr. Neiman does see a family physician, who referred him for counseling after finding no organic basis for the depression. Mr. Neiman attributes his depressed feelings to the loss of his wife. He states that they had a very close relationship and that he was unprepared for her sudden and unexpected death from a burst aneurysm. He states that he can be depressed anytime or any place, ranging from during meals, watching TV, going to the grocery store, or during the night upon waking up. He does not report any weight gain or loss or any particular pattern in sleep difficulties.

Because of the persuasiveness and rather random occurrence of his depressed thoughts and moods, the counselor suggests the possibility of a postponement strategy to Mr. Neiman. The counselor explains that the purpose of this procedure is to help him become less depressed for less of the time. Together, the counselor and Mr. Neiman also explore things Mr. Neiman might do during the times he feels happier as a result of this procedure—such as joining a bowling league, a civic organization, or volunteering his time at a local nonprofit organization. Since Mr. Neiman seems to have depressed thoughts and moods rather frequently, the counselor instructs him as follows:

> *Mr. Neiman, when you find yourself starting to get depressed about your wife's death, look at your watch or clock. Do whatever you can to postpone these thoughts or this bad mood for the next thirty minutes on your watch. Take a walk,*

get out somewhere, call a friend, watch TV, but do something for thirty minutes in order to postpone these thoughts. At the end of the thirty minutes, you can allow yourself to get into this mood. But the next time this happens and you start to feel depressed again, do the very same thing. Postpone it for at least thirty minutes.

(As the counselor works with Mr. Neiman, this time interval could gradually be increased to 40 minutes, 45, 50, and then 55.)

Cognitive Restructuring

Cognitive restructuring (Meichenbaum, 1972), also referred to as *rational restructuring* (Goldfried, DeCenteceo, & Weinberg, 1974), involves identifying and altering irrational or negative self-statements of clients. It has been used to help athletes modify high performance anxiety (Hamilton & Fremouw, 1985), to change unrealistic expectations of couples in marital therapy (Baucom & Lester, 1986), and to alter cognitions around food for bulimic clients (Wilson, Rossiter, Kleifield, & Lindholm, 1986). This strategy also has been used successfully in treating depression in children, adolescents and older adults (Matson, 1989; Yost, Beutler, Corbishley, & Allender, 1986), influencing career indecision (Mitchell & Krumboltz, 1987), treating phobias and panic disorders (Mattick & Peters, 1988; Clark & Salkovskis, 1989), and enhancing self-esteem (Pope, McHale, & Craighead, 1988; Warren, McLellarn, & Ponzoha, 1988).

Identification of Client Thoughts in Problem Situations

First, the counselor and client will want to explore the client's typical thoughts in troublesome situations. These thoughts may include self-enhancing (rational) and self-defeating (irrational) ones. In addition, the counselor can query the client about specific things he or she thinks about *before, during,* and *after* the problematic situations (Fremouw, 1977). If the client has trouble recalling specific thoughts, the counselor may want to ask the client to write down instances of problematic situations and corresponding negative self-statements as they occur during the week on a daily log sheet (see Figure 8-1). Although this inquiry process is similar to RET, it is more specific in that thoughts are linked to situations, and the antecedents and consequences of these situations.

FIGURE 8-1 Example of Daily Log

Name: _____	
Date: _____	
Week: _____	
Negative Self-Statements:	Situations:
1.	1.
2.	2.
3.	3.
4.	4.
5.	5.
6.	6.
7.	7.

SOURCE: M. Fremouw, *A Client Manual for Integrated Behavior Treatment of Speech Anxiety* (JSAS Catalogue of Selected Documents in Psychology, 1977). Reprinted by permission of the author.

Another way to help clients identify their thoughts in problem-related situations is to describe situations and ask them to attend to their inner dialogue. For example, "Imagine a very intense or traumatic situation. Listen to your internal dialogue. What is actually being said?" or "Imagine that you receive a telephone call from your boss and that she wishes to see you immediately. What is your internal dialogue like?"

Transactional Analysis counselors will use situations such as the above to help clients become more aware of who is talking in the dialogue. For example, is it a critical or nurturing parent, a reasonable, logical adult, an impulsive or spontaneous child, or a feeling child? (These are referred to in TA as *ego states.*) For example, the counselor could ask a client to imagine that she or he is about to give a presentation or take a test in an important class. The counselor asks the client:

"What is the inner dialogue?"

"What are the parent figures saying?"

"How is your child responding?"

Introduction and Use of Coping Thoughts

After the client has identified typical negative self-statements or thoughts surrounding problem situations, the client then learns to substitute a variety of coping self-statements or thoughts instead. Coping thoughts are incompatible with the self-defeating thoughts and are developed individually for each client. Coping thoughts are similar both in content and function to the assertive thoughts used in the thought-stoppage procedure. The use of coping thoughts is crucial to the overall success of the CR procedure. The awareness of negative or irrational self-statements is necessary but not usually sufficient to result in enduring change unless the client learns to produce incompatible self-instructions and behaviors as well (Meichenbaum, 1977).

In introducing coping thoughts, the counselor will emphasize their importance and their role in affecting the client's resulting feelings and behavior. The counselor will also need to model examples of coping thoughts in order to help clients discriminate clearly between coping and noncoping thought patterns. Often, it is helpful to teach clients a variety of coping thoughts to use at different times during problematic situations when the need to cope or intensity of a feeling may vary with the situation. For example, the client may find it useful to use particular coping thoughts *before* a problem situation as a planning tool to help to prepare to handle the situation most effectively. *During* the situation, the client may need to utilize coping thoughts that help to confront a challenge or to cope with a difficult moment or with feeling overwhelmed. *After* the situation, clients can learn coping thoughts to encourage themselves or to reflect on what they learned during the situation. A list of potentially useful coping statements for before, during, and after problem situations appears in Table 8–2. These statements, however, should never be prescribed by the counselor for the client! Clients appear to benefit far more when they individualize their own coping statements and choose ones that reflect both their preferences and realistic alternatives (Chaves & Barber, 1974).

Clients should be encouraged to "try on" various coping statements and to select ones that feel comfortable. As part of this process, clients need to verbalize aloud the use of a variety of coping thoughts. This type of practice is very important because it seems to reduce the client's initial awkwardness and to strengthen the client's ability to produce different self-talk. Gradually, as clients find coping thoughts that feel like they fit for them, they can practice saying them aloud in the natural sequence in which they will be used: before the situation to plan for it; during the situation to confront it head on and to cope with difficult feelings or moments; and after the situation to reward themselves for having coped and having learned something from the situation. As this kind of prac-

Table 8-2 Examples of Coping Thoughts Used in Cognitive Restructuring

Before Situation	*Preparing for a stressor* (Meichenbaum & Cameron, 1973a)	*Preparing for a provocation* (Novaco, 1975)	*Preparing for a painful stressor* (Turk, 1975)

Before Situation

Preparing for a stressor (Meichenbaum & Cameron, 1973a)

What is it you have to do?
You can develop a plan to deal with it.
Just think about what you can do about it. That's better than getting anxious
No negative self-statements; just think rationally.
Don't worry; worry won't help anything. Maybe what you think is anxiety is eagerness to confront it

Preparing for a provocation (Novaco, 1975)

What is it that you have to do?
You can work out a plan to handle it.
You can manage this situation. You know how to regulate your anger.
If you find yourself getting upset, you'll know what to do.
There won't be any need for an argument. Time for a few deep breaths of relaxation. Feel comfortable, relaxed, and at ease.
This could be a testy situation, but you believe in yourself.

Preparing for a painful stressor (Turk, 1975)

What is it you have to do?
You can develop a plan to deal with it.
Just think about what you have to do.
Just think about what you can do about it.
Don't worry; worrying won't help anything.
You have lots of different strategies you can call upon.

During Situation

Confronting and handling a stressor (Meichenbaum & Cameron, 1973a)

Just "psych" yourself up; you can meet this challenge.
One step at a time; you can handle the situation.
Don't think about fear; just think about what you have to do. Stay relevant.
This anxiety is what the counselor said you would feel. It's a reminder to use your coping exercises.
This tenseness can be an ally, a cue to cope. Relax; you're in control. Take a slow deep breath. Ah, good.

Confronting a provocation (Novaco, 1975)

Stay calm. Just continue to relax.
As long as you keep your cool, you're in control here.
Don't take it personally.
Don't get all bent out of shape; just think of what to do here.
You don't need to prove yourself.
There is no point in getting mad.
You're not going to let him get to you.
Don't assume the worst or jump to conclusions. Look for the positives.
It's really a shame that this person is acting the way she is.
For a person to be that irritable, he must be awfully unhappy.
If you start to get mad, you'll just be banging your head against the wall. So you might as well relax.
There's no need to doubt yourself. What he says doesn't matter.

Confronting and handling the pain (Turk, 1975)

You can meet this challenge.
One step at a time; you can handle the situation.
Just relax, breathe deeply and use one of the strategies.
Don't think about the pain, just what you have to do.
This tenseness can be an ally, a cue to cope. Relax. You're in control; take a slow deep breath. Ah, good.
This anxiety is what the trainer said you might feel. That's right; it's the reminder to use your coping skills.

	Coping with the feeling of being overwhelmed (Meichenbaum & Cameron, 1973a)	Coping with arousal and agitation (Novaco, 1975)	Coping with feelings at critical moments (Turk, 1975)
During Situation	When fear comes, just pause. Keep the focus on the present; what is it you have to do? Label your fear from 0 to 10 and watch it change. You should expect your fear to rise. Don't try to eliminate fear totally; just keep it manageable. You can convince yourself to do it. You can reason your fear away. It will be over shortly. It's not the worst thing that can happen. Just think about something else. Do something that will prevent you from thinking about fear. Describe what is around you. That way you won't think about worrying.	You're muscles are starting to feel tight. Time to relax and slow things down. Getting upset won't help. It's just not worth it to get so angry. You'll let him make a fool out of himself. It's reasonable to get annoyed, but let's keep the lid on. Time to take a deep breath. Your anger is a signal of what you need to do. Time to talk to yourself. You're not going to get pushed around, but you're not going haywire either. Try a cooperative approach. Maybe you are both right. He'd probably like you to get really angry. Well, you're going to disappoint him. You can't expect people to act the way you want them to.	When pain comes just pause; keep focusing on what you have to do. What is it you have to do? Don't try to eliminate the pain totally; just keep it manageable. You were supposed to expect the pain to rise; just keep it under control. Just remember, there are different strategies; they'll help you stay in control. When the pain mounts you can switch to a different strategy; you're in control.

	Reinforcing self-statements (Meichenbaum & Cameron, 1973a)	Self-reward (Novaco, 1975)	Reinforcing self-statements (Turk, 1975)
After Situation	It worked; you did it. Wait until you tell your therapist about this. It wasn't as bad as you expected. You made more out of the fear than it was worth. Your damn ideas—that's your problem. When you control them, you control your fear. It's getting better each time you use the procedures. You can be pleased with the progress you're making. You did it!	It worked! That wasn't as hard as you thought. You could have gotten more upset than it was worth. Your ego can sure get you in trouble, but when you watch that ego stuff you're better off. You're doing better at this all the time. You actually got through that without getting angry. Guess you've been getting upset for too long when it wasn't even necessary.	Good, you did it. You handled it pretty well. You knew you could do it! Wait until you tell the trainer about which procedures worked best.

Source: D. Meichenbaum and D. Turk, "The Cognitive-Behavioral Management of Anxiety, Anger, and Pain," in P.O. Davidson (Ed.), *The Behavioral Management of Anxiety, Depression and Pain.* Copyright 1976 by Brunner/Mazel, Inc. Reprinted by permission.

tice ensues, it is important for the counselor to obtain a check on the intensity of the client's affect. It is much more useful if the client practices the coping statements "with feeling" rather than just saying them aloud in a mechanical fashion. The client is always encouraged to try to internalize the meaning of the coping statement and not just to emit it by rote (Meichenbaum, 1977, p. 89).

Shift from Self-Defeating to Coping Thoughts

In this part of CR, the client learns to shift from self-defeating to coping thoughts during simulations and then *in vivo* problematic situations. Practice of this shift helps the client learn to view the presence of a self-defeating thought as a red light, a cue for an immediate switch to coping thoughts. The counselor models this part of the procedure first. For example, a counselor could model the shift from self-defeating to coping thoughts for a client who is waiting for an important job interview.

> *OK, I'm sitting here waiting for them to call my name for this interview. Wish I didn't have to wait so darn long. I'm getting really nervous. What if I blow it (self-defeating thought)?*
> *Now, wait a minute, that doesn't help (cue to cope). It will probably be only a short wait. Besides, it gives me a chance to sit down, relax, pull myself together, take some deep breaths, and review not only what I want to emphasize, but also what I want to find out about this employer. I'm going to be sizing up this person, too. It's not a one-way street (coping thoughts* before *the situation in the form of* planning).
>
> *OK, now they're calling my name. I guess it's really my turn now. Boy, my knees are shaking. What if I don't make a good impression (self-defeating thought and cue to cope)?*
> *Hey, I'm just going to do my best and see what I can learn from this, too (coping thought).*

After the counselor models the process of shifting from self-defeating to coping thoughts, the client tries it out, using the coping thoughts selected earlier. At first, the client can talk through the situation and make the shift covertly or subvocally. In an interpersonal situation involving another person such as the job interview, the counselor can assume the role of the other person (the employer) and use role-playing to help the client practice the shift. After clients are able to make this shift successfully in a self-directed manner during the session, they are ready to apply the same process to situations as they occur in their actual environment.

Reframing

Reframing is the gentle art of viewing a situation differently. Within the therapeutic context, it is much more than a Pollyanna view of life. In fact, reframing (also called reformulation) is the counselor's attempt to take the definition of the problem and redefine it in such a way as to open the door to viable solutions. Watzlawick (1978) notes that although the differences between the family's and therapist's definitions may appear trivial, that difference is decisive in solving the problem. Sometimes reframing amounts to redefining an unsolvable problem as solvable or viewing the problem as not a problem. Other times, the reframe cuts through unfounded assumptions about either the person or the problem and provides a fresh and uncomplicated approach to the problem. Madanes (1981) even includes bizarre behavior as reframable, suggesting that it be relabeled "as discourteous communication, in that others cannot understand it or in that it upsets others" (p. 130). Another example might be the relabeling of an overbearing mother's behavior as the inability to communicate an extraordinary amount of love for the child.

Therapeutic reframing is most effective when it redefines an offensive motive or behavior as inept but well intended, thus making the behavior more personally or socially acceptable. In most instances the offending person's behavior is either well intended or impersonal. It is the recipient who is most likely to define the offensive behavior as intended or inconsiderate. By removing the negative context, the difficulty between the offender and offended is far more easily resolved. Finally, an accurate and accepted reframe is often paradoxical in that the client cannot accept it without changing his or her behavior in a more problem-solving direction.

Case Illustration of Reframed Behavior:
The Case of Mark and Melissa

Mark and Melissa are a young couple who have been married five years. Their relationship is generally good, but Mark has a tendency to become verbally abusive when he is under stress. Melissa is a quiet, somewhat retiring person and becomes intimidated by Mark's aggressive outbursts. Recently she has decided that this situation must change and has convinced Mark to go to marriage counseling with her.

In the first session, the counselor had each describe the relationship and how they viewed the "problem" that brought them into counseling. In the second session, the counselor decided that the presenting problem, Mark's abusive outbursts, had two dimensions: (1) Mark's behavior; and (2) Melissa's intimidated response to Mark's outburst. The first intervention was to reframe the meaning of Mark's outburst so Melissa would not have to suffer the intimidation. To accomplish this, the counselor suggested to Melissa that Mark possessed some remnants of his childhood, namely, when he was under stress, he was prone to have "temper tantrums." When he had one of these temper tantrums, Melissa was to remember that the little boy was coming through and the adult Mark was inaccessible. This reframe accomplished two immediate results. Now that she though of Mark as having child-like tantrums, Melissa no longer felt intimated or responsible. Furthermore, having redefined his outbursts as temper tantrums, Mark began to reassess his behavior and his motives and gradually began to respond in more appropriate, adult-like ways.

Prescribing the Problem

Another form of cognitive restructuring is often referred to as prescribing the problem or symptom. The counselor's rationale for using this directive is that the client (or the family) are stuck in an irrational justification of destructive interaction patterns, but cannot recognize or accept that the justification is irrational. The rationale that the counselor presents to the client(s), however, is that this irrational pattern is necessary for the individual (or family) to maintain some sort of balance homeostasis. For example, you might insist that a little girl's temper tantrums serve the purpose of keeping the couple distracted from issues in the marriage. Given this useful behavior, the child is encouraged to continue her outbreaks of temper. Two things are accomplished by this kind of prescription:

1. By telling the child that she can continue her tantrums, the counselor is taking a presumably uncontrollable behavior and putting it under the control of the child. If the little girl does continue to have temper tantrums, she will be congratulated for doing something for the parents as though the tantrums were controllable. Thus, the only way for her to be "spontaneous" is to have the tantrums disappear.
2. By giving the tantrums a motive (to protect the parents from their own conflict), the prescription motivates all family members to "prove the counselor wrong" by having the tantrums disappear and having no marital issues appear.

In this example, the internal logic of the family system has been challenged, and the family will respond to preserve its integrity. Presumably, to acknowledge that there are marital problems will be more threatening than allowing the tantrums to continue, and the couple will do what is necessary to extinguish them. The alternative for the couple is to acknowledge marital problems and address those issues in counseling.

A less complicated form of prescribing the symptom comes from individual counseling practices and may be more familiar to the reader. The counselor is prescribing the symptom when he or she suggests that a client suffering from insomnia try to stay awake and even do some task rather than fall asleep. The point of this intervention is that we can be trapped into fighting ourselves when we try to control a spontaneous process (falling asleep). Trying to control its opposite (staying awake) somehow manipulates our internal processes such that we can "let go." Another example might be to warn the client not to expect to get over a crisis too quickly. By prescribing the symptom (the client's fear that the crisis will not recede), the counselor may actually help the client recover more quickly. Such is the paradoxical nature of the psyche.

Case Illustration of Problem Prescription: The Case of Julian and Margo

Julian and Margo are a dual-career couple. Julian is a physics professor at the state university. Margo is a Ph.D. chemist for a large pharmaceutical firm. Both are deeply committed to their careers as well as to their relationship. However, during the past few months, career demands have been heavy for both Julian and Margo. Consequently, they have given very little time to the relationship, and each feels guilty about this. The guilt feelings have grown into fears at this point, and both are worried that the relationship may soon be on the rocks.

The counselor decided that the best intervention was to prescribe the problem and advised Julian and Margo to suspend all relationship tendencies until their work demands began to ease. Although the couple found this difficult to accept, the counselor explained that it was the only sensible thing to do. They could not quit their jobs, and they could not devote time to the relationship while doing the jobs. Thus, the only solution was to put the relationship on hold deliberately. After much discussion, the couple agreed to try the counselor's prescription.

Within three weeks, they reported that the problem had begun to improve. It seems that once they were able to stop worrying about the fate of the relationship, the time they were together grew more positive, and a new focus on the relationship emerged.

Resisting Therapeutic Change

A final paradoxical intervention comes in the form of cautioning clients against change or warning them that they are improving too quickly. Fisch, Weakland, and Segal (1982) describe this technique with a variety of presenting problems. It can be used alone or as part of a more complex intervention (as was seen earlier with the child having tantrums). There are many cases in which the counselor can outline what needs to be done to improve a situation but can then add the perils of change. For example, a female client entered counseling with the complaint that she was not able to be productive at work. This was particularly disturbing since she considered herself a liberated professional woman. The counselor provided a powerful paradox by suggesting that perhaps she continued to experience a block at work because she was afraid of being taken seriously and was not yet ready to change.

Similarly, clients can be warned that they are improving too rapidly. For example, a client in divorce counseling might be cautioned if he or she is feeling "single" too soon (sooner than the statistics indicate is normal). If the person suffers a relapse, the counselor has buffered the setback by saying it is normal; if the person continues to change in a therapeutic direction, then the implication is that the client is making a better than normal recovery.

Case Illustration of Resisting Change: The Case of Sue

Sue is a twenty-nine-year-old divorcee of three months. She has made a dramatic adjustment to the divorce, a fact she attributes to her long and emotionally draining predivorce separation. Nevertheless, she sometimes wonders if she is moving too quickly.

The counselor picked up on this concern and decided to introduce a paradoxical resistance. Suggesting that she might be deceived by the rapid progress she has made, the counselor cautioned that Sue might encounter a temporary relapse during the course of her adjustment. She accepted this caution and thanked the counselor for the warning. The caution achieved two important results: (1) it was indeed possible that she would have a temporary relapse and should it happen, Sue would be less likely to fear that all her gains were imagined; and (2) the notion that she remained somewhat vulnerable led her to exercise some caution as she made new growth decisions. As a postscript, the relapse never happened.

A Final Point

Paradox is both subtle and sophisticated as a technique, and it takes a good amount of practice to master. On the other hand, you may find yourself saying, "The paradox could be true. Maybe the symptom *is* hiding another problem, or perhaps the person *is* afraid to change." If you had either of these reactions, you are experiencing an important aspect of the therapeutic paradox. A good paradox often addresses the truth. This is precisely why the technique is so powerful. Some proponents suggest that you not use paradox unless you firmly believe you are addressing the truth . . . a truth the client cannot yet share, except in symbolic form.

Client Reactions to Cognitive Strategies

Clients are likely either to love or despise cognitive strategies. Often there is no neutral ground when using these approaches. Clients who respond to these techniques are likely to be people who are intelligent, witty, present neurotic symptoms, generate pictures or internal dialogue easily, and value the art of logical thinking. Clients who are turned off to cognitive approaches may be in crisis or have more severe problems, want or expect a great deal of emotional support and warmth from the counseling relationship, process information kinesthetically, and react to issues and make decisions emotionally. It is difficult to use cognitive strategies successfully with clients who are resistant to them. Other types of interventions may be more useful with these clients.

In addition to the above reactions, there are other typical reactions which are likely to occur initially after introducing cognitive strategies. By anticipating these reactions, you will be better able to handle them when and if they occur.

One reaction has to do with the language or labels used by some counselors when using cognitive interventions. When the counselor describes the client's thoughts or beliefs as "irrational," "mistaken," or "illogical," clients are sometimes likely to perceive that they themselves, as well as their ideas, are being attacked. A client may say, "Who me—crazy? I'm not crazy." This may be especially true for some types of clients (rebellious teenagers or rigid adults, for example). Clients are also likely to have negative reactions if the counselor's labels are given in the context of a highly directive, active, and confrontational therapeutic style that is seemingly devoid of understanding and warmth.

There are several possible things you can do to circumvent this reaction from clients. One is to avoid the use of emotionally charged terms such as "crazy," "illogical," or "irrational" and substitute words such as "true and false," or "self-defeating," or "self-enhancing." One study (Baker, Thomas, & Munson, 1983) found that teenagers, for example, were much more amenable to a cognitive approach when the term "clean up your thinking" was used in place of "irrational thoughts."

Another way to avoid this potential pitfall is for you to remove yourself from the position of determining which of the client's beliefs are true or false. Instead, this procedure is performed by the *client*, thus eliminating the possibility of a power struggle or argument between you and your client.

A second rather typical client reaction is initial disbelief at the counselor's proclamation that their thoughts, rather than external events or other persons, cause distressing feelings. A client may say, "I told you I wouldn't feel this way if it weren't for *her*," or "for *it*" (it meaning an outside event). In fact, in initial interviews with clients, many of them believe that everything but their thinking is causing the problem—which is more likely to be blamed on a parent or spouse, family background, childhood upbringing, unconscious material, and so on (McMullin & Giles, 1981).

How can a counselor deal with a client's disbelief in a sensitive and yet informative manner? One way is to spend an adequate amount of time describing the rationale on which cognitive techniques are based, thus providing an adequate conceptualization of these strategies to the client. Often this may mean that the counselor devotes at least one entire session to educating the client about the nature of problems and possible corresponding treatment approaches. It is important for counselors to do this with clinical sensitivity in a way that avoids blaming or repudiating the client's ideas. As Meichenbaum (1977) observes, "(t)he purpose of providing a framework is not to convince the client—perhaps against his will—that any particular explanation of his problem is valid but rather to encourage him to view his problem from a particular perspective and thus accept and collaborate in the therapy that will follow" (pp. 150-151).

For cognitive interventions, it is important in your rationale to refute the "situation/people cause problems/feelings" theory and to subsequently explain how thoughts create undesired feelings and behaviors. This explanation usually is more helpful if realistic examples and analogies are used. For instance, McMullin and Giles (1981) use the following sorts of examples with clients:

When my daughter was three, she used to watch monster shows on TV and get scared. When she was five, she watched the same shows and laughed like crazy. The situations were the same, but the consequences were different. Why do you think this was so?

A New Yorker went to Texas to visit his friend. As they were driving in the desert, the New Yorker spotted what he thought was a boulder in the road and frantically tried to grab the wheel. The Texan, however, said, "Relax. It's just a mesquite bush." Do you see how it was what the New Yorker thought about the bush that caused his panic? (Snygg & Combs, 1949)

Two men overate one night and woke up the next morning feeling sick. One went to the doctor in a panic, and the other simply took it easy until he felt better. The first man was saying something pretty scary to himself. What do you think that might have been? (p. 34)

Clients can also be asked to describe examples from their life in which beliefs affect feelings or to provide examples of how a belief affects the behavior or feeling of a friend or relative. Another technique involves asking the client to describe a myth, fairy tale, or superstition they believed as a young child but no longer believe as an older child, teenager, or adult (McMullin & Giles, 1981).

Another way to help clients realize that their thoughts can affect feelings and behaviors is with the use of the *distancing* technique (Beck, 1976; McMullin & Giles, 1981). Using a list of either irrational beliefs or of beliefs that often contribute to emotional distress, the client is asked to pick one belief from the list (for example, Other people should do what I want them to do) and to imagine that this belief is "injected" into the head of a passer-by. The client is then asked to state how this person's behavior and feelings would be affected by having this new belief in his head.

Finally, there is always the possibility that cognitive interventions do not produce desired changes in clients' feelings and behaviors. If after repeated use of a cognitive procedure the client's level of distress does not diminish, the counselor's original assessment of the client's problem may have been inaccurate or incomplete. Perhaps in these instances, negative self-statements are not preceding or contributing to the client's feelings or behaviors. Some emotions and behavior may be acquired through conditioning and therefore are treated more appropriately with traditional behavioral procedures based on operant or classical conditioning. These types of strategies are described in the next chapter.

Summary

In this chapter, we discussed a variety of interventions that deal primarily with influencing changes in clients' cognitions or beliefs and "self-talk." Cognitive interventions attempt to reduce emotional distress and modify inappropriate behavioral patterns by correcting errors in clients' thoughts and beliefs.

A core cognitive intervention we described is the A-B-C-D-E analysis. In this technique, clients are taught to recognize that beliefs, not external events, cause distressing emotional and behavioral consequences. They are taught a variety of ways to dispute irrational beliefs.

A cognitive technique we described associated with Transactional Analysis is redecision work. This involves helping clients identify injunctions ("don'ts") they learned at an early age and any decisions they made based on such injunctions. Clients then learn to evaluate the appropriateness of early decisions for their present life and, if necessary, to revise the decision. Particular attention is paid to the thoughts and beliefs that support or underlie old and new decisions.

Cognitive-behavioral interventions we described include thought suppression techniques and cognitive restructuring. Thought suppression techniques include stimulus control, postponement strategies, and thought-stopping. The aim of these interventions is to help clients reduce or eliminate unpleasant or troublesome thoughts. In contrast to the A-B-C-D-E analysis and cognitive restructuring, thought suppression techniques help clients modify their thinking without analyzing the specific content of their maladaptive cognitions. Cognitive restructuring involves identification and alteration of negative or self-defeating thought patterns. Clients learn to use these thought patterns as a cue for using more adaptive thoughts, referred to as coping thoughts.

In all of the cognitive-based interventions, the client's acceptance of the rationale for the strategy is critical. It is important to emphasize to clients how certain kinds of thoughts and belief patterns can create emotional distress and can interfere with optimal performance in various situations.

Exercises

I. Conduct an A-B-C-D-E analysis for a problem of your own.

1. Identify an external event (person or problem situation) that consistently evokes strong and unpleasant feelings for you.

Identify and list in writing typical thoughts you have about this situation. Examine them. Do your usual thoughts indicate that you believe this situation is what causes your distressed feelings? If so, try to write examples of different or new thoughts about the situation in which you take responsibility for your feelings. For example, you might try using an "I message": "I feel_____," rather than "This situation or person makes me feel_____."

2. Identity the specific emotions or feelings that are distressing or uncomfortable. List them. Next, rate the usual intensity of such feelings on a 1 to 10 (1 = not intense; 10 = very intense) scale.

3. For each emotion or feeling you listed in #2 above, identify any thoughts or self-talk that goes on before and during the occurrence of these feelings. If this is difficult for you, ask yourself questions such as: What goes through my mind when I feel this way? What am I thinking about before and during these feelings?

    List these thoughts in writing for each emotion. Examine your list and categorize your thoughts as either rational, true beliefs or irrational, false beliefs. Remember that if the belief can be supported by data, facts, or evidence and can be substantiated by an objective observer, it is an RB. If it cannot be supported by evidence or facts to back up the belief, it is an IB.

    You may need to continue Exercise 3 during actual situations. As these distressing feelings actually occur, become aware of your thoughts surrounding the presence of these feelings.

4. Examine and challenge each IB you listed in Exercise 3 above on a sentence-by-sentence basis. Use questions such as the following to challenge each of these beliefs:
    What makes it so?
    Where is the proof?
    Let's be scientists—find the supporting data. Where is the evidence for that?
    Next, for each IB on your list, develop at least two "counters" for that belief. Recall that a counter is a statement that is directly opposite to the false belief, yet is a believable statement of reality. Make each counter as concise as possible. After developing these counters, repeat them aloud—first, mechanically, next with as much vigor and emotional intensity as possible. Finally, practice countering your IBs by whispering or thinking the counter to yourself. During the next two weeks, use the counters with actual situations. Each time you become

aware that you are starting to think an IB, whisper or think to yourself the counters you have developed to challenge that particular IB.

5. Become aware of any new effects of using this process over the next few weeks. Identify and list any *behavioral effects*—new or altered responses—as well as any *emotional effects*—new or altered feelings. Discover what has happened to the frequency and intensity of the feelings you listed earlier in Exercise 2.

II. TA Redecision Work

Use the list of injunctions and the outline of the process of re-decision work described on pp. 194-195 to identify any injunctions you used as the basis of an early decision. Determine whether this decision is still appropriate for you. If not, rewrite the decision in a way that makes it appropriate for the present. Develop a plan to put the new decision into effect, with particular consideration to any thoughts and beliefs that could undermine your plan and any thoughts and beliefs necessary to support your plan. Although you can complete this activity on your own, it might help to stimulate your thinking by sharing this process in a group setting.

III. Cognitive Restructuring

This activity can be done either for yourself or for another person.

1. Identify a situation in which your performance or behavior is altered or inhibited because of unproductive thought patterns. It may be something such as making a presentation in front of a group, a job interview, encountering a difficult client, taking a test, and so on.

2. During the next two weeks, keep a log of the kinds of thoughts that occur before, during, and after this situation whenever the situation (or thoughts and anticipation of it) occurs. Identify which of these thoughts are negative or self-defeating.

3. For each negative or self-defeating thought from your list in #2, develop an incompatible thought or a coping thought. Try to develop coping thoughts that will help you before, during, and after the problematic situation. You may find it helpful to refer to Table 8-2, but make sure that the coping thoughts are ones that are suitable for you. Try them out and see how they sound and feel. Practice saying them aloud, in the sequence in which you would actually use them in the situation. Use an appropriate level of emotion and intensity as you engage in such practice.

4. Practice making a deliberate shift from the negative or self-defeating thoughts to the coping thoughts. Learn to recognize and utilize the self-defeating thoughts as a signal to use the coping thoughts. First, talk yourself through the situation. Later, practice making this shift subvocally. Use role-play, if necessary, to help you accomplish this. Gradually, start to engage in this process whenever the trouble situation occurs *in vivo*.

IV. *Application of Cognitive Intervention Strategies*

In this exercise, you are given six client descriptions. Based on the information we give you, decide whether cognitive strategies would be appropriate or inappropriate treatments for each client. Explain your decision. An example is given. (Feedback follows the exercise.)

Example: The client is a young boy who is acting out in school (third grade) and, because of limited ability, is having difficulty working up to grade level. Cognitive interventions are not suitable for this client. Because of his age and limited ability, it would be too difficult for him to systematically apply logical reasoning to faulty thinking.

1. The client is a young male adult who is a senior in college. He feels depressed over the recent breakup of a long-standing relationship with his girlfriend.

2. The client is a six-year-old boy who is an only child. According to his teachers, he is having trouble interacting with the other children in his first-grade class and spends much of the time alone. His parents confirm that previous opportunities for interactions with other children have been very limited and have occurred on a sporadic basis.

3. The client is a middle-aged man who is referred to you by his family. In talking with him, you observe flat affect coupled with "loose" or incoherent talk. Occasionally, the client refers to acting on instructions he has been given by a saint.

4. The client is a middle-aged woman who is employed as an elementary school teacher. She was recently elected to a national office and reports feeling "terrified" of the prospect of having to get up and speak in front of other adults. She explains that she is constantly worried about making a mistake, forgetting her speech, or in some way embarrassing herself.

5. The client is a twelve-year-old seventh grader who comes in to talk to the school counselor because she doesn't think she's as

pretty or as smart as the other girls in her class and as a result feels "sad."

6. The client is a seventy-two-year-old retired woman who complains about her retired husband's "chronic dependency" on her. According to the client, her husband seems unable to get tasks accomplished without her help. The client is "well-defended," seems unable to identify any feelings she is having about this issue in her life, and appears to have strongly held beliefs, which are expressed in a rather dogmatic and rigid fashion.

Feedback for Exercises

IV. Application of Cognitive Intervention Strategies

1. This client is probably suitable for cognitive approaches and strategies. He is likely to be intelligent enough to apply logical reasoning and to understand the concepts of cognitive interventions. Additionally, it is probable that his distress over the recent relationship breakup is maintained by self-defeating thoughts or self-talk.

2. This client is not likely to benefit from cognitive approaches and strategies. First, he is probably too young to have mastered the kind of cognitive developmental tasks necessary in order to use a cognitive intervention effectively. Second, it appears that his presenting problem is more related to skill deficits and lack of opportunities to develop social skills than to inappropriate cognitions or beliefs.

3. Cognitive strategies are inappropriate for this client because of his flat affect, loose associations or stream of thinking, and the presence of auditory hallucinations, all of which suggest severe pathology.

4. Cognitive interventions are likely to be quite helpful for this client. Her stress and anxiety appear to be directly related to troublesome cognitions ("If I should fail, it will be awful."). Additionally, she is likely to have the intellectual capacity to understand the principles and rationale of cognitive strategies.

5. Cognitive strategies will probably be helpful to this client. She is just about at the age where she has probably mastered enough cognitive developmental tasks to understand the con-

cepts of these strategies and to apply logical reasoning to problem situations. Additionally, her "sad" feelings seem to be directly related to errors in thinking.

6. Cognitive strategies are probably not going to be too helpful for this client. Although she can probably understand the principles of these strategies, her strong defenses, lack of self-awareness, dogmatism, and need to disavow responsibility for any part of the relationship problem do not make her a very suitable candidate for cognitive strategies.

Discussion Questions

1. A basic assumption of any cognitive intervention is that thoughts cause feelings. What is your reaction to this assumption? What effect might your reaction have on your application of cognitive strategies with clients?

2. Discuss the characteristics of people you think would be very suitable for cognitive strategies. For what kinds of clients or problems might cognitive interventions not be appropriate?

3. In what ways might some clients resist working with a cognitive strategy? What might this resistant behavior mean? How could you handle it?

Recommended Readings

Ascher, L. M., Ed. (1989), *Therapeutic Paradox* (New York: Guilford).

Beck, A.T. (1976), *Cognitive Therapy and the Emotional Disorders* (New York: International Universities Press).

Bennett, D. (1976), *TA and the Manager* (New York: AMACOM).

Berne, E. (1964), *Games People Play* (New York: Grove Press).

Berne, E. (1961), *Transactional Analysis in Psychotherapy* (New York: Grove Press).

Ellis, A. (1971), *Growth Through Reason: Verbatim Cases in RET* (Palo Alto, CA: Science and Behavior Books; and Hollywood, CA: Wilshire Books).

Ellis, A. (1973), *Humanistic Psychotherapy: The RET Approach* (New York: Julian Press and McGraw-Hill Paperbacks).

Ellis, A. (1977), "RET: Research Data that Supports the Clinical and Personality Hypothesis of RET and Other Modes of Cognitive Behavior Therapy," *Counseling Psychologist* 7, 2–42.

Ellis, A. (1979), "Rational Emotive Therapy," in R. Corsini (Ed.), *Current Psychotherapies*, 2nd ed. (Itasca, IL: F.E. Peacock Publishers), 185–229.

Ellis, A. (1984), *Rational-Emotive Therapy and Cognitive Behavior Therapy* (New York: Springer Books).

Ellis, A., & Greiger, R. (1977), *RET: Handbook of Theory and Practice,* (New York: Springer Books).

Ellis, A., & Harper, R. A. (1975), *A New Guide to Rational Living* (Englewood Cliffs, NJ: Prentice-Hall; and Hollywood, CA: Wilshire Books).

Goulding, M., & Goulding, R. (1979), *Changing Lives through Redecision Therapy* (New York: Brunner/Mazel).

Harris, T. A. (1967), *I'm OK, You're OK* (New York: Harper & Row).

Madanes, C. (1981), "Children's Problems: Three Paradoxical Strategies," *Strategic Family Therapy*, Chapter 4 (San Francisco, CA: Jossey-Bass).

Maultsby, M. C. (1984), *Rational Behavior Therapy* (Englewood Cliffs, NJ: Prentice-Hall).

McMullin, R. E., & Giles, T. R. (1981), *Cognitive Behavior Therapy* (New York: Grune & Stratton).

Meichenbaum, D. (1977), *Cognitive Behavior Modification: An Integrative Approach* (New York: Plenum).

Meichenbaum, D., & Jaremko, M., Eds. (1983), *Stress Reduction and Prevention* (New York: Plenum).

Meyers, A. W. & Craighead, W. E., Eds. (1984), *Cognitive-Behavior Therapy with Children* (New York: Plenum).

Steiner, C. (1974), *Scripts People Live: Transactional Analysis of Life Scripts* (New York: Grove Press).

Walen, S., DiGiuseppe, R., & Wessler, R. (1980), *A Practitioner's Guide to RET* (New York: Oxford University Press).

Woollams, S., & Brown, M. (1979), *TA—The Total Handbook of Transactional Analysis* (Englewood Cliffs, NJ: Prentice-Hall).

Yost, E. B., Beutler, L. E., Corbishley, M. A. & Allender, J. R. (1986), *Group Cognitive Therapy: A Treatment Method for Depression in Older Adults* (New York: Pergamon Press).

9

Behavioral
Interventions

Thus far, we have discussed human problems in terms of how people feel and how they think. In this chapter, we address problems in terms of behavior, what people do, or fail to do. Behavioral interventions are intended to help clients change their behavior when that behavior fails to support their goals, ambitions, or values, or when that behavior contributes to negative outcomes. Behavioral helping strategies utilize theories and processes of learning. Although a large number of strategies can be classified as behavioral in nature and focus, perhaps the most common ones include social modeling approaches, skills training, operant conditioning and contracting, relaxation training, systematic desensitization, covert conditioning, and self-management techniques (Cormier and Cormier, 1991; Rimm and Masters, 1979). Behavioral interventions are relatively new approaches to the field of helping (the term "behavior therapy" was first introduced in 1954 by Skinner and Lindsley and in 1960 by Eysenck) and as such are still undergoing much evolution and metamorphosis. Contemporary behavioral practitioners, for example, rely heavily on many of the cognitive change strategies we discussed in the previous chapter.

Behavioral approaches also share much in common with other action-oriented approaches to helping, such as reality therapy developed by Glasser (1965). As Glasser and Zunin (1979) note, changes in behavior that occur from reality therapy strategies also involve learning. They observe that "(W)e are what we do, and to a great extent, we are what we learn to do, and our identity becomes the integration of all learned and unlearned behavior" (p. 316).

Behavioral interventions share certain common elements

1. Maladaptive behavior (that which produces undesirable personal or social consequences) is the result of learning, not illness, disease, or intrapsychic conflict.

2. Maladaptive behavior can be weakened or eliminated, and adaptive behavior can be strengthened or increased through the use of psychological principles, especially principles of learning that enjoy some degree of empirical support.

3. Behavior (adaptive or maladaptive) occurs in specific situations and is functionally related to specific events that both precede and follow these situations. For example, a client may be aggressive in some situations, without being aggressive in most situations. Thus, behavioral practitioners attempt to avoid labeling clients using arbitrary descriptors like "aggressive." Instead, emphasis is placed on what a client does or does not do that is "aggressive" and what situational events cue or precipitate the aggressive response, as well as events that strengthen or weaken the aggressive responses. A thorough assessment phase (or behavior analysis) similar to the process we described in Chapter 5 is a cornerstone of behavioral interventions.

4. Clearly defined outline or treatment goals are important for the overall efficiency of these interventions and are defined individually for each client. Thus, counselors attempt to avoid projecting their desires for change onto clients and also help clients specify precise outcomes they want to make as a result of counseling.

5. Helping interventions focus on the present rather than the past or future and are selected and adapted for each client and his or her set of problems and concerns. Behavioral approaches reject the "all-purpose counseling" notion that assumes that one method or approach is generally appropriate for most clients.

Characteristics of clients who seem to have the most success with behavioral interventions include:

- People with a strong goal orientation—motivated by achieving goals or getting results.

- People who are action-oriented—need to be active, doing something, participating in the helping process.

- People who are interested in changing a discrete and limited (two to three) number of behaviors.

Goals of Behavioral Interventions

The overall goal of behavioral interventions is to help clients develop adaptive and supportive behaviors to multifaceted situations. The term *behavior* includes covert or private events such as thoughts, beliefs, and feelings (when they can be clearly specified), as well as overt events or behaviors that are observable by others. Developing adaptive behavior often involves weakening or eliminating behaviors that work against the desired outcome (for example, eating snacks when you wish to lose weight), acquiring or strengthening desirable behaviors, (for example, asking for things that you want or need), or both. Unadaptive or maladaptive behaviors can be harmful to a person's health, lifestyle, or welfare. Adaptive behaviors help a person meet biological and social needs and avoid pain and discomfort (Wolpe, 1982).

Behavioral interventions have been used in many different settings (such as schools, business and industry, and correctional institutions), with a great variety of human problems (including learning and academic problems, motivational and performance problems, marital and sexual dysfunction, skills deficits, and anxiety), and with maladaptive habits (such as overeating, smoking, procrastination, and so on). In this chapter, we focus primarily on the behavioral techniques that we believe are most useful for working with individuals in noninstitutionalized settings. These include social modeling, behavioral rehearsal and skills-training approaches, relaxation training, systematic desensitization, and self-management interventions. Cognitive-behavioral strategies are not discussed because of their inclusion in the previous chapter.

Social Modeling

Social modeling, or observational learning (vicarious learning), refers to a process "in which the behavior of an individual or a group, *the model*, serves as a stimulus" for another individual who would imitate or adopt the thoughts, attitudes, or behaviors that the model presents (Perry and Furukawa, 1980, p. 131). Much of the work associated with social modeling has been contributed by Bandura (1977).

Much that we have learned as adults, we learned by watching others. It was a safe way to learn because we didn't have to take the risk of failing. It was informative because we could observe both the behavior and the payoff or the consequence of the behavior. Often it was entertaining. This observing habit is characteristic of all human beings. It can also be used to help people change, in which case it is called modeling. As a helping strategy, modeling is used to help a client conceptualize and acquire desired responses or to extinguish or weaken undesired behavioral responses by observing the behavior of another person, the model. This observation can be presented in a live modeling demonstration by the counselor, in symbolic form through written and media-taped models, or via the client's own imagination.

Live Modeling

In live modeling the desired behavioral response is performed in the presence of the client. Live models can include the counselor, teachers, or the client's peers. Usually the counselor will provide a modeled demonstration via a role-play activity, in which he/she takes the part of the client and demonstrates a different way that the client might respond or behave.

Live modeling can be a most versatile tool for the school counselor, the correctional counselor, or the family counselor, to name only a few. Scenarios can vary from (a) helping seventh graders understand how to begin thinking about careers; (b) helping high school students deal with peer pressures; and helping family members develop different responses to family issues and so on. The counselor's role can vary from (a) being an actor in the scenario to (b) being the choreographer of the scenario, to (c) being the narrator of the scenario. The following is a modeling session in which the counselor served as narrator. The scene is a group guidance session involving 12 seventh graders. The counselor has been working with six of the students on a project "using the library to learn about careers." The second six students are new to the group and are just beginning the project.

Counselor: Today, we have some new faces in our group. I think all of you already know each other. For convenience, I'm going to call you the "old timers" and the "new bunch." (*Talking to the new bunch*) The old timers have been working on a project to learn about jobs. I'm going to ask them to demonstrate some of the things they have learned. We will use something called a "fishbowl." What that means is that the old timers will sit in a small circle. The rest of us will sit outside the circle and observe the old timers as they talk about their project. We will do this for about fifteen minutes and then we will trade places. The "new bunch" will come into the inner circle and the old timers will sit around the outside. Any questions? (*Nervous noises, chairs moving, people getting settled. The old timers are familiar with this exercise. They were introduced to it when they were in the role of new bunch a few weeks earlier.*) Now, if everyone is ready, old timers, I would like for you to talk together about the topic: "Fifty ways to choose a career—all in the library."

Old Timers: A discussion begins, slowly at first, about how to use library to find out about careers. Different group members talk about how they got started, who in the library helped them find the right books, which books were most helpful, funny things they discovered about some careers, and so on. There is a lot of joking. It doesn't look like a great learning experience, but the point is made that the library is a resource for career information, who (by name) can be helpful, what can be learned. (*After about fifteen minutes, the counselor interrupts, summarizes what was said, and asks the two groups to trade places. Many groans, teasing, playful putdowns follow as students change seats.*)

Counselor: Now, new bunch, it's your turn. I'd like for you to show the old timers what you can do. This time the topic will be "Things I am going to do in the library to learn about jobs."

New Bunch: (*More groans, jokes, moving of chairs*) Talk begins slowly. Someone makes a joke. All laugh. Finally, someone gets into the spirit and says she would like to find out about becoming an astronaut. Everyone laughs. (*Counselor intervenes, commends student for her question, challenges group to come up with a plan for using the library to help her find out about becoming an astronaut.*) The group begins, more or less in earnest, and the information that characterized the first group's discussion comes out again, this time focusing on the topic of finding out about becoming an astronaut.

Live modeling is particularly useful in instances in which the client does not have response alternatives available. The modeled demonstration provides cues that the client can use to acquire those new responses. For example, a client who wishes to be more assertive may benefit from seeing the counselor or a peer demonstrate such behaviors in role-played situations. The following exchange between the counselor (model) and client (wishing to be more assertive) illustrates how such a session might go:

Counselor: Today, Nancy, I thought we might do a role-play, that's where you and I enact someone other than ourselves, and our "play" will be a scenario in which you are returning some unusable merchandise to a local store.

Nancy: That sounds awful. I don't like to have to return things to the store.

Counselor: I know. But you said you wished you could do that sort of thing without getting so upset. Don't worry. I'm going to play you and you are going to play the part of the store employee. O.K.?

Nancy: (laughing) Well, that's a little better. O.K.

Counselor: You will begin first, by asking me if I need some help.

Nancy (as employee): Hello, can I help you?

Counselor (as Nancy): Yes, I purchased this baptismal gown for my daughter's baby but after the baby was born, she realized it was too small. I'd like to exchange it if I may.

Nancy (as employee): How long ago did you purchase it?

Counselor (as Nancy): Two months ago, I'm afraid. I know your return policy is 30 days but I hope you will accept it in exchange.

Nancy (as employee): Well, since you only want to exchange it, I think we can do that.

Following the role-play, the counselor and Nancy discussed the interaction and then they conducted a second role-play, this time with Nancy as herself and the counselor as the store employee. Then they evaluated Nancy's performance and identified some ways she could improve. This was followed by a third role-play in which Nancy again was herself. Her performance in the third role-play was much improved and she felt successful. Live modeling in which the client is a participant is limited by the client's willingness to participate in an imagined situation as an actor. If your client is particularly withdrawn, you may wish to use other persons as the modeling participants.

Symbolic Modeling

Although live models have much impact on the client, they are sometimes difficult to use because the counselor cannot control the accuracy of the demonstration of the behavior being modeled. To correct for this, many counselors make use of symbolic models through videotapes, audiotapes, or films in which a desired behavior is introduced and presented. For example, symbolic models could be used with clients who want to improve their study habits. Reading about effective study habits of successful people and their scholastic efforts is a first step to help clients identify desired behaviors. Next, clients can listen to an audiotape or watch a videotape illustrating persons who are studying appropriately. Once effective symbolic models are developed, they can be stored easily and retrieved for future use by the same or different clients.

Covert Modeling

Covert modeling is a process in which the client imagines a model (either self or someone else) modeling the desired behavior (Cautela, 1976). This approach is also called "imaging" and has been used with great success by professional (and amateur) athletes. The first step is to work out a script that depicts the situation(s) and desired responses. For example, if a client desires to learn to communicate more successfully with a spouse instead of avoiding issues, scenes would be developed that depict the client having a successful discussion. One scene might be:

> It is a Friday night. You would like to go to a movie but your wife (husband) is very tired. You acknowledge your spouse's tiredness but suggest that a movie might prove relaxing as well as entertaining. Your spouse thinks about it for a moment and then agrees.

Imaging serves two purposes. It brings the appropriate behaviors into focus. It also serves to construct a success image into the person's self-concept. Both are desired outcomes. Perhaps the best example of this is the Olympic diver who, while standing on the board, imagines herself balancing, then springing, then turning, and finally entering the water, all perfectly. The behavior then follows the pattern established by the image. This procedure is also referred to as *covert self-modeling*, and has the potential for augmenting the client's personal involvement in the process and subsequently effecting greater facilitation of desired behavior (Rimm and Masters, 1979, p. 130).

Characteristics of the Modeled Presentation

The modeled presentation can affect the client's ability to attend to and remember the modeled demonstration. As Perry and Furukawa (1980) note, the counselor must present the model in such a way that it fits the client's intellectual strengths and weaknesses (p. 136). The first part of the modeled presentation should include instructions and cues about the features of the modeled behavior or activity. Prior instructions can minimize competition for the client's attention. A rationale for the use of modeling should also be given prior to the modeled display.

The scenarios or responses to be modeled should minimize the amount of stress in the presentation. Distressing and anxiety-provoking modeled stimuli may interfere with observation, processing, or retention.

Complex patterns of behaviors should be presented in modeled sequences. Modeling of too many behaviors at one time may be overwhelming for a client. The counselor can seek the client's input about the presentation of modeled responses to ensure that the ingredients and pace of the modeled demonstration are presented in a facilitative manner.

When the modeled behavior is particularly complicated, the counselor can facilitate retention of the modeled presentation "by having either the model or a narrator comment on the important features of the modeled behavior as well as on the general principle or rule which governs the model's performance" (Perry and Furukawa, 1980, p. 139). For example, consider the following situation supplied by Perry and Furukawa:

> *Suppose a model were demonstrating assertive behavior to a withdrawn, socially inept observer. The scene involves ordering dinner in a restaurant and discovering that the steak is too tough to eat. The model exhibits an assertive response in this situation by requesting the waitress to bring him another steak. The model can comment at this point: "That was an example of an assertive response. I was entitled to a good steak and was willing to pay for it. I explained the difficulty in an open and friendly manner to the waitress and asked her to bring me another steak. Afterwards I felt good about myself and enjoyed my meal." By listening to the model highlight the essential characteristics of an assertive response, the observer is more likely to remember the behavior and is in a better position to apply this form of response in a variety of different situations. As an additional aid to retention, the observer can be asked by the therapist to summarize the main features and general rules associated with the model's behavior. Several studies (for example, Bandura, Grusec, and Menlove, 1966) have found that observers who actively summarize the model's behavior are better able to learn and retain this information. (Perry and Furukawa, 1980, p. 139)*

Practice of the goal behavior or activity increases the effectiveness of the modeling procedure. Practice may help the client code and reproduce the modeled behaviors. In addition to practice in the counseling session, the counselor might assign homework to the client for practice outside the session. Self-directed practice can enhance the generalization of the modeling treatment from within the session to real-life situations. If a client experiences difficulty in performing a particular activity or behavior, instruction aids, props or counselor-coaching can facilitate successful performance.

Characteristics of Models

In selecting models, it is best to maximize model–client similarity. Clients are more likely to learn from someone whom they perceive as similar to themselves. Such characteristics as age, sex, prestige, ethnic background, and attitudes should be considered in selecting effective models. Similarity between model and client assures clients that the behaviors shown "are both appropriate to and attainable" (Perry and Furukawa, 1980, p. 136). With some clients there is no better model than the client. Hosford and deVisser (1974) have found that arranging conditions so that clients see themselves performing the desired response can be a very powerful learning tool. In their procedure, called *self-as-a-model,* the client's desired behavior is demonstrated to the client on videotape or audiotape. For example, a client who wishes to stop stuttering listens to and practices with a tape in which all stuttering has been edited out. Hosford, Moss, and Morrell (1976) indicate that having a client observe both inappropriate and appropriate behaviors may weaken acquisition of the desired responses and promote occurrence of the undesired behavior.

A coping model may be more helpful than a mastery model (Meichenbaum, 1971). A client may be able to identify more with a model who shows some fear or some struggle in performing than someone who comes across perfectly. For example, a very shy, timid person could be overwhelmed by a very assertive model. This client may improve more quickly if exposed to a model who starts quietly and gradually increases assertive behaviors. Clients also may learn more from modeling when exposed to more than one model. Multiple models may have more impact on a client, because the client can draw on the strengths and styles of several different persons (Kazdin, 1973). Warmth and nurturance by the model also facilitate modeling effects.

When modeling fails to contribute to desired client changes, reassess the characteristics of the selected model(s) and the mode and format of the modeled presentation. In many cases, modeling can provide sufficient cues for the client to learn new responses or to extinguish fears. In other instances, modeling may have more effect when accompanied by practice of the target response. Such practice can occur through role-play and rehearsal strategies, as described in the next section of this chapter.

Role-Play and Rehearsal

Role-play and rehearsal strategies promote behavior change through simulated or *in vivo* enactment of desired responses. Role-play and behavior rehearsal originated from Salter's conditioned reflex therapy (1949), Moreno's psychodrama technique (1946), and Kelly's fixed-role therapy (1955). Common elements in the application of role-play and rehearsal strategies include:

1. A reenactment of oneself, another person, an event, or a set of responses by the client
2. The use of the present, or the "here and now," to carry out the reenactment
3. A gradual shaping process in which less difficult scenes are enacted first, and more difficult scenes are reserved for later
4. Feedback to the client by the counselor and/or other adjunct persons

Depending on the therapeutic goal, role-playing procedures often are used by dynamic therapies as a method to achieve catharsis; by insight therapies as a means to bring about attitudinal changes; by Gestalt therapy as a tool to promote conflict resolution and self-awareness; and by behavior therapy as a way to facilitate behavior change. In this chapter we discuss role-play as a way to facilitate behavior change. Gestalt dialogue work and role-playing to promote attitudinal change were presented in Chapter 7.

Role-Play as a Method of Behavior Change

The strategy of behavior rehearsal uses role-play and practice attempts to help people acquire new skills and to help them behave more effectively under threatening or anxiety-producing conditions. Behavior rehearsal is used primarily in three instances:

1. The client does not have and needs to learn the necessary skills to handle a situation *(response acquisition)*.
2. The client needs to learn to discriminate between positive and negative application of the skills or between inappropriate and appropriate times and places to use the skills *(response facilitation)*.

3. The client's anxiety about the situation needs to be sufficiently reduced so that the client can use skills already learned, even though they are currently inhibited by anxiety *(response disinhibition).*

For example, if a client wants to increase self-disclosive behavior but doesn't know what self-disclosure is or hasn't learned the skills involved in self-disclosing, the client has a deficient repertoire in self-disclosure and needs to acquire certain skills (response acquisition). On the other hand, there are times when the skills are already in the client's repertoire, but the client needs clarification or discrimination training in when and how to employ the skills (response facilitation). We have all known persons who have self-disclosure skills but use the skills inappropriately. A person may self-disclose too much to someone who is disinterested and withhold personal information from a significant other. In another case, the client's anxiety perhaps has inhibited the skills (response disinhibition). In other words, a client may have learned the skills of appropriate self-disclosure but avoids self-disclosing because of anxiety the client feels in certain self-disclosive situations.

In addition to the practice effects gained from behavior rehearsal, the strategy can often give the counselor important clues about how the client actually behaves in real-life situations. This is particularly helpful in instances where the clients' self-reported descriptions of this behavior are at odds with the client's portrayed behavior under these somewhat simulated conditions. As Rimm and Masters (1979) note, "(c)ontradictions of this nature are not at all uncommon, and when they occur, it is likely that the role-played behavior is far more accurate than the client's verbal characterization of how he typically handles such a situation . . ." In this respect, behavior rehearsal "is an invaluable diagnostic technique . . ." (p. 68).

The "nuts and bolts" of behavior rehearsal consists of a series of graduated practice attempts in which the client rehearses the desired behaviors, starting with a situation that is manageable and is not likely to backfire. The rehearsal attempts may be arranged in a hierarchy according to level of difficulty or stress of different situations. Adequate practice of one situation is required before moving on to another scene. The practice of each scene should be very similar to the situations that occur in the client's environment. To simulate these situations realistically, use any necessary props and portray the other person involved with the client as accurately as possible. This portrayal should include acting out the probable response of this person to the client's new or different behavior.

Behavior rehearsal can be overt or covert. In covert behavior rehearsal, clients practice the target behavior by imagining themselves performing the response in certain situations. For instance, clients might imagine themselves successfully presenting an important speech or initiating a discussion with a friend or a boss. In overt rehearsal, the client acts out the target responses in role-played scenarios. Both covert and overt rehearsal seem to be quite effective (McFall & Twentyman, 1973). Probably a client could benefit from engaging in both of these forms of behavior rehearsal. Initially, the client might practice covertly and later act out the responses in role-played enactments. Covert rehearsal also can be used easily by clients as homework, since imaginary practice does not require the presence of another person.

Each scene should be practiced before moving on to the next scene. You can determine when a scene is rehearsed satisfactorily by three criteria proposed by Lazarus:

1. The client is able to enact the scene without feeling anxious.
2. The client's general demeanor supports the client's words.
3. The client's words and actions would seem fair and reasonable to an objective onlooker. (1966)

However, the rehearsal efforts may be limited unless accompanied by some form of feedback or analysis of performance.

Feedback is an important part of role-play and rehearsal strategies. Feedback is a way for the client to recognize both the problems and successes encountered in the practice attempts. According to Melnick (1973), feedback is a means of observing and evaluating one's performance and of initiating corrective action. However, feedback should not be used indiscriminately. Feedback may be more effective if the client is willing to change, if the feedback given is adequate but not overwhelming, and if the feedback helps the client identify other alternatives. (McKeachie, 1976). Feedback also should be nonpunitive, constructive, and directed toward behaviors the client can potentially change. Feedback also can be supplied by videotaped and audiotaped playbacks of the client's practices. These taped playbacks may be more objective assessments of the client's performance. At first you can go over the tapes together and point out the strengths and limitations apparent in the practice. Gradually, the client should be able to analyze the taped playback alone—providing self-analysis and self-reinforcement for his or her practice efforts.

Modeling, Rehearsal, and Feedback:
Components of Skill Training

It should be recognized that the strategies of modeling, rehearsal, and feedback can be combined as a skill-training package. These strategies often are used to teach clients problem-solving skills, decision-making skills, communication skills, and assertion skills. *Assertion training* is a means of overcoming social anxiety that inhibits a person's interactions with others (Wolpe & Lazarus, 1966). Typical assertion skills involve the ability to make requests, to refuse requests, to express opinions, to express positive and negative feelings, and to initiate, continue, and terminate social conversations. In assertion training, you begin by having the client identify one situation in which he or she wants to be more assertive. Then specify what assertive behaviors are involved and what the client would like to say or do. The situation is modeled and role-played consistently in the interview until the client can be assertive without experiencing any anxiety. Following successful completion of the task outside the interview, assertion training can continue for other kinds of situations involving self-assertion by the client. Successes at assertiveness will soon generalize to other situations as well; that is, it will be increasingly easier for clients to be assertive on their own without assistance and feedback.

As an illustration, suppose you are working with a student who reports a lack of assertive classroom behaviors. You and your client would first specify the desired assertive skills. You may need to observe the student in the classroom setting to identify these target behaviors. In counting the number of times the student engages in assertive classroom behavior (asking questions. voicing opinions, engaging in group discussion, giving reports, volunteering for blackboard work, initiating conversations with the teacher, and so on), you can obtain an accurate idea of the kind of assertive behaviors that are most prevalent in the client's repertoire and the ones the client needs most to strengthen. You can provide either live, symbolic, or covert models of these specific assertive behaviors. After the client has seen, listened to, read about, or imagined these modeled behaviors, the client can demonstrate and practice small steps of such assertive classroom behaviors in the interview. Following practice attempts in which the client is able to demonstrate repeated efforts of a given behavior within the interview, he or she should be encouraged to practice it on a daily basis in the classroom.

Case Illustration of Skill Training with Modeling and Rehearsal: The Case of Jack

Jack is a twenty-seven-year-old male who initially refers himself for counseling because of "depression." Assessment reveals that Jack feels depressed after discovering his wife of five years has had an affair during the last year. Jack now is depressed over the breakdown in the relationship, feels conflicted about the future of the relationship, and doesn't want marital counseling, at least initially. Assessment further reveals that Jack feels depressed about his own role in the relationship up to this time. He states that he lacks self-confidence, which makes him feel weak and powerless. He observes that his wife is the more dominant of the pair, and that he has let her make all the significant decisions during their marriage and handle important responsibilities. As counseling ensues, Jack becomes resentful about allowing himself to function like a "doormat" but seems unable to demonstrate any skills other than acquiescence or submissiveness. At this point, the counselor suggests the usefulness of some assertion training with Jack. He readily agrees.

First, the counselor explains the process of assertion training to Jack, noting that it involves a good bit of role-playing. The counselor also draws on paper a continuum of a possible range of behavior—"passive-assertive-aggressive"—to illustrate the differences between being passive, assertive, and aggressive. This distinction is very important, because formerly passive people often attempt to overcompensate initially in their interactions with others by behaving aggressively instead of assertively. In Jack's case, this could have a very negative effect on the marital relationship which he is trying to improve. The counselor explains that passivity is like being a doormat—people walk on you. In contrast, assertive behavior involves the right for Jack to ask for what he wants and refuse what he doesn't want without using dogmatic requests or violating the rights of others. The last two are examples of aggressive responses.

Next, Jack and the counselor identify a series of situations in which Jack has trouble behaving assertively. Most of these center around his wife, but several also involve his mother as well. Each situation is discussed thoroughly so that there is a good idea of what actually happens in each situation in the real-life circumstance. Next, Jack and the counselor arrange these situations in a hierarchy—starting with ones that are the least difficult or problematic for him to be assertive in and also present fewer negative consequences for assertiveness. Jack and the counselor identify eight situations, which Jack arranges in the following order:

1. Not following my wife into a store at the mall—going to a different store on my own
2. Choosing what to wear without asking for my wife's advice
3. Deciding where we will go out to eat
4. Deciding how we will spend Saturday night
5. Telling my mother I can't come over to see her
6. Telling my wife I don't want to do the same thing she does
7. Telling my mother I can't fix something for her
8. Telling my wife about behaviors that bother me.

At this point, Jack is ready to start working with the first situation on the list—that of going to look in a different store at the mall from the one his wife goes to.

Practice is often more efficient if one has an idea or a model to visualize in one's head, so the counselor can either assume the client's role—act out the situation—or can ask the client to do it the way he or she wants. In this case, the counselor first takes the role of Jack, and Jack takes the role of his wife. The counselor starts to follow his wife into a store and then tells her he is going to look in another store while she does her shopping. (The counselor has previously instructed Jack to respond like the wife). As the wife, Jack agrees that would be fine and suggests a meeting place.

Jack and the counselor then discuss the modeling—specifically, whether Jack would feel comfortable doing or saying what the counselor did and said or would want to modify his response in some way. As soon as Jack has a clear idea of exactly what he wants to do and say in this situation, the roles are reversed. The counselor takes the role of the wife, and Jack role-plays himself, telling her he is going to look in another store. Role-playing of this situation is continued until Jack feels comfortable enough to handle this situation without undue anxiety should it arise outside of counseling during the week. (If possible, it is preferable for the client to encounter succeeding situations in the hierarchy until most of the assertive training has been completed.)

As Booraem (1974) has noted, during skill training there is a tendency for counselors to terminate role-playing with too few trials, possibly because the counselor has a higher skill level than the client and becomes bored, or assumes clients are more comfortable with the new skills than they really are. The counselor may also want to discuss how the client can handle unexpected or varied responses from the other party. For example, in the above situation

Jack and the counselor discussed ways Jack could respond if his wife insisted he accompany her into the store she selected to browse in.

When Jack feels he is ready to complete this particular task in his real-life setting, he and the counselor review the task and the goal, or his desired response. The counselor helps Jack to remember his goals for this situation by writing them down and by audiotaping one of the better practice sessions he did with the counselor. This is very important, since there is some evidence that nonassertive people have less clear goals than assertive people (Flowers & Booraem, 1980). At the next session, the counselor reviews how Jack handled this situation in the real-life setting. Successive situations on Jack's hierarchy are then modeled and rehearsed in the same manner as described above. After each situation is modeled and rehearsed, Jack is encouraged to encounter the situation *in vivo*.

Anxiety Reduction Methods

Many clients presenting for help do so because of strong negative emotions labeled "fear" or "anxiety." Anxiety can take a variety of forms and be reflected in various ways and with different symptoms. Lehrer and Woolfolk (1982), for example, distinguish between *somatic anxiety*, which may manifest itself in body sensations such as stomach butterflies, sweaty palms, rapid pulse rate; *cognitive anxiety*, which may be apparent in an inability to concentrate and in intrusive, repetitive, panicky, or catastrophic thoughts; and performance or *behavioral anxiety*, typically manifested by avoidance of the anxiety-arousing situation.

While some amount of anxiety is thought to be helpful to successful performance, when it reaches an intolerable or uncomfortable level, a person usually seeks help for it. Various procedures are used for anxiety reduction. In this chapter, we describe two of the more common behavioral ones: relaxation training and systematic desensitization.

Relaxation Training

The most common form of relaxation training used by behavioral counselors is called *progressive relaxation* or *muscle relaxation* (Jacobson, 1938). Muscle relaxation has been used to treat a wide variety of disorders, including generalized anxiety and stress, headaches and psychosomatic pain, insomnia, and chronic illnesses such as hypertension and diabetes. Relaxation training is often used as an adjunct to short-term counseling and may be used by practitioners of other theoretical orientations to help clients feel as if they are doing something concrete for themselves. As Rimm and Masters (1979) note, relaxation can be a very effective way of establishing rapport and a sense of trust in the therapist's competence (p. 35). Muscle relaxation is also a major component of another widely used anxiety reduction procedure that we discuss in the next section, systematic desensitization.

The basic premise of using muscle relaxation to treat anxiety is that muscle tension exacerbates felt or experienced anxiety or stress. Consequently, an individual can experience a reduction in felt anxiety by learning to discriminate between tense and relaxed muscle groups and to relax various muscle groups upon cue or self-instructions. The procedure itself involves training clients to successively tense and relax various muscle groups in their bodies, to discriminate between sensations of tension and relaxation, and to induce greater relaxation through release of muscle tension and suggestion. Suggestion is enhanced by counselor comments throughout the procedure, directing the client's attention to pleasant sensations, heavy and warm sensations, and so on. These suggestions are not unlike hypnotic inductions; however, muscle relaxation is not hypnosis, and some clients may need to hear that they are not going to be hypnotized. After going through the procedure several times with the counselor's assistance, clients are encouraged to practice it on their own, daily if possible, and often with the use of audiotape recorded instructions as a guide. (Commercially prepared relaxation audiotapes are available, or the counselor can put the instructions on tape and give them to the client.)

Relaxation training needs to occur in a quiet environment free of distracting light, noise, and interruptions. The client should use a couch, reclining chair, or even a patio chaise lounge, if at all possible. (For relaxation training with a group of clients, try a padded floor with pillow support for the back and head.) The counselor uses a quiet, soothing tone of voice when delivering the relaxation instructions to clients. Each step in the process (that is, the alternate tensing and relaxation of each muscle group), takes about ten to fifteen seconds, with a ten- to fifteen-second pause between each of the steps (Morris, 1980). The entire procedure takes twenty to thirty minutes. It is very important not to rush through any of the procedure—an error committed frequently by persons inexperienced with this technique.

The specific process of progressive muscle relaxation is illustrated in the following instructions:

First study your right arm, your right hand in particular. Clench your right fist. Clench it tightly and study the tension in the hand and in the forearm. Study those sensations of tension. [Pause]

And now let go. Just relax the right hand and let it rest on the arm of the chair. [Pause] And note the difference between the tension and the relaxation. [ten-second pause]

Now we'll do the same with your left hand. Clench your left fist. Notice the tension [five-second pause] and now relax. Enjoy the difference between the tension and the relaxation. [ten-second pause]

Now bend both hands back at the wrists so that you can tense the muscles in the back of the hand and in the forearm. Point your fingers toward the ceiling. Study the tension, and now relax. [Pause] Study the difference between tension and relaxation. [ten-second pause]

Now clench both your hands into fists and bring them toward your shoulders. As you do this, tighten your biceps muscles, the ones in the upper right part of your arm. Feel the tension in these muscles. [Pause] Now relax. Let your arms drop down again to your sides. See the difference between the tension and the relaxation. [ten-second pause]

Now we'll move to the shoulder area. Shrug your shoulders. Bring them up to your ears. Feel and hold the tension in your shoulders. Now, let both shoulders relax. Note the contrast between the tension and the relaxation that's now in your shoulders.

We'll work on relaxing the various muscles of the face. First, wrinkle up your forehead and brow. Do this until you feel your brow furrow. [Pause] Now relax. Smoothe out the forehead. Let it loosen up. [ten-second pause]

Now close your eyes tightly. Can you feel tension all around your eyes? [five-second pause] Now relax those muscles, noting the difference between the tension and the relaxation [ten-second pause]

Now clench your jaws by biting your teeth together. Pull the corners of your mouth back. Study the tension in the jaws. [five-second pause] Relax your jaws now. Can you tell the difference between tension and relaxation in your jaw area? [ten-second pause]

Now, press your lips together. As you do this, notice the tension all around the mouth. [Pause] Now relax those muscles around the mouth. Just enjoy the relaxation in your mouth area and your entire face. [Pause] Is your face as relaxed as your biceps? [Muscle group comparison]

Now we'll move to the neck muscles. Press your head back against your chair. Can you feel the tension in the back of your neck and in the upper back? Hold the tension. Now let your head rest comfortably. Notice the difference. Keep on relaxing. [Pause]

Now continue to concentrate on the neck area. See if you can bury your chin into your chest. Note the tension in the front of your neck. Now relax and let go.

Now direct your attention to your upper back area. Arch your back like you're sticking out your chest and stomach. Can you feel tension in your back? Study that tension. [Pause] Now relax. Note the difference between the tension and the relaxation.

Now take a deep breath, filling your lungs, and hold it. See the tension all through your chest and into your stomach area. Hold that tension. [Pause] Now relax and let go. Let your breath out naturally. Enjoy the pleasant sensations. [ten-second pause]

Now think about your stomach. Tighten the abdominal muscles. Hold this tension. Make your stomach like a knot. Now relax. Loosen these muscles now. [ten-second pause] Is your stomach as relaxed as your back and chest? (Muscle group comparison)

Focus now on your buttocks. Tense your buttocks by holding them in or contracting them. Note the tension that is there. Now relax—let go. [ten-second pause]

I'd like you now to focus on your legs. Stretch both legs. Feel tension in the thighs. [five-second pause] Now relax. Study the difference again between the tension in the thighs and the relaxation you feel now. [ten-second pause]

Now concentrate on your lower legs and feet. Tighten both calf muscles by pointing your toes toward your head. Pretend a string is pulling your toes up. Can you feel the pulling and the tension? Note that tension. [Pause] Now relax. Let your legs relax deeply. Enjoy the difference between tension and relaxation. [ten-second pause]

Now, I'm going to go over again the different muscle groups that we've covered. As I name each group, try to notice whether there is any tension in those muscles. If there is any, try to concentrate on those muscles and tell them to relax. Think of draining any residual tension out of your body. Relax the muscles in your feet, ankles, and calves. [Pause] Let go of your knee and thigh muscles. [Pause] Loosen your hips. [Pause] Loosen the muscles of your lower body. [Pause] Relax all the muscles of your stomach, waist, lower back. [Pause]

Drain any tension from your upper back, chest, and shoulders. [Pause] Relax your upper arms, forearms, and hands. [Pause] Relax your face. [Pause] Let all the muscles of your body become loose. Drain all the tension from your body. [Pause] Now sit quietly with your eyes closed.

Now I'd like you to think of a scale from 0 to 5, where 0 is complete relaxation and 5 is extreme tension. Tell me where you would place yourself on that scale now. *

Following the muscle relaxation procedure, the counselor may ask the client to rate his or her felt level of tension on a 1 to 10 or 1 to 100 scale. (The 1 to 100 scale is also employed in systematic desensitization.) It is important to remember that many clients have developed a state of chronic muscular tension which may not disappear after only one or two attempts at muscle relaxation. Occasionally, an individual may not benefit from muscle relaxation or may not be able to complete all of the muscle group exercises due to certain physical disabilities, such as neck or back pain or injuries. In these instances, the counselor can omit certain muscle groups from the procedure or can substitute a different form of relaxation training, such as yoga, biofeedback, meditation, or sensory relaxation.

Successful use of relaxation requires that the counselor apply the procedure with each client in an individualized way. For example, some clients may need more or less time to tense and relax muscles; others may prefer much less dialogue from the helper. Counselors also need to ensure that clients are only tensing one muscle group at a time while keeping their other muscles relatively relaxed. Additional tips regarding this procedure can be found in sources such as Cormier and Cormier (1991) and Rimm and Masters (1979).

Systematic Desensitization

Systematic desensitization is an anxiety-reduction technique developed by Wolpe (1958; 1982) and based on the learning principles of classical conditioning. This type of learning involves the pairing (occurring close together) of a neutral event or stimulus with a stimulus that already elicits a reflexive response such as fear. Desensitization employs *counterconditioning*—the use of learning

* From *Interviewing and Helping Skills for Health Professionals* by L.S. Cormier, W.H. Cormier, and R.J. Weisser, Jr., pp. 265–266. Copyright © 1984 by Wadsworth, Inc. Reprinted by permission of the publisher, Wadsworth Health Services Division, Monterey, CA.

procedures to substitute one type of response for another—to desensitize clients to high levels of felt fear or anxiety. In desensitization, a counteracting stimulus such as relaxation is useful to overcome anxiety on a step-by-step basis. Wolpe (1982) explains this process as follows:

> *A physiological state that is inhibiting of anxiety is induced in the [client] by means of muscle relaxation; [the client] is then exposed to a weak anxiety-arousing stimulus for a few seconds. If the exposure is repeated, the stimulus progressively loses its ability to evoke anxiety. Successively stronger stimuli are then introduced and similarly treated. (p. 133)*

Desensitization is often the first treatment of choice for *phobias* (experienced fear in a situation in which there is no obvious external danger) or any other disorders arising from fear attached to specific external events (Rimm & Masters, 1979; Morris, 1980). It is particularly useful in instances where the client has sufficient skills to cope with the situation or perform a desired response but avoids doing so or performs below par because of interfering anxiety and accompanying arousal.

On the other hand, desensitization is inappropriate when the target situation is inherently dangerous (such as sky diving) or when the person lacks appropriate skills to handle the target situation. In the latter case, modeling, rehearsal, and skills-training approaches are more desirable. Counselors can determine whether a particular client's anxiety is irrational or is the result of a truly dangerous situation or a skills deficit by engaging in a careful assessment of the presenting problems. Effective desensitization usually also requires that a client be able to relax and to engage in imagery, although occasionally responses other than relaxation or imagery are used in the procedure.

The procedure itself involves three basic steps and, on the average, takes about ten to thirty sessions to complete, depending on the client, the problem, and the intensity of the anxiety. The basic steps involved in desensitization are:

1. Training in deep muscle relaxation
2. Construction of a hierarchy representing emotion-provoking situations
3. Graduated pairing through imagery of the items on the hierarchy with the relaxed state of the client

Training in deep muscle relaxation follows the procedure we discussed earlier. If the client is unable to engage in muscle relaxation, some other form of relaxation training such as yoga or meditation may be used.

Hierarchy construction

Hierarchy construction involves identification of various situations that evoke the conditioned emotion to be desensitized, such as anxiety. It may involve either situations the client has already experienced or anticipates experiencing in the future. The counselor and client can discuss these situations in the counseling sessions, and the client can also keep track of them as they occur in the *in vivo* setting with written notations. As each different situation is identified, it is listed separately on a small index card.

There are three possible types of hierarchies one can use in desensitization, depending upon the parameters and nature of the client's problem. The three hierarchy types are: spatio-temporal, thematic, or personal. The *spatio-temporal hierarchy* consists of items that relate to physical or spatial dimensions, such as distance from a feared object, or time dimensions, such as time remaining before a feared or avoided situation such as taking a test. Spatio-temporal hierarchies are particularly useful in reducing client anxiety about a particular stimulus object, event, or person.

Thematic hierarchies consist of items representing different parameters surrounding the emotion-provoking situation. For example, one client's fear of heights may be greater or less depending on the contextual cues surrounding the height situation and not just on distance from the ground. Or a client's social anxiety may vary with the type and nature of various interpersonal interactions.

Personal hierarchies consist of items representing memories or uncomfortable ruminations about a specific person. Dengrove (1966) suggests that personal hierarchies are very useful in desensitizing a client to conditioned emotions produced either by a loss-related situation such as loss of one's job or dissolution of a relationship through death, divorce, separation, and so on. Personal hierarchies can also be used to countercondition a client's avoidance behavior to a particular person who, perhaps because of negative interactions, has become aversive to the client. Table 9-1 provides an illustration of these three different types of hierarchies.

Regardless of which type of hierarchy is used, each hierarchy usually consists of ten to twenty different items. After each item is listed on a separate index card, they are arranged by the client in a graduated order from the lowest or least anxiety-provoking item to the highest or most anxiety-producing item. The ordering process is also facilitated by a particular scaling and spacing method.

TABLE 9-1 Three Different Hierarchies Used in Systematic Desensitization

Spatial-Temporal (Test-Anxiety)	*Thematic (Sensitivity to Criticism)*
1. It is two weeks before an examination.	1. Friend on the street: "Hi! How are you?"
2. A week before an examination.	2. Friend on the street: "How are you feeling these days?"
3. Four days before an examination.	3. Sister: "You've got to be more careful so they don't put you in a hospital."
4. Three days before an examination.	4. Wife: "You shouldn't drink beer while you are taking medication."
5. Two days before an examination.	5. Mother: "What's the matter? Don't you feel good?"
6. One day before an examination.	6. Wife: "It's just you yourself. It's all in your head."
7. The night before an examination.	7. Service station attendant: "What are you shaking for?"
8. The examination paper lies face down before her.	8. Neighbor borrowing rake: "Is there something wrong with your leg? Your knees are shaking."
9. Awaiting the distribution of examination papers.	9. Friend on the job: "Is your blood pressure okay?"
10. Standing before the unopened doors of the examination room.	10. Service station attendant: "You are pretty shaky; are you crazy or something?"
11. In the process of answering an examination paper.	
12. On the way to the university on the day of the examination.	

Personal (Termination of Intimate Relationship)

1. You have been with Susie every day for the last month. You're sitting holding her in your arms and feeling like she's the only woman you'll ever love like this.	7. You call Susie up late at night. The phone rings constantly without any answer. You wonder where she is.
2. You and Susie are sitting on the floor in your apartment, drinking wine and listening to your records.	8. You call Susie to ask her out for dinner and she turns you down—says she doesn't feel well.
3. You've just returned from taking Susie to her first race. She's ecstatic about the experience.	9. You're walking down the street by the court. You see Susie playing there with another person. You wonder why she hasn't told you about him.
4. You and Susie are studying together in the library.	10. You go over to Susie's. She isn't there. You wait until she comes. She sees you, goes back to the car, and drives away.
5. You and Susie are drinking beer at the local pub.	11. You call Susie on the phone. She says she doesn't want to see you anymore, that she never really loved you, and hangs up on you.
6. You and Susie aren't spending every day together. Sometimes she wants to study alone now. You're in the library by yourself studying.	

Sources: J. Wolpe, *The Practice of Behavior Therapy*, 3rd Ed. (New York: Pergamon Press, 1982), p. 152; J.N. Marquis and W.G. Morgan, *A Guidebook for Systematic Desensitization* (Palo Alto, CA: Veterans Workshop, Veterans Administration Hospital, 1969), p. 28; W.H. Cormier and L.S. Cormier, *Interviewing Strategies for Helpers: Fundamental Skills and Cognitive-Behavioral Interventions*, 3rd Ed. (Monterey, CA: Brooks/Cole, 1991).

Although there are several possible, the most commonly used scaling method in desensitization is referred to as SUDS or *subjective units of disturbance* (Wolpe & Lazarus, 1966). The SUDS scale ranges from 0 to 100. Zero represents absolute calm or no emotion; 100 represents panic or extreme emotion. The client is asked to specify a number between 0 and 100 that best represents the intensity of his or her emotion for each item. Effective hierarchies usually consist of items at all levels of the SUDS scale. If there are more than ten SUDS spacing between any two items, probably another item needs to be inserted.

The pairing (interposition) process. After the hierarchy has been constructed and the client has been trained in muscle relaxation or some variation thereof, the counselor and client are ready to begin the pairing process. The pairing process in systematic desensitization can be summarized in the following steps:

1.   The counselor and client discuss and agree on a signaling process which the client can use to let the counselor know if and when he or she experiences any anxiety during the pairing process. A common signaling system is to ask the client to raise an index finger if any anxiety (or other conditioned emotion) is felt.

2.   A state of relaxation is then induced for the client.

3.   When the client is deeply relaxed (this will be apparent to the counselor by such things as deeper and slower respiration rate, changes in skin color, body posture, and so on), the counselor describes the first (least emotion-provoking) item on the hierarchy to the client and asks the client to imagine that item as he or she actually perceives it. The first time the scene is presented, it is presented briefly, for about ten seconds, assuming the client does not signal anxiety prior to this time. If the client does not signal anxiety at the end of ten seconds, the counselor instructs the client to stop visualizing the scene and to either relax or to imagine a pleasant, somewhat neutral scene, such as being on a warm, sandy beach. After a pause of about thirty seconds, the counselor can present the same scene again.

4.   The counselor then presents the same item again. On the second presentation, the duration of the exposure is increased to about thirty seconds. The second presentation of a same scene should also include as much detailed description as the counselor gave the first time; simply saying "Imagine that scene again" does not give the client enough information (Watts, 1974).

5.   If no anxiety is indicated by the client during the second scene presentation, the counselor has the option of presenting the same scene one more time or of moving up the hierarchy and presenting the next scene. Typically, an item can be considered suc-

cessfully completed with two successive "no-anxiety" presentations (Marquis, Morgan, & Piaget, 1973). However, items that are very emotionally arousing, such as those at the upper end of the hierarchy, may require three successive "no-anxiety" repetitions.

Each successive scene on the hierarchy is presented according to the process just described. In the event that an item does evoke anxiety from the client, the client is instructed to terminate the image, to imagine a pleasant or relaxing scene instead, and to continue to concentrate on relaxing and warm images and sensations. After a pause of one or two minutes, the same scene is presented again, as long as the counselor is confident that the client is once again deeply relaxed. If no anxiety is indicated after two more presentations of this scene, the counselor moves on to the next item. If, however, an item continues to elicit anxiety after three successive presentations, this may indicate either a problem in the hierarchy or in the client's visualization.

As Cormier and Cormier (1991) note, there are at least three things a counselor can do to eliminate continued anxiety resulting from presentation of the same item: add a new, less anxiety-provoking item to the hierarchy; present the same or the previous item to the client again for a shorter time period: or assess if the client is revising or drifting from the scene during the imagery process.

One word of caution to beginning attempts with the pairing process in desensitization. Rimm and Masters (1979) observe:

> *Especially with beginning therapists, there is a strong tendency to "reinforce" the [client] for not signaling anxiety. This may manifest itself in the therapist's saying (sometimes with a note of relief in [the] voice), "Good" . . . This practice may inadvertently encourage clients not to report anxiety even when they really feel it during a scene presentation, particularly if the counselor remains silent following the client's anxiety signals. One way to avoid this practice is to use a standardized instruction at all times regardless of whether the client does or does not signal anxiety such as "Now I want you to stop imagining that scene."*

Each desensitization session involving the pairing process described above typically begins with the last item successfully completed during the previous session and ends with a no-anxiety item. The pairing process is usually terminated in each session after successful completion of three to five hierarchy items or after a duration of twenty to thirty minutes (shorter for children), although occasionally a client may be able to concentrate for a longer time period and complete more than five items successfully

Because the pairing process may occur over several weeks, it is important for the counselor to keep accurate written notations about each item as it is presented to the client. A simple recording system using index cards has been proposed by Goldfried and Davison (1976) (see Figure 9-1). The counselor writes the date, item number, and a description of the item on each card. Underneath the item description is space for the counselor to indicate the duration of each presentation and to record with a + or a − whether the client did not signal anxiety (plus sign) or did report anxiety (minus sign). Note on the card shown in Figure 9-1 that two successive no-anxiety visualizations (+ 30 and + 40) occurred before this item was terminated. As items are successfully completed without anxiety within the counseling session, it is assumed that the client will be able to confront them in the *in vivo* setting also without experiencing undue anxiety or discomfort. However, clients are usually cautioned not to attempt to encounter the hierarchy situations *in vivo* until 75 to 80 percent of the hierarchy desensitization process has been successfully completed.

Case Illustration of Anxiety Reduction Strategies: The Case of Pam

Pam is a nine-year-old third grader who has recently refused to go to school in the morning. According to her parents, about a month ago, she got very upset at school and begged her teacher to send her home; her teacher did so. In the last two weeks, Pam has become physically ill on school mornings and protests strongly

FIGURE 9-1 Notation Card   (Adapted from M.R. Goldfried and G.C. Davison, *Clinical Behavior Therapy*, New York: Holt, Rinehart & Winston, 1976.)

Item No. 5

Date: 2–7–XX

ITEM DESCRIPTION

It is one week before your speech. You are trying to organize your material and are wondering if you'll be able to deliver a well-prepared speech that is evaluated highly by your instructor

+ 10   - 15   + 20   - 25   + 30   + 40

---

when her parents insist it is time to leave. Her teacher reports that she continues to have periods of being upset and of crying at school. Her parents are perplexed, since Pam has always enjoyed school and seems relatively well adjusted in other areas of her life.

Assessment reveals that probably Pam did become upset initially in school one day for unknown reasons. Unfortunately, her feelings of anxiety and stress were terminated by being sent home, rather than being encouraged to stay at school and cope with the upsetting situation. Pam has now learned that by staying at home, she can successfully avoid any feelings of stress that she associates with school. The counselor explains to the parents how this may have occurred and suggests systematic desensitization as a treatment method, after first checking out Pam's ability to engage in imagery by asking Pam to imagine several scenes, such as playing on a warm, sandy beach or walking on a hiking trail at a campground.

The next thing Pam and the counselor do is to train Pam in the use of a relaxation procedure. The counselor uses deep muscle relaxation and follows the format and instructions described earlier on pp. 234–236.

After Pam is able to utilize successfully the relaxation procedure, Pam and the counselor discuss possible stress-arousing situations related to school. With a client of Pam's age, the counselor uses words such as "situations or things about school that upset or bother you or make you feel sick" rather than "produce anxiety." In Pam's situation, she becomes more upset as the time for school approaches, so a spatio-temporal hierarchy is constructed with time as the significant dimension. The following items comprise the hierarchy for Pam:

1. It's Friday night. School's over with for a whole weekend, but in two and a half days it will be here again.
2. It's Saturday. I start to do some homework and think about school coming up on Monday.
3. It's Sunday night. I don't want the weekend to be over. I start to get a funny feeling in my stomach.
4. It's Monday morning. I wake up feeling sick. I don't want to go to school. The whole week lies ahead of me.
5. It's breakfast time but I don't feel hungry. All I can think about is feeling sick to my stomach and wanting to stay here.
6. My mom insists I get dressed for school. I pull my jeans on as slowly as possible. My stomach feels worse. My heart starts to race.
7. It's almost time to leave. I have to get all my books and papers together. My heart feels like it's pounding a mile a minute.

8. My dad has started the car. I can hear it and I don't want to go. I rush into the bathroom and throw up.

9. I'm riding in the car. All I can think about is how awful I feel. I start crying. I can't stop.

Once the relaxation training and hierarchy construction are completed, the real work of systematic desensitization began with Pam. During the first session of actual desensitization, the counselor explained a signaling system to Pam and then spent about fifteen minutes helping Pam become relaxed. When she was relaxed, the counselor presented the first hierarchy item to Pam—"It's Friday night. School's over with for a whole weekend but in two and a half days it will be here again"—reminding Pam to raise her index finger if or when she felt at all bothered or uncomfortable imagining this situation. After fifteen seconds, Pam signaled. The counselor spent about three minutes having Pam become very relaxed again and then presented the same item. Pam signaled after twenty-five seconds. The counselor then presented the item again, and this time Pam did not signal during the entire fifty-second presentation. Following this, the counselor repeated instructions for Pam to feel relaxed and then presented the same item one more time. Again, Pam did not signal during the entire fifty-second presentation. The counselor recorded the following information on the systematic desensitization note card and the sequence of this item to indicate the number of times and the time of anxiety and no anxiety:

Item #1:   -15   -25   +50   +50

Since this item was concluded successfully, and because of the need to keep the sessions about thirty minutes long due to Pam's age, the counselor decided to terminate this first session with this item. The second session began with this item again after relaxation training. Pam did not signal any discomfort during either of the two successive fifty-second presentations. The counselor presented the second item; Pam signaled anxiety after twenty seconds but did not signal during the next two fifty-second presentations, so the counselor went on to the third item.

Pam signaled discomfort for the third item after ten seconds and twenty seconds, but not during the following two fifty-second presentations. The counselor recorded this information on the systematic desensitization note card:

Item #2:   -20   +50   +50
Item #3:   -10   -20   +50   +50

This session was terminated after successful completion of Item #3.

The counselor began the fourth session with Item #4. Pam signaled discomfort after 8 seconds, 15 seconds, 20 seconds, and 25 seconds. At this point, the counselor stopped the process to discuss what might be going on.

Together, Pam and the counselor decided there was too large a time gap between Items #3 and #4 and inserted the following item into the hierarchy: "It's the middle of the night. I wake up suddenly in a sweat thinking about school the next morning." The counselor then presented this item to Pam, who was able to imagine it without any discomfort on the second and third presentations.

A total of twelve sessions were required before Pam and the counselor had successfully worked through all of the items on the hierarchy. (The number of sessions would usually be fewer for an adult client because of a longer attention span.) During this time, both Pam and the parents reported that Pam was not fighting about going to school. They also reported that although Pam occasionally seemed to invent an excuse such as a cough to avoid school, she was no longer becoming physically ill on school mornings. Her teacher reported that, although Pam occasionally appeared distressed initially when dropped off at school, she did not exhibit further fear or avoidance during the school day.

Self-Management

Many people are legitimately concerned about the long-term effects of helping. In an effort to promote enduring client changes, counselors have become more concerned with client self-directed change. In a recent survey of thirty-six counselors, self-change methods were ranked as the top form of intervention predicted to increase during the next decade (Karoly, 1982). This interest has led many counseling researchers and practitioners to explore the usefulness of a variety of helping strategies called self-control, self-regulation, or self-management (Cautela, 1969; Kanfer, 1970, Mahoney, 1971).

The primary characteristic of a self-management strategy is that the client administers the strategy and directs the change efforts with minimal assistance from the counselor. Self-management strategies are very useful in dealing with a number of client problems and may promote generalization to life settings of what clients learn in the interview. Kanfer (1980) observes that self-management methods are most effective when they help clients acquire new behaviors; they are used less frequently once new behavior patterns are developed. However, as he points out, the same methods are still available for use in future occasions when the same client faces different issues (p. 336). Self-management strategies are among the best strategies designed to strengthen client investment in the helping process. Self-management may eliminate the counselor as a "middle" person and ensure greater chances of client success because of the investment made by the client in the strategies for change.

Uses of Self-Management Interventions

According to Kanfer (1980), self-management techniques are most easily applied when clients are concerned about their problems and can anticipate some improvement in their life by resolution of the existing problem (p. 349). Self-management interventions actually have a variety of uses. Rimm and Masters (1979) have noted that they are particularly useful when the client's environment offers little or no *perceived* positive reinforcement for desired behaviors. The range of behaviors that this could describe might include smoking, improper diet, avoidance of necessary activities (such as homework), excessive TV viewing, and so on. Generally speaking, the self-management approach is most effective when the client is highly motivated to change but believes that a lack of willpower prevents the change. What self-management offers is a highly structured situation that relieves the client of the responsibility to organize for change. Self-management interventions typically involve self-directed manipulation of antecedent conditions, behaviors, and/or consequences. In this section of the chapter we describe three useful self-management intervention methods: self-monitoring, self-reward, and self-contracting.

Self-Monitoring

Recent emphases in behavioral approaches suggest the efficacy of a number of self-control procedures, of which self-monitoring is the primary one. Self-monitoring involves two processes: self-observation and self-recording. In *self-observation*, an individual notices or discriminates aspects of his or her behavior. In *self-recording*, the individual uses specified procedures to record these observations. Self-monitoring involves having clients count and/or regulate given habits, thoughts, or feelings. Self-monitoring seems to interfere with the learned habit by breaking the stimulus-response association and by encouraging performance of the desired response—which is then often reinforced by the individual's sense of progress following its accomplishment. Self-monitoring also seems to promote behavior change by promoting client *awareness* of selected behaviors and habits. As Kanfer (1980) notes, "(a) person who is asked to observe and record his own behavior is helped immediately to become more aware of its occurrence" (p. 354). Such awareness helps clients to obtain more concrete information about their problems and to collect objective evidence of changes in the response over time.

There are two issues which affect the self-monitoring strategy—reactivity and reliability. *Reactivity* means that the process of noticing one's own behavior closely can cause the behavior to change. *Reliability* refers to the accuracy with which the client counts the behavior. One simple way to increase the accuracy of the client's recording is to have the client ask another person to record with him. For therapy purposes, the counselor and client should attempt to structure the self-monitoring in a way that maximizes the reactivity. Therefore, in implementing the procedure, they will need to consider what, how, and when to self-monitor.

What to monitor An initial step involves selection of the behavior to monitor. Usually individuals will achieve better results with self-monitoring if they start by counting only one behavior—at least initially. Clients may, for example, count positive feelings about themselves or thoughts of competency. The counting encourages greater frequency of these kinds of thoughts and feelings. Clients may count the number of times they tell themselves to do well on a task or they may count the number of behaviors related to goal achievement: the number of times they tell their spouse "I love you," the number of times they initiate conversations, or participate in class discussions, and so forth. The type of behavior the client monitors can also affect the degree and direction of reactivity that occurs from self-monitoring. Self-monitoring seems to increase positively valenced (socially desirable) behaviors and to decrease negatively valenced (socially undesirable) behaviors (Fremouw & Brown, 1980). Self-monitoring of neutral behaviors results in nonsignificant or inconsistent behavior change. For this reason, it is important to have clients monitor behaviors they value and care most about changing. If a client wishes to stop smoking, self-monitoring of this behavior could be very useful. Simply asking a person who doesn't wish to give up smoking to monitor this habit is not likely to be effective (McFall, 1970).

How to monitor The particular method the client uses to count the target response will depend on the nature of the selected response. Generally, clients will count either the frequency or duration of a response. If they are interested in knowing *how often* the response occurs, they can use a frequency count to note the number of times they smoke, talk on the telephone, initiate social conversations, or think about themselves positively. Sometimes it is more useful to know the *amount of time* the behavior occurs. A person can count the duration of a behavior in these cases. For example, clients might count how long they studied, how long they talked on the telephone, or the length of depressed periods of thought. Occasionally, clients may find it useful to record both the frequency and duration of a response. In choosing to count the occurrences of a behavior either by the number or by the amount of time, there is a simple "rule of thumb" recommended by Watson and Tharp:

> *If it is easy to count the number of separate times you perform the target behavior, count that. If it is not easy, or if the target behavior runs on for several minutes at a time, count the amount of time you do it. (1972, p. 82)*

In some cases where the target response occurs very often or almost continuously or when the onset and termination of the target responses are hard to detect, the frequency and duration methods of recording may not be too useful. In these instances, clients could record with an *interval method.* In the interval method of recording, they could divide the time for recording (8:00 A.M. to 8:00 P.M.) into time intervals such as thirty minutes, one hour, two hours, and so on. During each time interval. they simply record the presence or absence of the behavior with a "yes" if the behavior occurred or a "no" if it did not. Mahoney and Thoresen (1974) refer to this as the "all-or-none" recording method. Ciminero, Nelson, and Lipinski (1977) suggest the information gleaned by the "all-or-none" interval recording method may be increased if clients are instructed to rate each interval using a number system to indicate how often the target response occurred. For example, using a five-point scale, they could rate the occurrence of a response as a 0, 1, 2, 3, or 4, depending on whether the response occurred never, occasionally, often, very frequently, or always. Clients also can record the *intensity* of an event with the use of a rating scale. Things such as pain, fear, depression, and so on may be recorded more appropriately by using a numerical system in which each number has a precise meaning according to a prearranged scale. Rating scales are most useful for self-monitoring of feelings and mood states. Typical rating scales used in self-monitoring contain 5 to 9 numerical points (Watson & Tharp, 1981). For example, a client could list events in which she felt calm or anxious and then rate the extent of the experienced feelings, using a 1 to 5 rating scale, such as:

1 = complete calm
2 = a little anxious
3 = somewhat anxious
4 = very anxious
5 = complete panic

According to Watson & Tharp (1981), "(r)ating scales can produce better self-understanding because they help put events into full perspective"[*] (p. 63). For instance, in the example described above, the monitoring gives the client information about when she felt calm and when she felt anxious. Clients are helped to see that they are not anxious *all* the time, and that often their anxiety may not be as intense as they imagine it to be.

Clients will need to record with the assistance of some "device" for recording. These can range from simple devices, such as note cards, logs, and diaries for written recordings, to more mechanical devices such as a golf wrist counter, a kitchen timer, a wristwatch, or a tape recorder. The device may increase the reactivity of self-monitoring if it is obtrusive, yet it should not be so noticeable that it is embarrassing or awkward for clients to use (Nelson, Lipinski, & Boykin, 1978). The device should be simple to use, convenient, portable, and economical.

When to record The timing of self-monitoring can influence the change produced by this strategy. Generally, there are two times when clients can record—before the response occurs (pre-behavior monitoring) or after the response (post-behavior monitoring) (Bellack, Rozensky & Schwartz, 1974). If the clients wish to use self-monitoring to decrease a response, pre-behavior monitoring may be most effective; post-behavior monitoring may be more helpful when the goal is to increase a behavior. The rule of thumb for the timing of self-monitoring can be stated to clients as follows:

1. *To decrease the monitored behavior:*
   Since you want to decrease the number of cigarettes you smoke (or the number of self-critical thoughts you have), each time you have the urge to smoke but don't (or start to criticize yourself but refrain from doing so), then count this on your log.

---

[*] This and all other quotes from this source are from *Self-Directed Behavior: Self-Modification for Personal Adjustment*, 3rd Ed. by D.L. Watson and R.C. Tharp. Copyright © 1981 by Wadsworth, Inc. Reprinted by permission of the publisher, Brooks/Cole Publishing Company, Monterey, CA.

2. *To increase a behavior:*
   Since you want to increase the number of times you verbally express your opinions to someone else (or the number of positive, self-enhancing thoughts), count and record on your log immediately after you express an opinion (or as soon as you are aware of thinking something positive about yourself or your accomplishments).

Counting, or quantifying, behaviors is the initial step in self-monitoring. The second, and equally important, step in self-monitoring is charting or plotting the behavior counts over a period of time. This permits clients to see progress that might not otherwise be apparent. It also permits clients to set daily goals that are more attainable than the overall goal. Clients can take weekly cumulative counts of self-monitored behaviors and chart them on a simple line graph. After graphing the data, the public display of the graph may set the occasion for both self- and external reinforcement.

After initial recording efforts are successful in initiating change, it is useful for clients to continue recording in order to maintain change. Often clients' motivation to continue self-monitoring can be enhanced if they reward their efforts for self-monitoring. We discuss the self-reward strategy in the next section.

Self-Reward

Research suggests that the effects produced by self-monitoring may be greater and more permanent if self-monitoring is accompanied by other therapeutic strategies, such as self-reward, self-punishment, and self-contracting (Mahoney, Moura, & Wade, 1973). Self-monitoring can always be combined with other helping strategies as a way to collect data concerning the occurrence of goal behaviors. As we noted in the previous section, self-monitoring can also be used intentionally to induce therapeutic change. However, the therapeutic gains from self-monitoring may be maximized with the explicit use of other self-management strategies to increase or decrease a response.

Self-reward involves the self-presentation of rewards following the occurrence of a desired behavior. Self-reward is intended to strengthen a behavior. It is assumed that self-reward functions like external reinforcement. A *reinforcer* is something that, when administered following a target response, tends to maintain or increase the probability of that response in the future. Self-reward is a very complicated process involving a number of variables. For example, as Watson and Tharp (1981, p. 204) point out:

(W)hen you reinforce your behavior, you are calling your own attention to it. You are giving yourself clear information. clear feedback (Castro & Rachlin, 1980). You are making the behavior more vivid, even more vivid than in self-recording alone. You are teaching yourself to discriminate between correct and incorrect performances. You are reminding yourself of your long-term goals and of your rules for getting there (Nelson, Sprong, Hayes, & Graham, 1979). You are learning self-awareness (Catania, 1975).

There are two ways clients can use self-reward. First, they can give themselves rewards after engaging in specified behaviors. For example, clients could imagine being on a sailboat after doing daily exercises or could buy themselves treats after daily studying. Or they could remove something negative after performing the desired behaviors. For instance, an overweight client could remove a "fat picture" from the wall after losing a certain number of pounds. In most cases we recommend the first approach (self-presentation of a positive stimulus) because it is more positive than the second. The first approach, which may be referred to as positive self-reward, has been validated by more research studies than the negative procedure (Mahoney, Maura, & Wade, 1973).

There are three major factors involved in helping a client use a self-reward strategy: what to use as rewards, how to administer the rewards, and when to administer the rewards.

Type of rewards First you will want to help clients select appropriate rewards. Rewards can be things, people, activities, or even images and ideas. Watson and Tharp (1981) observe that "(t)he most important reinforcers are those that will eventually maintain [a] new behavior, once it is solidly in place" (p. 169). These reinforcers can be used to support steps or achievement of subgoals and are logical rewards because they use the same rewards the client is striving toward. For instance, a student who wants to graduate with honors may use good grades as a reward to reinforce harder work or increased studying. One of the authors rewarded a specified number of completed exercise workouts with the purchase of exercise shoes, warm-up suits, and so on. If such "logical" reinforcers do not seem to be available, any pleasant event or image can serve as a reinforcer.

The most effective self-rewards are perhaps similar to what Glasser and proponents of reality therapy term *positive addictions*—different from conventional addictions in that they bring both short- and long-term benefits, not just immediate gratification and delayed pain. According to Glasser (1976), a positive addiction is anything you do regularly that is also noncompetitive, easy to do, beneficial to you, and results in both self-improvement and self-acceptance.

Specific types of rewards include verbal-symbolic, imaginal, and material rewards. An example of a *verbal-symbolic reward* is self-praise, such as thinking, "I really did that well." *Imaginal rewards* involve visualizing or fantasizing scenes that produce pleasure and satisfaction. *Material rewards* include tangible events, such as an enjoyable activity, a purchase, or tokens or points that can be exchanged for something. Rewards also can be current or potential. A *current reward* is something enjoyable that occurs on a daily basis, such as eating, reading, getting the mail, etc. A *potential reward* is something that could occur in the future that would be satisfying and enjoyable. Taking a trip or going out for a gourmet meal are examples of potential rewards.

Clients should be encouraged to select a variety of rewards, including both current and potential, material, imaginal, and verbal-symbolic, to prevent one reward from losing its potency or impact. Counselors can help clients select rewards by having them identify some ongoing and potentially satisfying thoughts and activities. Clients can identify events that are reinforcing to them by completing a reinforcement survey such as the one in Table 9-2.

An occasional client may have difficulty in identifying rewards. For example, a client may be too busy or too depressed to find reinforcers or may be unable to find reinforcers that are either affordable or do not duplicate reinforcements already being received. In lieu of using a very enjoyable activity as a reward, this client might choose a more mundane daily activity, such as answering the telephone or walking up or down stairs. Using a frequently occurring activity as a reward is based on the *Premack principle*, which states that a high-probability behavior can be used to reinforce a low-profitability behavior (Premack, 1965). For instance, something a student engages in frequently, such as getting up from the desk, can be made contingent on something the student does infrequently, such as completing assignments or work problems. As Watson and Tharp (1981) note, "(t)he point of the Premack effect is that an activity does not have to feel good in order to be useful as a reinforcer; however, clients should avoid selecting aversive activities as the high-frequency behavior they are too likely to stop engaging in that activity if they could" (p. 172). Neutral behaviors such as brushing teeth, drinking a glass of water or soda, or answering the phone are all possible choices.

The rewards clients select should be potent but not so valuable that the client would not give them up in the event the target behavior was not performed. In other words, the reinforcer should

TABLE 9-2 Example of Reinforcement Survey

1. What will be the *rewards of* achieving your goal?
2. What kind of praise do you like to receive, from yourself or from others?
3. What kinds of things do you like to have?
4. What are your major interests?
5. What are your hobbies?
6. What people do you like to be with?
7. What do you like to do with those people?
8. What do you do for fun?
9. What do you do to relax?
10. What do you do to get away from it all?
11. What makes you feel good?
12. What would be a nice present to receive?
13. What kinds of things are important to you?
14. What would you buy if you had an extra $20? $50? $100?
15. On what do you spend your money each week?
16. What behaviors do you perform every day? (Don't overlook the obvious or the commonplace.)
17. Are there any behaviors that you usually perform instead of the target behavior?
18. What would you hate to be?
19. Of the things you do every day, which would you hate to give up?
20. What are your favorite daydreams and fantasies?
21. What are the most relaxing scenes you can imagine?

D.C. Watson and R.J. Tharp, *Self-Directed Behavior: Self-Modification for Personal Adjustment,* 3rd Ed. (Monterey, CA: Brooks/Cole. 1981), p. 170.

be strong enough to make working for it worthwhile and, at the same time, not so indispensable that the client refuses to put it "in contingency"—or to use it only after the specified response occurs (Watson & Tharp, 1981, p. 176).

Delivery of rewards After selecting rewards, clients will need to work out ways to administer the rewards. They should know what has to be done in order to present themselves with a reward. The counselor might encourage them to reward themselves for *gradual* progress toward the desired goal. Daily rewards for small steps are more effective than one delayed reward for a great improvement.

Timing of rewards Clients also need to present the rewards at certain times in order to maximize the self-reward strategy. The reward should come only *after* target behavior has been performed in order to have the most impact (Homme, Csanyi, Gonzales, & Rechs, 1969). Ideally, the reinforcement should occur immediately after performing the specified behavior. Immediate doses of reinforcement are more effective than delayed rewards. Providing clients with extra immediate reinforcement can tip the balance and cause them to change long-term behaviors. As Watson and Tharp explain:

> *If the dieter arranges the reinforcement of, say, watching an enjoyable TV program immediately after (or even during) self-restraint, dieting is more likely to be observed than if he or she depends entirely on the long-range rewards of being slim someday. In other words, it is the TV program that right now competes with an extra bowl of spaghetti, not the dim dream of slimness in what, at the moment, may appear as a faraway future. (1981, p. 179)*

Immediate reinforcement is especially critical in cases where the undesired behavior consists of consummatory or fear responses. For example, an ice cream cone or piece of candy you eat right now is more reinforcing than the change in the scale next week or the drop in your clothing size next month. Similarly, it feels better to avoid a feared situation right now than to engage in it and think about how good it will feel afterwards to administer the reward.

If a client selects material rewards that aren't portable enough to be carried around for immediate use, they might consider the following intermediate options as immediate rewards:

1. Tell a significant other about your behavior to elicit their encouragement. Social reinforcement can be very powerful in helping clients to find extra opportunities to be reinforced and also to ward off urges and temptations.

2. Assign so many points to each occurrence of the desired behavior; after accumulating a specified number of points, trade it in for a reinforcer. Points (sometimes called tokens) are useful because they make it possible to employ a variety of reinforcers and also make it easy to increase a behavior gradually (Watson & Tharp, 1981, pp. 181–182).

3. Engage in imagined or verbal-symbolic rewards; see, hear, and feel what it is like to be ten pounds slimmer, or praise yourself covertly for refusing that second helping or for resisting the temptation to snack. Although extensive or material rewards are useful in cases where clients might not otherwise perform the target response, imaginal and verbal-symbolic rewards are especially useful in helping clients maintain changes and have some advantages

over extensive or material rewards. For instance, these rewards are always available, depend only on the client's judgment of acceptable performance, can always be applied without delay, and may be more powerful or increase a client's sense of personal satisfaction if the target behavior is an especially valued one (Williams & Long, 1983, p. 83).

Cautions in self-reward strategies Self-reward strategies will be most effective if the following conditions exist:

1. The total amount of reinforcement the client receives for engaging in the desired behavior is greater during the self-management program than it was before.

2. Extensive or material rewards are not used exclusively, but were adequately supplemented with imagined and verbal-symbolic rewards.

3. A variety of different rewards is selected in order to avoid satiation or wearing out of one or two reinforcers.

4. The rewards selected by a client are not punishing in any way to other people.

5. Different reinforcers are used for each target behavior the client wishes to change with a self-management program.

6. If selected rewards require the assistance or cooperation of significant others, the client first obtains agreement from that other person and also informs the other person exactly what he or she is supposed to do. Otherwise, the client may end up getting lectured, nagged, or otherwise pressured instead of encouraged or praised! (Watson & Tharp, 1981; Williams & Long, 1983).

Sometimes self-reward is used in conjunction with another self-management strategy: self-contracting.

Self-Contracting

Clients who are able to identify and own their behaviors often acknowledge that their current actions are resulting in some undesirable consequences. They state how they would like the consequences to be different (goals). They may or may not realize that in order to change the consequences, they must first modify the behaviors producing them. Behavior change of any kind can be a slow, painful process requiring much time and effort on the client's part. Therefore, getting clients to make behavior changes is not easy. You must first obtain the client's *commitment* to change.

The contract is a useful technique for gaining the cooperation and commitment of the client. Both behavioral and reality therapists rely on contracts to help strengthen the client's commitment to action. Commitment is a very important part of behavior change and of action plans because "it encourages and reinforces the client to take action steps" (Gilliland, James, and Bowman, 1989, p. 223). The contract specifies what actions the client agrees to take in order to reach the desired goal. Furthermore, it contains a description of the conditions surrounding the action steps: *where* the client will undertake such actions; *how* (in what manner) the client will carry out the actions, and *when* (by what time) the tasks will be completed. Because these contract terms are specified and carried out by the client, we refer to this self-management strategy as *self-contracting.* The most effective contracts have terms that are completely acceptable to the client, are very specific, and reflect short-range goals that are possible for the client to attain (Kanfer, 1980). Contracts also should be formulated in writing. The writing of the contract enables the client to take an initial action step—that of planning. Contracts may be more successful if the behaviors required in the contract are first rehearsed by the client.

Self-contracts often are more successful when they are accompanied by self-reward. In other words, clients are more likely to commit themselves to a contract if they know there will be some kind of reward resulting from achievement of the contract terms. Encourage clients to provide their own reinforcements. This reward is made contingent upon successful completion of the contract; that is, the client must successfully complete the contract terms before engaging in the selected reward.

In some cases, a self-contract also may include sanctions that the client administers for failure to meet the contract terms. However, the rewards and sanctions should be balanced, and a self-contract that emphasizes positive terms may be more effective. When clients do not fulfill terms of their self-contract, it is important not to accept excuses, and at the same time not to emphasize the client's failure (Glasser, 1972). Instead, try to maintain a relationship with the client that emphasizes your own involvement and concern. Instead of focusing on what the client did not do or should have done, help the client reexamine goals, level of commitment, and the nature and terms of the contract. If the contract is realistic and the client is committed to pursuing it, "(t)hen it is the therapist's role to facilitate success by accepting no excuses or reasons for nonperformance while maintaining an accepting, positive, empathic involvement" with the client (Gilliland, James, and Bowman, 1989, p. 224)

Self-contracts are very useful in working with children and adolescents because they are so concrete. When contracts are used with children and adolescents, several additional guidelines are pertinent (Homme, Csanyi, Gonzales, & Rechs, 1969; Kanfer, 1980):

1. The required behavior should be easy for the child to identify.

2. The total task should be divided into subtasks, and initial contracts should reward completion of each component or subtask. Other steps can be added later, after each successive target behavior is well established.

3. Smaller, more frequent rewards are more effective in maintaining the child or adolescent's interest in working for change than larger, less frequently administered rewards.

4. In the case of a self-contract, rewards controlled by the child or teenager are generally more effective than those dispensed by adults. For example, a child who completes his workbook pages at school by lunchtime may dispense a variety of accessible rewards to and for himself, such as free time, visiting the library, drawing, and so on. This helps the child to view the reward "as recognition of accomplishments and not as payment for obedience" (Kanfer, 1980, p. 351).

5. Rewards follow rather than precede performance of the target behavior. In other words, the client must complete the specified activity first before engaging in any part of the reward.

6. The client must view the contract as a fair one which, in an equitable way, balances the degree of work and energy expended and the resulting payoffs or consequences.

7. The most effective self-contracts for children and adolescents facilitate their overall growth and development and are used daily. As Kanfer (1980) explains: "(t)he very essence of the effectiveness of the contract procedure, as of many other self-management techniques, lies in the fact that it becomes a rule for everyday conduct. Neither contract management nor other methods can be reserved for use only as special occasions, on weekends, or in difficult situations" (p. 352).

Client Commitment to Self-Management

A critical problem in the effective use of any self-management strategy is having the client use the strategy regularly and consistently. There is some evidence that people who benefit from self-management use self-management strategies on a very consistent basis (Perri & Richards, 1977; Heffernan & Richards, 1981).

Clients may be more likely to carry out self-management programs given the presence of certain conditions, including the following:

1. The use of the self-management program will provide enough advantages or positive consequences to be worth the cost to the client in terms of time and effort. The self-management program must do more than simply meet the status quo.

2. Clients believe in their capacity to change. Since beliefs create reality, the belief that they can change helps clients to try harder when they get "stuck" or are faced with an unforeseen difficulty in their self-change problem (Watson & Tharp, 1981, p. 37).

3. Clients' utilization of self-management processes reflects their own standards of performance, not the standards of the counselor or of significant others. As Karoly (1982) notes, "self-management efforts are unlikely to be maintained if clients are merely learning how to behave in accordance with standards that are foreign to them" (p. 22). Karoly recommends that an important ingredient of a self-management program, particularly for clients who are ambivalent about their choices, is *values clarification.*

4. Clients use personal reminders about their goals whenever tempted to stray off the intervention plan. A written list of self-reminders that clients can carry around at all times may prove helpful in this respect.

5. If the client secretly harbors an escape plan ("I'll study every day except when my friend drops over" or "I'll diet every day except on Sundays"), this should be made explicit. Concealed escape plans are likely to wreak havoc onto the best-conceived self-management programs. As Watson and Tharp (1981) observe, some escape clauses may be particularly detrimental to change, for instance, when they are too lenient or when one slip reactivates an irresistible craving. However, these authors recommend that any plan "should clearly state all intended escapes, whether or not they are wise" (p. 40).

6. The self-management program is directed toward maintenance as well as initial acquisition of target behaviors. For this to occur, the counselor must take into account the client's complete lifestyle. As Karoly (1982) notes,

> *Self-management requires more than a temporary change in setting conditions or the acquisition of specific strategies. For therapeutic change to be maintained, the individual must be prepared, by virtue of his or her mode of information processing, the adequacy of active coping skills, and by dint of having selected a supportive social setting (friends, co-workers,*

spouse, etc.) to deal with unforeseen challenges, conflicts, pe-
riods of deprivation, and/or the periodic malfunctioning of
"best laid plans." (p. 22)

7. The client's use of the program may be strengthened by
enlisting the support and assistance of other persons—as long as
their roles are positive, not punishing. Former clients, peers, or
friends can aid the client in achieving goals through reinforcement
of the client's regular use of the self-management strategies and
reminders to resist "temptations."

8. The counselor maintains some minimal contact with the
client during the time the self-management program is being carried out. Counselor reinforcement is quite important in successful
implementation of self-management efforts.

You as counselor can provide reinforcement (anything that
serves to increase the frequency of a desired response) easily
through oral approval ("That's great." "I like that.") or by knowledge of progress ("You did very well." "You did the task perfectly." "You've done a great job in improving your study habits.").
Have the client drop in or telephone you during the course of the
self-management program. This enables you to provide immediate
encouragement to the client.

Case Illustration of Self-Management
Interventions: The Case of Juan

Juan is a fourteen-year-old boy who has scored very high on ability
tests but has performed in school consistently below his ability.
Juan admits that his poor grades for the most part are due to what
he calls "inability to apply myself." When asked by the counselor
to define and give examples of this, Juan notes that he rarely takes
homework home, or if he does, he doesn't complete it. He also
rarely "cracks a book" and doesn't always know what he is tested
on. Juan is interested in going to college and is starting to realize
that his bad grades will adversely affect this possibility unless he
pulls them up. He is concerned because he does not know how to
change what he refers to as "my bad study habits."

The counselor explains some of the rationale and process of a
self-management program to Juan, who seems amenable to trying
it. The counselor notes that Juan, rather than the counselor, will be
in charge of setting goals for his performance and monitoring it.
This aspect appeals to Juan, who states that he is tired of having so
many other people on his back about doing better in school.

Because Juan's present base rate for studying is almost zero,
initially the counselor discusses some realistic goals Juan might

want to set for himself as part of a self-contract that also makes use of self-reward and self-monitoring. Juan decides on the following goals and action steps for his self-contract:

> *Goal:* To improve my grade point average during the next nine-week grading period from a 1.9 to a 2.9.

> *Action Steps:* To take assigned reading home from school and read completed assignments.

Additionally, he completes a reinforcement survey such as the one presented on p. 253 and selects eight potential rewards he could use daily for completion of each of these two action steps. (Recall that in self-reward, it is important for clients to select rewards that can be used frequently and immediately following the desired behavior.) Additionally, Juan includes a "bonus clause" in his self-contract which specifies an additional reward to be used weekly. Juan's self-contract is illustrated in Figure 9-2.

After completing the terms of the contract, the counselor emphasizes that Juan will need to use the rewards each time he actually completes an action step—but only if the action step is completed as specified in the contract. The counselor also emphasizes that Juan can vary choice of rewards from the ones listed in the contract and should avoid using the same reward each day. Juan and the counselor also agree to review the terms of the contract in two weeks to see if the contract is realistic and workable, at which time it would also be important to build in some new rewards to prevent satiation.

The counselor also explains how Juan can use self-monitoring to keep track of his progress on the action steps and to strengthen his commitment to work toward his goal. The counselor suggests that Juan use a daily log to record completion of each action step and the specific reward Juan chose to use for successful completion of each action step. The counselor also discusses whether Juan wants to use any outside source to verify completion of the tasks. Juan decides to use himself to verify completion of reading assignments but suggests he might be more motivated to do his homework if it had to be checked and verified by some other source. Juan and the counselor decide to have the teachers who give a homework assignment verify Juan's completion of it on his log whenever he turns the assignment in. The counselor asks Juan to come back with his completed log sheet at the end of the first week. The log Juan presented at the end of Week 1 is shown in Figure 9-3.

Name of person making contract _____

Date of contract _____ April 1, 1987

Goals of Contract: To improve my grade point average during the (target behavior) next nine-week period from 1.9 to 2.9 (criterion level)

Action Steps:
1. To take assigned reading home from school and read assignments
2. To complete daily homework assignments

Bonus: If at the end of each school week I have completed all assigned reading and homework, I will go to a game, a concert, or movie on the weekend.

Rewards:
1. Go out with the guys an extra 30 minutes.
2. Watch a sports event on TV.
3. Listen to my favorite music an extra 30 minutes.
4. Go out and get a pizza.
5. Work out at the gym.
6. Buy a new record or tape.
7. Relax—loaf—do nothing for an hour
8. Talk on the phone to a friend.

Date contract will be reviewed _____ April 15, 1987

Signatures: _____ Juan P. (client)

_____ Mrs. Henry (counselor)

Figure 9–2

Name _____ Juan P. _____

Behavior being observed:

1. _____ Completion of assigned reading _____

2. _____ Completion of assigned homework _____

Verification Sources: Juan (#1)

Teachers (#2)

Week	Date	Behavior	Rewards Used	Verified by
1	April 2	Complete reading assignments in English.	TV—sports	1. Juan
		Complete homework in math and science.	Phone	2. J.W., math teacher 3. A.P., science teacher
1	April 3	Complete reading assignments in English.	New record	1. Juan
		Complete homework in math.	Listen to music	2. J.W., math teacher
1	April 4	Complete reading assignments in social studies.	TV—sports	1. Juan
		Complete homework in science.	Relax-loaf	2. A.P., science teacher
1	April 5	Complete reading assignments in English.	Workout-gym	1. Juan
		Complete homework in math and science.	Pizza	2. J.W., math teacher 3. A.P., science teacher

Figure 9–3

Juan continues to engage in self-monitoring and review his log with the counselor on a weekly basis. At the end of the first two weeks, they also review the contract terms which Juan finds "manageable." They insert some different rewards into the contract and schedule another review of the contract two weeks later.

Client Reactions to Behavioral Strategies

Behavioral strategies are often very appealing to clients, particularly in initial stages of counseling when clients are "hurting" and want something to be done for them. The specificity, concreteness, and emphasis on action that these interventions offer help clients feel as if something important is being done on their behalf. Even non-behavioral counselors sometimes use a behavioral strategy such as relaxation to capitalize on this phenomenon, which can increase the counselor's credibility with the client and the client's sense of trust that counseling can and will make a difference.

As the helping process continues, some of the clients' initial enchantment with the procedures may wear off as they discover the different and often painful work of changing fixed and established behavior patterns. Successful use of behavioral strategies requires a significant investment of time and energy from clients—daily practice, homework assignments, and so on. Often, too, after sudden spurts of "quick and easy" behavior change, the clients' behavior stabilizes at a certain plateau, and clients can then become easily discouraged about further change attempts.

To counteract these potential pitfalls, counselors who rely heavily on behavioral approaches during the helping process must also generate involvement with the client through a positive therapeutic relationship that attempts to strengthen the client's investment and commitment to action. Additionally, counselors who use behavioral approaches must find ways to strengthen a client's compliance with the demands of the strategy. Compliance can be enhanced in a number of ways, in addition to the use of involvement as mentioned above. Additional techniques for fostering compliance include creating a positive expectancy set, providing detailed instructions about the use and benefits of a strategy, having the client rehearse the strategy, and having the client visualize and explore beneficial aspects of change.

Summary

In this chapter, we described a variety of intervention strategies based upon action-oriented helping approaches such as behavioral counseling and reality therapy. These approaches focus on direct modification of a client's behavior and rely heavily on principles of learning to facilitate behavior change.

The modeling and rehearsal strategies we described are major components of skill training programs such as assertion training, job interview skills training, and social skills training. These strategies are most useful when clients have skill deficits or lack effective skills for selected situations.

Anxiety reduction strategies such as muscle relaxation, sensory relaxation, and systematic desensitization are useful for dealing with the behavioral excess of fear, worry, and anxiety. Muscle relaxation is used as either a single strategy or as a part of systematic desensitization.

Self-management intervention programs are the wave of the future. Clients are put in charge of their change program; the counselor acts as a facilitator of that process. Common components of a self-management program include self-monitoring, self-reward, and self-contracting.

Behavioral approaches are initially very appealing to clients because of their specificity and concreteness. A major problem with continued use of these strategies is to obtain the client's commitment to new and different actions and responses.

Exercises

I. Modeling

Listed below are four hypothetical clients who might derive benefit from a modeling strategy. Based on the description given about each client, select the model that might be most effective for the client. (Feedback follows the chapter exercises.)

1. The client is a black male in a graduate program who is avoiding a required statistics course because of his fear of math.
   a. An older black male who has already made it successfully.
   b. A white male who has overcome his fear of statistics.
   c. A black male about the same age, also enrolled in a graduate program that requires statistics.
2. The client is a young, white, male veteran who lost a leg in combat and is trying to learn to get around in a wheelchair without soliciting assistance from other people.

   a. A female who has been in a wheelchair since birth.
   b. A white male who also is a veteran.
   c. An older white male who is successfully employed.

3. The client is a middle-aged woman who is enrolled in a special treatment program because she is an alcoholic.
   a. Another middle-aged woman who has successfully overcome alcoholism through this program.
   b. Another woman who is also an alcoholic.
   c. The woman's husband or a close relative.

4. The client is a young woman who is institutionalized in a state hospital because she has refused to go out of her house, believing that people were after her.
   a. Another institutionalized patient who is in the pre-release program.
   b. A staff psychiatrist.
   c. A female staff aide.

II. Behavior Rehearsal

With a partner, try out the process of behavior rehearsal. One of you should take the client's role, and the other can assume the role of the helper. Have the client present a problem in which the desired change is to acquire a skill or to extinguish a fear. The counselor should try out the behavior rehearsal strategy to help the client meet this goal. Here are the things to remember to do:

1. Specify the target behavior(s).
2. Determine the situations in which the skills need to be used or the fear needs to be reduced.
3. Arrange these situations on a hierarchy, starting with the least difficult or least anxiety-producing situations and gradually moving up to situations of greater difficulty, complexity, or threat.
4. Beginning with the first situation on the hierarchy, have the client engage in covert rehearsal of the target response(s). Following this practice attempt, ask the client to analyze it.
5. Using the same situation, have the client engage in a role-play (overt) rehearsal. Give the client feedback about the strengths and limitations of this practice. Supplement your feedback with an audiotape or videotape analysis, as feasible.
6. Determine when the client has satisfactorily demonstrated the target skills or reduced anxiety within the interview rehearsals. Assign homework consisting of *in vivo* rehearsal of this one situation.
7. Repeat Steps 4 through 6 for the other situations on the hierarchy.

III. Relaxation

Using triads or small groups, practice providing muscle relaxation training for someone in the group. You can utilize the instructions found on pp. 234–236 as a guide. After the procedure, obtain feedback both from your role-play "client" and from observers. Some of the items you may wish to solicit feedback about include:

    a. Your voice—pitch, tempo, volume

    b. The pacing or speed with which you took the person through the procedure

    c. The clarity of your instructions

After you have practiced with this strategy and received feedback from another person, you may want to put the instructions for muscle relaxation on an audiotape and critique it yourself.

IV. Systematic Desensitization

    Instructions:

        1. Match each of the client descriptions listed below with the type of hierarchy that would be most appropriate to use with that particular client. Explain your choice. Be sure to give a rationale for your choice. (Feedback is given following the chapter exercises.)

        2. Pick one of the client descriptions from this list and develop a corresponding hypothetical hierarchy for the client. Consult with a colleague or instructor after your hierarchy is completed.

    Type of Hierarchy

        a. Spatio-Temporal

        b. Thematic

        c. Personal

    Client Descriptions

    _ 1. The client is very stressed after the recent dissolution of a five-year relationship.

    _ 2. The client becomes increasingly anxious about a speech as the time of the speech draws closer.

    _ 3. The client becomes anxious in situations that involve other people.

    _ 4. The client becomes more anxious as she gets farther away from her house.

    _ 5. The client is very upset after the death of her spouse two years ago.

V. Self-Management

This exercise is designed to help you modify some aspect of your helping behavior with the use of a self-management program.

1. Select and define a behavior you wish to increase or decrease that, when changed, will make you a better helper. The behavior may be an overt one, such as using more silence or asking open questions instead of closed questions. Or the behavior may be covert, such as reducing the number of apprehensive thoughts about seeing clients or increasing some self-enhancing thoughts about your helping potential.
2. Record the occurrence of the behavior for a week or two to obtain a baseline measure; the baseline gives you the present level of the behavior before applying any self-management strategies.
3. After obtaining some baseline data, deliberately try to increase or decrease the behavior (depending on your goal) using self-monitoring. Remember: pre-behavior monitoring to decrease a response and post-behavior monitoring to increase a response. Do this for about two weeks. Does the behavior change over time in the desired direction? If so, you may want to continue with self-monitoring for a few weeks. Charting and posting the data will help you see visible progress.
4. You may want to augment any behavior change produced by self-monitoring with self-reward or self-contracting. Work out a self-reward plan or write out a self-contract.
5. Continue to self-record the occurrence of the behavior during Step 4; then compare these data with the data you gathered during baseline (Step 2). What changes occurred?
6. How did your use of self-management affect this helping behavior?

Feedback for Exercises

I. Modeling

1. Probably the best choice would be C. This model would be similar to the client in race, age, sex, and educational goals.
2. We would choose B, who, even though he is not in a wheelchair, is similar to the client in race, sex, age, and can identify with the cause of the client's disability, since he is also a veteran.
3. Model A, who is similar to the client in age, race, sex, and problem.
4. Model A, who is similar to the client in terms of patient status, but who has been able to deal with the problems to the point of being near release from the institution.

IV. Systematic Desensitization

1. The most appropriate hierarchy for this client is C (Personal), because the client is dealing with the effects of a loss.
2. The most appropriate hierarchy for this client is A (Spatio-temporal), with time as the significant dimension because the client's anxiety becomes greater as the time for the speech gets closer.
3. The most useful hierarchy for this client is B (Thematic), because the client's social anxiety varies with the context surrounding other persons.
4. The most useful hierarchy for this client is A (Spatio-temporal), with distance as the significant dimension, because the client's anxiety becomes greater as the distance from her home increases.
5. The most appropriate hierarchy for this client is C (Personal), because the client is dealing with the effects of a significant loss.

Discussion Questions

1. Behavioral approaches assume that much maladaptive behavior is acquired through learning. What is your reaction to this assumption?

2. In what ways does learning occur through counseling?

3. In using behavioral approaches with clients, to what extent do you think that you are treating real problems or merely symptoms?

Recommended Readings

Cormier, W. H., & Cormier, L.S., (1991), *Interviewing Strategies for Helpers: Fundamental Skills and Cognitive-Behavioral Interventions*, 3rd ed., (Pacific Grove, CA: Brooks/Cole).

Eisler, R.M., & Fredericksen, L.W. (1980), *Perfecting Social Skills: A Guide to Interpersonal Behavior Development* (New York: Plenum).

Fremouw, W.J., & Brown, J.P., Jr. (1980), "The Reactivity of Addictive Behaviors to Self-Monitoring: A Functional Analysis," *Addictive Behaviors* 5, 209–217.

Glasser, W. (1976), *Positive Addiction* (New York: Harper & Row).

Heffernan, T., & Richards, C.S. (1981), "Self-Control of Study Behavior: Identification and Evaluation of Natural Methods," *Journal of Counseling Psychology* 28, 361–364.

Kanfer, F.H., & Goldstein, A.P., Eds. (1980), *Helping People Change*, 2nd ed. (New York: Pergamon Press).

Karoly, P., & Kanfer, F.A., Eds. (1982), *Self-Management and Behavior Change* (New York: Pergamon Press).

Lazarus, A.A. (1981), *The Practice of Multimodal Therapy* (New York: McGraw-Hill).

Rimm, D.C., & Masters, J.C. (1979), *Behavior Therapy: Techniques and Empirical Findings*, 2nd ed. (New York: Academic Press).

Watson, D.L., & Tharp, R.G. (1981). *Self-Directed Behavior: Self-Modification for Personal Adjustment*, 3rd ed., (Pacific Grove, CA: Brooks/Cole).

Williams, R.L., & Long, J.D. (1983), *Toward a Self-Managed Lifestyle*, 3rd ed., (Boston: Houghton-Mifflin).

Wolpe, J. (1982), *The Practice of Behavior Therapy* (New York: Pergamon Press).

10

System Interventions

The past ten years have witnessed a maturing of the systems therapy movement. Its roots are in the 1950s, when Bateson was first conducting his studies of the treatment of schizophrenia. Stimulated by Bateson's early thinking, the next twenty years witnessed an explosion of new concepts on the functioning of the family. These concepts have begun to crystallize into four recognizable schools of family therapy: the *object relations* school which includes writers such as Framo (1982) and Zuk (1975); the *family systems* school, represented by Bowen (1978); the *structural family therapy* school, identified in the writings of Minuchin and Fishman (1981); and the *strategic intervention* school, a ranging group of scholars that includes the Mental Research Institute of Palo Alto (MRI) group (Weakland, Fisch, Watzlawick and Bodin, 1974; Jackson, 1961; Haley, 1963; 1973; 1976); the Milan *systemic therapy* school (Palazzoli, Cecchin, Prata, and Boscolo, 1978), and the *Nathan W. Ackerman Institute* group who strongly reflect the Milan approach (Hoffman, 1981). These four groups reflect a theoretical continuum that extends from a highly psychoanalytic basis (object relations) to an ecological basis (Foley, 1989). All four schools occupy prominent social positions in the practice of marriage and family therapy in the United States today. Common to each of these approaches is the concept of the family as a system.

Interpersonal Systems Thinking

The fundamental notion of interpersonal systems can be likened to ecological systems in which all elements are interrelated, and in which change at any level of those interrelated parts will lead to alteration of the total system.

Thus, the family that seeks change through family therapy may be affected by interventions at almost any point. Beyond this most fundamental notion, there are other systemic issues that arise and affect the progress of therapy.

Cohesive interpersonal systems develop a self-sustaining quality. The integral parts (members) of the system seek to maintain the system, even when the system is failing to meet the needs of individual members. Thus, the family in therapy is, at the same time, seeking change and resisting change.

Dysfunctional systems tend to develop rigid boundaries. The psychological boundaries that define the family (separate the family from other social units, for example, neighbors) identify and sustain the family unit. Because dysfunctional families experience greater vulnerability, the systemic tendency is to become more rigid and resistant to change. Thus, the dysfunctional family finds change to be more difficult to accomplish than the family with more flexible boundaries.

The internal organization of the cohesive system is defined by systemic "rules." Systemic rules are a euphemism for interactions between individual members so predictable that one might think a rule exists to govern the behavior. An example might be the manner in which the father reenters the family system each evening (no one is to disturb him until he has had time to read his paper or drink a beer) or the manner in which a particular child is disciplined (only the mother may discipline Billy). Such rules contribute to the family's tendency to sustain the system. When rules are broken, the violator may be dealt with by the entire system or by a designated enforcer. For example, if the father is an incorrigible grouch, family rules will evolve that attempt to control those stimuli that will put him in a bad mood. Strong pressure will be exerted on maverick family members to keep them from breaking the rules that might lead to father's bad temper.

These brief illustrations suggest that the family functions as an integral system. When therapeutic treatment is sought, the counselor must make the decision either to treat family members individually, or to treat the family as a system. When treating the system, the counselor's conceptual approach must reflect an awareness of governing rules, structure, and other ecological factors. For this reason, systemic therapy has evolved by using traditional interventions in new ways or by developing new kinds of interventions that are more effective with system change.

The major portion of this book has addressed counseling interventions in an individual context. By increasing the number of individuals involved in any intervention, interpersonal dynamics (current and historical) becomes a significant dimension of the therapy process. This fact has led to the emergence of communications approaches. Furthermore, the fact that family system rigidity is related to the group's level of dysfunction has caused theorists to search for more effective interventions. Thus, the structural and strategic approaches have emerged. The first of these, *structural therapy*, has focused on redefining the system by altering interpersonal rules and boundaries. The second, *strategic therapy*, has developed cognitive interventions to a high level.

In this chapter we shall explain how many individual interventions are also adaptable and effective in achieving better communication, structural change, and strategic change. In addition, attention will be directed to systemic interventions that are associated with the newer family approaches.

Altering Communication Patterns

Family or group dysfunctions may be approached from different directions. Sometimes the underlying issue appears to be a fundamental misunderstanding among members. This misunderstanding may relate to members' expectations, roles, or responsibilities. When communication appears either to have broken down or fails due to lack of communication skills, the counselor may use a variety of interventions to teach or develop insight among family or group members. Nichols (1984) has observed that most of the techniques used by communications family therapy consist of teaching rules of clear communication, analyzing and interpreting communicational patterns, and manipulating interactions through a variety of strategic maneuvers.

Communication Skill-Building

Often communication skill-building begins with an introduction to basic rules of communication. These "rules" are really guidelines to sending and receiving clear and concise messages. Gestalt therapy, reality therapy, and rational emotive therapy all emphasize these rules. In addition, the work of Jackson and Weakland (1961) and programs such as the Minnesota Couples Communication Program have contributed to communication rules training. Effective communications rules are fairly simple. They include: (a) speaking in the first person singular; (b) speaking for self; and (c) speaking directly to the person for whom the communication is intended.

These "simple" rules often prove to be rather difficult to master, particularly when they run counter to the individual's habitual patterns of communication. Consequently, the acquisition of a new pattern may require instruction, rehearsal, evaluation, and continued practice. (These elements of skill training are discussed in Chapter 9.) For example, some people develop a communication style in which the personal pronoun "I" is almost never used. In its place, the impersonal second person (you) or the collective (people) is used. This is illustrated by a brief dialogue between Bob and his wife, Janet.

Janet: Bob, are you going to cut the grass tomorrow?

Bob: You know people don't cut the grass on Sunday.

Janet: Well, I just thought it would be good to cut it before Monday.

Bob: Well, that's just not what one does on Sunday.

The counselor might point out to Bob that when he uses such referents as "people" and "one," he is speaking in terms that Miller, Nunnally, and Wackman (1975) call *underresponsible.* This notion of underresponsible communication is the same as the Gestaltist notion of *claiming ownership.* In other words, if Bob were to say, "You know I don't cut the grass on Sunday," he would be taking responsibility for the claim rather than attributing it to unknown "people."

Underresponsible communication is a style. It does not necessarily reflect an intention to avoid responsibility, although it can. The counselor might work with Bob and Janet to increase Bob's awareness both of his style and the consequences of his style.

Counselor: Bob, when you say, "People don't cut the grass on Sunday," aren't you also saying "I don't cut the grass on Sunday?"

Bob: Right.

Counselor: What would happen if you just said, "I don't want to cut the grass on Sunday?"

Bob: Nothing, I guess. Maybe Janet wouldn't understand why.

Counselor: Could you tell her why if she didn't understand?

Bob: Yeah, I guess so.

Counselor: Why don't you tell Janet why you don't want to cut the grass?

Bob: O.K. I don't want to cut the grass on Sunday because I don't think it looks good to the neighbors.

Counselor: Janet, is it different when Bob says it that way?

Janet: Yes, I like it better when Bob tells me what he is thinking, but I think it is silly to feel that way.

The third other type of communication style is the *indirect message.* Janet answered the counselor's question and then added her opinion of Bob's view by saying, "I think it is silly to feel that way." By tacking this opinion onto her answer, she is actually communicating to Bob *through the counselor.* Speaking directly to the person for whom the communication is intended is responsible communication. When the message is made through another person (children, friend, neighbor), the communicator is, once again, using an underresponsible style. In this case, the counselor might turn to Janet and say:

Counselor: Janet, you answered my question, and then you said something to me that Bob needed to hear.

Janet: What do you mean?

Counselor: You told me your opinion of Bob's reason for not cutting grass on Sunday. I think you really wanted Bob to hear your opinion. Is that right?

Janet: Well, yes, I guess so.

Counselor: Then turn to Bob and tell him.

Janet: He already knows now. (*Janet resists being responsible.*)

Counselor: I know, but this is just for practice.

Janet: I don't think you need to worry about what the neighbors think. They all work on Sunday.

At this point, the counselor interrupts the dialogue to review what was happening in the two communication styles and how underresponsible styles lead to ambiguity, confusion and frustration. This is the teaching time and is as important as the rehearsal. During this time, the counselor can appraise each person's style, the consequences of that style, and its apparent effect on the other person. Sometimes the lesson is enhanced by asking the participants to exaggerate their underresponsible style (be even more under-responsible!).

One particularly common communication problem that becomes evident in counseling is what Fogarty (1976) has labeled the "distancer/pursuer" system. This dynamic emerges over time when one partner pursues and the other distances or avoids communicating. This systemic issue is illustrated in a case described by Bernard and Hackney (1983, pp. 52-53).

Case Illustration of Distancer/Pursuer: The Case of Sheila and Eric

Eric was attracted to Sheila because she was outgoing and fun. Since he was somewhat shy, he admired this friendly quality in her. Sheila found Eric attractive because he was "the strong, silent type." She also liked his gentleness, which made him different from many of the men she had dated. After a year of dating, they were married. They both felt they had found a mate who would complement them, someone who would bring out new things in themselves.

After a year, Sheila found herself edgy with Eric when they went to social gatherings. Although he wished to be friendly, he still acted aloof and distant. At home they also seemed to have "stuck" at an intermediate level of closeness. Eric didn't offer all the information Sheila wanted. He didn't think to tell her about little details at work, funny things that happened. In an attempt to open him up, she would ask questions and more questions. Eric was not comfortable with what felt like an intrusion on his privacy. He wished Sheila were more like him. He was also beginning to feel that Sheila thought he was inadequate.

Ten years later, the scene looks quite different. Sheila is belligerent about her husband's quietness. "You never tell me anything. You don't want me in your world. What do you think it is like to live with a stranger?" Eric has become totally withdrawn. Sheila's role is to nag. Eric's role is to hide.

Eric, and Sheila's communication difficulties are a product of personal qualities each brought into the marriage. They are complicated and intensified by the couple's lack of awareness of the systemic and personal issues that are involved. Sensitizing Eric and Sheila to the systemic issues will address part of the problem. This may be accomplished by pointing out the pattern and helping them see that it is not Eric's withdrawal or Sheila's demands but the interaction of their unique characteristics.

Awareness should also be focused on interpersonal qualities, since partial awareness of one's needs, motives, or intentions is a frequent source of miscommunication. Miller, Nunnally, and Wackman (1975, p. 31) use an exercise they call the Awareness

Wheel to help couples become aware of these interpersonal patterns. Each communicated message has five stages of development. The first stage is *sensing*, or receiving data into awareness (for example, awareness of discomfort). Stage two *is thinking* about that data (Why am I uncomfortable? What is the source?). The third stage, *feeling*, involves affective processing of the cognitive processes of stage two (How do I feel about being made uncomfortable by that?). In the fourth stage, *intentions*, the individual determines what should be done to respond to the thought and feeling stages (What do I want to change? How should things be?). In the final stage, the individual reaches the level of *action* (What am I going to do?). This is a circular sequence, with the action stage leading back into the sensing stage and beginning the process all over again. (It might help you to draw these stages out in a circular pattern with arrows pointing from each stage to the next.)

This procedure can be used with couples as a means for analyzing each person's communication process. Typically, one or more stages is either weak or missing entirely from the process. The counselor can ask partners to select a topic and use the five stages to organize their messages. For example:

Sensing: I sense that you are irritated.
Thinking: This makes me wonder if I did something to make you mad.
Feeling: I'm nervous and uncomfortable with that thought.
Intending: I would like for you to be friendly and warm.
Acting: I will ask you if I did something to upset you. If I did, I will apologize. If I didn't, I will ask what I could do to make your day more pleasant.

An insecure person might be highly sensitive (stage one) and unaware of the thinking or feeling stages. On the other hand, the spouse might be action-oriented (stage five) but relatively unaware of stages one and three. In such an example, neither partner could communicate effectively until they were able to identify internal dimensions of their messages. First, one must know the message, and then it can be communicated.

Accurate and responsible communication is only half the goal of good communication patterns. If a message is responsibly and clearly sent, but the receiver does not comprehend, then communication has failed. This may happen if the message is too threatening or if the receiver is preoccupied or otherwise blocked from perceiving the intent of the message. The person trying to communicate the message cannot know this without some feedback from the receiver. In other words, the communicator must know if the receiver (a) hears, and (b) hears accurately, what is being said. Miller, Nunnally, and Wackman (1975) refer to this as a "shared meaning," and they have developed a communication exercise for partners to use whenever they believe miscommunication is occurring. The shared-meaning exercise is a conversation in slow motion. The communicator is asked to phrase a communication (restricting it to not more than two or three parts). After stating the message, the communicator asks, "What did you hear me saying?" The receiver tries to repeat the elements of the communication and asks, "Is that what you meant to say?" If the message was perceived accurately, the communicator adds whatever is required to complete the message. If the message was perceived inaccurately, then the communicator corrects the misperception and proceeds.

Not all communication problems are caused by underresponsible patterns, of course. Very often, the problem has an interpersonal dimension which has developed over time. As a result of her past frustrations, a wife may have come to the conclusion that her husband does not care to communicate. This may cause her to assume a defensive stance when she needs to communicate. Whether or not her perception is accurate, by communicating defensively, she elicits a certain kind of response from her husband. This response, which is in part due to her approach, may give her further reason to think she is right. Such a sequence of events is referred to as systemic. In other words, the couple are locked into a systemic pattern that always leads to a predictable outcome. The counselor must recognize when poor communication is a systemic problem and develop an intervention that addresses the systemic issue rather than the communication issue. This can be done by observing how the couple interact in the session, identifying patterns and intervening in the pattern development. But if the problem is unique to the home environment, the best means for observation is to ask the couple to enact a typical encounter by role-playing.

Role-Playing

Role-play or role-enactment has already been discussed in Chapter 7 as a useful intervention in individual counseling. It is also used in working with families when a particular event or experience must be "relived" in order to be more real. Thus, the therapist may decide to ask a family member to enact a problematic encounter or to enact the role of another family member. This provides an immediate stimulus to which family members can react. It gives the counselor an opportunity to observe sequences and can lead to discussion of individual perceptions of the family system, individual differences, or conflicting loyalties.

Family members may be surprised by the content that is provoked in role-plays. Often they are able to see the other person's point of view more easily through an enactment than by having the person discuss viewpoints. Role-play also allows the counselor to intervene, ask why the scene develops as it does, and offer alternative patterns the couple might try when they become locked into a sequence of events.

Negotiation

Many families find negotiation and decision making to be a time when communication is most likely to break down. In family therapy, negotiation is an ongoing process that involves both therapy process issues and family issues. Consequently, the therapy setting provides an ideal opportunity for the counselor to observe family negotiation skills and to provide strategies the family can use to improve communication and negotiation.

Gottman, Notarius, Gonso, & Markman (1976, pp. 62-63) have developed an exercise that will help build negotiation skills.

Called the Family Meeting, the exercise is divided into three parts: (a) gripe time, (b) agenda building, and (c) problem solving. The counselor should preface the exercise by explaining that all family members can have gripes and resentments and that these gripes are viewpoints rather than truths. They are the way the individual views the moment, the situation, or the relationship. They can change, and if ignored, they can get worse. It is important that each person's viewpoint be respected and aired. The counselor can help ensure each person's cooperation by introducing rules for griping.

DO'S	DON'TS
Do state clearly and specifically the gripes you have about other family members.	Don't try to defend yourself by showing that the other person is wrong.
Do be honest and constructive when you gripe.	Don't sulk and withdraw.
Do listen and accept gripes as legitimate feelings.	Don't respond to gripes with a gripe of your own. Don't assume you know what the other person means; make sure you know.

After all family members have been allowed time to express their gripes (and this may require some encouragement from the counselor), the family moves into the second stage, agenda building. The purpose of agenda building is to evaluate the relative importance of gripes that have been expressed and select one or more that family members believe should be remedied. The counselor is an active arbitrator during this process, helping family members define specific dimensions of a particular gripe.

Having identified and defined a particular gripe, the family moves into the problem-solving stage. The problem-solving stage is characterized by identification of positive behaviors that will address the complaint(s) and the writing of a contract that (1) specifies behaviors each family member will change, and (2) specifies incentives designed to increase the frequency of desired behaviors.

Altering Family Structure

Family structure refers to the patterns of interaction, the rules and roles that emerge to support these patterns, and the alliances that result from these rules and roles. All structure begins with family transactions which, when repeated, become patterns. As interaction patterns become well established, they begin to dictate how, when, and with whom family members will interact. For example, a young child falls, skins his knee, and runs to mother for comfort. As this scene repeats itself over and over again, a nurturing alliance forms between mother and child. Thus, mother assumes a nurturant (role) posture and the child learns to seek mother when hurt (rule). The alliance between mother and child defines a subsystem within the family.

All families have subsystems which are determined by interaction patterns, rules, roles, and alliances. The spousal subsystem is the obvious beginning point. When the first child is born, two things happen. The spousal subsystem accommodates a new parental subsystem, and mother-child and father-child subsystems emerge. Subsystems become differentiated from one another by boundaries. Additional children, grandparents, and other family relatives develop alliances within the larger family structure to the point that many subsystems emerge, with individuals occupying significant roles within more than one subsystem. There is a random as well as systematic dimension to the development of family structure. Consequently, families are often at a loss to explain how certain rules or subsystems became so powerful or how they could be changed.

Recognizing the powerful impact structure has on family functioning, a group of family therapists began working with the structure. Significant among these therapists were Salvador Minuchin, Braulio Montalvo, and Jay Haley. They developed a scenario for working with the family based on five basic goals for the counseling process:

1. Joining with the family
2. Generating and observing the interaction
3. Diagnosing the family structure
4. Identifying and modifying interactions
5. Reconstructing boundaries

These goals are accomplished through a variety of techniques and interventions, some of which require family cooperation and others of which are therapist manipulations.

Joining with the Family

The first of these objectives, *joining,* refers to social identification with each family member. This is accomplished in a number of small but significant ways: addressing each member by name; shaking hands with each member (including even the smallest); touching the baby; and so forth. This individual and personal contact is seen as quite important to the later process of therapy, since each family member has been given a personal acknowledgment by the therapist. Nichols notes that:

> It is particularly important to join powerful family members as well as angry ones. Special pains must be taken to accept the point of view of the father who thinks therapy is hooey, or of the angry teenager who feels like a hunted criminal. It is also important to reconnect with such people at frequent intervals, particularly as things begin to heat up in later sessions. (1984, p. 491)

Joining does not mean that the therapist is catering to powerful family members. Rather, it means that the therapist is acknowledging all family members, all of the time, even when a particular member's effect may be negative.

Generating and Observing Interactions

After the family has been joined (in the first session and in succeeding sessions), the therapist turns to the task of setting up and observing family interactions. One of the real benefits of working with family units is that they allow the therapist the opportunity to observe them in realistic interactions (as opposed to the individual client who must report interactions). Some interactions are totally spontaneous sequences that emerge when the family is dealing with a current issue. Since spontaneous interactions may not develop, the therapist must help the family become involved in interactions that are representative. One of the first of these is the physical alignment the family displays at the beginning of each session.

Recognizing Physical Alignments

Prior to each session, the therapist arranges a sufficient number of chairs in a circle. As family members enter the room, they are encouraged to sit where they wish. The therapist observes closely who chooses to sit by whom, what kind of negotiation occurs when two members want the same chair, or who moves chairs (increasing or decreasing distance). This early expression of family dynamics frequently is the metaphor for the family's dysfunctioning system.

As the session progresses and subsystems become more apparent through interactions, the therapist may ask specific family members to exchange chairs, thus physically altering a boundary separating subsystems. Or if the therapist senses that the family has excluded a member, he or she may physically move to sit beside that excluded member, again realigning the dynamics of the therapy scene. As therapy progresses in later sessions, family members become aware of this realignment activity and begin to realize that such alterations do change the dynamics of the family interaction.

Using the Family Genogram

One of the better ways of helping the family recognize its intergenerational structure is the genogram, a type of diagram. The intervention uses the symbols to represent family members, typically over three generations (see Figure 10-1). The intervention begins by explaining to family members how the genogram is drawn, and then proceeding to draw the family's genogram with their assistance.

FIGURE 10-1   The Family Genogram

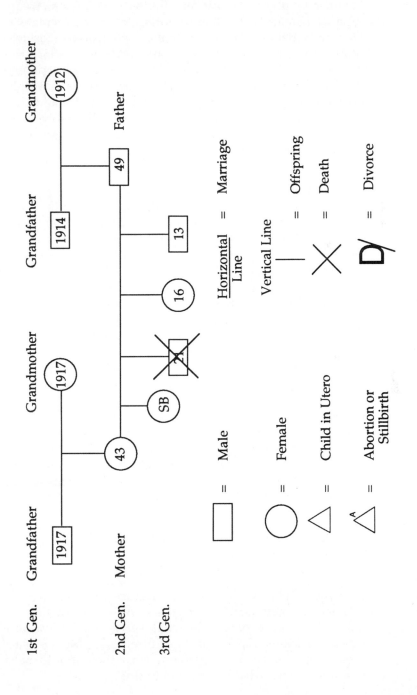

Once the genogram has been drawn, you may use it to examine the other pertinent facts about the interrelationship of family members, including "physical location of family members, frequency and type of contact, emotional cutoffs, issues that create conflict of anxiety, nodal events, and degree of openness or closeness" among family members (Sherman and Fredman, 1986, p. 83). This discussion yields a "family history" as well as a pictoral format. Both may be used to help family members gain insight into the family's functioning, to repair cutoffs, and to make adjustments in organizational patterns. The genogram is probably most used by counselors of a Bowenian orientation, but is a useful intervention for all schools of family therapy.

Family Sculpture

Family sculpture (Duhl, Kantor, & Duhl, 1973) also provides diagnostic insights and generates family awareness of perceptions, structure, and sequences. Perhaps a better label would be family choreography (Papp, 1976) because the exercise calls for one family member to choreograph family members' involvement with one another in a typical scene. It can be used to enact current family sequences or to reenact scenes from the past. Through family sculpture or choreography, family members are "placed" both in activities and spatial relationship to one another. As the director (the family member who is choreographing the scene) assigns, moves or directs interactions, all family members respond both to the direction and to the director's perceptions of their interactive relationships.

In the family therapy case of Bob and Jeannette, the therapist used family sculpting as a means to generate awareness of each spouse's perceptions of their problem. The situation that was selected for enactment was the end-of-day scene in which father and mother each arrived home from work.

Case Illustration of Family Sculpture:
The Case of Bob and Jeannette

Therapist: Bob, I'd like you to produce the scene at home when you and Jeannette arrive from work. We'll assume the kids are also home. Place each person in whatever is the typical activity they would be doing. Do this without discussion. Merely place them in a particular space, and tell them what they should be doing. Do you understand what I want you to do?

Bob: I'm not sure. Do I just say, "Jeannette, you yell at the kids or something like that?"

Therapist: If that is what Jeannette typically does, yes. And then go on to tell the kids what they should be doing.

Bob: O.K. Jeannette, you are sitting in the living room with a martini. Tommy (seven years old), you are downstairs watching cartoons with Karen (nine years old). Then Tommy, you and Karen come to the living room when I arrive home. After I sit down with Mommy, you start talking and demanding attention. Mommy and I try to have a conversation, but you won't let us.

Therapist: O.K. everyone, act out that scene that Bob just described.

The family members begin to act out their parts. Just as Bob sits down and begins to talk to Jeannette, Tommy comes in to ask Mom a question. Bob waits until Jeannette answers, at which time Tommy asks another question. Enter Karen, who proceeds to tell Mom that Tommy ate all the potato chips. Mom responds, and it becomes obvious that Jeannette and the children are the focal unit. Bob, trying to look patient, asks the children to return to their activities so he and Mom can talk. The children leave and Jeannette turns to Bob and tells him that the children need some parent time after being away from them all day. Bob responds impatiently that he needs some "spouse" time and accuses her of not noticing that.

Diagnosing the Family Structure

In the discussion that followed this scene, Jeannette and Bob discussed their reactions. Jeannette was somewhat surprised that Bob was wanting relationship time with her but was unable to have it because the kids were intervening. She indicated that such interventions didn't bother her as much as they apparently bothered Bob. Instead, she had been presuming that his reactions to her (this scene was a common one in their home) were merely reflecting a bad day at work. Bob, on the other hand, thought Jeannette understood his relationship needs but was opting to take care of the children. He assumed that her choice was in reaction to feeling guilty that she had been away from the kids all day. As they discussed their individual perceptions, each became aware of the other's needs, motivations, and misperceptions. Throughout this type of interaction, the counselor also observes and watches for ways the couple might sabotage their negotiations

This diagnosing involves the recognition of dysfunctional sequences and the behaviors that maintain the sequences. It also includes recognition of boundaries and how they are creating or sustaining problematic behavior sequences. Diagnosing family interactions does not involve specific therapeutic interventions. However, Minuchin has developed a "family blueprint" which allows the counselor to diagram family boundaries. This approach is discussed at length in *Families and Family Therapy* (Minuchin, 1974). The reader who wishes to develop family diagnostic skills would want to include Minuchin's work.

Identifying and Modifying Interactions

Having determined what sequences appear to be maintaining the dysfunctional interactions, the structural family counselor proceeds to bring the family's attention to the sequence. This calls for *intensifying* the interaction such that family members cannot ignore or avoid the issue.

Intensification   Minuchin (1974, p. 310) provides an example of intensification while working with the family of an anorexic girl. In the dialogue, the daughter (Loretta) has accused her mother of being too money conscious, and the mother responds:

Mother: Sophia tells me, "Don't do these things. You're killing yourself." Now you, Loretta, you tell me this, see? How many aspirin? I'll get them for you, because when you get nervous, you stop eating. Right away, no food. Not get up from the bed. You don't want to see nobody. You don't want to talk to nobody. And Mama cries.

(Therapist insists on conflict)

Minuchin: Is your mother saying that you are blackmailing them?

Loretta: That's not— . . .

(Therapist increases stress between mother and daughter)

Minuchin: That's what she's saying. She's saying that you are controlling her by having temper tantrums and not eating.

This style of intensifying conflict keeps family members to the task of resolving old issues rather than their typical style of brushing up against the issue and then retreating from it.

Confrontation Another way in which the therapist modifies interaction sequences is through confrontation and direction. In the following example, the parents are attempting to deal with a three-year-old child who is throwing a temper tantrum. The therapist is observing and eventually intervening.

Mother: Janice, please settle down or we are going to have to spank you. *(Janice wails louder.)*

Father: Janice, you heard what your mother said. *(Mother places Janice on her lap and begins to soothe her. Janice continues to wail and resist. Father turns to the therapist and shrugs.)*

Therapist: Aren't you going to do anything? Are you just going to let her continue to disrupt us?

Father: What should we do?

Therapist: You tell me. You're the parent. *(Father turns to mother, who tries to soothe Janice.)*

Therapist: Well, do something.

Father: (to mother) Let me have her. *(Mother hands Janice over to father.)*

Father: Janice, stop now or you will have to go to the other room (waiting room). *(Janice doesn't stop.)*

Therapist: (to mother) Does he really mean that he will send her away until she stops?

Mother: I don't know.

(Father carries Janice to waiting room and returns. Janice wails for five minutes.)

Mother: Don't you think we should go check on her?

Father: I don't know.

Therapist: She can't hurt herself out there.

Father: Right, she's just mad.

In this interaction, the therapist is forcing the parents to confront the issue. Mother attempts to intervene, and father withdraws. The therapist turns to father and challenges him to stay involved. Father becomes involved by threatening the child with removal, but then does not follow through. At that point the therapist increases the tension by asking mother if father intends to do what he threatened. This confronts father, and he follows through. The parents then begin to waver as daughter turns up the intensity from the other room. The therapist assures them that the daughter is really all right, and they regain their resolve to "win."

The process of identifying and modifying interactions is one way in which the therapist is attempting to alter the family structure by altering sequences of behavior. A second approach involves the manipulation of subsystem boundaries.

Reconstructing Boundaries   As the therapist works with families, the concept of *family identity* becomes increasingly apparent. Families develop qualities that define their internal structure and interdependent characteristics. One family may be so cohesive that individual identities are relegated to a low priority, while the total family unit is elevated to the highest priority. In such a family, often referred to as *enmeshed*, group activities are emphasized over individual activities, the welfare of the family unit is emphasized over the individual, the group "will" is more important. (Minuchin illustrated this by squeezing the teenage daughter's wrist and asking how many family members feel the pain. All but one raised their hands, and that person was apologetic for not feeling the pain.)

Family enmeshment is one end of a family organization continuum. The other end of the continuum is represented by the *disengaged* family. In disengagement, family members have little or no connection to one another. The family group identity is deemphasized, and individualization is held supreme. In the disengaged family, members' activities are planned without consultation or consideration of other family members. Group activity is a rare occurrence.

Within the family system, boundaries function to differentiate between subsystems. Thus, in normal families boundaries allow members to function in appropriate roles and to interact with other subsystems. But families can generate many different types of subsystems, and often these subsystems exist to maintain a dysfunctional situation. For example, one parent may create an alliance with one or more children that effectively excludes the other parent from decision making or other family functions. In such situations, the therapist may wish to intervene in the system in ways that will reintegrate the excluded parent. This can be done through assignments or through physical manipulation of family spatial arrangements (as discussed under *Family Sculpture*).

The use of assignments in the therapy setting to manipulate subsystem boundaries resembles family sculpture in one respect. For example, if the therapist believes parents are failing to respect the sibling subsystem by interfering or invading the system, the therapist might "invite the invading parents to join the therapist in an observing, 'adult' group 'because children think differently these days than in our time and may have solutions that we couldn't even imagine.'" (Minuchin & Fishman, 1981, p. 149) By creating an "adult observer" group, the therapist has pulled the parents away from the sibling subsystem and assigned them the role of observer. Since one cannot be an effective observer and participant at the same time, the therapist has created a new boundary separating parents from siblings.

The therapist also manipulates the spatial relationships that reflect boundaries between subsystems. It was noted earlier that the therapist may use the seating arrangements in the counseling room as a means of observing how subsystems operate. By moving family members to other chairs, thus altering the spatial arrangements, the therapist also alters the spatial expression of boundaries. For example, imagine a therapy scene in which the clients are a step-family composed of mother, teenage son, and stepfather. The step-family has existed for about twelve months. During this time mother has created an obvious boundary between herself and son, and the stepfather. This may have been done by her insistence on being the disciplining parent. It may be reflected in her sitting between son and stepfather. By moving the stepfather's chair in such a way that he now sits beside stepson, the therapist has made a symbolic intervention into the family system. This intervention can be extended by asking the mother to become an observer of step-father/stepson interactions, thus encouraging these interactions to happen, and removing mother from active involvement.

By altering family structure, the objective is to interrupt habitual and dysfunctional sequences and patterns in such a way that the family must create new patterns. With the therapist's help, these new patterns can be more functional and constructive for family relationships and individual needs.

Working with Families Strategically

The area of strategic family therapy includes a diversified group of family therapists, among whom are Jay Haley, Milton Erickson, Maria Selvini Palazzoli, Lynn Hoffman, Paul Watzlawick, John Weakland, Richard Fisch, and Cloe Madanes. With this variety of major contributors, one might expect the approach to be diffuse; in fact, strategic therapists have a significant core of agreement in their approaches.

By way of comparison with the structural therapy group, strategic therapists emphasize problem definition (including how the family perceives itself and its problems); brief or short-term therapy; interventions that focus upon redefinition of the problem or perception; and interventions that affect sequences outside the session. It should also be said that strategic therapists often use structural interventions, just as structural therapists use strategic interventions.

The term *strategic therapy* was coined by Jay Haley in describing the work of Milton Erickson. Erickson developed "a specific approach to fit whatever the problem at hand ... pragmatic and flexible. He believed that people's problems are unique and infinitely variable. He intervened forcefully to block symptoms and to provoke patients to behave in new, more adaptive ways. He assumed full accountability for what happens in treatment." (Nichols, 1984, p. 427) Haley was one of the first to bring Erickson's work to the attention of professionals.

Another source of strategic thinking was the Brief Therapy Center, part of the Mental Research Institute of Palo Alto, California. Led by Don Jackson, this group came from a communications orientation to change, and it included Richard Fisch, Paul Watzlawick, and John Weakland. They emphasized a close examination of how people tend to conceptualize their problems and how families tend to generate unworkable solutions to those problems; when the solution does not work, the next solution is more of the first solution. The reader will note that many of the interventions used in strategic therapy do not originate in the more traditional individual therapies, nor does the rationale for using interventions have a parallel in most individual approaches.

Preparing for the Intervention

Although the ultimate goal of strategic family therapy is to prescribe an intervention that will cause change, the process leading to that objective is critical if strategic therapy is to work. Joining with each family member is very important, just as it is with structural family therapy. Indeed, family interactions in early sessions will be closely scrutinized by the strategic therapist. Typically, once a brief social interaction has been completed between the therapist and each family member, the therapist sets the stage for counseling. This is similar to what a counselor does in individual counseling: alerting the family to observers for taping; receiving demographic data; having clients sign consent forms. An additional condition set on strategic therapy that is often not part of individual counseling is an agreement that counseling will last a certain number of sessions, usually no more than ten. By definition, strategic therapy is brief therapy.

Defining the problem Because of the limit put on the number of counseling sessions, it is very important that the problem be well defined. In many ways, strategic family therapists mirror a behavioral approach in defining the family's problem. There are four guidelines the counselor should follow in defining the problem.

1. Each family member must contribute to the definition without having to become argumentative or defensive.
2. The problem must be stated in specific behavioral language.
3. If there is more than one problem, the most troublesome must be identified and that made the target of counseling.
4. Unsuccessful attempts to solve the problem are described in detail.

Although each family member will see the problem from his or her own perspective, usually there is some agreement about the behavioral manifestation of the problem. For example, a father might see his teenage son's behavior as disrespectful, while the son experiences his father as overbearing. With the counselor's help, however, they might both be able to agree that they can define the problem as "the number of times they get into explosive arguments." Thus, the problem becomes the frequency of their arguments rather than each person's bad attitude. If the arguments tend to gravitate toward a specific theme; for example, the son getting home too late with the family car, then the problem would be defined as getting home too late. It is important not to rush this phase of counseling and to be willing to negotiate and renegotiate until one problem is identified as the goal of counseling.

Finally, it is imperative that the counselor collect information regarding attempted solutions that have failed. There are several reasons for doing this. First, a great amount can be learned about the family system by hearing them describe their attempts to solve their problems. This information will be essential when attempting to identify an appropriate intervention for the family. Second, this discussion of failed solutions establishes the fact that the family does, indeed, have a problem that it has been unable to solve. Since most families continue to deny their problem even in counseling, this admission is important. Third, the process establishes that the counselor respects the efforts put forth by the family thus far. The counselor is saying, "I know you take your problem seriously and that you have already invested considerable energy in trying to solve it. Furthermore, I won't frustrate you by asking you to do what you have already tried without success." Finally, this part of the counseling process gives the counselor another opportunity to watch the family operate and to determine the distribution of power in the family; for example, alliances.

Setting realistic goals It is not enough for the family and counselor to define the problem. The family must also agree on what degree of improvement would be considered a therapeutic success. The description of success must be as concrete and well-defined as the description of the problem. Using our example of father and teenage son, it would not be appropriate to switch from "too many arguments" as the problem to "having a better relationship" as the measure of success. Rather, the goal might be "going from five arguments a week to one." Once the arguments were under control, it might be appropriate to work toward positive goals such as "spending more leisure time together." The consequence of reducing the number of arguments added to spending more enjoyable time together might result in having a better relationship, but this cannot be measured and therefore is not considered an appropriate counseling goal.

Directives for Change

The crux of strategic family therapy is the *therapeutic directive,* or intervention. Most strategic directives are paradoxical in nature; that is, they may seem to defy logic. The rationale behind the paradoxical directive is that most problems are more emotional than logical. Therefore, a solution that follows the typical laws of logic completely misses the point and simply will not work. Watzlawick, Weakland, and Fisch (1974) also note that most attempted solutions are linear, that is, Event B is expected to be caused by or a function of Event A. For example, if a child is grounded for the weekend for misbehaving, the problem is presumed to have been addressed by the punishment, grounding. But what if the child misbehaves again? The linear solution might be to ground the child for an entire week. In this illustration, can it be said that grounding had the desired effect? Grounding (punishment) was intended to produce good behavior in the future, a *linear* solution. These types of solutions are called more-of-the-same solutions, and rarely work. Paradoxical interventions attempt to come at the problem from a different perspective.

In Chapter 8, we discussed paradoxical interventions as cognitive interventions. Their effect is to reformat the individual's frame of reference in such a way that misbehavior *appears to the child* to be illogical or inappropriate, rather than something that might be punishable. For more information on this topic, we refer to you the excellent original sources that are dedicated exclusively to a discussion of the strategic intervention (Watzlawick, Weakland, & Fisch, 1974; Haley, 1973; Madanes, 1981).

Summary

As we have noted, systemic interventions do not originate in the traditional theories of counseling or personality. Instead, they derive from an ecological epistemology that many trained therapists find both unique and highly effective. The systemic orientation begins with a set of assumptions about human behavior that include: (a) a self-sustaining quality known as *homeostasis;* (b) the tendency of dysfunctional systems to develop rigid boundaries; and (c) an internal system organization that is determined by systemic "rules" as defined by repeated behavioral interaction patterns.

Effective counseling with social systems begins by recognizing these conditions and then developing interventions that address the system character rather than individual psychological characteristics. The dominant approaches are represented by communication-oriented therapists, structurally-oriented therapists, and strategic therapists. In almost all cases, systems therapists feel free to draw upon interventions from all three orientations and from individual therapy orientations as well.

Systems therapy fits quite well into the five-stage model for the helping process. Particular emphasis is placed on assessment as well as intervention. A frequent admonition of the systems therapist is that the problem cannot be treated until it has been identified. Systems thinking has particular relevance in working with couples and families. Indeed, many family interventions make no sense unless you think of the family as an eco-system that is self-reinforcing and self-sustaining. Therefore, we strongly recommend that you become well informed in family systems approaches if you plan to work with families or use family interventions.

Exercises

1. Consider your family of origin. On a sheet of paper, write the names of your parents first. Then, as you add the names of siblings, place the names nearest that parent with whom you think there was a primary identification. Draw lines connecting the subsystems you believe were operating in your family.

2. This is a two-part exercise. With a group of three to four class members, define yourselves as a family. Each person should assume a family member role: father, mother, oldest sibling, and so on. Given this "system," the family should discuss and make plans for a week-long vacation at the beach. After the plan has been finalized, step out of your roles and analyze the process and the system.

   In the second part of the exercise, the family is to repeat the same exercise, assuming the same roles. However, one family member in this exercise is to be a dysfunctional member (exhibiting a marginal level of functioning). Given this condition, repeat the planning of the vacation. Once the plan has been finalized, step out of your roles once again and analyze the process and the system. How did a dysfunctional family member alter the system? How did the individual family member roles accommodate this change?

3. In the Case Illustration of Eric and Sheila (p. 276) the communication problem was identified as the product of personal qualities each brought into the marriage. Identify two or three individual goals for both Eric and Sheila that would have a positive effect on the communication problem.

Discussion Questions

1. In a small group of class members, discuss what you think would be the most difficult type of family problem to work with. As you discuss the problem(s), consider whether you would choose to work with individuals or the total family in addressing the problem(s).

2. In this chapter we compared the family's system to an ecological system. In what ways are the two similar? How is this illustrated by the "empty nest" syndrome?

3. In a group of employees who have worked together in the same office area for ten years, what kinds of systemic rules are likely to be developed? How easy would it be to alter those rules?

4. In this chapter, very little attention is given to soliciting input from members of the system regarding goal-setting. Why wouldn't the counselor ask members of the system to help identify counseling goals?

Recommended Readings

Foley, V.D. (1989) Family Therapy, in Raymond J. Corsini and Danny Wedding, Eds. *Current Psychotherapies*, 4th Ed. (Itasca, IL: F.E. Peacock).

Haley, J. (1973), *Uncommon Therapy* (New York: W.W. Norton).

Haley, J. (1976), *Problem-Solving Therapy* (New York: McGraw-Hill).

Hoffman, L. (1981), *Foundations of Family Therapy* (Cambridge, MA: Harvard University Press).

Minuchin, S. & Fishman, H.C. (1981), *Family Therapy Techniques* (Cambridge, MA: Harvard University Press).

Satir, V. (1967), *Conjoint Family Therapy* (Palo Alto, CA: Science and Behavior).

Sherman, R. & Fredman, N. (1986), *Handbook of Structured Techniques in Marriage and Family Therapy* (New York: Brunner/Mazel).

Watzlawick, P., Weakland, J., & Fisch, R. (1974), *Change: Principles of Problem Formation and Problem Resolution* (New York: W.W. Norton).

___11___

Termination and Follow-up

In Chapter 2 we described termination as one of the five stages of counseling. This suggests that it functions as part of the therapeutic process and is not just a significant moment in the counseling relationship. The dynamics of termination are some indication of just how important the treatment of this stage can be. It has been described as a "loss experience" (Goodyear, 1981), an "index of success" (Pate, 1982), a "recapitulation of the multiple preceding goodbyes in life" Hansen, Stevic, & Warner, 1986), and a mixture of sadness and pleasure (Pietrofesa, Hoffman, Splete, & Pinto, 1984). However one wishes to describe termination, the emotional dynamics of letting go, trusting their gains, and facing future potential with only partially tested new skills present clients with multiple undercurrents of feeling.

The counselor also experiences pride and regret when a successful counseling relationship ends. Or if the relationship has been something less than successful, the counselor probably feels unfinished or even unsure of the manner in which the counseling case was conducted. In this chapter, we shall consider termination as a therapeutic stage and shall address such issues as who determines when termination should occur, problems in the termination process, and characteristics of successful termination.

The Termination Stage

Termination is not so much an ending as it is a transition from one set of conditions to another. Pate has caught the spirit of this, saying:

When counseling is viewed as a process in which an essentially competent person is helped by another to solve problems of living, solving the problem leads to termination, not as a trauma, but as another step forward in client growth. (1982, p. 188)

At some level, both the counselor and client know from the beginning of the counseling relationship that it will end eventually. But the knowledge that counseling ultimately will end provides no guidelines for making the decision. This raises the question, "What are the determinants of when counseling should terminate?" The answer to this question is based both upon theoretical orientations and counselor/client interactions.

Theoretical Determinants of Termination

The counselor operates out of some theoretical view of what counseling is meant to accomplish and how clients change through counseling. This theoretical viewpoint may be formalized (identified with a recognized counseling theory) or it may be idiosyncratic to the counselor's life view. The person-centered therapist might view termination as a decision to be made by the client. On the other hand, Pate observes that:

One point of view builds on the developmental nature of counseling and the goal of client self-actualization. Such a view might (wrongly) lead to the conclusion that a counseling relationship was always growth producing and thus ideally would continue. (1982, p. 189)

A somewhat different position is reflected in family therapy practice. Madanes explains that:

After the presenting problems are solved, the therapist must be willing to disengage quickly, with the idea of keeping in touch occasionally with the family and to be available if problems arise. (1981, p. 121)

Finally, "brief therapy" proponents take the position that counseling should be limited to a specified number of sessions (often ten sessions). In this case the therapist may contract with the client in the initial session to terminate at a specific point in time.

In each of these examples, the question of when termination should occur may be answered by the counselor's theoretical stance. However, it should be noted that many counselors do not feel bound to theoretical directives regarding the termination issue. When theoretical determinants are not used, the counselor tends to rely upon intuition or other variables.

Pragmatic Determinants of Termination

In practical terms, counseling ends when either the client, the counselor, or the process indicates that termination is appropriate. Even in psychoanalysis, clients have input into the decisions, as Lorand has observed:

> *Often patients themselves bring up the matter of terminating by asking how much longer they will need to come. Sometimes they are more definite and may state, for instance, that they will not come back in the fall. This gives the analyst an opportunity to discuss a tentative time limit for winding up the analysis. (1982, p. 225)*

When Clients Terminate

Clients may elect to terminate for a number of reasons. They may feel that their goals have been accomplished. They may feel that the relationship (or the counselor) is not being helpful or may even be harmful. They may lack the financial means to continue. Or they may move to a new community or they may finish the school year. Whatever the client's reason for terminating, it should be emphasized that the counselor's legal and ethical responsibilities do not end with the client's announcement. Preparation for termination and possible referral are issues that must be addressed. These topics will be discussed in greater detail later in the chapter.

When the Counselor Terminates

Often the counselor is the first person to introduce the notion that counseling is approaching termination. This decision may be based upon the client's progress toward identified counseling goals, or the counselor may determine that his or her expertise does not match the client's needs.

When counseling has been predicated upon a behavioral or other form of contract, progress toward the goals or conditions of the contract presents a clear picture of when counseling should end. Although clients are in the best position to experience counseling-based change, they are not always in the objective position needed to recognize change. Thus, the counselor may need to say to the client, "Do you realize that you have accomplished everything you set out to accomplish?" Ordinarily, the counselor can see this event approaching several sessions earlier. It is appropriate to introduce the notion of termination at that time, thereby allowing the client an opportunity to adjust to the transition. A fairly simple observation such as, "I think we probably have three or perhaps four more sessions and we will be finished" is enough to say. It provides an early warning, opens the door for discussion of progress and goal assessment, and focuses the client's attention upon "life after counseling."

Occasionally, as a case unfolds, the counselor may become aware that the demands of the client's problem call for skills or qualities the counselor does not possess. For example, after a few sessions a client may reveal that she is a binge-purge eater. If the counselor is unacquainted with the treatment procedures for such a condition, the client should be referred to a professional who is recognized as competent with this complaint. Or the client may present a dilemma that poses value conflicts for the counselor such that the counselor could not meet the client's needs without experiencing personal value contradictions. An example might be when a pregnant client is considering abortion, and the counselor is unable to support an objective examination of this solution. In such cases, the counselor is ethically bound to refer the client to another professional who is able to provide appropriate services. Obviously, this involves termination and transition to another counselor.

Premature Termination

Sometimes counselors suggest that counseling terminate before an appropriate point has been reached. Because many clients rely heavily upon the counselor to be the best judge of such matters, clients may go along with the counselor's recommendation, and the relationship may end prematurely. It has already been suggested that there are some very legitimate reasons why the counselor may decide to terminate counseling and refer the client to another professional. Aside from these situations, three precipitating conditions (Bernard, 1979) can lead the counselor to inappropriate premature termination:

1. The counselor experiences interpersonal discomfort.
2. The counselor fails to recognize and conceptualize the problem.
3. The counselor accurately conceptualizes the problem but becomes overwhelmed by it.

Personal discomfort may result from the counselor's fear of intimacy or inexperience with intense counseling relationships. With good supervisory assistance, this situation will remedy itself through continued counseling exposure and awareness. If the counselor's conceptual skills are weak or if the counselor's approach to all problems is to minimize the situation, then the result may be premature termination because the counselor fails to understand the client. This situation obviously calls for a careful reassessment of the counselor's decision to become a helper and whether additional training and supervision can remedy the situation. The third reason for premature termination is that the counselor accurately conceptualizes the problem but becomes overwhelmed by its complexity.

Finally, the special case of the counselor-in-training or the counselor who relocates should be mentioned. In most cases, counselor trainees provide services in a practicum setting that conforms to university semester or quarter schedules. When counselor trainees know that their practicum will end at a certain date and the client will either be terminated or referred to another counselor, ethical practice dictates that the client be informed in the first session that a terminal date already exists. This allows the client a choice to enter into what might be brief counseling or potential long-term counseling with the condition of referral, or to seek another counselor who does not impose this terminal limitation on the counseling relationship.

The solution is a bit different with the counselor who relocates to another geographical area. If the move decision occurs after the counseling relationship has been established, the counselor's ethical expectation is to provide and facilitate a successful referral of the client to another acceptable counselor. Sometimes, the transition is not completed in a successful referral, however. Pistole (1991) writes of the situation in which the client renews contact with the former counselor by mail, renewing the prospect of a continuing counseling communication. She discusses the pros and cons of such a situation including the counselor's ethical dilemma in whether or not to answer such communications. Pistole suggests that the ethically proper situation probably is not to respond under such conditions.

The Termination Report

Whether counseling is brief or long term, a summary report of the process is appropriate and desirable for several reasons. Assuming that the client may have future need for counseling, the termination report provides an accurate summation of the client's responsiveness to counseling and to specific types of interventions. Should the client request the counselor to provide information to other professionals (physician, psychiatrist, psychologist), the report provides a base for the preparation of that information.

The case can usually be summarized in two or three typewritten pages and should include the client's name, address, date that counseling began, date counseling concluded, number of sessions, presenting problem(s), types of counseling interventions used and their effectiveness, client reaction to the counseling relationship over time, client reaction to termination, and the counselor's assessment of client's future needs. The termination report is a confidential document and must not be released without the client's written permission.

Termination as a Process

The termination process involves several steps. The first is a careful assessment by the counselor and client of the progress that has been made and the extent to which goals have been achieved. Depending on the results of this assessment, the counselor will take one of two directions: termination or referral. Assuming termination is the appropriate choice, the counselor and client may proceed to discuss in depth the gains that have been or may yet be translated into changes in the client's environment, making plans for follow-up, and finally, saying goodbye (Pate, 1982, p. 188). Typically, the termination process is characterized by cognitive discussions interspersed with emotional moments. When termination is appropriate, the process has a constructive, positive quality.

Assessing Progress

Assessment or evaluation may be either formal or informal. If the counselor began the counseling process by asking the client to identify specific goals, or if they developed some form of counseling "contract," then the assessment of change may take a rather formal character. Each goal that had been set becomes a topic to discuss, changes related to that goal are identified, perhaps environmental consequences that grow out of those changes are enumerated, and so forth. In this approach to assessment, there is a sense of structure as the counselor and client review the relationship. When counseling has involved couples or families, the assessment becomes even more complex, for each member's change is considered in the process and system changes are identified.

Patterson and Eisenberg (1983) make the point that termination is not difficult to assess for many clients: "The client reports changes that have occurred, indicates a clear sense of having acquired what was wanted from the experience, and shows clear signs of being ready to end counseling" (p. 112). This more informal approach is augmented by the counselor's judgment or intuition that the process has evolved to a natural ending point. Usually this intuitive judgment can be tested with a casual statement such as, "I think we are about to complete our work. What do you think?" Particularly when the counselor leaves open the possibility of one or two more sessions, the client who is ready to terminate will acknowledge that imminent probability.

Summarizing Progress

It may seem redundant to suggest that the assessment of progress should be followed by some sort of summary of that progress by the counselor. The rationale for providing a summary is twofold. First, hearing one's progress from another person or another perspective is quite different from hearing oneself describe progress. Most clients benefit from the counselor's statement, even though it is not new information. As one client described it, "I know I have made a lot of progress, but it sure helps to hear you say it, too." The second reason for a summary is that the counselor can inject some cautions if some counseling gains need to be reinforced or monitored by the client. This is related to future client efforts to preserve or generalize the progress that has been achieved.

Generalizing Change

Having identified the changes that have occurred directly or indirectly through counseling, the counselor and client should turn to how those new behaviors, attitudes, or relationships can be generalized to the client's world. This step in the process calls upon the client to extend beyond the immediate gains to potential future gains. The counselor might introduce this with questions such as, "In what other situations could you anticipate using these social skills you have acquired?" or "If your husband should develop some new style of obnoxious behavior next month, how do you think you might handle it?" The basic goal of the implementation step is to test the client's willingness and ability to adapt learned skills or new attitudes to situations other than those that provoked the original problem.

Planning for Follow-Up

Follow-up in counseling refers to the nature and amount of professional contact that occurs between the counselor and client after termination has occurred. Some counseling approaches place greater emphasis upon follow-up than others. For example, Minuchin has taken the position that a family therapist is like a family physician. Over the years, the family will encounter new crises and problems and will reenter counseling as these situations demand. Thus, counseling is viewed as a service that can extend, intermittently, over a portion of the client's lifetime. Other approaches, most notably those that emphasize self-actualization, view counseling as a developmental experience, the object of which is to facilitate the client's growth and capability of dealing with new problems more effectively. In this context, future returns to counseling are not expected, although they certainly are acceptable.

There is also an ethical aspect to follow-up. Even when the counselor and client agree that sufficient progress has been made to justify termination, it is appropriate for the counselor to: (a) make his or her future services available; and (b) explain to the client how future contact can be made. In so doing, the counselor has established a link, however tenuous, between the client's present state and future needs. This link can also be an effective intervention for those clients who believe termination is appropriate but experience anxiety at the prospect.

It is often effective for the counselor to suggest a three-month or six-month "checkup." Depending on the client's response to the suggestion, the counselor can even schedule an appointment or suggest that the client call to make an appointment if needed. This is an effective bridging intervention in that it gives the client a sense of security and relationship continuation, even when counseling has terminated. The counselor might also suggest to the client that should the appointment not seem necessary in three month's time, a phone call to cancel the appointment would be appreciated. Our experience has been that clients are responsible about either keeping the appointment or canceling it. Even when they call to cancel, the telephone contact provides some follow-up information on how the client is adapting.

Finally, if counseling outcomes include post-counseling activities that the client has decided to pursue, the counselor might want to follow up on the success of these goals. For example, if a client decides to make a career change that involves future job interviewing, then the counselor might ask the client to keep him informed of progress, either through a letter or telephone contact.

The Referral Process

Client referral is a special form of termination. Shertzer and Stone (1980) define it as "the act of transferring an individual to another person or agency for specialized assistance not available from the original source" (p. 327). To this definition might be added: or when the service provider cannot continue providing counseling either for ethical or personal reasons. The referral involves a number of steps: (1) identifying the need to refer; (2) evaluating potential referral sources; (3) preparing the client for the referral; and (4) coordinating the transfer.

The Need to Refer

Some mention has already been made of the various reasons one might want to refer a client. The most prominent reason is when the client needs some specialized form of counseling. This does not mean that the client is seriously stressed, although that can be the case for referral. It is more likely that the client needs a specific form of counseling that the counselor does not offer (for example, career counseling or marital counseling). Because clients rarely are informed consumers of the various forms of counseling, counselors should be keenly attuned to specialized needs and their own ability to provide quality services.

If you have not been trained in family counseling, if you are intimidated by the prospect of working with a family group, or if you prefer one-to-one relationships, then you should not present yourself as a family therapist. The point is that the counselor may recognize the need to refer long before the client does.

Even when the counselor recognizes the need, the task remains to help the client come to the same conclusion, or referral will not be effective.

Clients may resist the idea at first suggestion. After all, having risked themselves by sharing their fears or vulnerabilities, they probably would prefer not to have to go through the same process with yet another counselor.

Evaluating Potential Sources

It is important that counselors be familiar with potential referral sources in the community. Some communities publish a helping services directory that lists public agencies, services they provide, fees, and how referral can be accomplished. The Yellow Pages of the telephone directory also provide information on both public and private sources under such headings as: Psychologists, Physicians, Marriage and Family Therapists, Counselors (Counseling), and Psychotherapy. Such lists or directories provide little more than names and possible affiliations. For example, a listing under Marriage, Family, Child, and Individual Counselors might read:

> Ralph T. Meduzzo, Ph.D.
> Communication and change at the
> Center for Psychotherapy
> *Marriage Enrichment
> *Divorce Bereavement
> *Family Mediation
> Call for appointment: 319-2650

Just what can be learned from this listing? Dr. Meduzzo offers psychotherapy for improving marriage, surviving divorce, and resolving family issues. What is not known is: (a) the kind of training Dr. Meduzzo received; (b) whether his doctorate was earned in psychotherapy, as opposed to chemistry or speech therapy; (c) his therapeutic orientation (individual vs. family; client-centered, rational-emotive, behavioral, psychoanalytic); or (d) his skill level or success rate with different types of problems. The best way to know answers to such questions is through exposure to different sources and feedback from clients and professional peers. Lacking that, the counselor might want to call Dr. Meduzzo and ask him such questions. After obtaining this information, the counselor should ask if he is receiving referrals and what procedures he prefers to follow when a case is referred to him.

Over time, counselors can build up their own listing of referral sources that is based on direct experience. Such a listing is by far the best resource when the need to refer a client arises.

Coordinating the Transfer

Whenever the counselor is referring a client to another professional, it is hoped that the referral will occur successfully and without undue strain on the client. If the client is highly anxious or if the counselor thinks the client might not accept the referral, special attention should be devoted to the client's concerns. In addition, successful referrals require that the counselor make contact with the receiving professional and provide information that will facilitate the referral process.

Preparing the Client

Preparing the client for referral involves both details of the referral and the client's anxieties about the new relationship. It helps if the counselor has discussed the case with the referring professional and can assure the client that painful details may not have to be repeated. It also helps if the counselor can tell the client something about the referring professional, including personal characteristics, professional competency, and the professional's receptiveness to the referral. Referral details may include making the first appointment for the client, explaining how to get to the new counselor's office, telephone numbers, professional fees, and so on.

Communication with the Receiving Professional

Before any referral recommendation is made, the counselor must determine whether the receiving professional is willing or able to accept the referral. This can be accomplished most effectively through telephone communication. Usually the receiving professional will want a written case summary, in addition to the information received by telephone. The termination report described earlier will provide sufficient information to meet this requirement. Before sending any written material, however, the counselor must obtain written consent from the client to provide this information. Most counseling centers use a standard consent form.

Blocks to Termination

Counseling can be such an intimate and valued personal experience for both the counselor and client that the thought of ending the relationship is most unattractive. From the counselor's perspective, a client who grows, overcomes obstacles, and accomplishes goals is an immensely rewarding experience. Added to this, counselor/client relationships often assume a personal as well as professional dimension. Counselors begin to like clients and appreciate their humanness and finer qualities. Clients often experience counselors in ways they wish could have happened in their familial

```
┌─────────────────────────────────────────────────────────────┐
│                  COUNSELING ASSOCIATES, INC.                  │
│         CONSENT FOR RELEASE OF CONFIDENTIAL INFORMATION       │
│                                                               │
│   Date: _____                                        │
│                                                               │
│   Client's Name: _____  Date of Birth: _____  │
│                                                               │
│   Permission is hereby granted to COUNSELING ASSOCIATES,      │
│   Inc. to release psychological, medical, social,             │
│   educational, and other clinical information regarding the   │
│   client named above to the following professional therapist  │
│   and/or clinic.                                              │
│                                                               │
│      Person/Clinic to                                         │
│      receive information: _____ │
│                                                               │
│      Address: _____ │
│                                                               │
│      City, State, Zip: _____ │
│                                                               │
│      Signature: _____ │
│                                                               │
│      Name of signer (please print): _____ │
│                                                               │
│                                                               │
│      Relationship to client: _____ │
│      (if client is minor)                                     │
└─────────────────────────────────────────────────────────────┘
```

relationships. In this context, termination often means saying good-bye to a very good friend. For these reasons, it is wise to be aware of professional and personal resistance to termination, whether it originates with the client or the counselor.

Client Resistance to Termination

Patterson and Eisenberg make the point that often the counselor becomes ". . . an anchor—a source of security in a (sea) of stress. The experience of being prized by the counselor (and) the restoration of hope . . . create strong attachment bonds. Letting go can cause (some clients) to suffer an intense stress" (1983, p. 113). It should be noted that ordinarily clients are not terminated when external stress is at a high level. But the memory of those peak stress moments is very real for clients, and resistance is partially stimulated by that memory.

According to psychoanalytic thinking, "The most desirable state of affairs is for the patient to slowly wean himself away, for him to eventually accept his limitations and be willing to relinquish the desires which cannot be realized" (Lorand, 1982, p. 225). Other theoretical approaches tend to emphasize a more direct counselor involvement in the process of acceptance. In all cases, the counselor must evaluate the client's degree of concern with the prospect of termination and respond therapeutically.

Client resistance to termination may be based on a fear of facing future (undefined) problems or crises, uncertainty that counseling gains are real, or intense liking of the counselor. The resistance can take the form of a relapse into old dysfunctional patterns, identification of new counseling goals the client would like to work on, manipulative anger toward the counselor (that the counselor feels should be addressed), or efforts to postpone or drag out the date of termination.

Counselor Resistance to Termination

It is a little more surprising that counselors often resist terminating with clients, even though the client has reached a logical hiatus in the counseling process. And yet, most counselor resistance is totally understandable. Take the counselor trainee for example. When a trainee has a successful counseling experience with a cooperative and diligent client, the overpowering sense of accomplishment is almost too rewarding to conclude. It is not unusual for the supervisor to have to keep reminding the counselor that the relationship is ready for termination.

Counselors in practice also form real human attachments to clients. In fact, it can be argued that counselor investment in the person of the client is a prerequisite to successful counseling. When this is part of the relationship, letting go has an emotional impact. Goodyear has identified eight conditions that can lead to the counselor's experience of loss at the point of termination.

1. When termination signals the end of the significant relationship.

2. When termination arouses the counselor's anxieties about not having been more effective with the client.

3. When termination arouses guilt in the counselor about not having been more effective with the client.

4. When the counselor's professional self-concept is threatened by the client who leaves abruptly and angrily.

5. When termination signals the end of a learning experience for the counselor (for example, the counselor may have been relying on the client to learn more about the dynamics of a disorder or about a particular subculture).

6. When termination signals the end of a particularly exciting experience of living vicariously through the adventures of the client.

7. When termination becomes a symbolic recapitulation of other (especially unresolved) farewells in the counselor's life.

8. When termination arouses in the counselor conflicts about his or her own individuation. (1981, p. 348)

While the counselor trainee may have a supervisor who can point to any apparent resistance, what does the professional counselor do? In the first place, most experienced counselors know, at some level of consciousness, when the relationship has grown quite important. This is a cue to the counselor that peer consultation or supervision would be both appropriate and desirable. The more human counselors are, the more susceptible they are to personal intrusions in their professional practice. Having a colleague who can provide a level of objectivity through discussion and taped supervision is a valuable asset.

Case Illustration of Termination: the Case of Margaret

In the following case illustration, Margaret, twenty-nine and separated, initiated counseling to work through her anger toward her estranged husband. The case illustration begins with excerpts from the first session through the final session, since termination was considered a constant in the counseling process. The case was seen in a college counseling center. The first session occurred three weeks before Christmas.

First Session

The first session began with the counselor orienting Margaret to the conditions she could expect, including confidentiality, the necessity to be tape-recorded, the existence of a university supervisor who would be involved in the case, and so forth. In addition, the counselor raised the issue of termination in the first session:

Counselor: In addition, Margaret, I think we should be aware that the university schedule will cause some breaks in our sessions and will mean that we must plan to terminate in mid-May, if we're still meeting then.

Margaret: When will the breaks come?

Counselor: Well, the counseling center will be closed from December 15 until January 10. And we will be closed for spring break the week of March 11. Since it is already December 5, we can meet next week and then we will meet again on January 12. We also need to take a moment to talk about terminating. I know that sounds premature, but neither you nor I plan to continue the counseling relationship forever.

Margaret: Right, but how long does counseling usually take?

Counselor: Well, that depends. Most clients here at the center take ten to fifteen sessions. Occasionally, they take longer. I think we should plan on ten sessions and then make a decision about termination.

Fourth Session

As the fourth session was about to end, the topic of termination was initiated by the client.

Margaret: Right now I really feel like things are getting better, but that feeling worries me because I'm not sure.

Counselor: What is it about a good feeling that makes you worry?

Margaret: Oh, it's not the good feeling. Maybe I'm afraid to trust the feeling or the progress, I guess. I mean, what happens if I am just fooling myself and we decide to terminate and then I discover I was wrong?

Counselor: Well, first of all, if you discovered you were wrong, we'd just change our plans and continue with counseling. But it doesn't usually work out that way. Most of the time, when the client has that feeling for several weeks, it's real. I am glad you raised the question, however. We're almost halfway through our agreed-upon ten sessions. We don't have to do anything about that except to be aware that we will be terminating sometime in the foreseeable future.

The counselor took this opportunity to extend the client's awareness of the termination process. In effect, this discussion became the starting point for the termination process in this case. The seed of awareness was planted, and the client took that awareness with her at the end of the session. Three sessions later, the awareness had grown and matured.

Seventh Session

Nearing the end of this session, which had been a difficult but significant session, the counselor introduced the termination topic again.

Counselor: Well, you have worked hard today. How do you feel about your progress?

Margaret: Truthfully, I'm exhausted, but I feel good about what's happening. I'm starting to feel in control of myself, and that's a precious feeling.

Counselor: About a month ago, you mentioned that one of your fears was feeling too optimistic about your improvement. Do you still feel that way?

Margaret: No, and isn't that interesting? I think I was just feeling shaky then.

Counselor: What about the idea of terminating? Do you feel shaky about that?

Margaret: (*Laughing*) Well, you still owe me three sessions. I'm not ready to terminate today. But, unless the bottom falls out, I don't think I will need another ten sessions.

Counselor: (*Chuckling*) No, if you had another ten sessions, you'd probably begin to lose ground.

Margaret: What do you mean? Do people lose ground if they stay too long?

Counselor: I think so. There's a time to leave your parents, a time to leave your training, and in our case, a time to leave counseling. If we don't make that break when it's time, then you could grow dependent, and that would be self-defeating.

In this dialogue, the counselor is able to present the therapeutic effects of appropriate termination in such a way that it is seen as a normal, developmental process, like growing up. That does not remove all the client's fears, but it does place termination in a context that is anything but catastrophic.

Ninth Session

The counselor begins this session by introducing the topic of termination.

Counselor: Well, Margaret, this is our next to last session. How shall we use it?

Margaret: We could cry.

Counselor: You're right. There is some sadness about the prospect.

Margaret: This has been so meaningful for me. I really feel like I have grown. When I think about what a basket case I was last December, I can't believe the changes.

Counselor: Are you doubting again?

Margaret: No, no, that was just an expression. I'm very pleased . . . not totally confident, maybe . . . but I'm not a basket case either.

Counselor: That's right. You have discovered your strengths.

Margaret: When you say that, it feels good, but I'm not sure if I could say what they are. Maybe that's how I'd like to use today.

Counselor: You mean talking about the strengths you have been discovering?

Margaret: Yes, that's what I want to do.

The counselor introduced termination at the beginning of this session to allow the client time to process her feelings about the imminent ending of the relationship. The client might have dwelt upon the sadness of ending a meaningful relationship, she could have negotiated an extension, or she could cement the gains through discussion and review. In this case, Margaret chose the latter.

Tenth and Final Session

Margaret began this session with the acknowledgment that it was the final session.

Margaret: Well, this is it.

Counselor: What do you mean?

Margaret: This is the last time I'll be seeing you, I think.

Counselor: I think so, too.

Margaret: It's been good. I've learned a lot. And I really have valued getting to know you.

Counselor: And it has been a very meaningful experience for me too.

(Later in the session)

Counselor: Before we close today, I want you to know that I would like to hear from you in six months or so. Just a note telling me how things have been going would be fine. Would you do that?

Margaret: Yes, I will. What if I run into some new problems?

Counselor: If that happens, you can call and set up an appointment.

In this final session, the counselor provided a bridge to aid the transition by asking Margaret to get back in touch in six months with an informal progress report. This is as much for the client's benefit as it is for the counselor, for it says, "I'm not just dropping you from my appointment book and my world. You will remain my client in absentia." Secondly, the counselor has provided a termination structure that allows the client to make contact for future needs, should they arise. This would seem to be assumed, but clients often do not take this privilege for granted or are shy about such a move.

Summary

Often, termination is viewed as the moment when counselor and client conclude a successful counseling relationship. We have tried to dispel this notion and replace it with a broader definition of termination as a stage in the counseling process. As a stage, termination can be as critical to successful counseling as was the relationship-building first stage.

Indeed, termination of a relationship deserves as much time and care as is devoted to creation of a relationship. Consequently, when termination is an imminent possibility, the counselor and client should begin discussing the matter several sessions prior to the last session. Many desirable consequences accrue from this discussion. The client becomes increasingly aware of new strengths and skills, the counselor is able to reinforce those gains, future demands and expectations can be considered, fears and concerns can be assessed. The process addresses unfinished business and enhances a sense of completion. In all of this, the counselor has responsibility to see that the client's well-being is protected and preserved. When termination occurs through referral, the counselor has primary responsibility to see that the transfer to the receiving professional is handled smoothly and sensitively.

Successful termination must be seen as part of successful treatment. Without it, even the most impressive gains of therapy are tempered in the client's perception and future needs may be negatively affected.

Exercises

1. Class members should divide into groups of three. Each should assume a role: counselor, client, or observer. The observer's responsibility is to record both the counselor's and client's behaviors during the exercise. Both the counselor and client should select a role from the following lists. Do not reveal your role to the other person.

Counselor	*Client*
1. Resisting termination	1. Resisting termination
2. Encouraging termination	2. Requesting termination
3. Uncertain about termination	3. Uncertain about termination

   Conduct a ten-minute counseling session simulation using the roles you selected. Following the session, discuss your reactions to one another. The person who observed then should provide feedback to each of you regarding the dynamics he or she observed.

2. In the following role-play, one person should be the counselor. the second should be the client, and the third will be an observer/recorder.

   The role-play is a client who is being referred to a psychologist. The reason for the referral is that the counselor has realized that the client's problems are beyond his or her level of competence to treat. The client has seen the counselor for two sessions. Allow ten minutes for this role-play.

   Following the role-play, discuss among yourselves the dynamics of the interaction. What did you learn from this experience? What interpersonal skills were required?

Discussion Questions

1. What are the pros and cons of early discussion of termination?

2. What types of clients are most in need of gradual introduction to the idea of termination?

3. In the chapter, reference is made to premature termination. What are some of the conditions that might lead to premature termination?

4. Discuss the idea of counselor resistance to termination. Do you possess any characteristics that might cause you to resist terminating a client?

5. Discuss the ways in which referral is similar to termination. How is referral different from termination? What are the interpersonal dynamics of each?

Recommended Readings

Bernard, J. M. (1979), "Supervisor Training: A Discrimination Model," *Counselor Education and Supervision 19*, 60-68.

Goodyear, R. K. (1981), "Termination as a Loss Experience for the Counselor," *The Personnel and Guidance Journal 59*, February, 347-350.

Lanning, W. & Carey, J. (1987), "Systematic Termination in Counseling," *Counselor Education and Supervision 26*, 168-173.

Lorand, S. (1982), *Techniques of Psychoanalytic Therapy* (New York: St. Martin's Press).

Madanes, C. (1981), *Strategic Family Therapy* (San Francisco: Jossey-Bass).

Pistole, C. (1991), "Termination: Analytic Reflections on Client Contact after Counselor Relocation," *Journal of Counseling and Development 69*, 337-340.

12
Special Issues in Counseling

The content of this book is based upon the assumption that the counseling process is predictable. Many problems or concerns are widely shared by people. In view of this assumption, much of the book has focused on those strategies and interventions that have grown out of the accumulated research and wisdom of many helpers. These experiences make it possible for us to predict certain problems that most counselors face at one time or another in their interactions with clients. Counseling is also predictable in that certain behaviors are more facilitative, more therapeutic, than others. Some counselor behaviors might even be anti-therapeutic.

However, there is some inherent danger in these assumptions. They can gloss over the real differences that exist between persons, groups, and cultures. "The erroneous belief that all Asians are the same, all Blacks are the same, all Hispanics are the same, or all American Indians are the same has led to numerous therapeutic problems" (Sue & Sue, 1990, p. 94). Larson (1982) has observed that all individuals carry three identities: an individual identity, a group identity, and a universal identity.

> If viewed only in the context of his or her universality, . . . a person loses his or her individuality; if viewed only in the context of his or her individuality, the person loses a sense of connectedness with humanity; if viewed only in the context of group membership, an individual is stereotyped. The delicate task in counseling is to integrate all three views when working with clients. (p. 844)

Within this context, all counseling must be concerned with: the individual identity (what sets this person apart as unique); the group identity (what qualities this person carries as a function of his/her membership in a particular group or groups); and the client's universal identity (that which this book addresses as "the client").

There are any number of ways to examine individual and group identity. One's gender, racial, or ethnic roots, psychological characteristics, and physical characteristics all fall into the category of group identity. Each set of characteristics influences the others in such a way as to produce highly idiosyncratic results which we may address as individual identity. As you can see, one's identities can become a highly complex concept, perhaps more complex than the counselor's ability to respond. Bernard and Goodyear (1992) suggest that these many nuances can be grasped best by using a metaphor of the snapshot proposed by McGoldrick, Pierce, and Giordano (1982). They proposed that:

> *Real people are too complex to treat. But a person with a phobia (a snapshot) or a family with a disruptive child (the family photo) is within our grasp. This is true not only for diagnostic categories but also for cultural phenomena. Therefore, our understanding of Hispanic or gay or physically disabled becomes a cognitive shorthand for a variety of constructs. (p. 199)*

One of the first issues counselors must face is the challenge to perceive as accurately as possible the personhood of the client, including individual, group, and universal qualities, while at the same time, filtering out biases, prejudices, and myths. Three areas particularly contribute to this challenge. They are: (a) racial and ethnic differences; (b) gender differences; and (c) physical differences.

Racial and Ethnic Issues

While most of your initial counseling contacts may be with persons from the same culture as your own, you will soon encounter clients from cultures different from your own. *Culture* is sometimes used interchangeably—and erroneously—with *race* and *ethnicity*. As Moore (1974) observed:

> *Great races do have different cultures. Ethnic groups within races differ in cultural content. But, people of the same racial*

origin and of the same ethnic groups differ in their cultural matrices. All browns, or blacks, or whites, or yellows, or reds are not alike in the cultures in which they live and have their being. (p. 41)

Culture has proved to be a difficult concept to define, perhaps because its influence is so pervasive. It has been defined in terms of social structure, kinship systems, personality, psychological adjustment, ethnic diversity, and socioeconomic status, to name a few. For our purposes, we shall use Axelson's (1985, p. 7) definition of group life, "A cultural system is the process that a group of people have developed for satisfying needs, for solving problems, and for adjusting to both the external environment and to each other." With this definition in mind, counseling cannot occur outside of a culture. It may be the counselor's culture that is used, or it may be the client's culture. If the counselor's culture is the medium, then, unless the client is of the same cultural background, the process of counseling will miss the target at best, or be irrelevant and useless at worst. There is no substitute for working in the client's cultural medium if counseling is to be effective.

How does one determine the client's cultural background? Bernard and Goodyear (1992) have posited a number of questions the counselor may use in determining what is known about the client's cultural world view (see Table 12-1).

TABLE 12-1 Sources of cultural identity

Historical

What is the client's racial (ethnic) identity?
What is the history of the client's race (ethnic group) in this country?
What is most likely to be the client's experience with persons of the counselor's race (ethnic group)?

Language:

What is the primary language spoken by the client?
If English is a second language, how difficult is it for the client to comprehend subtle nuances of the English language?
In what ways can the counselor be sure that the client understands what is said?
In what ways can the counselor be sure that he/she understands the client?
Even when English is the common language, are communication patterns different?
Does silence mean the same thing to the counselor and client?
Are questions experienced by the client in ways that the counselor intends?
Do families have a particular hierarchy through which all communications must flow?

Social structure:

Do client and counselor define family membership similarly?
What are the boundaries for the client's family?

continued

How important are members of extended family to the client?
Are nonrelatives considered family to the client?
What are the child-rearing practices within the client's culture?
What roles do elderly family members play?

Social identity:

What is the client's level of acculturation?
To what degree does the client identify with cultural heritage?
How mainstream American is the client?
Does the client aspire to be culturally mainstreamed?
Are the client's parents acculturated into American society?
Does the client's family have issues regarding acculturation?

Religious identity:

What is the role of religion in this client's life?
Does religion mean the same to the client as it does to the counselor?
How does the client understand his/her problems? Bad luck? Result of sin? God's wrath?
    As unrelated to his/her religious beliefs?

Socioeconomic identity:

What is the apparent socioeconomic status of the client?
Is socioeconomic status the main source of the client's problems?
Is the client's socioeconomic status significantly different from the counselor's?
Is the client's socioeconomic status significantly different from the majority of the members of the client's cultural group?
To what does the client attribute socioeconomic status?

Gender roles:

What are the predominant gender roles within the client's culture?
Does the gender of the counselor pose dissonance for the client?
Is the client congruent with gender roles for his or her cultural group?

Therapeutic readiness:

Does the client's culture enhance readiness for the therapeutic encounter?
What is the value of self-disclosing in the client's culture?
Does the client understand his or her role in counseling?

Success orientation:

How does the client define "success?"
What is the relationship of education to success?
What is the relationship of industry to success?
What is the relationship of family to success?
What is the relationship of material gains to success?
What is the relationship of title or job to success?
What is the relationship of life style to success?

Time orientation:

What is the client's concept of time?
Do problems seem imminent or more diffuse?
What value does the client place on the past? The present? The future?
What value does the client place on timeliness?

Table 12-1 has been adapted from Bernard, J.M. & Goodyear, R.K. (1992, pp. 202-203), *Fundamentals of Clinical Supervision*, Boston: Allyn & Bacon.

Bernard and Goodyear make the point that the ultimate purpose of considering culture questions is to allow the counselor to do a better job of the basic tasks of counseling. People from a different cultural background may react quite differently to silence, or to eye contact, or to the opposite sex than the counselor. Without this knowledge the counselor risks misinterpreting the client's response, misdiagnosing the problem, and mishandling the case. Sue and Sue (1990, p. 94) illustrate the importance of this type of understanding, noting that "Research now suggests that a minority individual's reaction to *counseling*, the *counseling process*, and to the *counselor* is influenced by his/her cultural/racial identity and not simply linked to minority-group membership." Many of the questions in Table 12-1 will be answered in the normal progression of counseling. Still, you must be alert and sensitive to this type of information. Only through such sensitivity will you be able to recognize, understand, and respect the cultural world view of the client.

Gender Role Issues in Counseling

It was noted earlier that counseling cannot occur outside a culture. Because gender roles are always a dimension of culture, gender role (as differentiated from sex) issues necessarily emerge in the counseling relationship. Our expectations of one another, when based on gender, will affect the counseling relationship. Role stereotyping is also a cultural phenomenon. Thus, the culture(s) of the participants must also be taken into account. To paraphrase Larson (1982), the counselor and client bring to the counseling relationship individual, group, and universal gender role perspectives. Bernard and Goodyear (1992) offer some of the likely encounters that smack of gender issues:

> The female client with an overbearing, rigid father enters therapy with a male therapist, hoping this time to gain approval; the male client who expresses no emotion to his male friends and colleagues enters therapy with a male therapist; the couple who have become frightened because the man has become physically abusive enter therapy with a female therapist; the male client who has not been successful establishing an intimate relationship with a female enters therapy with a female therapist. (p. 213)

These illustrations are stereotypic in their own right, for they offer the most dramatic examples of gender role conflict in counseling.

The possibility for more subtle gender issues to creep into the counseling relationship is far more insidious, and more likely. It is probably a safe generalization to say that males generally have not been encouraged to understand and appreciate the female world view, nor have females been encouraged to understand and appreciate aspects of the male world view. In male-dominated cultures, neither gender is encouraged to reach this level of sensitivity. Perhaps the solution is for each gender to attempt to interpret itself, honestly and accurately, to the other. Gilligan (1982) has attempted to do this, as have a number of other feminist authors (Good, Gilbert, & Scher, 1990; Mintz & O'Neil, 1990).

Earlier we suggested that minority status is determined, not numerically, but by the relative power or powerlessness of the group in question. Women are certainly not a numerical minority, but there is general consensus that they are not the power holders in most societies. This cultural condition serves both to oppress women and to teach them about the manipulation of power. Such issues can be the source of many problems that are seen in counseling for they strike at one's identity and self-esteem. It is essential that the counselor function with a high level of consciousness about these kinds of issues.

Nor is it simply a female issue. Males also develop distorted perspectives of themselves, of females, and of relationships. To think that one is superior (or inferior), empowered (or unempowered), privileged (or disenfranchised), on the basis of gender is psychological bondage. The apparent gains from *thinking* one is superior, empowered, or privileged conceal other less desirable consequences for the beholder, consequences that frequently lead one into counseling.

Psychology offers two alternatives to working with gender issues. The first emphasizes movement toward psychological androgyny (for example, Foxley, 1979), while the second invites a keener understanding and appreciation of gender uniqueness (for example, Gilligan, 1982).

Counselors should be aware of both alternatives and keep a constant vigil to detect gender stereotyping that emanates from within, from the client, and from the culture.

Finally, we should acknowledge the presence of communication pattern differences that exist between males and females. These patterns are related to gender roles and reveal themselves in ways that might seem so normal as to go unnoticed. For example, on a recent Sunday morning television program that featured four news correspondents, three male and one female, the communication went as follows: Speaker 1 (male) introduced the topic and raised a question. Speaker 2 (male) volunteered a response. Speaker 3 (female) asked Speaker 2 a question about his response. Speaker 2 answered. Speaker 3 started to react to Speaker 2's answer and was interrupted by Speaker 4. This pattern continued throughout the program.

Question: Was it coincidental that Speaker 3 (female) was not the first to respond to a new question or was some sort of deference occurring? Was it coincidental that the male speakers interrupted the female speaker while she did not interrupt their responses, or was some unspoken rule operating? Other patterns also emerge when comparing gender communications. For example, when faced with a demand situation, males have a greater tendency to move directly to decision-making, while females are more inclined to move to affect. Such differences are manifested in the counseling relationship and should be recognized as culturally role-determined. For a more thorough examination of this topic, the reader is referred to *Language, Gender, and Society* (Thorne, Kramarae, & Henley, 1983).

Physical Disabilities Issues

All other things being equal, when working with clients who have physical disabilities, the "problem" is the environment in which the person must function rather than the client's disability. But when was the last time all other things were equal? Again, we return to the effect of culture, the majority culture (those persons whose physical disabilities are not restrictive) and the minority culture (those persons who have a restrictive physical disability). What expectations does the majority culture in this case have for a blind person? A person confined to a wheelchair? A person with severe hearing loss? Do we assume the same interpersonal "rules" apply? Does the disabled person have different affective reactions to stress, frustration, or success? Should the counselor think about these issues prior to meeting his or her first client with disabilities? And how might that be done?

Hulnick and Hulnick (1989) suggest that a first step is to view disabilities as functional limitations rather than as problems to be overcome. Lombana (1989, p. 178) adds that "If we come to a point where we accept the notion that all of us possess functional limitations in one area or another, we can stop thinking in terms of providing 'different' services for people with disabilities. Instead, we can build on the skills we already possess and think in terms of changing the environment in ways which would benefit everyone." If we think of counseling as a wellness activity intended to enhance the client's quality of life, then what are the implications for working with clients with disabilities? In a study of quality of life factors, Scherer (1988) identified two personal factors that disabled clients considered to have the most impact on improved quality of life: perceived control over their quality of life (empowerment) and the desire for assimilation into society. In light of such findings, Roessler (1990) suggests that counselors should adopt a quality of life perspective which ensures "that rehabilitation interventions do not overemphasize personal factors and underemphasize environmental or social conditions" (p. 88).

The literature on counseling disabled clients suggests some mutual bonds with racial and ethnic minorities and with gender issues. Culturally determined perspectives frequently are inaccurate and depersonalizing. Individual qualities frequently are disassociated from cultural determinants. Biases and misperceptions often intrude into the counselor-client relationship. The solution for counselors would also appear to be similar. Become aware of the cultural contributions, the group identity issues, and the individual factors. Try not to see a disability, see a person.

Resistance Issues in Counseling

Resistance is actually a rather common issue in the therapeutic relationship. Resistance means that either the client or the counselor is "less than fully committed to effecting positive behavioral changes" (Cavanaugh, 1982, p. 240), or that client reactions are "essentially irrational and emotional" (Blocher, 1987, p. 119) or that the client system is seeking to maintain homeostasis (see Chapter 10). Clients are resistant because they are conflicted about change. They may not perceive the need to change, they may not see the usefulness of a particular change, or they may see change as more threatening (or less desirable) than the status quo.

It is important for helpers to understand how difficult and painful the change process can be for clients. Cavanaugh (1982) reminds us that "(t)he pain of growth in counseling is analogous to what a person in physiotherapy experiences when muscles are being stretched and exercised in new ways. There is almost always a price to pay for becoming stronger, and sometimes the price is dear" (p. 241). Because of this, it is often helpful if counselors expect rather than deny any conflict the client brings to counseling about change. Otherwise, the counselor and client are likely to get in a power struggle over the client's investment in the goals of helping. Counseling is on shaky ground when the counselor wants more for clients than they want for themselves. In these instances, the counselor often fights with the client (in the client's behalf) but, in doing so, the client loses an important ally (Cormier & Cormier, 1991, p. 577).

One way to make sure your expectations do not supersede those of the client is to recognize that the client will have both approach and avoidance behaviors and feelings; that is, responses that propel the client both toward and away from change simultaneously. Usually, one side of this "push-pull" conflict may be stronger or more resourceful. You can help clients work through this conflict in several ways. One way is to use some of the Gestalt dialogue strategies we presented in Chapter 7. Have the client "play out" the polarity and notice which side feels stronger. If it is the avoidance side, work on strengthening the approach side.

Another strategy is to use the empty-chair technique (Chapter 7) or the TA redecision strategy (Chapter 8) as a way for clients to identify their self-talk associated with both sides of the conflict. What do they say to themselves that facilitates their change efforts, and what do they say that discourages change? For example, a client may want to lose twenty-five pounds yet appears hesitant about depriving herself of certain foods over the next three months. Through use of these strategies, she may discover self-talk that supports the desired changes: "I'll look so much better when I get this weight off" or "It will feel so good to wear smaller-size clothing." At the same time, the client may find self-talk that she uses to sabotage this change: "Oh, one piece of pie today won't hurt that much" or "Well, I already indulged in one cookie—why not another?" The counselor can help the client turn around the negative self-statements so that they support rather than discourage change. For example, "Well, I did indulge in one cookie, but that's not a good enough reason to eat four more."

Clients also resist change because their present behavior, even though dysfunctional, is meeting a need or providing a payoff that the client is hesitant about giving up. As Cavanaugh (1982) explains, "When people enter counseling with maladaptive behavior, there is always a compelling reason for it, a reason that will not be exorcised merely by the act of entering counseling. People will cling to maladaptive behavior until there is good reason to believe that the substitute behavior will be equally satisfying or anxiety reducing" (p. 244).

There are a great many payoffs clients receive for maladaptive behavior, including money, attention from significant others, immediate (versus delayed) gratification of needs, avoidance of work or stress, and control. Additionally, clients derive comfort and security from their present behavior which, though painful, is also predictable. As Gottman and Leiblum (1974) observe, "Symptoms may be subjectively distressful, but they may produce a certain degree of consistency . . . in an otherwise unpredictable world" (p. 108). For this reason, helpers are usually advised not to tear down what they cannot replace.

Sometimes, too, clients exhibit resistance because they were never committed to counseling in the first place. This is seen more often with clients who are involuntary or are required to seek help. These clients may feel coerced to change and, because of this, will do their best to defeat the helper. Other countertherapeutic motives that bring people into counseling include getting verification that they do not need to change, obtaining support for a decision they have made, satisfying other persons in the hope this will get them "off their back," and finding someone else to blame for their problem (scapegoating) (Cavanaugh, 1982).

In these instances, the therapist has a variety of potential maneuvers. One is to include significant others in the helping process—particularly those who have a vested interest in having the client change—by utilizing a systemic intervention approach as described in Chapter 10. A second choice is to reduce the number of sessions or to terminate helping until the client makes some attempt to commit himself or herself to the helping process. As Fisch, Weakland, and Segal (1982) note, "(t)he therapist cannot deal effectively with patient resistance unless he is prepared to exercise this ultimate option should it become necessary" (p. 23). In exercising this option. however, the therapist must proceed carefully, being certain that the client does not construe termination as punishment, but rather as the therapist's concern and unwillingness not to have the client waste time and/or money (Gottman & Leiblum, 1974, p. 113).

In cases where it becomes apparent that the client is resistant simply to "outdo" or "do in" the therapist, there is always the option of a paradoxical intervention. As mentioned in Chapter 10, in these interventions the client is encouraged either to produce symptomatic behavior at will or to avoid trying to get better. The paradox conveyed to clients is that the client can change by remaining unchanged. This reduces pressure on clients who feel coerced to change and, at the same time, takes away the opportunity to defeat the helper. In using paradoxical interventions effectively, therapists must avoid becoming frustrated, defensive, or counteroppositional.

A most important principle to remember in dealing with highly resistant clients is never to fight with them. As Shelton and Levy (1981) note, when a therapist accepts the client's resistance, "the client is caught in a position where resistance becomes cooperation" (p. 72). Paradoxical interventions, though highly effective, are usually reserved for use in situations of major noncompliance and only after more direct methods of dealing with the resistance have been tried (Papp, 1980).

A final strategy that may be useful for some highly resistant or involuntary clients is to attempt to get them interested in participating in counseling. Sometimes this can be achieved by renegotiating the implicit contract. Ask clients whether they are bothered by anything in addition to what they were sent or referred for. The object of this strategy is to identify a complaint that *this* client is interested in changing.

Therapists must also consider the possibility that sometimes they, rather than clients, are the contributing source to lack of movement in the helping process. When counselors are resistant, they are often not any more aware of it than their clients—at least initially. Yet signs of therapist resistance are very similar to those of client resistance. For example, resistant counselors may cancel or postpone appointments, be late, daydream, be forgetful, or be overly eager to refer or to terminate the counseling.

Counselors can be resistant for a variety of reasons. Some may find the client attractive and resist terminating, while others dislike the client and opt for premature termination (Cavanaugh, 1982). Still others may behave in resistant ways because their need to control, convert, or punish the client is stronger than their need to be therapeutic or helpful (Cavanaugh, 1982, p. 260). Therapist resistance is often greater with novice helpers who are concerned or anxious about their competence or with more seasoned helpers who are often very good and because of this become overextended and subsequently burned out. In both cases, helpers are taking on too much responsibility. Anxious counselors may do too much work for the client in an attempt to alleviate their own discomfort. Overworked helpers may become responsible for too many clients and attempt to be all things to all people. Both kinds of counselors need to learn to set realistic limits for themselves with clients in order to avoid therapist-generated resistance and burn-out and fatigue.

Counselor Burn-Out and Self-Renewal

Beginning counselors are likely to feel alternately excited and anxious about their work with clients. Such feelings, which are usually very energized, often last as long as the newness and intensity of the counselor's work do not wear off. As counselors continue to see a number of clients each day, sometimes these feelings of excitement and anxiety change to discouragement and dread. When this occurs, the counselor may be experiencing a phenomenon called burn-out. Burn-out has been defined as a state of "physical, emotional, and mental exhaustion" (Corey, Corey, & Callanan, 1988, p. 56). Symptoms and signs of burn-out include any or all of the following:

Restlessness, boredom
Physical or emotional depletion
Helplessness or discouragement
Irritability
Lethargy, fatigue
Negative attitudes about themselves, their clients, or their work

Reasons for counselor burn-out are multiple, including being overworked, performing tedious tasks, and being strained with personal or family problems. Counselors who seem most susceptible to burn-out are those who work in isolation, whose work is limited to one type of activity or one type of clientele, and above all, those who experience a lack of therapeutic success (Farber & Heifetz, 1982).

Burn-out is an important issue for helpers because of its potential effects on the therapeutic relationship. Burned-out counselors move away from clients, and clients gradually sense the distance. Such distance deprives the client of necessary security and acceptance. Such distance also makes counselors vulnerable to missing important information shared by clients (Cavanaugh, 1982, p. 265).

There are a variety of things you can do to both prevent burn-out and to deal with it effectively if and when it occurs. First, recognize how and by whom the problem has been created. If it is created solely by you, let the client know it is your problem. As Cavanaugh (1982) states, "(w)hen a problem arises in counseling, it is very important for the person to know whose problem it is" (p. 266). Otherwise, clients are likely to conclude—erroneously—that they are responsible for the distance they are experiencing in the relationship. If some of it is created by a client—such as a client who storytells, rambles, or is so repressed that little or no affect surfaces—consider changing your approach, using a different intervention strategy, using a log or a journal, rescheduling to another time, or using the skills of self-disclosure and immediacy to express your concerns.

Another way to prevent or deal with burn-out is to vary your work environment so that you do not become satiated with one type of activity or clientele. If you only do intake interviews or only see status offenders, for example, very soon the sheer predictability of your sessions will create boredom and lethargy on your part. Planning for variety in your work, expressing rather than repressing negative feelings about your work, and exchanging job responsibilities with a colleague are all examples of ways to make your work setting more stimulating (Corey, Corey, & Callanan, 1988).

A third way to prevent and handle burn-out is to become involved with a close-knit support system of friends and colleagues. This is especially important for counselors who work alone or in relatively isolated settings. Becoming involved in peer-group meetings, participating in growth experiences, meeting regularly with friends and colleagues, and attending ongoing professional education and training seminars are all useful ways to stay in contact with other persons (Corey, Corey, & Callanan, 1988)

A fourth way to manage burn-out is to take care of yourself. Counselors who are fatigued because of lack of sleep, improper exercise and diet, too much work and too little play, are more susceptible to burn-out. Developing activities and interests other than counseling, setting and keeping priorities in mind, eating and sleeping well, exercising on a regular basis, and providing for time to yourself will help you be less vulnerable to burn-out (Corey, Corey, & Callanan, 1988).

Finally, it is important to remember that you are not a "bottomless pit." Counselors are persons, too, who need to periodically fill up their pot or find ways to replenish themselves. One way you can do so is to recognize that helping involves taking as well as giving!

It is easy, in our culture, to construe helping as giving and to construe giving as virtuous. Thus, helping becomes virtuous. The implication is that the truly virtuous person is a giver by nature and not a taker by nature. In fact, to be labeled a taker would not be a very favorable judgment. The cultural supports for giving are around us all of the time. Everyone is familiar with expressions like "Give 'til it hurts," "Give that another might live," or "Give to your United Way." There is a sense of unity, purpose, and goodwill in social giving.

With such powerful supports for the virtue of giving, we begin to wonder if there is anything at all to be said for taking. Some thoughts do come to mind. If the world were filled with givers, who would be left to take from them? And if there were no one to take, how could the giver give? And if the giver could not give, then he or she could not be a giver. So, in a very real sense, the giver is dependent upon the taker in order to fulfill the giving role.

The spirit of taking is very much the same as the spirit of giving. Indeed, unless the two complement each other, both the giving and the taking are frustrating experiences. The point is that we really should respect the role of the taker more than we seem to. In the real world, relationships are immature when one person is only a giver and the other person is only a taker. Mature relationships are give *and* take relationships.

How does all this relate to counseling? Are we implying that a good counselor is a taker as well as a giver? Yes we are!

What does the counselor take from clients? Certainly, the counselor does not take anything and everything that clients may offer. Some limitations the counselor may impose may be based upon ethical reasons or professional reasons. It may not be in the best interests of the counseling relationship, for example, for the counselor to accept a concurrent social relationship with the client. But we are here more concerned with what the counselor can take. A highly skilled marriage counselor was asked, "What do you take from your clients?" Her answer was, "I take from my clients every time they come back. They give me a new sense of my credibility. I trust the message in their coming back. I also take the power they give me. When I offer a strategy that I believe will work, and they accept my suggestion, I have the sense that they are giving me a lot of power over their lives."

Clients do give the counselor influence. They also give the counselor a level of confidence, respect, and professional stature. It is very important that you, as a counselor, not reject this gift. It will affect the client's perception of you as a counselor/professional. But there is another, perhaps more important, dimension. We believe that it is very important for you to be able to say, "I accept my clients' views of me and my competence, even though they may not agree with my own views." A fundamental issue is at stake here. If you are to respect your clients as human beings, you must also respect their views. After all, it is possible that your own views of yourself might be just a little bit off.

You will also want to accept your clients' views on their problems. After all, they have gained in some ways from living their lives, no matter how stressed those lives may be. If you give your client credibility as a helper in the counseling relationship, in return you will receive a co-worker who is committed to change. Asking your client for possible solutions, strategies, or different ways of framing the problem often yields excellent and surprising results. It also demystifies the counseling process, and that is always desirable.

Summary

Now, for a final thought as we come to the end of this journey with you. Helping others is an honorable involvement. Many of us decided to become counselors because we saw it as a way of becoming better helpers. Or at least we saw counseling as a preferred way of helping. Anyone who has ever seen a person in mental anguish knows the pull of that experience. Anyone who has counseled a person through such a period knows the beautiful feelings that come from having helped.

It is this feeling that most people acknowledge when asked, "Why do you want to be a counselor?" But this is not the most important or even the first question that should be asked of the potential counselor. That question, we believe, is "Do you know what counseling means?" In conclusion, we would like you to view counseling as a giving-and-taking process for all parties involved—both for the counselor and for the person in counseling. Your openness to taking and your willingness to let the client be a giver opens doors that otherwise would remain closed. It allows the relationship to be a real and maturing one. It allows you to see your client more as a real person. And it allows your client the same view of you. It gives your client a more honest perception of what a normally functioning person can be. And, above all, it allows you to replenish and renew yourself when your stamina, your energy, and your ability to use yourself therapeutically are ebbing away.

Exercises

I. Gender Role Issues

In the Gender Role section of this chapter, we discussed communication patterns and how they reveal underlying power relationships between the sexes. One of the problems in detecting such patterns is the unchallenged nature of these communication patterns, if not to say the power issues. In this exercise, you are to look for existing communication patterns between males alone, between males and females, and between females alone.

A. At a social event in which both males and females are present, remove yourself sufficiently from the interaction to allow yourself to study the communication patterns that are occurring naturally. There are three categories of communication that you should examine:

1. Communication within sexes.
   a. When one male states an opinion, how does the second male respond?
   b. When one female states an opinion, how does the second female respond?

2. Communication between sexes.
   a. When one male states an opinion in the presence of both another male and another female, who responds first? How does that person respond?
   b. When one female states an opinion in the presence of both another male and another female, who responds first? How does that person respond?

3. Types of responses.
   a. It has been suggested in the literature that when a male makes a statement to a second male, the response from the second male is likely to be a statement. Did you find this to be true?
   b. It has also been suggested in the literature that when a male makes a statement to a female, the response from the female is likely to be a question. Did you find this to be true?
   c. Do you find any power connotations in your observations? Deference? Reinforcement to continue speaking?

II. Cross-Cultural Counseling

This exercise calls for the use of triads to simulate cross-cultural counseling sessions and is adapted from Pedersen's (1977) triadic model of cross-cultural counseling.

1. One person serving as the helper pairs up with another person functioning as the client. The client and counselor should be as culturally dissimilar as possible. Consider such factors as cultural affiliation, race, ethnicity, nationality, socioeconomic level, age, sex, sex-role orientation, and lifestyle in selecting these dyads.

2. A third person, or "anti-helper," who is also culturally dissimilar from the counselor is selected. This third person also should be matched as well as possible to the client in terms of the same factors listed in #1 above.

3. The third person attempts to use the cultural similarity with the client to side with the client and to disrupt the work of the helper. Thus, the task of the anti-helper is to maintain the client's problem and work against solutions recommended by the helper. Ways that the anti-helper might engage in this task

include confusing, distorting, distracting, discrediting, or frustrating the helper. At the same time, it is important for the antihelper to have a high degree of acceptance and empathy for the client.

4. The task of the helper is to attempt to align with the client and against the problem and to pull in one direction toward a solution of the issue.

5. The task of the client is to present a hypothetical or simulated problem (as opposed to a real problem where actual counseling might be more appropriate) and to choose which alternative—the cross-cultural helper or the same culture anti-helper—offers the most meaningful ally. In order to do this, it is important for the client to feel free to reject an inauthentic anti-helper just as easily as he or she might reject a nonempathic or misinformed helper.

6. All three persons engage in a ten-minute role-play interview. It is important during the role-play for all three to interact with one another, rather than just the helper and the client.

7. Following the role-play, both the anti-helper and the client provide immediate feedback to the helper. The feedback should be positive as well as negative.

8. Following the feedback, the same triad conducts another ten-minute role-play interview so that the helper has another opportunity to interact with the client and to incorporate the feedback received following the initial role-play session.

9. After the second role-play, the helper, client, and anti-helper exchange views about the effects of the second session. Which session was more effective? The more effective session will be the one in which a helper—client coalition forms against the anti-helper. Least effective counseling occurs in a client—anti-helper coalition, thereby isolating the helper.

10. New triads are formed in order to allow others to experience different roles in subsequent role-plays.

IV. Managing Resistance

Select a partner who can role-play a client for you. Engage in a ten-minute role-play interaction. The client's task is to present an immediate and concrete problem that needs to be solved. Your task is to provide some ideas or recommendations about the problem for the client to consider. The client should counter or refute each of your suggestions or respond with "Yes, but . . ." After the interaction is over, discuss how you felt to have your input resisted by the client. In what ways were your feelings evident in your responses and behavior?

V. Counselor Burn-Out and Self-Renewal

1. Can you recall the last time in your life when you felt burned out? If not about counseling, then maybe you felt that way about a job, a class, or a relationship. What feelings did you have? What signs or behaviors were present that suggested you were experiencing burn-out? How did you try to deal with this phenomenon? Was it effective or not?

2. Based on what you learned from the experience in #3, list some signs or symptoms you need to be alert to for yourself that may indicate the onset of burn-out in your role as a counselor.

3. Brainstorm some ways you believe would be most effective for you to (a) prevent burn-out; and (b) handle burn-out if it occurred.

Discussion Questions

1. When in conversation with several of your colleagues, you become aware that one of them refers to Italian-American clients as overly emotional, dramatic, and too volatile to deal with effectively in counseling. How do you react? Suppose you heard similar information from your supervisor. What would your reaction be?

2. According to Pedersen (1977), the function of counseling is to establish a temporary coalition with the client and against the client's identified problem. Under what conditions will this process occur when counseling clients who are from the same culture as the helper? From a different culture?

3. Assume that you have been working with a client for two months. At the end of two months, the client is functioning in the same way as before counseling started. What does this suggest to you about possible resistance? How would you deal with it?

4. Discuss some direct and indirect ways to manage resistance in clients.

5. Experienced helpers talk a great deal about burn-out. Do you believe their concern is justified, or do you feel it is an over-

rated phenomenon? Support your views with an explanation and rationale.

Recommended Readings

Foxley, C.H. (1979), *Nonsexist Counseling: Helping Women and Men Redefine Their Roles* (Dubuque, IA: Kendall/Hunt).

Gilligan, C. (1982), *In a Different Voice: Psychological Theory and Womens' Development* (Cambridge, MA: Harvard University Press).

Good, G.E., Gilbert, L.A., & Scher, M. (1990), "Gender Aware Therapy: A Synthesis of Feminist Therapy and Knowledge about Gender," *Journal of Counseling and Development 68*, 376-380.

Larson, P.C. (1982), "Counseling Special Populations," *Professional Psychology 13*, 843-858.

Lee, C.C. & Richardson, B.L., Eds. (1991), *Multicultural Issues in Counseling: New Approaches to Diversity* (Alexandria, VA: American Association for Counseling and Development Press).

McGoldrick, M., Pearce, J.K., & Giordano, J., Eds. (1982), *Ethnicity and Family Therapy* (New York: Guilford).

Mintz, L.B. & O'Neil, J.M. (1990), "Gender Roles, Sex, and the Process of Psychotherapy: Many Questions and Few Answers," *Journal of Counseling and Development, 68*, 381-387.

Roessler, R.T. (1990), "A Quality of Life Perspective on Rehabilitation Counseling," *Rehabilitation Counseling Bulletin 34*, 82-90.

Sue, D.W. & Sue, D. (1990), *Counseling the Culturally Different: Theory and Practice* (New York: John Wiley & Sons).

Thorne, B., Kramarae, C., & Henley, N., Eds. (1983), *Language, Gender, and Society* (Cambridge, MA: Newbury House).

Appendix A

Ethical Standards, American Counseling Association*

(Approved by Executive Committee upon referral of the Board of Directors, January 17, 1981.)

Preamble

The American Personnel and Guidance Association (now ACA) is an educational, scientific, and professional organization whose members are dedicated to the enhancement of the worth, dignity, potential, and uniqueness of each individual and thus to the service of society.

The Association recognizes that the role definitions and work settings of its members include a wide variety of academic disciplines, levels of academic preparation and agency services. This diversity reflects the breadth of the Association's interests and influence. It also poses challenging complexities in efforts to set standards for the performance of members, desired requisite preparation or practice, and supporting social, legal, and ethical controls.

The specification of ethical standards enables the Association to clarify to present and future members and to those served by members, the nature of ethical responsibilities held in common by its members.

The existence of such standards serves to stimulate greater concern by members for their own professional functioning and for the conduct of fellow professionals such as counselors, guidance and student personnel workers, and others in the helping professions. As the ethical code of the Association, this document establishes principles that define the ethical behavior of Association members.

Section A: General

1. The member influences the development of the profession by continuous efforts to improve professional practices, teaching, services. and research. Professional growth is continuous throughout the member's career and is exemplified by the development of a philosophy that explains why and how a member functions in the helping relationship. Members must gather data on their effectiveness and be guided by the findings.

2. The member has a responsibility both to the individual who is served and to the institution within which the service is performed to maintain high standards of professional conduct. The member strives to maintain the highest levels of professional services offered to the individuals to be served. The member also strives to assist the agency, organization, or institution in providing the highest caliber of professional services. The acceptance of employment in an institution implies that the member is in

agreement with the general policies and principles of the institution. Therefore the professional activities of the member are also in accord with the objectives of the institution. If, despite concerted efforts, the member cannot reach agreement with the employer as to acceptable standards of conduct that allow for changes in institutional policy conducive to the positive growth and development of clients, then terminating the affiliation should be seriously considered.

3. Ethical behavior among professional associates, both members and non-members, must be expected at all times. When information is possessed that raises doubt as to the ethical behavior of professional colleagues, whether Association members or not, the member must take action to attempt to rectify such a condition. Such action shall use the institution's channels first and then use procedures established by the state Branch, Division, or Association.

4. The member neither claims nor implies professional qualifications exceeding those possessed and is responsible for correcting any misrepresentations of these qualifications by others.

5. In establishing fees for professional counseling services, members must consider the financial status of clients and locality. In the event that the established fee structure is inappropriate for a client, assistance must be provided in finding comparable services of acceptable cost.

6. When members provide information to the public or to subordinates, peers or supervisors, they have a responsibility to ensure that the content is general, unidentified client information that is accurate, unbiased, and consists of objective, factual data.

7. With regard to the delivery of professional services, members should accept only those positions for which they are professionally qualified.

8. In the counseling relationship the councilor is aware of the intimacy of the relationship and maintains respect for the client and avoids engaging in activities that seek to meet the counselor's personal needs at the expense of that client. Through awareness of the negative impact of both racial and sexual stereotyping and discrimination, the counselor guards the individual rights and personal dignity of the client in the counseling relationship.

Section B: Counseling Relationship

This section refers to practices and procedures of individual and/or group counseling relationships.

The member must recognize the need for client freedom of choice. Under those circumstances where this is not possible, the member must apprise clients of restrictions that may limit their freedom of choice.

1. The member's primary obligation is to respect the integrity and promote the welfare of the client(s), whether the client(s) is (are) assisted individually or in a group relationship. In a group setting, the member is also responsible for taking reasonable precautions to protect individuals from physical and/or psychological trauma resulting from interaction within the group.

2. The counseling relationship and information resulting therefrom [must] be kept confidential, consistent with the obligations of the member as a professional person. In a group counseling setting, the counselor must set a norm of confidentiality regarding all group participants' disclosures.

3. If an individual is already in a counseling relationship with another professional person, the member [must] not enter into a counseling relationship without first contacting and receiving the approval of that other professional. If the member discovers that the client is in another counseling relationship after the counseling relationship begins, the member must gain the consent of the other professional or terminate the relationship, unless the client elects to terminate the other relationship.

4. When the client's condition indicates that there is clear and imminent danger to the client or others, the member must take reasonable personal action or inform responsible authorities. Consultation with other professionals must be used where possible. The assumption of responsibility for the client's behavior must be taken only after careful deliberation. The client must be involved in the resumption of responsibility as quickly as possible.

5. Records of the counseling relationship, including interview notes, test data, correspondence, tape recordings, and other documents, are to be considered professional information for use in counseling and they should not be considered a part of the records of the institution or agency in which the counselor is employed unless specified by state statute or regulation. Revelation to others of counseling material must occur only upon the expressed consent of the client.

6. Use of data derived from a counseling relationship for purposes of counselor training or research shall be confined to content that can be disguised to ensure full protection of the identity of the subject client.

7. The member must inform the client of the purposes, goals, techniques, rules of procedure and limitations that may affect the relationship at or before the time that the counseling relationship is entered.

8. The member must screen prospective group participants, especially when the emphasis is on self-understanding and growth through self-disclosure. The member must maintain an awareness of the group participants' compatibility throughout the life of the group.

9. The member may choose to consult with any other professionally competent person about a client. In choosing a consultant, the member must avoid placing the consultant in a conflict of interest situation that would preclude the consultant's being a proper party to the member's efforts to help the client.

10. If the member determines an inability to be of professional assistance to the client, the member must either avoid initiating the counseling relationship or immediately terminate that relationship. In either event, the member must suggest appropriate alternatives. (The member must be knowledgeable about referral resources so that a satisfactory referral can be initiated.) In the event the client declines the suggested referral, the member is not obliged to continue the relationship.

11. When the member has other relationships, particularly of an administrative, supervisory and/or evaluative nature with an individual seeking counseling services, the member must not serve as the counselor but should refer the individual to another professional. Only in instances where such an alternative is unavailable and where the individual's situation warrants counseling intervention should the member enter into and/or maintain a counseling relationship. Dual relationships with clients that might impair the member's objectivity and professional judgment (e.g., as with close friends or relatives, sexual intimacies with any client) must be avoided and/or the counseling relationship terminated through referral to another competent professional.

12. All experimental methods of treatment must be clearly indicated to prospective recipients and safety precautions are to be adhered to by the member.

13. When the member is engaged in short-term group treatment/training programs (e.g., marathons and other encounter-type or growth groups), the member ensures that there is professional assistance available during and following the group experience.

14. Should the member be engaged in a work setting that calls for any variation from the above statements, the member is obligated to consult with other professionals whenever possible to consider justifiable alternatives.

Section C: Measurement and Evaluation

The primary purpose of educational and psychological testing is to provide descriptive measures that are objective and interpretable in either comparative or absolute terms. The member must recognize the need to interpret the statements that follow as applying to the whole range of appraisal techniques including test and nontest data. Test results constitute only one of a variety of pertinent sources of information for personnel, guidance, and counseling decisions.

1. The member must provide specific orientation or information to the examinee(s) prior to and following the test administration so that the results of testing may be placed in proper perspective with other relevant factors. In so doing, the member must recognize the effects of socioeconomic, ethnic and cultural factors on test scores. It is the member's professional responsibility to use additional unvalidated information carefully in modifying interpretation of the test results.

2. In selecting tests for use in a given situation or with a particular client, the member must consider carefully the specific validity, reliability, and appropriateness of the test(s). *General* validity, reliability and the like may be questioned legally as well as ethically when tests are used for vocational and educational selection, placement. or counseling.

3. When making any statements to the public about tests and testing, the member must give accurate information and avoid false claims or misconceptions. Special efforts are often required to avoid unwarranted connotations of such terms as *IQ* and *grade equivalent scores*.

4. Different tests demand different levels of competence for administration, scoring, and interpretation. Members must recognize the limits of their competence and perform only those functions for which they are prepared.

5. Tests must be administered under the same conditions that were established in their standardization. When tests are not administered under standard conditions or when unusual behavior or irregularities occur during the testing session, those conditions must be noted and the results designated as invalid or of questionable validity. Unsupervised or inadequately supervised test-taking, such as the use of tests through the mails, is considered unethical. On the other hand, the use of instruments that are so designed or standardized to be self-administered and self-scored, such as interest inventories, is to be encouraged.

6. The meaningfulness of test results used in personnel, guidance, and counseling functions generally depends on the examinee's unfamiliarity with the specific items on the test. Any prior coaching or dissemination

of the test materials can invalidate test results. Therefore, test security is one of the professional obligations of the member. Conditions that produce most favorable test results must be made known to the examinee.

7. The purpose of testing and the explicit use of the results must be made known to the examinee prior to testing. The counselor must ensure that instrument limitations are not exceeded and that periodic review and/or retesting are made to prevent client stereotyping.

8. The examinee's welfare and explicit prior understanding must be the criteria for determining the recipients of the test results. The member must see that specific interpretation accompanies any release of individual or group test data. The interpretation of test data must be related to the examinee's particular concerns.

9. The member must be cautious when interpreting the results of research instruments possessing insufficient technical data. The specific purposes for the use of such instruments must be stated explicitly to examinees.

10. The member must proceed with caution when attempting to evaluate and interpret the performance of minority group members or other persons who are not represented in the norm group on which the instrument was standardized.

11. The member must guard against the appropriation, reproduction, or modifications of published tests or parts thereof without acknowledgment and permission from the previous publisher.

12. Regarding the preparation, publication and distribution of tests, reference should be made to:

a. Standards for Educational and Psychological Tests and Manuals, revised edition, 1974, published by the American Psychological Association on behalf of itself, the American Educational Research Association and the National Council on Measurement in Education.

b. The responsible use of tests: A position paper of AMEG, APGA, and NCME. *Measurement and Evaluation in Guidance*, 1972, 5, 385-388.

c. "Responsibilities of Users of Standardized Tests," APGA, *Guidepost*, October 5, 1978, pp. 5-8.

Section D: Research and Publication

1. Guidelines on research with human subjects shall be adhered to, such as:

a. *Ethical Principles in the Conduct of Research with Human Participants*, Washington, D.C.: American Psychological Association, Inc., 1973.

b. Code of Federal Regulations, Title 45, Subtitle A, Part 46, as currently issued.

2. In planning any research activity dealing with human subjects, the member must be aware of and responsive to all pertinent ethical principles and ensure that the research problem, design, and execution are in full compliance with them.

3. Responsibility for ethical research practice lies with the principal researcher, while others involved in the research activities share ethical obligation and full responsibility for their own actions.

4. In research with human subjects, researchers are responsible for the subjects' welfare throughout the experiment and they must take all

reasonable precautions to avoid causing injurious psychological, physical, or social effects on their subjects.

5. All research subjects must be informed of the purpose of the study except when withholding information or providing misinformation to them is essential to the investigation. In such research the member must be responsible for corrective action as soon as possible following completion of the research.

6. Participation in research must be voluntary. Involuntary participation is appropriate only when it can be demonstrated that participation will have no harmful effects on subjects and is essential to the investigation.

7. When reporting research results, explicit mention must be made of all variables and conditions known to the investigator that might affect the outcome of the investigation or the interpretation of the data.

8. The member must be responsible for conducting and reporting investigations in a manner that minimizes the possibility that results will be misleading.

9. The member has an obligation to make available sufficient original research data to qualified others who may wish to replicate the study.

10. When supplying data, aiding in the research of another person, reporting research results, or in making original data available, due care must be taken to disguise the identity of the subjects in the absence of specific authorization from such subjects to do otherwise.

11. When conducting and reporting research, the member must be familiar with, and give recognition to, previous work on the topic, as well as . . . observe all copyright laws and follow the principles of giving full credit to all to whom credit is due.

12. The member must give due credit through joint authorship, acknowledgment, footnote statements, or other appropriate means to those who have contributed significantly to the research and/or publication, in accordance with such contributions.

13. The member must communicate to other members the results of any research judged to be of professional or scientific value. Results reflecting unfavorably on institutions, programs, services, or vested interest must not be withheld for such reasons.

14. If members agree to cooperate with another individual in research and/or publication, they incur an obligation to cooperate as promised in terms of punctuality of performance and with full regard to the completeness and accuracy of the information required.

15. Ethical practice requires that authors not submit the same manuscript, or one essentially similar in content, for simultaneous publication consideration by two or more journals. In addition, manuscripts published in whole or in substantial part in another journal or published work should not be submitted for publication without acknowledgment and permission from the previous publication.

Section E: Consulting

Consultation refers to a voluntary relationship between a professional helper and help-needing individual, group or social unit in which the consultant is providing help to the client(s) in defining and solving a work-related problem or potential problem with a client or client system. (This definition is adapted from Kurpius, DeWayne, Consultation theory and process: An integrated model. *Personnel and Guidance Journal,* 1978, 56.)

1. The member acting as consultant must have a high degree of self-awareness of his/her own values, knowledge, skills, limitations, and needs in entering a helping relationship that involves human and/or organizational change and . . . the focus of the relationship [must] be on the issues to be resolved and not on the person(s) presenting the problem.

2. There must be understanding and agreement between member and client for the problem definition, change goals, and predicted consequences of interventions selected.

3. The member must be reasonably certain that she/he or the organization represented has the necessary competencies and resources for giving the kind of help that is needed now or may develop later and that appropriate referral resources arc available to the consultant.

4. The consulting relationship must be one in which client adaptability and growth toward self-direction are encouraged and cultivated. The member must maintain this role consistently and not become a decision maker for the client or create a future dependency on the consultant.

5. When announcing consultant availability for services. the member conscientiously adheres to the Association's *Ethical Standards*.

6. The member must refuse a private fee or other remuneration for consultation with persons who are entitled to these services through the member's employing institution or agency. The policies of a particular agency may make explicit provisions for private practice with agency clients by members of its staff. In such instances. the clients must be apprised of other options open to them should they seek private counseling services.

Section F: Private Practice

1. The member should assist the profession by facilitating the availability of counseling services in private as well as public settings.

2. In advertising services as a private practitioner, the member must advertise the services in such a manner so as to accurately inform the public as to services. expertise, profession, and techniques of counseling in a professional manner. A member who assumes an executive leadership role in the organization shall not permit his/her name to be used in professional notices during periods when not actively engaged in the private practice of counseling.

The member may list the following: highest relevant degree, type and level of certification or license, type and/or description of services, and other relevant information. Such information must not contain false, inaccurate, misleading, partial, out-of-context, or deceptive material or statements.

3. Members may join in partnership/corporation with other members and/or other professionals provided that each member of the partnership or corporation makes clear the separate specialties by name in compliance with the regulations of the locality.

4. A member has an obligation to withdraw from a counseling relationship if it is believed that employment will result in violation of the *Ethical Standards*. If the mental or physical condition of the member renders it difficult to carry out an effective professional relationship or if the member is discharged by the client because the counseling relationship is no longer productive for the client. then the member is obligated to terminate the counseling relationship.

5. A member must adhere to the regulations for private practice of the locality where the services are offered.

6. It is unethical to use one's institutional affiliation to recruit clients for one's private practice.

Section G: Personnel Administration

It is recognized that most members are employed in public or quasi-public institutions. The functioning of a member within an institution must contribute to the goals of the institution and vice versa if either is to accomplish their respective goals or objectives. It is therefore essential that the member and the institution function in ways to (a) make the institution's goals explicit and public; (b) make the member's contribution to institutional goals specific; and (c) foster mutual accountability for goal achievement.

To accomplish these objectives, it is recognized that the member and the employer must share responsibilities in the formulation and implementation of personnel policies.

1. Members must define and describe the parameters and levels of their professional competency.

2. Members must establish interpersonal relations and working agreements with supervisors and subordinates regarding counseling or clinical relationships, confidentiality, distinction between public and private material, maintenance, and dissemination of recorded information, work load and accountability. Working agreements in each instance must be specified and made known to those concerned.

3. Members must alert their employers to conditions that may be potentially disruptive or damaging.

4. Members must inform employers of conditions that may limit their effectiveness.

5. Members must submit regularly to professional review and evaluation.

6. Members must be responsible for in-service development of self and/or staff.

7. Members must inform their staff of goals and programs.

8. Members must provide personnel practices that guarantee and enhance the rights and welfare of each recipient of their service.

9. Members must select competent persons and assign responsibilities compatible with their skills and experiences.

Section H: Preparation Standards

Members who are responsible for training others must be guided by the preparation standards of the Association and relevant Division(s). The member who functions in the capacity of trainer assumes unique ethical responsibilities that frequently go beyond that of the member who does not function in a training capacity. These ethical responsibilities are outlined as follows:

1. Members must orient students to program expectations, basic skills development, and employment prospects prior to admission to the program.

2. Members in charge of learning experiences must establish programs that integrate academic study and supervised practice.

3. Members must establish a program directed toward developing students' skills, knowledge, and self-understanding, stated whenever possible in competency or performance terms.

4. Members must identify the levels of competencies of their students in compliance with relevant Division standards. These competencies must accommodate the para-professional as well as the professional.

5. Members, through continual student evaluation and appraisal, must be aware of the personal limitations of the learner that might impede future performance. The instructor must not only assist the learner in securing remedial assistance but also screen from the program those individuals who are unable to provide competent services.

6. Members must provide a program that includes training in research commensurate with levels of role functioning. Para-professional and technician-level personnel must be trained as consumers of research. In addition, these personnel must learn how to evaluate their own and their program's effectiveness. Graduate training, especially at the doctoral level, would include preparation for original research by the member.

7. Members must make students aware of the ethical responsibilities and standards of the profession.

8. Preparatory programs must encourage students to value the ideals of service to individuals and to society. In this regard, direct financial remuneration or lack thereof must not influence the quality of service rendered. Monetary considerations must not be allowed to overshadow professional and humanitarian needs.

9. Members responsible for educational programs must be skilled as teachers and practitioners.

10. Members must present thoroughly varied theoretical positions so that students may make comparisons and have the opportunity to select a position.

11. Members must develop clear policies within their educational institutions regarding field placement and the roles of the student and the instructor in such placements.

12. Members must ensure that forms of learning focusing on self-understanding or growth are voluntary, or if required as part of the education program, are made known to prospective students prior to entering the program. When the education program offers a growth experience with an emphasis on self-disclosure or other relatively intimate or personal involvement, the member must have no administrative, supervisory, or evaluating authority regarding the participant.

13. Members must conduct an educational program in keeping with the current relevant guidelines of the American Counseling Association and its Divisions.

Appendix B

Integrative
Practice Exercises

Learning to counsel is somewhat like learning any other complex task. It involves acquiring a set of skills, mastering a set of subtasks, and eventually putting everything together in some integrated fashion. Perhaps you can recall what the process of learning to drive a car was like for you. At first, the mere thought of being able to drive a car was probably an overwhelming idea. Now you drive and hardly pay any attention to the process because it is so familiar and has become such a part of you. In between the initial overwhelming idea of learning to drive and your current state of driving with relative comfort and ease, you practiced and mastered a variety of skills related to driving. You learned how to steer the car, use the accelerator, use the clutch, brake the car, and while doing all of this, watch out for other drivers. And you learned all of this in a relatively short time period—although certainly not overnight.

Now it is time to try to put some things together for yourself—to take what you have learned in somewhat isolated fashion and integrate it in a meaningful way. The purpose of these exercises is to help you put the parts together in a conceptual framework that allows you to make even greater sense of the helping process for yourself. At the same time, it is important to realize that your ability to synthesize the tools and stages of counseling will necessarily stretch beyond the experience of these exercises, particularly if you are not yet in a field or job experience in which you can apply the tools with actual clients.

While simulation such as role-playing can be an invaluable way to learn under conditions of reduced threat, it is not a substitute for actual encounters and interactions with persons whose lives are distressed, whose emotions are conflicted, and who are sitting in front of you somewhat expectantly, relieved, and scared, all at the same time. As you accumulate actual counseling experience, your understanding and integration of the tools and stages of helping will continue to grow, just as you will also continue to grow and develop personally and professionally.

In this appendix, we present a variety of exercises designed to help you pull together the skills and strategies we have presented in this book into some meaningful whole. Additionally, we believe that completion of these activities will enable you to understand better the counseling process as it unfolds over an extended period of time with a client.

EXERCISE 1

In this exercise, we present three client cases. After reading each case, respond to the questions following the cases. In your responses, indicate issues that may arise in each of the five stages of the counseling process as well as your ideas for dealing with these issues effectively. You may wish to jot down your ideas in writing or use a partner or small group to help you brainstorm with this material.

Case 1. Sally is a college freshman at a large university; she is overwhelmed by the size of the university, having lived in a small town all her life. She is concerned about her "shyness" and feels it is preventing her from making friends. She reports being uncertain about how to "reach out" to people. She is concerned about her performance on tests; although she believes her study habits are adequate, she reports that she "blows" the tests because she gets so uptight about them.

Case 2. Mr. and Mrs. Yule have been married for two years. Both are in their sixties, and this is their second marriage; their previous spouses had died within the last ten years. Mr. and Mrs. Yule are concerned that they "rushed into" this second relationship without adequate thought. They report that they argue constantly about everything. They feel they have forgotten how to talk to each other in a "civil" manner. Mrs. Yule states that she realizes her constant nagging upsets Mr. Yule; Mr. Yule discloses that his spending a lot of time with his male buddies irritates Mrs. Yule.

Case 3. Arthur is a third-grader at Malcolm Elementary School. Arthur is constantly "getting into trouble" for a number of things. Arthur admits that he starts a lot of fights with the other boys. He says he doesn't know why or how, but suddenly he is punching them. Only after these fights does he realize his anger got out of hand. Arthur realizes his behavior is causing some of the other kids to avoid him, yet he believes he would like their friendship. He is not sure how to handle his temper so that he doesn't lash out at his peers.

Rapport-Relationship

    1. List specific issues that may arise with this client in terms of establishing rapport and an effective helping relationship.

    2. How might this particular client respond initially to the counselor?

    3. How might this client respond to the counselor after several sessions?

Assessment of Problems

    4. List what seem to be the major problem areas for this client. Consider the affective, behavioral, cognitive, and interpersonal dimensions.

    5. What seem to be the client's main strengths. resources, and coping skills?

    6. Can you identify any probable payoffs of the client's dysfunctional or problematic behavior?

Goal-Setting

    7. What might this client seek or expect from counseling?

    8. What seem to be the ideal outcomes for this person?

    9. How different might your choice of outcomes for this client be from the client's choice of outcomes? If the difference is great, what impact might this have on the helping process?

Intervention Strategies

    10. Develop a list of possible intervention strategies that might be most useful in working with this particular client. Provide a rationale for your selection.

    11. What theoretical approach underlies each of the intervention strategies on your list?

12. Would you *generally* favor using affective, cognitive, behavioral, or systemic strategies with this person? Why?

Termination and Follow-Up

13. What are some indicators you would look for that suggest this client is ready to terminate counseling?

14. How would you help this client plan for transfer of learning from the counseling situation to the person's actual environment? What potential obstacles in his or her environment need to be anticipated?

15. How would you follow up on the progress of this client once the helping process is terminated?

EXERCISE 2

Select one of the three cases described in Exercise 1 to use for the purpose of conducting an extended series of role-play counseling sessions. Enlist the help of a colleague or classmate who can meet with you regularly over the next five weeks. This person's task is to assume the role of the client from one of these cases and to "become" this client in the sessions with you. Your task is to meet with this person for five scheduled sessions during the next five weeks.

The first session should be directed toward establishing rapport and building an effective therapeutic relationship with this person. The second session should be an assessment interview and should reflect the content presented in Chapter 4. In the third session, try to help the client develop outcome goals, using the process and skills described in Chapter 5. In the fourth session, based on the assessed problem areas and defined goals, select one or two intervention strategies from Chapters 7-10 and implement these strategies with the client. Also in this session, begin to prepare the client for termination. In the fifth and last session, help the client summarize and evaluate the helping process and plan for changes in his or her environment. Terminate the counseling process and develop a follow-up plan.

At a minimum, audiotape each session—videotape if possible. After each interview, assess and rate your behavior using the corresponding part of the Counseling Strategies Checklist that follows. Your instructor or supervisor may also want to assess your performance. Your "client" can also provide you with informative feedback. Use this feedback and your ratings to determine which skills and parts of the helping process you have mastered and which areas need additional improvement and practice.

THE COUNSELING STRATEGIES CHECKLIST (CSC)

The CSC is divided into six parts: (I) The Process of Relating; (II) Assessment; (III) Goal-Setting; (IV) Intervention Strategies; (V) Termination and Follow-Up; and (VI) Individual Skills Summary. The first five parts correspond to each of the five stages of the counseling process. Each of these parts can be used to observe, evaluate, and rate sessions for each of these stages in the counseling process. For example, Part I, the Process of Relating, is used primarily to assess rapport and relationship-building sessions. Part II, Assessment, is used to evaluate assessment interviews, and so on. Part VI, The Individual Skills Summary, is a compilation of all the individual verbal and nonverbal skills associated with each of these stages of counseling. It can also be used following each corresponding type of session to determine the presence or absence of the skills associated with a particular stage of counseling.

Using the Counseling Strategies Checklist

Each item in the CSC is scored by circling the most appropriate response, either Yes, No, or N.A. (not applicable). The items are worded such that desirable responses are Yes or N.A. No is an undesirable response.

After you have observed and rated each interview, sit down and review the ratings. Where noticeable deficiencies exist, you should identify a goal or goals that will remedy the problem. Beyond this, you should list two or three Action Steps that permit you to achieve this goal.

PART I: THE PROCESS OF RELATING

1. The counselor maintained eye contact with the client.
   Yes   No   N.A.
2. The counselor's facial expressions reflected the mood of the client.
   Yes   No   N.A.
3. The counselor demonstrated some variation in voice pitch when talking.
   Yes   No   N.A.
4. The counselor used intermittent one-word vocalizations ("mm-hmm") to reinforce the client's demonstration of goal-directed topics or behaviors.
   Yes   No   N.A.
5. The counselor made verbal comments that pursued the topic introduced by the client.
   Yes   No   N.A.
6. The subject of the counselor's verbal statements usually referred to the client, either by name or the second-person pronoun, "you."
   Yes   No   N.A.
7. A clear and sensible progression of topics was evident in the counselor's verbal behavior; the counselor avoided rambling.
   Yes   No   N.A.
8. The counselor made statements that reflected the client's feelings.
   Yes   No   N.A.
9. The counselor verbally stated his or her desire and intent to understand.
   Yes   No   N.A.
10. Several times (at least twice), the counselor shared his or her own feelings with the client.
    Yes   No   N.A.
11. At least one time during the interview, the counselor provided specific feedback to the client.
    Yes   No   N.A.
12. The counselor encouraged the client to identify and discuss his or her feelings concerning the counselor and the interview.
    Yes   No   N.A.
13. The counselor voluntarily shared his or her feelings about the client and the counseling relationship.
    Yes   No   N.A.

14. The counselor expressed reactions about the client's strengths and/or potential.
    Yes   No   N.A.
15. The counselor made responses that reflected his or her liking and appreciation of the client.
    Yes   No   N.A.

PART II: ASSESSMENT

1. The counselor asked the client to provide basic demographic information about himself or herself.
   Yes   No   N.A.
2. The counselor asked the client to describe his or her current concerns and to provide some background information about the problems.
   Yes   No   N.A.
3. The counselor asked the client to list and prioritize problems.
   Yes   No   N.A.
4. For each identified problem, the counselor and client explored the
   _____ affective dimensions of the problem.
        Yes   No   N.A.
   _____ cognitive dimensions of the problem.
        Yes   No   N.A.
   _____ behavioral dimensions of the problem.
        Yes   No   N.A.
   _____ interpersonal dimensions of the problem.
        Yes   No   N.A.
   _____ intensity of the problem (frequency, duration, or severity).
        Yes   No   N.A.
   _____ antecedents of the problem.
        Yes   No   N.A.
   _____ consequences and payoffs of the problem.
        Yes   No   N.A.
5. The counselor and client discussed previous solutions the client had tried to resolve the problem.
   Yes   No   N.A.
6. The counselor asked the client to identify possible strengths, resources, and coping skills the client could use to help resolve the problem.
   Yes   No   N.A.

PART III: GOAL-SETTING

1. The counselor asked the client to state how he or she would like to change his or her behavior ("How would you like for things to be different?")
   Yes   No   N.A.
2. The counselor and client decided together upon counseling goals.
   Yes   No   N.A.
3. The goals set in the interview were specific and observable.
   Yes   No   N.A.
4. The counselor asked the client to state orally a commitment to work for goal achievement.
   Yes   No   N.A.

5. If the client appeared resistant or unconcerned about achieving change, the counselor discussed this with the client.
Yes   No   N.A.

6. The counselor asked the client to specify at least one action step he or she might take toward his or her goal.
Yes   No   N.A.

7. The counselor suggested alternatives available to the client.
Yes   No   N.A.

8. The counselor helped the client to develop action steps for goal attainment.
Yes   No   N.A.

9. Action steps designated by counselor and client were specific and realistic in scope.
Yes   No   N.A.

10. The counselor provided an opportunity within the interview for the client to practice or rehearse the action step.
Yes   No   N.A.

11. The counselor provided feedback to the client concerning the execution of the action step.
Yes   No   N.A.

12. The counselor encouraged the client to observe and evaluate the progress and outcomes of action steps taken outside the interview.
Yes   No   N.A.

PART IV: STRATEGY SELECTION AND IMPLEMENTATION

1. The counselor suggested some possible strategies to the client based on the client's stated goals.
Yes   No   N.A.

2. The counselor provided information about the elements, time, advantages, and disadvantages of each strategy.
Yes   No   N.A.

3. The counselor involved the client in the choice of strategies to be used.
Yes   No   N.A.

4. The counselor suggested a possible sequence of strategies to be used when more than one strategy was selected.
Yes   No   N.A.

5. The counselor provided a rationale about each strategy to the client.
Yes   No   N.A.

6. The counselor provided detailed instructions about how to use the selected strategy.
Yes   No   N.A.

7. The counselor verified if the client understood how the selected strategy would be implemented.
Yes   No   N.A.

PART V: TERMINATION AND FOLLOW-UP

1. The counselor and client engaged in some evaluation or assessment of the client's attainment of the desired goals.
Yes   No   N.A.

2. The counselor and client summarized the client's progress throughout the helping process.
   Yes   No   N.A.
3. The counselor identified client indicators and behaviors suggesting termination was appropriate.
   Yes   No   N.A.
4. The counselor and client discussed ways for the client to apply or transfer the learnings from the helping interviews to the client's environment.
   Yes   No   N.A.
5. The counselor and client identified possible obstacles or stumbling blocks the client might encounter after termination and discussed possible ways for the client to handle these.
   Yes   No   N.A.
6. The counselor discussed some kind of follow-up plan to the client.
   Yes   No   N.A.

PART VI: INDIVIDUAL SKILL SUMMARY

Instructions: Check (✓) any of the skills that were utilized by the counselor in the observed interview. Use the space under Comments to record your qualitative assessment of the use of this skill. For example, how appropriately and effectively was it used?

Skills of Counseling	Comments
Rapport-Relationship	
Nonverbal attending	
Verbal attending	
Paraphrase	
Reflection	
Self-Disclosure	
Immediacy	
Pacing	
Assessment	
Questions	
Open	
Closed	
Clarifying	
Goal-Setting	
Confrontation	
Ability Potential	
Instructions	

Strategy Implementation

Information-Giving

Modeling

Rehearsal/Practice

Feedback

Termination

Summarization

References

Anderson, C.A., Lepper, M.R., & Ross, L. (1980). "Perseverance of Social Theories. The Role of Explanation in the Persistance of Discredited Information," *Journal of Personality and Social Psychology, 39*, 1037–1049.

Ascher, L.M., Ed., (1989), *Therapeutic Paradox* (New York: Guilford).

Axelson, J.A. (1985), *Counseling and Development in a Multicultural Society* (Pacific Grove, CA: Brooks/Cole).

Baker, S.B. & Butler, J.N. (1984), "Effects of Preventative Cognitive Self-Instruction on Adolescent Attitudes, Experiences and State Anxiety," *Journal of Primary Prevention 5*, 10-14.

Baker, S.B., Thomas, R.N. & Munson, W.W. (1983), "Effects of Cognitive Restructuring and Structured Group Discussion as Primary Prevention Strategies," *School Counselor 31*, 26-33.

Bandura, A. (1969), *Principles of Behavior Modification* (Englewood Cliffs, NJ: Prentice-Hall).

Bandura, A. (1977), *Social Learning Theory* (Englewood Cliffs, NJ: Prentice-Hall).

Bandura, A., Grusec, J.E. & Menlove, F.L. (1966), "Observational Learning as a Function of Symbolization and Incentive Set," *Child Development 37*, 499-506.

Barrett-Leonard, G.T. (1981), "The Empathy Cycle: Refinement of a Nuclear Concept," *Journal of Counseling Psychology 28*, 91-100.

Baucom, D.A. & Lester, G.W. (1986), "The Usefulness of Cognitive Restructuring as an Adjunct to Behavioral Marital Therapy," *Behavior Therapy 17*, 385-403.

Beck, A.T. (1976), *Cognitive Therapy and the Emotional Disorders* (New York: International Universities Press).

Belkin, G.S. (1984), *Introduction to Counseling* (Dubuque, IA: Wm. C. Brown).

Bellack, A., Rozensky, R. & Schwartz, J. (1974), "A Comparison of Two Forms of Self-Monitoring in a Behavioral Weight Reduction Program," *Behavior Therapy 5*, 523-530.

Bergin, A.E., & Lambert, M.J. (1978). "The Evaluation of Therapeutic Outcomes," in S.L. Garfield & A.E. Bergin (Eds.), *Handbook of Psychotherapy and Behavior Change: An emperical analysis* (pp. 139–189). New York: John Wiley.

Bernard, J.M. (1979), "Supervisor Training: A Discrimination Model," *Counselor Education and Supervision 19*, 60-68.

Bernard, J.M. & Goodyear, R.K. (1992), *Fundamentals of Clinical Supervision* (Boston: Allyn & Bacon).

Bernard, J.M. & Hackney, H. (1983), *Untying the Knot: A Guide to Civilized Divorce* (Minneapolis, MN: Winston).

Biglain, A. & Campbell, D. (1981), Depression, in J.L. Shelton & R.L. Levy (Eds.), *Behavioral Assignments and Treatment Compliance* (pp. 111-146) (Champaign, IL: Research Press).

Blocher, D.H. (1987), *The Professional Counselor* (New York: Macmillan).

Booraem, C.D. (1974), "Differential Effectiveness of External versus Self Reinforcement in the Acquisition of Assertive Responses," Unpublished doctoral dissertation, University of Southern California.

Bowen, M. (1978), *Family therapy in clinical practice* (New York: Jason Aronson).

Brammer, L.M. & Shostrom, E.L. (1982), *Therapeutic Psychology*, 4th Ed. (Englewood Cliffs, NJ: Prentice Hall).

Brooks, D.K., Jr. and Gerstein, L.H. (1990), "Counselor Credentialing and Interprofessional Collaboration," *Journal of Counseling and Development* 68, 477-484.

Carkhuff, R.R. & Anthony, W.A. (1979), *The Skills of Helping* (Amherst, MA: Human Resource Development Press).

Cashdan, S. (1988), *Object Relations Therapy* (New York: W.W. Norton).

Castro, L. & Rachlin, H. (1980), "Self-Reward, Self-Monitoring, and Self-Punishment as Feedback in Weight Control," *Behavior Therapy* 11, 38-48.

Catania, A.C. (1975). "The Myth of Self-Reinforcement," *Behaviorism, 3*, 192–199.

Cautela, J.R. (1969), Behavior Therapy and Self Control: Techniques and Implications, in C. Franks, Ed., *Behavior Therapy: Appraisal and Status* (pp. 323-340) (New York: McGraw-Hall).

Cautela, J.R. (1976), "The Present Status of Covert Modeling," *Journal of Behavior Therapy and Experimental Psychiatry* 6, 323-326.

Cavanaugh, M.E. (1982), *The Counseling Experience* (Pacific Grove, CA: Brooks/Cole).

Celotta, B. & Telasi-Golubscow, H. (1982), "A Problem Taxonomy for Classifying Clients' Problems," *Personal Guidance Journal 61*, 73-76.

Chaves, J. & Barber, T. (1974), "Cognitive Strategies, Experimental Modeling, and Expectation in the Attenuation of Pain," *Journal of Abnormal Psychology 83*, 356-363.

Ciminero, A., Nelson, R. & Lipinski, D. (1977), Self-Monitoring Procedures, in A. Ciminero, K. Calhoun, & H. Adams, Eds., *Handbook of Behavior and Assessment* (New York: Wiley), pp. 195-232.

Clark, D.M. and Salkovskis, P. M. (1989) *Cognitive Therapy for Panic and Hypochondriasis* (New York: Pergamon Press).

Corey, G., Corey, M.S., & Callanan, P. (1988), *Issues and Ethics in the Helping Professions* (Pacific Grove, CA: Brooks/Cole).

Cormier, W.H., and Cormier, L.S., (1991), *Interviewing Strategies for Helpers: Fundamental Skills and Cognitive Behavioral Interventions*, 3rd Ed. (Pacific Grove, CA: Brooks/ Cole).

Cormier, L.S., Cormier, W.H., & Weisser, R.J. (1984), *Interviewing and Helping Skills for Health Professionals* (Monterey, CA: Wadsworth).

Corrigan, J.D. Dell, D.M., Lewis, K.N. & Schmidt, L.D. (1980), "Counseling as a Social Influence Process: A Review," *Journal of Counseling Psychology 27*, 395-441.

Corsini, R.J. (1989), Introduction (Chapter One) in Raymond J. Corsini and Danny Wedding, Eds. *Current Psychotherapies* (Itasca, Il: F.E. Peacock).

Corsini, R.J. and Wedding, D., Eds. *Current Psychotherapies* (Itasca, Il: F.E. Peacock).

Crowley T.J. (1970), "The Conditionability of Positive and Negative Self-Reference Emotional Affect Statements in a Counseling—Type Interview," Unpublished doctoral dissertation, The University of Massachusetts.

Cummings, A.L. (1989), "Relationship of Client Problem to Novice Counselor Response Modes," *Journal of Counseling Psychology 36*, 331-335.

Deffenbacher, J.L. (1985), "A Cognitive-Behavioral Response and a Modest Proposal," *Counseling Psychologist, 13*, 261-269.

Dengrove, E. (1966), "Treatment of Non-Phobic Disorders by the Behavioral Therapies," Paper presented at the Association for Advancement of Behavior Therapy, New York.

Devine, D.A. & Fernald, P.S. (1973), "Outcome Effects of Receiving a Preferred Randomly Assigned, or Non-Preferred Therapy," *Journal of Consulting and Clinical Psychology 41*, 104-107.

Dinkmeyer, D. & Dinkmeyer, D., Jr. (1982), *Developing Understanding of Self and Others, D-1 & D-2*, rev. ed. (Circle Pines, MN: American Guidance Service).

Dixon, D.N. & Glover, J.A. (1984), *Counseling: A Problem-Solving Approach* (New York: Wiley).

Donley, R.J., Horan, J.J. & DeShong, R.L. (1990), "The Effect of Several Self-Disclosure Permutations on Counseling Process and Outcome," *Journal of Counseling and Development 67*, 408-412.

Doster, J.A. & Nesbitt, J.G. (1979), Psychotherapy and Self-Disclosure, in G.J. Chelune, Ed., *Self-Disclosure: Origins, Patterns, and Implications of Openness in Interpersonal Relationships* (San Francisco: Jossey-Bass).

Duhl, F.J., Kantor, D., & Duhl, B.S. (1973), Learning, Space and Action in Family Therapy: A Primer of Sculpture, in D.A. Bloch, Ed., *Techniques of Family Therapy* (New York: Grune & Stratton).

Dye, H.A. & Hackney, H. (1975), *Gestalt Approaches to Counseling* (Boston: Houghton Mifflin).

Egan, G. (1990), *The Skilled Helper*, 4th Ed., (Pacific Grove, CA: Brooks/Cole).

Ekman, P. & Friesen, W.V. (1967) "Head and Body Cues in the Judgment of Emotion: A Reformulation," *Perceptual and Motor Skills 24*, 711-724.

Ekman, P. & Friesen, W.V. (1969) "Nonverbal Leakage and Clues to Deception," *Psychiatry 32*, 88-106.

Elder, J.P., Edelstein, B.A. & Fremouw, W.J. (1981), "Client by Treatment Interactions in Response Acquisition and Cognitive Restructuring Approaches," *Cognitive Therapy and Research 5*, 203-210.

Ellis, A.E. (1971), *Rational-Emotive Therapy and its Application to Emotional Education* (New York: Institute for Rational Living).

Ellis, A.E. (1984), *Rational-Emotive Therapy and Cognitive Behavior Therapy* (New York: Springer).

Epstein, N.B. & Bishop, D.S. (1981), "Problem-Centered Systems Therapy of the Family," *Journal of Marital and Family Therapy 7*, 23-31.

Farber, B.A. & Heifetz, L.J. (1982), "The Process and Dimensions of Burnout in Psychotherapists," *Professional Psychology 13*, 293-301.

Figley, C.R. & Nelson, T.S. (1990), "Basic Family Therapy Skills, II: Structural Family Therapy," *Journal of Marriage and Family Therapy 16*, 225-239.

Fisch, R., Weakland, J.H. & Segal, L. (1982), *The Tactics of Change: Doing Therapy Briefly* (San Francisco: Jossey-Bass).

Flowers, J.V. & Booraem, C.D. (1980), Simulation and Role-Playing Methods, in F.A. Kanfer & A.P. Goldstein, Eds., *Helping People Change* (New York: Pergamon), pp. 172-209.

Fogarty, T.F. (1986), "Marital Crisis," in P G. Guerin, Ed., *Family Therapy: Theory and Practice* (New York: Gardner Press).

Foley, V.D. (1989), Family Therapy, in R.J. Corsini & Danny Wedding, Eds., *Current Psychotherapies*, 4th ed. (Itasca, IL: F.E. Peacock).

Fong, M.L. & Cox, B.G. (1983), "Trust as an Underlying Dynamic in the Counseling Process: How Clients Test Trust," *Personnel and Guidance Journal 62*, 163-166.

Forman, S.G. (1980), "A Comparison of Cognitive Training and Response Cost Procedures in Modifying Aggressive Behavior of Elementary School Children," *Behavior Therapy 11*, 594-600.

Foxley, C.H. (1979), *Nonsexist Counseling: Helping Women and Men Redefine Their Roles* (Dubuque, IA: Kendall/Hunt).

Framo, J. (1982), *Family Interaction: A Dialogue Between Family Therapists and Family Researchers* (New York: Springer).

Frederick, S.L. (1988), "Learning to Empathize with Resistance," *Journal of Counseling and Development 67*, 128.

Fremouw, W.J. (1977), "A Client Manual for Integrated Behavior Treatment of Speech Anxiety," *JSAS Catalogue of Selected Documents in Psychology 1*, 14 MS. 1426.

Fremouw, W.J. & Brown, J.P. Jr. (1980), "The Reactivity of Addictive Behaviors to Self-Monitoring: A Functional Analysis," *Addictive Behaviors 5*, 209-217.

Frey, D.H. (1972), "Conceptualizing Counseling Theories: A Content Analysis of Process and Goal Statements," *Counselor Education and Supervision 11*, 243-250.

Gazda, G.M., Asbury, F.S. Balzer, F.J., Childers, W.C., & Walters, R.P. (1984), *Human Relations Development: A Manual for Educators*, 3rd Ed. (Boston: Allyn & Bacon).

Gendlin, E.T. (1969), "Focusing," *Psychotherapy: Theory, Research and Practice 6*, 14-15.

Gendlin, E.T. (1984), The Client's Edge: The Edge of Awareness, in J.M. Shlien & R.F. Levant, Eds., *Client-Centered Psychotherapy and the Person-Centered Approach* (New York: Praeger).

Gilliland, B., James, R., and Bowman, J. (1989), *Theories and Strategies in Counseling and Psychotherapy*, 2nd Ed. (Englewood Cliffs, NJ: Prentice-Hall).

Gilligan, C. (1982), *In a Different Voice: Psychological Theory and Womens' Development* (Cambridge, MA: Harvard University Press).

Gilmore, S. (1973), *The Counselor-in-Training* (Englewood Cliffs, NJ: Prentice-Hall).

Gladding, S.T. (1988), *Counseling: A Comprehensive Profession* (Columbus, OH: Merrill).

Gladstein, G. (1983), "Understanding Empathy: Integrating Counseling, Development and Social Psychology Perspectives," *Journal of Counseling Psychology 30*, 467-482

Glasser, W. (1965), *Reality Therapy* (New York: Harper & Row).

Glasser, W. (1972), *The Identity Society* (New York: Harper & Row).

Glasser, W. (1976), *Positive Addiction* (New York: Harper & Row).

Glasser, W. & Zunin, L.M. (1979), Reality Therapy, in R.J. Corsini, Ed., *Current Psychotherapies*, 2nd Ed., (Itasca, IL: F.E. Peacock), pp. 287-316.

Goldfried, M.R. & Davison, G.C. (1976), *Clinical Behavior Therapy* (New York: Holt, Rinehart & Winston).

Goldfried, M.R. DeCenteceo, E.T., & Weinberg, L. (1974), "Systematic Rational Restructuring as a Self-Control Technique," *Behavior Therapy 5*, 247-254.

Goldstein, A.P. (1980), Relationship-Enhancement Methods, in F.H. Kanfer & A.P. Goldstein, Eds., *Helping People Change* (New York: Pergamon Press), pp. 18-57.

Good, G.E., Gilbert, L.A., & Scher, M. (1990), "Gender Aware Therapy: A Synthesis of Feminist Therapy and Knowledge about Gender," *Journal of Counseling and Development 68,* 376-380.

Goodyear, R.K. (1981), "Termination as a Loss Experience for the Counselor," *Personnel and Guidance Journal 59,* 347-350.

Gordon. R.L. (1969), *Interviewing: Strategy, Techniques and Tactics* (Homewood, IL: Dorsey).

Gottman, J.M., & Leiblum, S.R. (1974), *How To Do Psychotherapy and How To Evaluate It* (New York: Holt, Rinehart & Winston).

Gottman, J.M., Notarius, C., Gonso, J. & Markman, H. (1976), *A Couple's Guide to Communication* (Champaign, IL: Research Press).

Graves, J.R. & Robinson, J.D. (1976), "Proxemic Behavior as a Function of Inconsistent Verbal and Nonverbal Messages," *Journal of Counseling Psychology 23,* 333-338.

Greenberg, L.S. (1979), "Resolving Splits: Use of the Two Chair Technique," *Psychotherapy: Theory, Research and Practice 16,* 316-324.

Hackney, H. (1973), "Goal-Setting: Maximizing the Reinforcing Effects of Progress," *The School Counselor 20,* 176-181.

Hackney, H. (1974), "Facial Gestures and Subject Expression of Feeling," *The Journal of Counseling Psychology 21,* 163-178.

Hackney, H. (1978), "The evolution of empathy," *The Personnel and Guidance Journal 55,* 35-39.

Hackney, H. & Cormier, L.S. (1988), *Counseling Strategies and Interventions.* 3rd Ed. (Englewood Cliffs, NJ: Prentice-Hall).

Haley, J. (1963), *Strategies of Psychotherapy* (New York: Grune & Stratton).

Haley, J. (1973), *Uncommon Therapy* (New York: W.W. Norton).

Haley, J. (1976), *Problem-Solving Therapy* (New York: McGraw-Hill).

Haley, J. (1980), *Leaving Home* (New York: McGraw-Hill)

Halstead, R.W., Brooks, D.K., Goldberg, A., & Fish, L.S. (1990), "Counselor and Client Perceptions of the Working Alliance," *Journal of Mental Health Counseling* 12, 208-221.

Hamilton, S.A. & Fremouw, W.J. (1985), "Cognitive-Behavioral Training for College Basketball Foul-Shooting Performance," *Cognitive Therapy and Research 9,* 479-484.

Hansen, J.C., Stevic, R.R., & Warner, R.W., Jr., (1986), *Counseling: Theory and Process,* 3rd ed. (Boston: Allyn & Bacon).

Haynes, S.N., Jensen, B.M., Wise, E. & Sherman, D. (1981), "The Marital Intake Interview: A Multimethod Criterion Validity Instrument," *Journal of Consulting and Clinical Psychology 49,* 379-387.

Heffernan, T. & Richards, C.S. (1981), "Self-Control of Study Behavior: Identification and Evaluation of Natural Methods," *Journal of Counseling Psychology 28,* 361-364.

Hill, C.E., Siegelman, L., Gronsky, B.R., Sturniolo, F., & Fretz, B.R. (1981), "Nonverbal Communication and Counseling Outcome," *Journal of Counseling Psychology 28,* 203-212.

Hoffman, L. (1981), *Foundations of Family Therapy* (Cambridge, MA: Harvard University Press).

Holdstock, T.L. & Rogers, C.R. (1977), Person-centered theory, in R.J. Corsini, Ed., *Current Personality Theories,* (Itasca, IL: Peacock), Chapter 5, pp. 125-151.

Homme, L., Csanyi, A., Gonzales, M. & Rechs, J. (1969), *How to Use Contingency Contracting in the Classroom* (Champaign, IL: Research Press).

Hosford, R. & de Visser, L. (1974), *Behavioral Approaches to Counseling: An Introduction* (Washington, D.C.: American Personnel and Guidance Association Press).

Hosford, R., Moss, C. & Morrill, G. (1976), The Self-as-a-Model Technique: Helping Prison Inmates Change, in J.D. Krumbolts & C.E. Thorsen, Eds., *Counseling Methods* (New York: Holt, Rinehart & Winston), pp. 487-495.

Hulnick, M.R. & Hulnick, H.R. (1989), "Life's Challenges: Curse or Opportunity? Counseling Families of Persons with Disabilities," *Journal of Counseling and Development 68*, 166-170.

Hutchins, D.E. (1979), "Systematic Counseling: The T-F-A Model for Counselor Intervention," *Personnel and Guidance Journal 57*, 529-531.

Hutchins, D.E. (1982), "Ranking Major Counseling Strategies with the T-F-A Matrix System," *Personnel and Guidance Journal 60*, 427-431.

Hutchins, D.E. (1984),"Improving the Counseling Relationship," *Personnel and Guidance Journal 62*, 572-575.

Iberg, J.R. (1981), Focusing, in R.J. Corsini, Ed., *Handbook of Innovative Psychotherapy* (New York: Wiley).

Ivey, A.E. (1988), *Intentional Interviewing and Counseling*, 2nd Ed. (Pacific Grove, CA: Brooks/Cole).

Ivey, A.E. & Gluckstern, N. (1976), *Basic Influencing Skills: Participant Manual* (Amherst, MA: Microtraining Associates).

Ivey, A.E., Ivey, M.B., and Simek-Downing, L. (1987), *Counseling and Psychotherapy: Integrating skills, theory and practice*, 2nd Ed. (Englewood Cliffs, NJ: Prentice-Hall).

Jackson, D.D. (1961), Interactional Psychotherapy, in M.T. Stein, Ed., *Contemporary Psychotherapies* (New York: Free Press).

Jackson, D.D. & Weakland, J.H. (1961), "Conjoint Family Therapy: Some Consideration of Theory, Technique and Results," *Psychiatry 24*, 30-45.

Jacobson, E. (1938), *Progressive Relaxation* (Chicago: University of Chicago Press).

Jessop, A.L. (1979), *Nurse-Patient Communication: A Skills Approach* (North Amherst, MA: Microtraining Associates).

Jevne, R. (1981). "Counselor Competencies and Selected Issues in a Canadian Counselor Education Program," *Canadian Counselor, 15*, 57–63.

Johnson, D.W. (1981). *Reaching out: Interpersonal effectiveness and self-actualization* (2nd ed.). Englewood Cliffs, NJ: Prentice-Hall.

Johnson, R. (1986), *Inner Work: Using Dreams and Active Imagination for Personal Growth* (New York: Harper & Row).

Kanfer, F.H. (1970), "Self-Monitoring: Methodological Limitations and Clinical Applications," *Journal of Consulting and Clinical Psychology 35*, 148-152.

Kanfer, F.H. (1980), Self-Management Methods, in F.H. Kanfer & A.P. Goldstein, Eds., Helping People Change (New York: Pergamon), pp. 309-355.

Karoly, P. (1982), Perspectives on Self-Management and Behavior Change, in P. Karoly & F.H. Kanfer, Eds. Self-management and Behavior Change (New York: Pergamon), pp. 3-31.

Kasdin, A.E. (1973), "Covert Modeling and the Reduction of Avoidance Behavior," *Journal of Abnormal Psychology 81*, 89-95.

Kelly, G. (1955), *The Psychology of Personal Constructs*, Vols. I and II (New York: . W. Norton).

Knapp, M. (1978), *Nonverbal Communication in Human Interaction*, 2nd Ed. (New York: Holt, Rinehart & Winston).

Krumboltz, J.D. (1966), "Behavioral Goals for Counseling," *Journal of Counseling Psychology, 13*, 133-159.

Krumboltz, J.D. & Thoresen, C.E. (1969), *Behavioral Counseling: Cases and Techniques* (New York: Holt, Rinehart & Winston).

L'Abate, L. (1981), "Toward a Systematic Classification of Counseling and Therapy Theorists, Methods, Processes, and Goals. The E-R-A Model," *Personnel and Guidance Journal 59*, 263-266.

Laing, J. (1988), "Self-Report: Can It Be of Value as an Assessment Technique?" *Journal of Counseling and Development 67*, 60-61.

Lanning, W. & Carey, J. (1987), "Systematic termination in counseling," *Counselor education and supervision, 26*, 168-173.

Larson, P.C. (1982), "Counseling Special Populations," *Professional Psychology 13*, 843-858.

Lazarus, A.A. (1966), "Behavioral Rehearsal vs. Non-Directive Therapy vs. Advice in Effecting Behavior Change," *Behavior Research and Therapy 4*, 209-212.

Lazarus, A.A. (1971), *Behavior Therapy and Beyond* (New York: McGraw-Hill).

Lazarus, A.A. (1981), *The Practice of Multimodal Therapy* (New York: McGraw-Hill).

Lee, C.C. & Richardson, B.L., Eds. (1991), *Multicultural Issues in Counseling: New Approaches to Diversity* (Alexandria, VA: American Association for Counseling and Development Press).

Lehrer, P.M. & Woolfolk, R.L. (1982), "Self-Report Assessment of Anxiety: Somatic, Cognitive, and Behavioral Modalities," *Behavioral Assessment 4*, 167-177.

Lloyd, M.E. (1983), "Selecting Systems to Measure Client Outcome in Human Service Agencies," *Behavioral Assessment 5*, 55-70.

Loesch, L.C., Crane, B.B., & Tucker, B.B. (1978), "Counselor Trainee Effectiveness: More Puzzle Pieces," *Counselor Education and Supervision 17*, 195-204.

Lombana, J.H. (1989), "Counseling Persons with Disabilities: Summary and Projections," *Journal of Counseling and Development 68*, 177-179.

London, P., (1964), *The Modes and Morals of Psychotherapy* (New York: Holt, Rinehart & Winston).

Long, L. Paradise, L. & Long, T. (1981), *Questioning: Skills for the Helping Process* (Pacific Grove, CA: Brooks/Cole).

Lorand, S. (1982), *Techniques of Psychoanalytic Therapy* (New York: St. Martin's Press).

Madanes, C. (1981), *Strategic Family Therapy* (San Francisco: Jossey-Bass).

Mahoney, M.J. (1971), "The Self-Management of Covert Behavior: A Case Study," *Behavior Therapy 7*, 510-521.

Mahoney, M.J., Maura, N. & Wade, T. (1973), "The Relative Efficacy of Self-Reward, Self-Punishment, and Self-Monitoring Techniques for Weight Loss," *Journal of Consulting and Clinical Psychology 40*, 404-407.

Mahoney, M.J. & Thoresen, C.E. (1974), *Self-Control: Power to the Person* (Pacific Grove, CA: Brooks/Cole).

Marquis, J.N., Morgan, W.G., & Piaget, G. (1973), *A Guidebook for Systematic Desensitization*, 3rd Ed., (Palo Alto, CA: Veteran's Workshop).

Matson, J.L. (1989), *Treating Depression in Children and Adolescents* (New York: Pergamon Press).

Mattick, R.P. & Peters, L. (1988), "Treatment of Severe Social Phobia: Effects of Guided Exposure with and without Cognitive Restructuring," *Journal of Consulting and Clinical Psychology 56*, 251-260.

Maultsby, M.C. (1984), *Rational Behavior Therapy* (Englewood Cliffs, NJ: Prentice-Hall).

Maurer, R.E. & Tindall, J.H. (1983), "Effect of Postural Congruence on Client's Perception of Counselor Empathy," *Journal of Counseling Psychology 30*, 158-163.

McCordick, S.M., Kaplan, R.M., Smith, S. & Finn, M.E. (1981), "Variations in Cognitive Behavior Modifications for Test Anxiety," *Psychotherapy: Theory, Research and Practice 18*, 170-178.

McFall, R.M. (1970), "Effects of Self-Monitoring on Normal Smoking Behavior," *Journal of Consulting and Clinical Psychology 35*, 135-142.

McFall, R.M. & Twentyman, C. (1973), "Four Experiments on the Relative Contributions of Rehearsal, Modeling, and Coaching to Assertion Training," *Journal of Abnormal Psychology 81*, 199-218,

McGoldrick, M., Pearce, J.K., & Giordano, J., Eds. 1982, *Ethnicity and Family Therapy* (New York: Guilford).

McKeachie, W.J. (1976), "Psychology in America's Bicentennial Year," *American Psychologist 31*, 819-833.

McLean, P.D. (1976), Therapeutic Decision-Making in the Behavioral Treatment of Depression, in P. O. Davidson Ed., *Behavioral Management of Anxiety, Depression, and Pain* (New York: Brunner/Mazel), pp. 54-90.

McMullin, R.E. & Giles, T.R. (1981), *Cognitive-Behavior Therapy: A Restructuring Approach* (New York: Grune & Stratton).

Meador, B. & Rogers, C.R. (1984), Person-Centered Therapy, in R.J. Corsini, Ed., *Current Psychotherapies* (Itasca, IL: Peacock), pp. 142-205.

Meichenbaum, D.H. (1971), "Examination of Model Characteristics in Reducing Avoidance Behavior," *Journal of Personality and Social Psychology 17*, 298-307.

Meichenbaum, D.H. (1972), "Cognitive Modification of Test Anxious College Students," *Journal of Consulting and Clinical Psychology 39*, 370-380.

Meichenbaum, D.H. (1977), *Cognitive-Behavior Modification: An Integrative Approach* (New York: Plenum).

Meichenbaum, D.H. & Cameron, R. (1973), "Stress Inoculation: A Skills Training Approach to Anxiety Management," Unpublished manuscript, University of Waterloo, Ontario, Canada.

Meichenbaum, D.H. & Turk, D. (1976), The Cognitive-Behavioral Management of Anxiety, Anger, and Pain, in P.O. Davidson, Ed., *The Behavioral Management of Anxiety, Depression and Pain* (New York: Brunner/Mazel).

Melnick, J. (1973), "A Comparison of Replication Techniques in the Modification of Minimal Dating Behavior," *Journal of Abnormal Psychology 81*, 51-59.

Miller, M.J. (1990), "The Power of 'OCEAN': Another Way to Diagnose Clients," *Counselor Education and Supervision 29*, 283-290.

Miller, S., Nunnally, E.W., & Wackman, D.B. (1975), *Alive and Aware: Improving Communication in Relationships* (Minneapolis: Interpersonal Communication Programs).

Mintz, L.B. & O'Neil, J.M. (1990), "Gender Roles, Sex, and the Process of Psychotherapy: Many Questions and Few Answers," *Journal of Counseling and Development 68*, 381–387.

Minuchin, S. (1974), *Families and Family Therapy* (Cambridge, MA: Harvard University Press).

Minuchin, S. & Fishman, H.C. (1981), *Family Therapy Techniques* (Cambridge, MA: Harvard University Press).

Mitchell, L.K. & Krumboltz, J.D. (1987), "The Effects of Cognitive Restructuring and Decision-Making Training on Career Indecision," *Journal of Counseling and Development 66*, 171–174.

Moore, B.M. (1974), "Cultural Differences and Counseling Perspectives," *Texas Personnel and Guidance Journal 3*, 39–44.

Moreno, J.L. (1946), *Psychodrama* (Vol. 1) (New York: Beacon House).

Morris, R.J. (1980), Fear Reduction Methods, in F.H. Kanfer & A.P. Goldstein, Eds., *Helping People Change* (New York: Pergamon), pp. 248-293.

Morse, C.L. & Bockoven, J. (1989), Improving the Efficacy of DUSO-R through the use of a Children's Intake Interview, *Elementary School Guidance and Counseling 24*, 102-111.

Moursund, J. (1985), *The Process of Counseling and Psychotherapy* (Englewood Cliffs, NJ: Prentice Hall).

Nelson, R.O., Lipinski, D.P. & Boykin, R.A. (1978), "The Effects of Self-Recorders' Training and the Obtrusiveness of the Self-Recording Device on the Accuracy and Reactivity of Self-Monitoring," *Behavior Therapy 9*, 200-208.

Nelson, R.O., Sprong, R.T., Hayes, S.C. & Graham, C.A. (1979, December), "Self-Reinforcement: Cues or Consequences?" Paper Presented at the annual meeting of the Association for the Advancement of Behavior Therapy, San Francisco.

Nichols, M. (1984), *Family Therapy: Concepts and Methods* (New York: Gardner).

Novaco, R.W. (1975), *Anger Control: The Development and Evaluation of an Experimental Treatment* (Lexington, MA: Heath).

Nugent, F.A. (1990), *An Introduction to the Profession of Counseling* (Columbus, OH: Merrill).

Osberg, T.M. (1989), "Self-Report Reconsidered: A Further Look at its Advantages as an Assessment Technique", *Journal of Counseling and Development 68*, 111-113.

Ost, L.G., Jerremalm, A. & Johannson, J. (1981), "Individual Response Patterns and the Effects of Different Behavioral Methods in the Treatment of Social Phobia," *Behavior Research and Therapy 19*, 1-16.

Palazzoli, M., Cecchin, G., Prata, G. & Boscolo, L. (1978), *Paradox and Counterparadox* (New York: Jason Aronson).

Papp, P. (1976), Family Choreography, in P.J. Guerin, Ed., *Family Therapy: Theory and Practice* (New York: Gardner), pp. 465-479.

Papp, P. (1980), "The Greek Chorus and Other Techniques of Paradoxical Therapy," *Family Process 19*, 45-57.

Pate, R.H. (1982), Termination: End or Beginning? in W.H. Van Hoose & M.R. Worth, Eds., *Counseling Adults: A Developmental Approach* (Pacific Grove, CA: Brooks/Cole).

Patterson, L.E. & Eisenberg, S. (1983), *The Counseling Process,* 3rd Ed. (Boston: Houghton Mifflin).

Pederson, P.B. (1977), "The Triad Model of Cross-Cultural Counselor Training," *The Personnel and Guidance Journal 56,* 94-100.

Perri, M.G. & Richards, C.S. (1977), "An Investigation of Naturally Occurring Episodes of Self-Controlled Behavior," *Journal of Counseling Psychology 24,* 178-183.

Perry, M.A. & Furukawa, M.J. (1980), Modeling Methods, in F.H. Kanfer & A.P. Goldstein, Eds., *Helping People Change* (New York: Pergamon), pp. 131-171.

Pietrofesa, J.J., Hoffman, A., Splete, H.H. & Pinto, D.V. (1984), *Counseling: An Introduction,* 2nd Ed. (Boston: Houghton Mifflin).

Pistole, C. (1991), Termination: Analytic Reflections on Client Contact After Counselor Relocation, *Journal of Counseling and Development 69,* 337-340.

Pope, A.W., McHale, S.M. & Graighead, N.E. (1988), *Self-Esteem Enhancement with Children and Adolescents* (New York: Pergamon Press).

Premack, D. (1965), Reinforcement Theory, in D. Levin, Ed. *Nebraska Symposium on Motivation,* pp. 123-180 (Lincoln, NE: University of Nebraska Press).

Rimm, D.C. & Masters, J.C. (1979), *Behavior Therapy: Techniques and Empirical Findings,* 2nd ed. (New York: Academic Press).

Roessler, R.T. (1990), "A Quality of Life Perspective on Rehabilitation Counseling," *Rehabilitation Counseling Bulletin 34,* 82-90.

Rogers, C.R. (1957), "The necessary and sufficient conditions of therapeutic personality change," *Journal of Consulting Psychology 21,* 95-103.

Rogers, C.R. (1977), *Carl Rogers on Personal Power: Inner Strength and its Revolutionary Impact* (New York: Delacorte).

Rogers, C.R. & Rablen, R.A. (1958), "A Scale of Process in Psychotherapy," Unpublished manuscript. University of Wisconsin. (Available in mimeo from Center of Studies of the Person, La Jolla, CA).

Rowe, W., Murphy, H.B., & DeCsipkes, R.A. (1975), "The Relationship of Counseling Characteristics and Counseling Effectiveness," *Review of Educational Research 45,* 231-246.

Rychlak, J.F. (1973), *Introduction to Personality and Psychotherapy* (Boston: Houghton Mifflin).

Salter, A. (1949), *Conditioned Reflex Therapy* (New York: Farrar, Straus & Giroux).

Satir, V. (1967), *Conjoint Family Therapy* (Palo Alto, CA: Science and Behavior).

Shelton, J.L. & Levy, R.L. (1981), *Behavioral Assignment and Treatment Compliance* (Champaign, IL: Research Press).

Scherer, M. (1988), "Assistive Device Utilization and Quality of Life in Adults with Spinal Cord Injuries or Cerebral Palsy," *Journal of Applied Rehabilitation Counseling 19,* 21-28.

Sherman, R. & Fredman, N. (1986), *Handbook of Structured Techniques in Marriage and Family Therapy* (New York: Bruner/Mazel).

Shertzer, B.E. & Stone, S.C. (1980), *Fundamentals of Counseling,* 3rd Ed. (Boston: Houghton Mifflin).

Sluzko, C.E. (1978), Marital Therapy from a Systems Theory Perspective, Chapter 7 in Thomas J. Paolino, Jr. and Barbara S. McCrady, Eds., *Marriage and Marital Therapy* (New York: Brunner/Mazel).

Smith, M.L. and Glass, G.V. (1977), "Meta-Analysis of Psychotherapy Outcome Studies," *American Psychologist 32*, 752-760.

Snygg, D., & Combs, A. (1949). *Individual Behavior*. New York: Harper & Row.

Spooner, S.E. & Stone. S. (1977), "Maintenance of Specific Counseling Skills over Time," *Journal of Counseling Psychology 24*, 66-71.

Strong, S. (1968), "Counseling: An Interpersonal Influence Process," *Journal of Counseling Psychology 15*, 215-224.

Strong, S. & Claiborn, C. (1982), *Change Through Interaction: Social Psychology Processes of Counseling and Psychotherapy* (New York: Wiley-Interscience).

Strong, S. & Schmidt, L. (1970), "Expertness and Influence in Counseling," *Journal of Counseling Psychology 17*, 81-87.

Sue, D.W. (1981), *Counseling the Culturally Different: Theory and Practice* (New York: Wiley).

Sue, D.W. & Sue, D. (1990), *Counseling the Culturally Different: Theory and Practice*, 2nd ed. (New York: Wiley).

Sweeney, G.A. & Horan, J.J. (1982), "Separate and Combined Effects of Cue-Controlled Relaxation and Cognitive Restructuring in the Treatment of Musical Performance Anxiety," *Journal of Counseling Psychology 29*, 486-497.

Swenson, C.H. (1968), *An Approach to Case Conceptualization* (Boston: Houghton Mifflin).

Teyber, E. (1989), *Interpersonal Process in Psychotherapy* (Pacific Grove, CA: Brooks/Cole).

Thompson, C.L. and Rudolph, L.B. (1988), *Counseling Children*, 2nd Ed. (Belmont, CA: Brooks/Cole).

Thorne, B., Kramarae, C., & Henley, N., Eds, (1983), *Language, Gender, and Society* (Cambridge, MA: Newbury House).

Turk, D. (1975), "Cognitive Control of Pain: A Skills Training Approach for the Treatment of Pain," Unpublished master's thesis, University of Waterloo, Ontario, Canada.

Turock, A. (1980), "Immediacy in Counseling: Recognizing Clients' Unspoken Messages," *Personnel and Guidance Journal 59*, 168-172.

Valerio, H.P. & Stone, G.L. (1982), "Effects of Behavioral, Cognitive, and Combined Treatments for Assertion as a Function of Differential Deficits," *Journal of Counseling Psychology 29*, 158-168.

Walen, S., DiGiuseppe, R. & Wessler, R. (1980), *A Practitioner's Guide to Rational-Emotive Therapy* (San Francisco: Jossey/Bass).

Warren, R., McLellarn, R. & Ponzoha, C. (1988), "Rational-Emotive Therapy vs. General Cognitive Behavior Therapy in the Treatment of Low Self-Esteem and Related Emotional Disturbances," *Cognitive Therapy and Research 12*, 21-38.

Watson, D.L. & Tharp, R.G. (1972), *Self-Directed Change: Self-Modification for Personal Adjustment* (Pacific Grove, CA: Brooks/Cole).

Watson, D.L. & Tharp, R.G. (1981), *Self-Directed Change: Self-Modification for Personal Adjustment*, 3rd Ed. (Pacific Grove, CA: Brooks/Cole).

Watts, F.N. (1974), "The Control of Spontaneous Recovery of Anxiety in Imaginal Desensitization," *Behavioral Research and Therapy 12*, 57-59.

Watzlawick, P. (1978), *The Language of Change* (New York: Basic Books).

Watzlawick, P., Weakland, J., & Fisch, R. (1974), *Change: Principles of Problem Formation and Problem Resolution* (New York: W.W. Norton).

Weakland, J. Fisch, R., Watzlawick, P., & Bodin, A. (1974), "Brief Therapy: Focused Problem Resolution," *Family Process 13*, 141-168.

Webster's New Universal Unabridged Dictionary, Deluxe 2nd Ed. (1983) (New York: Simon & Schuster).

White, P.E. and Franzoni, J.B. (1990), "A Multidimensional Analysis of the Mental Health of Graduate Counselors in Training," *Counselor Education and Supervision 29*, 258-267.

Williams, R.L. & Long, D.J. (1983), *Toward a Self-Managed Lifestyle, 3rd Ed.* (Boston: Houghton Mifflin).

Wilson, G.T., Rossiter, E., Kleifield, E.I. & Lindholm, L. (1986), "Cognitive Behavioral Treatment of Bulimia Nervosa: A Controlled Evaluation," *Behavior Research & Therapy 24*, 277-288.

Wolpe, J. (1958), *Psychotherapy by Reciprocal Inhibition* (Stanford, CA: Stanford University Press).

Wolpe, J. (1982), *The Practice of Behavior Therapy*, 3rd Ed. (New York: Pergamon).

Wolpe, J. & Lazarus, A.A. (1966), *Behavior Therapy Techniques* (New York: Pergamon).

Yost, E.B., Beutler, L.E., Corbishley, M.A. & Allender, J.R. (1986), *Group Cognitive Therapy: A Treatment Method for Depression in Older Adults* (New York : Pergamon Press).

Zajonc, R.B. (1980) "Feeling and Thinking: Preferences Need No Inferences," *American Psychologist 35*, 151-175.

Zuk, G. (1975), *Process and Practice in Family Therapy* (Haverford, PA: Psychiatry and Behavioral Science Books).

Index